'The current geopolitical situation, with its growing crises of immigration and the widespread displacement and upheaval of entire populations, makes this project powerfully topical and urgent. *Hospitalities* will be an indispensable volume for students and scholars of philosophy, literature, literary theory, history, sociopolitical theory, and aesthetic theory.'

– Sheila Teahan, *Michigan State University*

'The north-south and south-south take of the collection is an innovative and important angle which helps develop notions of hospitality. Not only does it add to the plurality of hospitalities in a new and radical way that should inform all forms of hospitality, but it also opens up a dialogue between different notions of hospitality by productively challenging ontological generalisations.'

– Cordula Lemke, *Free University of Berlin*

HOSPITALITIES

This collection of imaginative essays traces notions of hospitality across a sequence of theoretical permutations, not only as an urgent challenge for our conflicted present but also as foundational for ethics and resonant within the play of language. The plural form of the title highlights the inter-implication of hospitality with its exclusive others, holding suspicious rejection in tension with the receptiveness that transforms socio-cultural relations. Geographically, the collection traverses the globe from Australia and Africa to Britain, Europe and the United States, weaving exchanges from south to north, as well as south to south, and thoughtfully remapping our world. Temporally, the chapters range from the primordial hospitality offered by the earth, through the Middle Ages, to contemporary detention centres and the crisis of homelessness. Thematically, hospitality embraces sites of dwelling and the land, humans and animals in their complex embodiment, spectres and the dead, dolls and art objects. This text openly welcomes the reader to participate in shaping fresh critical discourses of the hospitable, whether in literary and linguistic studies, art and architecture, philosophy or politics.

Merle A. Williams is Professor Emerita of English at the University of the Witwatersrand in Johannesburg, South Africa, and a research associate of the African Centre for the Study of the United States.

Transdisciplinary Souths
Russell West-Pavlov (*Universität Tübingen, Germany*)
Molly Brown (*University of Pretoria, South Africa*)
Guadalupe Valencia García (*Universidad Nacional Autónoma de México, Mexico City, Mexico*)
Philip Mead (*University of Melbourne, Australia*)
Dilip Menon (*University of the Witwatersrand, Johannesburg, South Africa*)
Sudesh Mishra (*University of the South Pacific, Suva, Fiji*)
Sunita Reddy (*Jawaharlal Nehru University, New Delhi, India*)
Fernando Resende (*Universidade Federal Fluminense, Niterói/Rio de Janeiro, Brazil*)
Jing Zhao (*Xi'an Jiaotong-Liverpool University, Suzhou, China*)

How might we theorise, think, articulate and critically/creatively inhabit the multiple and overlapping Souths of today's world? How do we enable these Souths to speak to each other, question each other, in ways that complement and expand the work upon which they are already embarked with each other? It is becoming increasingly clear that in order to better understand and contribute to the multiple processes and ways of becoming-Souths, a radically transdisciplinary approach to the study and analysis of, critical interventions in, and dialogues within and between Souths needs to be implemented. Intersectional thinking at the crossroads of race and ethnicity, class and labour, gender and corporeality, not to mention climate change and ecological destruction, demands a combination of perspectives and methodologies to deal adequately with complex planetary dilemmas. This series offers a hospitable forum for innovative intellectual inquiry that seeks to break out of extant disciplinary frameworks so as to address new questions emerging from contemporary Souths. Facilitating cross-border exchanges and polyglot negotiations between the most disparate fields of intellectual and scientific inquiry, thereby resisting the disciplining effect of enclave-thinking, the series aims to contribute to the transformation of knowledge production and associated practices across multiple Souths.

As a gesture of international solidarity, the series editors of 'Transdisciplinary Souths' donate their royalties to the charitable organisation PRO ASYL e.V. in Frankfurt am Main. PRO ASYL supports the cause of asylum seekers by providing public advocacy and legal advice.

Hospitalities
Transitions and Transgressions, North and South
Edited by Merle A. Williams

For more information about this series, please visit: www.routledge.com/Transdisciplinary-Souths/book-series/TRDS

HOSPITALITIES

Transitions and Transgressions, North and South

Edited by Merle A. Williams

LONDON AND NEW YORK

First published 2020
by Routledge
2 Park Square, Milton Park, Abingdon, Oxon OX14 4RN

and by Routledge
52 Vanderbilt Avenue, New York, NY 10017

Routledge is an imprint of the Taylor & Francis Group, an informa business

© 2020 selection and editorial matter, Merle A. Williams; individual chapters, the contributors

The right of Merle A. Williams to be identified as the author of the editorial material, and of the authors for their individual chapters, has been asserted in accordance with sections 77 and 78 of the Copyright, Designs and Patents Act 1988.

All rights reserved. No part of this book may be reprinted or reproduced or utilised in any form or by any electronic, mechanical, or other means, now known or hereafter invented, including photocopying and recording, or in any information storage or retrieval system, without permission in writing from the publishers.

Trademark notice: Product or corporate names may be trademarks or registered trademarks, and are used only for identification and explanation without intent to infringe.

British Library Cataloguing-in-Publication Data
A catalogue record for this book is available from the British Library

Library of Congress Cataloging-in-Publication Data
Names: Williams, Merle A., editor.
Title: Hospitalities : transitions and transgressions, North and South / edited by Merle A. Williams.
Description: First Edition. | New York : Routledge, 2021. | Series: Transdisciplinary souths | Includes bibliographical references and index.
Identifiers: LCCN 2020042017 (print) | LCCN 2020042018 (ebook) | ISBN 9780367557027 (hardback) | ISBN 9780367631833 (paperback) | ISBN 9781003112433 (ebook)
Subjects: LCSH: Hospitality—History.
Classification: LCC GT3410 .H67 2021 (print) | LCC GT3410 (ebook) | DDC 395.309—dc23
LC record available at https://lccn.loc.gov/2020042017
LC ebook record available at https://lccn.loc.gov/2020042018

ISBN: 978-0-367-55702-7 (hbk)
ISBN: 978-0-367-63183-3 (pbk)
ISBN: 978-1-003-11243-3 (ebk)

Typeset in Bembo
by Apex CoVantage, LLC

For Geoff and Ed, Philip and Debby: in response to their loving hospitality

CONTENTS

List of contributors xi
Acknowledgements xv

1 Hospitalities: transitions and transgressions, north and south 1
 Merle A. Williams and Russell West-Pavlov

2 Welcoming and pluralism in the romances of Chrétien,
 Wolfram and Gottfried 23
 Donald R. Wehrs

3 Guests, hosts, ghosts: towards an ethics of gothic writing 41
 Dale Townshend

4 'A wandering to find home': Samuel Beckett's *Molloy*
 and the unhomeliness of home 59
 Mike Marais

5 Defying closure: hospitality, colonialism and mobility beyond
 the limits of the nation in Sol Plaatje's *Mhudi* 75
 Rebecca Fasselt

6 Home is where the heart is: a creative and theoretical reflection 95
 Jane Taylor

7 Hélène Cixous's mourning of loss and the loss of mourning:
 from Algerian apprehensions to *Hyperdream* – and beyond 108
 Merle A. Williams

8 Inhospitable life: security and migrancy in Atticus Lish's
   Preparation for the Next Life   126
   David Watson

9 Being a guest: from uneasy tourism to welcoming dogs
   in Marie NDiaye's *Ladivine*   143
   Judith Still

10 Indigenous hospitality: Kim Scott's fiction, multinaturalism
   and absolute conditional hospitality   163
   Russell West-Pavlov

11 'Yes to who or what arrives': hospitality and property in
   contemporary art   184
   Anthea Buys

Index   *203*

CONTRIBUTORS

Anthea Buys is a writer, curator and researcher working across the fields of art criticism, fiction and curating. She is a PhD candidate at the University of the Witwatersrand and a research associate of the Centre for Visual Identities in Art and Design at the University of Johannesburg. From 2014 until 2017, she was the Director of Hordaland Kunstsenter in Bergen, Norway, following a visiting PhD fellowship in the schools of Art History and Architecture at Columbia University (2013–2014). From 2017 until 2019 she was a co-founding director of the Bergen-based platform Weekend Server, an alternative institution and production house facilitating experimental artistic work. Essays on art and literature have been published in a variety of academic journals, essay collections and monographs, as well as in the media.

Rebecca Fasselt is a senior lecturer in the Department of English at the University of Pretoria, where she teaches African and postcolonial literature. She is particularly interested in the literary and cultural connections between South Africa and other parts of Africa. She has also published on Afropolitanism, African chick lit, the short story in South Africa post-2000 and first-person plural narration. Her articles have appeared in *English Studies in Africa*, *Feminist Theory*, *Research in African Literatures*, *Ariel*, the *Journal of Southern African Studies*, the *Journal of Commonwealth Literature* and *Poetics Today*. She is currently completing a monograph on African migration narratives.

Mike Marais, who teaches literary studies at Rhodes University in Makhanda (formerly Grahamstown), South Africa, is the author of *Secretary of the Invisible: The Idea of Hospitality in the Fiction of J. M. Coetzee* (2009). His research interests include the intersections between ethics and aesthetics in modern fiction.

Judith Still is Professor of French and Critical Theory at the University of Nottingham and a Fellow of the British Academy. She is the author of *Justice and Difference in the Work of Rousseau* (1993), *Feminine Economies: Thinking against the Market in the Enlightenment and the Late Twentieth Century* (1997), *Derrida and Hospitality* (2010; Gapper Prize winner in 2011), *Enlightenment Hospitality: Cannibals, Harems and Adoption* (2011) and *Derrida and Other Animals: The Boundaries of the Human* (2015). She is also the editor of *Men's Bodies* (a special issue of *Paragraph*, 2003), and co-editor with Michael Worton of *Intertextuality* (1990) and *Textuality and Sexuality* (1993); with Solange Ribeiro of *Feminisms: Brazilian Perspectives* (1999); with Margaret Atack, Diana Holmes and Diana Knight of *Women, Genre and Circumstance* (2012); and with Shirley Jordan of *Disorderly Eating in Contemporary Women's Writing* (a special issue of the *Journal of Romance Studies*, 2020), amongst other volumes. She is currently working on the French works of the Franco-American Enlightenment writer Crèvecœur, with particular reference to Indigenous peoples, enslavement and animals. She is President of the Society for French Studies (UK and Ireland) and on the editorial board of *French Studies*, *Nottingham French Studies* and the *Journal of Romance Studies*.

Jane Taylor is the Andrew W. Mellon Professor of Aesthetic Theory and Material Performance at the Centre for Humanities Research, University of the Western Cape. She has for some years been involved in public scholarship, curating and the arts. She currently directs a creative arts hub, the Laboratory of Kinetic Objects, and has helped to launch the Barrydale Festival, a forum for rural arts focusing on aesthetics, artificial intelligence and puppetry. She has held visiting positions at the Universities of Chicago, Oxford and Cambridge, as well as Northwestern University and the University of California at Berkeley. Working with artist William Kentridge and the Handspring Puppet Company, she has written several plays for puppets, including the influential *Ubu and the Truth Commission* (1998). She has also composed a puppet play about the early history of neurology for the Renaissance scholar Stephen Greenblatt (*After Cardenio*, in the *South African Theatre Journal*, 2012). Her recently completed monograph on William Kentridge's production of Shostakovich's *The Nose* at the New York Metropolitan Opera is entitled *William Kentridge: Being Led by the Nose* (2017). Jane Taylor is the author of two novels, *Of Wild Dogs* (2005) and *The Transplant Men* (2009).

Dale Townshend is Professor of Gothic Literature in the Manchester Centre for Gothic Studies, Manchester Metropolitan University. He has co-edited various collections of essays on Gothic themes: with Glennis Byron, *The Gothic World* (2013); with Angela Wright, *Ann Radcliffe, Romanticism and the Gothic* (2014) and *Romantic Gothic: An Edinburgh Companion* (2015); with Michael Carter and Peter N. Lindfield, *Writing Britain's Ruins* (2017). His most recent publications include *Gothic Antiquity: History, Romance, and the Architectural Imagination, 1760–1850* (2019) and Volumes I and II of *The Cambridge History of the Gothic*, co-edited with Angela Wright (2020). He is currently completing a monograph on Matthew Gregory Lewis (forthcoming in 2023) and editing the posthumous works of Ann Radcliffe for *The Cambridge Edition of the Complete Works of Ann Radcliffe* (forthcoming in 2026).

David Watson is an associate professor in the Department of English at Uppsala University, where he specialises in American literature and culture. He has published on nineteenth-century and modernist American poets, nineteenth-century and contemporary novelists, and issues in transnational and translation studies. He is currently completing a monograph on *The Security Imaginary: Contingency and Vulnerability in Twenty-First Century US Fiction*. His most recent publications examine failed states and the world novel, as well as the role of contingency within neoliberal narratives.

Donald R. Wehrs is Hargis Professor of English Literature at Auburn University, Auburn, Alabama, USA, where he teaches comparative literature, eighteenth-century studies and literary theory. He is author of three monographs on twentieth-century Anglophone and Francophone African fiction: *African Feminist Fiction and Indigenous Values* (2001), *Pre-Colonial Africa in Colonial African Narratives* (2008) and *Islam, Ethics, Revolt* (2008). He has edited or co-edited four collections: *Levinas and Twentieth-Century Literature* (2013) and with David P. Haney, *Levinas and Nineteenth-Century Literature* (2009); with Mark J. Bruhn, *Cognition, Literature, and History* (2014); and with Thomas Blake, *The Palgrave Handbook of Affect Studies and Textual Criticism* (2017). In addition, he has published book chapters and journal essays on Shakespeare, Cervantes, postcolonial fiction, British eighteenth-century studies, medieval romance, comparative literature and literary theory.

Russell West-Pavlov is Professor of Anglophone Literatures at the University of Tübingen, Germany, and Research Associate at the University of Pretoria, South Africa. He is convenor of an extensive BMBF/DAAD research network on Global South Studies (2015–2020) and a founding convenor of the Interdisciplinary Centre for Global South Studies at the University of Tübingen. Major book publications include *Temporalities* (Routledge, 2013), *Eastern African Literatures* (2018), *German as Contact Zone* (2019) and *AfrikAffekt* (2020). He has recently edited *The Global South and Literature* (2018).

Merle A. Williams is Professor Emerita of English at the University of the Witwatersrand in Johannesburg and a research associate of the African Centre for the Study of the United States, specialising in cultural exchange in the fields of literature and the visual arts. She is the author of *Henry James and the Philosophical Novel: Being and Seeing* (reprinted in 2009), and is completing a scholarly text of *The Awkward Age* for the Cambridge Edition of the *Complete Fiction of Henry James*. An invited collection of her critical essays on James is in preparation, while the edited volume *Cultures of*

Populism is forthcoming in 2021. She has recently co-edited special issues for the *Journal of Literary Studies*, *English Studies in Africa* and *Safundi: The Journal of South African and American Studies*. A range of articles and book chapters explore the relations between literature and philosophy, Romantic poetry (especially Shelley), nineteenth-century and modernist fiction, and trauma studies. She has held visiting research positions in Germany, Sweden and the United States.

ACKNOWLEDGEMENTS

Hospitalities would, quite simply, not have come to fruition without the sharp insight and consistent involvement of Russell West-Pavlov, who is also general editor of the new series on 'Transdisciplinary Souths' which this volume will launch. He has astutely guided the progress of this essay collection from its tentative conception, through various practical vicissitudes, to the preparation of the final manuscript; this project is the richer for his participation. I am also grateful to Martin Middeke of the University of Augsburg for his encouragement at a crucial stage, as well as a range of valuable suggestions. Lara Buxbaum assisted generously with a searching review of the initial submissions, while Kylie Crane has thoughtfully and meticulously copyedited the full text. Anya Heise-von der Lippe intervened at just the right moment to secure the production schedule.

I would like to thank the two anonymous reviewers for their incisive appraisal of the completed manuscript. Their responses have amply embraced the literary, cultural, historical and theoretical diversity of this collection, while confirming the authors' sense that such an enquiry is at once necessary and timely.

Hospitalities has been supported by the German Academic Exchange Service (DAAD) with funds from the German Federal Ministry for Education and Research (BMBF), under the aegis of Thematic Network Project 'Literary Cultures of the Global South' (2015–2020) (Grant No. 57373684)/'Futures under Construction in the Global South' (2019–2020) (Grant No. 57419920). I am grateful to Russell West-Pavlov, yet again, for his hospitality in inviting me to the University of Tübingen for a two-month fellowship at the end of 2018. It was during this period that we drafted the framing chapter on 'Hospitalities: Transitions and Transgressions, North and South', thus bringing into focus the central concerns of the volume. The university, in turn, demonstrated its hospitality by providing resources and enabling me to exchange ideas with welcoming colleagues in several different disciplines.

For permission to reproduce the cover images, I wish firstly to thank Thierry Geoffroy for *The Emergency Will Replace the Contemporary*, 2012, tent, acrylic spray paint, 150 cm x 210 cm x 210 cm © Thierry Geoffroy/Colonel; Collection Kunsthalle Mannheim; VG Bild-Kunst Bonn 2020; photograph © Russell West-Pavlov. The accompanying cover image, showing Gordon Matta-Clark's installation *Splitting*, 1974, Englewood, New Jersey, is reproduced by courtesy of the Estate of Gordon Matta-Clark and the Centre canadien d'architecture/cca.qc.ca; VG Bild-Kunst Bonn 2020. Permission has been granted for the reproduction of the same image in the concluding chapter by Anthea Buys entitled '"Yes to who or what arrives": Hospitality and Property in Contemporary Art' (184–202). This chapter includes two further images by Dutch artist Constant (Nieuwenhuys), for which I thank the Fondation Constant/Stichting Constant. The first of these is *Ontwerp voor een zigeunerkamp in Alba*, 1956, 13,7 cm x 125,0 cm x 125,0 cm, aluminium, oil paint, plexiglass, steel, wood; Collection Kunstmuseum Den Haag NL; photographer Tom Haartsen; © Constant/Fondation Constant, c/o VG Bild-Kunst Bonn 2020 (also DACS, London). The second is entitled *Erotic Space*, 1971, 165,0 cm x 175,0 cm, linen, oil paint; Collection Kunstmuseum Den Haag NL; photographer Tom Haartsen; © Constant/Fondation Constant, c/o VG Bild-Kunst Bonn 2020 (also DACS, London).

I am grateful to Sebastian Baden (Kunsthalle Mannheim), Caroline Dagbert (Centre canadien d'architecture/Canadian Centre for Architecture, Montreal, representing the Estate of Gordon Matta-Clarke), Thierry Geoffroy, and Uta Raschke (VG Bild-Kunst, Bonn) for their friendly and helpful assistance in obtaining high resolution visual material and for dealing with reproduction rights.

A closing word of appreciation is due to Aakash Chakrabarty and Brinda Sen, our editors at Routledge, for their kindness, understanding and commitment in meeting a demanding publication timetable for *Hospitalities*, despite the logistic challenges posed by the coronavirus pandemic. We warmly recognise their professional dedication.

1

HOSPITALITIES

Transitions and transgressions, north and south

Merle A. Williams and Russell West-Pavlov

What might be the purpose of drawing together a fresh collection of critical essays on hospitality just at this moment? An obvious reply could suggest that the challenge of hospitality has remained incontestably current, predominantly through multiple evasions, aberrations and downright abuses across the globe. While this piece was being written, international powers were conducting a proxy war in the Yemen that wilfully sealed in defenceless civilians, consigning them to humanly induced starvation. At the same time, President Donald Trump had decided that barbed wire was 'beautiful', dispatching thousands of troops to bar the southern border of the United States to a straggling caravan of diverse, but increasingly weary, migrants, refugees and asylum seekers from Central America. Scores of adults and children from North Africa continue to brave the Mediterranean, risking their freedom and their lives, to cross over into the perceived security and opportunity of Europe. These are only a few illustrative examples taken from a world in more widespread upheaval than ever before. What we see today, however, is only a fraction of predicted (and predictable) future disturbances. The figures for forcibly displaced populations were relatively stable between 2000 and 2010. However, they have been rising steeply ever since, from 42.5 million in 2011, to 59.5 million in 2014, to 68.5 million in 2017, and 70.8 million in 2018, according to the annual series of the United Nations High Commission for Refugees (UNHCR) 'Global Trends' reports (UNHCR 2011, 2014, 2017, 2019). Global warming, which shows no signs of abating (WMO 2018; IPCC 2018), and its attendant consequences such as resource conflicts, are expected to lead to a volume of forced displacement at least three times the 2018 magnitude by 2050 (Rigaud et al. 2018). By the end of the twenty-first century, rising sea levels may have caused the inundation of areas currently inhabited by 25 per cent of the world's population (Nealon 2016, 121). Clearly, in the decades to come, issues of displacement, hospitality – and, above all, inhospitability – will assume proportions that are now scarcely imaginable. Introducing her 2013 essay on 'Hospitality – Under Compassion and Violence', Anne Dufourmantelle starkly proposes that 'hospitality has become the gateway to hell'. Figuring a mythical scene of strict judgement and selection, she emphasises that hospitality marks 'not an invitation for a better life – at most, it offers a shelter – but a fully armed technological gate, serving as a limit and a threshold' (Dufourmantelle 2013, 13). She therefore contends that 'questioning ourselves on the conditions of hospitality has never been more important', recalling 'how Derrida forever opened the *question* of hospitality' (ibid.).

Dufourmantelle's remarks, while keeping in clear view prevailing geopolitical and humanitarian concerns, equally highlight the urgency of sustaining an engagement with the *question* of hospitality. In a dialogue entitled 'Hospitality, Justice and Responsibility', Derrida firmly declares that he is interested in unconditional hospitality 'in order to understand and to transform what is going on today in our world' (Derrida 1999b, 70). He proceeds to distinguish a socially structured, conditional hospitality of invitation from the visitation or 'absolute surprise' of pure unconditional hospitality. The 'pure gift' or 'pure hospitality', he insists, should consist of an 'opening without horizon of expectation' (ibid.).

> It may be terrible because the newcomer may be a good person, or may be the devil; but if you exclude the possibility that the newcomer is coming to destroy your house – if you want to control this and exclude in advance this possibility – there is no hospitality.
>
> (ibid.)

These are the stakes that dominate contemporary political debates about hospitality around the world. The essays in this collection accept the challenge, which is most starkly explored in David Watson's chapter with its attentiveness to prevailing migration regimes. The title 'Hospitalities' points to multiple variations, fissions and refractions within the framework of the hospitable, some benign and some undeniably threatening. Each discussion moves within the circuit of transition, because hospitality self-evidently involves crossing thresholds or entering unstable liminal spaces, not to mention the often unpredictably shifting relational dynamics between host and guest. Yet transitions unavoidably become transgressions, because the very notion of hospitality is self-contaminating in its play between the pure and the conditional, with each manifestation necessarily underwriting, yet undermining, the other. In his *Adieu to Emmanuel Levinas*, Derrida painstakingly examines the complex statement in *Totality and Infinity* that intentionality (or 'consciousness of something') is 'attention to speech or welcome of the face, hospitality' (Levinas 1969, 299; as quoted in Derrida 1999a, 22). In other words, responsiveness to the Other who appears in a dimension of 'height' or compelling appeal, calling forth the engaged accountability of the self, is the fundamental expression of hospitality. This Derrida duly interprets as 'ethicity itself for Levinas, the whole and principle of ethics' (Derrida 1999a, 50). Yet, in the absence of a contrary, such paramount hospitality requires receptivity to the rampantly unethical; even a torturer counter-intuitively attests to the humanity that he seeks to destroy (ibid.).

Borrowing from Jean-Luc Nancy, it would thus seem that 'hospitality' represents an intriguing instance of 'being singular plural' (perhaps a further justification for the construct of 'hospitalities'?), an assemblage of a gerundive verb or a noun with two juxtaposed adjectives, but without any 'determined syntax' (Nancy 2000, 28). Moreover, the singular already presupposes the plural because the Latin *singuli* 'designates the "one" as belonging to the "one by one"' (ibid.: 32). The singular is primarily '*each* one and, therefore, also *with* and *among* all the others. The singular is plural'. 'Hospitality' is thus 'hospitalities'. Finally, 'the singular is each time *for* the whole, in its place and in light of it' (ibid.), just as each particular act of practising hospitality paradoxically invokes the imbrication of the pure form with the conditional version. This aporia can be construed as a radical heterogeneity between two nonetheless indissociable terms, in the same way as justice, in Derrida's account, must stand outside or transcend the contingencies of 'the law' or 'the right'. Yet striving for justice depends upon the law as process, with its liability to 'deconstruction, transformations, revolutions, reformations, improvement, [and] perfectibility' (Derrida 1999a, 72-73). Derrida crystallises his perception of such aporetic conjunctions accordingly:

> For me, however, the *aporia* is not simply paralysis, but the *aporia* or non-way is the condition of walking: if there was no *aporia* we wouldn't walk, we wouldn't find our way; path-breaking implies *aporia*. This impossibility to find one's way is the condition of ethics.
>
> (ibid.: 73)

These reflections have close affinities with Derrida's treatment of the 'pervertible' or 'perverting' relationship between the laws of conditional hospitality and the Law of absolute hospitality, a preoccupation that indirectly informs a cross-section of the essays in this collection. At first sight, the laws of conditional hospitality appear straightforward, predicated as they are upon ancient recognitions of a pact rooted in 'familial or genealogical right' that passes down generations, as well as being able to call participants by their names, hence acknowledging that 'a proper name is never purely individual' (Derrida 2000b, 23). These pacts also presuppose a degree of reciprocity. Conditional hospitality thus consists in the potential inhospitality of 'interrogating the new arrival' against a background of considered inclusions and exclusions (ibid.: 27). The host is 'master at home', regarding anyone who encroaches on his prerogatives and *ipseity* (or sovereign selfhood) as an 'undesirable foreigner', 'virtually as an enemy' (ibid.: 53-55). The analogies with contemporary immigration policies in many nation-states hardly need elaboration, especially where issues of sovereignty and anticipated reciprocity are entailed, not to mention the ubiquitous threat of terrorism in all its forms (whether within the state or invading from beyond its borders).

The contrast between such laws and the law (or Law) of absolute hospitality remains striking, even though it has become familiar to scholars. Derrida argues that

> absolute hospitality requires that I open up my home and that I give not only to the [approved] foreigner . . . but to the absolute, unknown, anonymous other, that I *give place* to them, that I let them come, that I let them arrive, and take place in the place I offer them, without asking of them either reciprocity (entering into a pact) or even their names.
>
> (ibid.: 25)

The diction is quite different. Not only are all conditions suspended, but openness transfuses the description, as do 'giving' and 'taking place' with the full range of their literal and figurative connotations. Hospitality is fashioned as the inchoate event of coming, of arrival. Derrida reframes this formulation as a pressing appeal:

> Let us say yes *to who or what turns up*, before any determination, before any anticipation, before any *identification*, whether it has to do with a foreigner, an immigrant, an invited guest, or an unexpected visitor, whether or not the new arrival is the citizen of another country, a human, animal, or divine creature, a living or dead thing, male or female.
>
> (ibid.: 77)

Hospitality hence exceeds the reassuring parameters of given categories of humanity, resisting gender discrimination, encompassing animals, welcoming at once the dead and intimations of divinity. In concert with Derrida's earlier statement, there is also an embrace of hospitality to land or the environment as boundaries between the living and the non-living blur, thus incorporating the making and taking place *of* place as such. These notions of openness acquire form in radically concrete ways in the perforated, shattered or sectioned houses produced by the architect-sculptors examined in Anthea Buys's chapter. Architectural topography imaginatively renders visible the more abstract topologies of the absolute law. The antinomy inherent in *The* law of hospitality with its 'universal singularity' is opposed to the 'structured multiplicity' of the laws of the conditional instantiation, with their divisibility and propensity for historico-geographical dispersion. 'The law, in the absolute singular, contradicts laws in the plural, but on each occasion it is the law *within* the law, and on each case *outside the law* within the law' (Derrida 2000b, 79). This comprises the 'strange . . . plural grammar of *two plurals that are different at the same time*' – but also, one might add, from a certain perspective singular plural (ibid.: 81). Transition and transgression are endemic to the conundrum of hospitable performance, whether pure or conditional, transcendently anomic or subject to legal regulation.

These perplexities are compounded, if enriched, by the ambiguously shifting etymology of hospitality, notably with regard to the functions of 'host' and 'guest'. 'Hospitality' derives from the Latin *hostis*, which means both 'stranger' or 'foreigner' and 'enemy', more specifically someone not directly covered by the articles of an established pact of amity. This conjunction prompts Derrida to coin the neologism 'hostipitality' in order to capture the residual suspicion and violence latent in the hospitable enterprise. In his 2000 essay under this title, he focuses on the German word *Hospitalität*, which he claims to be of 'a troubled and troubling origin, [carrying] its own contradiction incorporated into it, a Latin word which allows itself to be parasitised by its opposite, "hostility", the undesirable guest [*hôte*]which it harbors as the self-contradiction in its own body' (Derrida 2000a, 3). The root of 'host' and 'guest' is just as entangled, troubled and troubling. The contemporary French word *hôte* (which derives obliquely from the Latin *hospes* or 'guest') can mean both 'host' and 'guest'. The Indo-European root is ★*ghosti-s* ('guest' or 'stranger'), which devolves through the Old French *oste/hoste* to become the reversible 'host-guest'. However, the passage as a loan word from Old French to Middle English has effectively confined the current English meaning to 'host' or the person providing the hospitality. Judith Still has aptly noted a similar paring down in the French feminine form *hôtesse*, which signifies only 'hostess' and bears implicit testimony to a gendered hierarchy. If 'hostess' is not applied in its merely commercial sense, Still suggests that a woman enjoys only a delegated authority on behalf of the master of the house, with her physical, intellectual and emotional resources deployed on his behalf, frequently to facilitate interactions between men (Still 2013, 21).

It would be tempting to view these etymological errancies as a characteristically European phenomenon, but an intriguing parallel is to be found in the Semitic context too. In Gil Anidjar's 2002 compilation of Derrida's seminars on 'hostipitality', the Biblical Abraham or Ibrahim is foregrounded as a seminal figure within the matrix of hospitality. He is the '*ger* (stranger, *hôte* [perhaps more literally the temporary dweller or sojourner]) . . . who is destined by God to be . . . an immigrant, a foreign body abroad' (Derrida 2002, 401). Derrida tentatively proposes affinities with the Arabic *giwār*, a 'noun of action' subtending both 'protection and neighborliness' for someone who is '*gār*, protected, [or a] customer' on the model of the Hebrew *ger*, as 'protected by the tribe or the community' (Derrida 2002, 401). He then posits connections with the position of the *dakhīl* or the 'inmate, hôte to whom protection is due, stranger, passing traveller. The right of the *dakhīl* would be a right to asylum witnessed everywhere in the Semitic world' (ibid.). Encouraging as these indications appear to be, the argument turns back on itself when confronted with the Arab lexicographers contributing to the *Encyclopaedia of Islam*: the root *gwr* is deemed to reinforce the 'almost universal semantic link' between 'stranger, enemy' (like the Latin *hostis*) and *hôte* in conveying 'the sense of hostility, injustice' (ibid.: 401–2). There is not only an antinomy between *The* law and the laws of hospitality, but the very notion deconstructs itself into its opposite which remains a prerequisite for its intelligible meaning.

In a typically Derridean remark, these proliferating oppositions, contraries and aporias fold over into the role of the subject under the sign of hospitality. In his *Adieu*, Derrida traces the subtle modulation in Levinas's thinking about subjectivity from 'host' (in Levinas 1969, 299) to 'hostage' (in Levinas 1998,

112, 114, 117, 128, 141, 158, 167). The self that freely welcomes the face of the Other through speech and in ethical action becomes the subject persecuted and obsessed by its responsibilities, under general accusation and committed to substituting itself for the suffering of its fellow creatures (Levinas 1998, 111-12; Derrida 1999a, 57). This subject endures persistent trauma, even as it accepts its ineluctable accountability as an 'I', an irreducible first person, for the pervasive anguish of all human beings. Such a seemingly excessive mission is attuned to the exacting demands of pure hospitality to '*who or what turns up*', but it is further correlated with the impossibility of achieving forgiveness. From one perspective, receiving guests presupposes forgiving any 'failing, fault, offense, [or] even sin' (Derrida 2002, 380) before they cross the threshold; pretence, resentment and grudging toleration are clearly at odds with the ethos of the hospitable. Yet the host in turn stands in need of forgiveness, not only because welcoming in the Levinasian spirit is infinite, but also because the host could always and undeniably give more. Honouring a proffered invitation should consequently not occlude openness to the visitation traced by 'messianic surprise', fraught with what is 'unforeseen, unforeseeable [*imprévu, imprévisible*], unpredictable . . . [and] unawaited [*inattendu*]' (Derrida 2002, 380-81). Still, there is a further turn of the screw because forgiveness – if it *is* to be possible at all – must forgive only the unforgivable rather than some commonplace misdemeanour, infraction or venality (ibid.: 385). Assertions of this kind touch on the hyperbolical, while concentrating concerns that run across the essays in this volume. If conditional hospitality, at least, implies boundaries and transactions with another (even if that other lies within the self), where are limits to be imposed, and when has the putative host done enough? Can an invitation actually be circumscribed so as to foreclose the shock of visitation? When is hospitality reduced to a cheap, cynical sham? Alternatively, casting the subject as hostage transmutes quite readily into narratives of flagrant exploitation and misappropriation, whether attempted or perceived. The *arrivant* carries no guarantee of being a 'good person' instead of 'the devil', intent on wrecking established decencies and convivialities. Homes and hosts are not immune to violation, although guests (especially strangers and migrants) confront the same predicament.

The idea of 'home', then, is tightly woven into the fabric of hospitality and the conception of this essay collection, as evinced with particular force in Mike Marais's searching contribution. In *Totality and Infinity*, Levinas follows the growth of the self to ethical awareness after a transformative pre-linguistic encounter with a feminine Other whose intimate welcome prepares the way for habitation in the world and ultimately the fully fledged response to the face of the Other. The founding of the home in this fashion is explicitly linked to interiority and 'the welcoming par excellence, welcoming in itself – the feminine being' (see Levinas 1969, 157; Derrida 1999a, 43). Whether this approach should be read as 'classical androcentrism', to adopt Derrida's phrase, or a 'sort of feminist manifesto' is a moot point (Derrida 1999a, 44); Levinas has frequently been called to account for his attitude to gender difference and his preoccupation with 'paternity' during this phase of his career. In a discussion of hospitality, though, it seems important to accord due recognition both to the cogency of feminist arguments and to strategies of multivocal reading that remain alert to ambivalence. A vital consequence of the feminine intervention, however, is to destabilise any incipiently complacent possession of the self in its recently inaugurated dwelling at home. Derrida comments that

> we must be reminded of this implacable law of hospitality: the *hôte* who receives (the host), the one who welcomes the invited or received *hôte* (the guest), the welcoming *hôte* who considers himself the owner of the place, is in truth a *hôte* received *in* his own home. He receives the hospitality that he offers in his own home; he receives it *from* his own home – which, in the end, does not belong to him. The *hôte* as host is a guest. The dwelling opens itself to itself, to its essence, as a 'land of asylum or refuge'.
>
> (ibid.: 41-42)

Once again, this seismic displacement is the work of 'feminine being', disrupting masculine egotism and acquisitiveness. At the same time, the notion of 'home' is unmoored from fixity, crossing again with the journeying of Abraham/Ibrahim whose holy progress as *ger* renders him a foreigner in need of asylum and the most generous of hosts, attended even by angels (Genesis 18:2–5). Conceptually speaking, it is the guest who constitutes the host as host and *vice versa*. These questions gain added purchase with regard to the earth at large, offering a vivid reminder that those who purport to dominate the planet are received in their own home, which does not belong to them, although they benefit from – or abuse – its hospitality as refuge. Here the call for human or human-animal hospitality spreads to matters of planetary hospitality, as understood from time immemorial by Indigenous cultures, such as those treated in Russell West-Pavlov's chapter.

In *Sharing the World*, Luce Irigaray frankly exposes the delusion of an empty hospitality confined to guest rooms which replicate the 'enclosed space partly defined around a void' (Irigaray 2008, 23) that prospective hosts have unwittingly reserved for themselves. She suggests that 'we cannot perceive the place in which we live, because it is cluttered with our objects, our projections, our repetitions, our habits and tautologies' (ibid.: 23-24). Against this insidious misrepresentation of home, she sets the making of a dynamically transient and fragile third world between the existing, individually crafted worlds inhabited by the self and the other. Her feminist argument is anchored in a recuperation of primary maternal hospitality as a basis for returning to

> something still more original, . . . the woman in the mother, . . . an identity different from ours, without any link of past dependence on it, allow[ing] us to prepare the space and the time in which it will be possible for us to enter into the presence of the other, with the other.
>
> (ibid.: 114)

Irigaray's text carries no direct citations, but it takes shape as a riposte to Heidegger's concept of *Mitsein* and as a modification of Levinasian relations between the self and the Other: the hospitality of sharing is paramount. The initial approach to the other occurs synaesthetically in darkness rather than light by listening to a touch that persists as virginal with respect to words and is passive regarding response (ibid.: 21). Self and other in their own worlds of perception, resonant past experience and auto-affection are obliged to accommodate mutual impenetrability while reaching out for contact. Yet there is an acknowledgement that the self's existence is received from the other 'through a gesture where doing and letting do, being and letting be, activity and passivity intertwine' (ibid.: 77). This rewriting of the approach of the Levinasian Other, which commands through its nakedness, produces a duality in the present as 'I open myself to an other Being who prevents my world from closing up in a totality that includes all beings' (ibid.: 79). This avoidance of Enlightenment certitudes generates a transcendental moment in which the self is incomprehensible to itself, yet arrives at a profound disclosure (ibid.: 79). The duration of the third intermediate world is transient in its puzzling, but deeply affecting, grace. Irigaray's concerted feminist variation on Levinasian or Derridean themes contributes a refreshingly collaborative dimension to the complexities of hospitality. She soberly recognises the retrograde power of prevailing mind-sets and the probability of rebuff; however, it is sharing that drives her theory, that is, sharing as aspiration and sharing as transcendental principle. This kind of yearning for an accomplished sharing despite repeatedly thwarted endeavours subtextually shadows the dystopian situations frequently examined in this collection.

Jean-Luc Nancy's account of being singular plural redirects the debate about hospitality from discrete, yet intermittently touching, life-worlds in search of healing contact to a single world in ceaseless self-creation *'out of nothing'*: it 'springs forth everywhere and in each instant, simultaneously' (Nancy 2000, 83). Every being 'belongs to the (authentic) origin, each is originary (the springing forth of the springing forth itself), and each is original (incomparable, underivable)' (ibid.). Nonetheless, all share the originarity and originality which is itself the origin. This egalitarian version of sharing fosters a virtuous circularity in which 'we' define 'being with', while 'being with' defines us. However, this plurality is consistently held in balance with singularity. Nancy ventures that 'what interests' or 'touches us' in the arts is 'the exposition of an access concealed in its opening, an access that is, then, "inimitable", untransportable, untranslatable *because* it forms, each time, an absolute point of translation, transmission, or transition of the origin *into origin*' (ibid.: 14).

The uniqueness of personal vision endorses the dynamic commonality of worldliness. Nancy's essay was composed in the summer of 1995 in dialogue with a shattering list of 'proper names', bearing in mind Derrida's insight that 'a proper name is never purely individual': Bosnia-Herzegovina, Chechnya, Rwanda, Nigeria, Afghanistan – and numerous others. The roll call remains disturbingly current, while leaving scope for including more recent emblematic names. It moves Nancy to compassion, once more stressing 'with' as the Latinate prefix 'com'; here 'compassion' should be glossed as 'the contact of being with one another in this turmoil' or 'the disturbance of violent relatedness' (ibid.: xii-xiii). The ontology of 'being-with' is therefore an ontology of bodies, steadfastly eschewing the lures of idealist self-preoccupation. These bodies are not only human but encompass every body, whether 'animate, inanimate, sentient, speaking, thinking, having weight' (ibid.: xii-xiii). Moreover, a body is seen as 'outside': 'next to, against, nearby, with a(n) (other) body, from body to body', in the perpetual dis-position or mobility of all bodies. Crucially, a body goes from itself to itself; 'whether made of stone, wood, plastic, or flesh, a body is the sharing of and the departure from self, the departure toward self, the nearby-to-self without which the "self" would not even be "on its own" ["à part soi"]' (ibid.: 84).

Nancy's philosophy of bodies is vastly hospitable in its inclusivity, refusing as it does to distinguish between the human and the non-human, living and non-living. Disposition or displacement becomes the precondition of being at home in a singular-plural world. Similarly, bodies are at home in and with themselves, acting as host-guests that leave themselves only to return to themselves as irreplaceable points of origin in a network that confirms shared originariness. For Derrida, the interruption of the self by the self as other is intrinsic to hospitality, just as Levinas interrupts phenomenological praxis in *Totality and Infinity* to address the 'enigma' of the face that will found his ethics (see Derrida 1999a, 51-53). Each of the chapters in this collection is alive to those interruptions, dispositions and transitions that advance or obstruct hospitality in environments of affirmed singular plurality or elicited compassion as 'the disturbance of violent relatedness'. The innovation of the project is to reinscribe the investigation of hospitality within a north-south and south-south mapping, both literally and figuratively. From the latter perspective, hosts and guests operate as actors within a magnetic field of diverse attractions and repulsions; these forces are analysed in their concreteness and their relationality. By the same token, the openness of the collection launches a dialogue between chapters which focus on the north, those dedicated to the global south and those which cross boundaries. Given the unprecedented influx of foreign refugees and asylum-seekers in recent years, there has often been a tendency to prioritise cosmopolitanism and the 'migrant crisis' in Europe, as, for instance, in Thomas Claviez's discerning *The Conditions of Hospitality* (2013). Yet hospitality should encourage a broadening of the frame of reference, as Judith Still does in engaging with North Africa, especially Algeria and Morocco, in *Derrida and Hospitality* (2013). These pieces freely traverse an eclectic diversity of spaces and times, from medieval Europe in Donald R. Wehrs's chapter, to nineteenth-century South Africa and contemporary Australia in the contributions by Rebecca Fasselt and Russell West-Pavlov. Immigration policy in today's United States (David Watson) meets Gothic spectrality in Britain (Dale Townshend), while transgressive transitions between Algeria and France burst longitudinal restraints by crossing over into the dream visitations that the dead pay to the living (Merle A. Williams). North-south and south-south are porous frames that invite infiltrations, as well as unpredictable reconfigurations.

Engaging with the north–south and south–south axes, together with the assorted human or cultural flows that they plot, cannot but raise the loaded question of the relation between the ethics and the politics of hospitality. This question is again central to the chapters that follow. Although Derrida insists that there is a *'formal injunction'* to derive a politics and a law from ethics, the rest is left undetermined

> or still to be determined beyond all knowledge, beyond all presentation, all concepts, all possible intuition, in a singular way, in the speech and responsibility *taken* by each person, in each situation, and on the basis of an analysis that is each time unique – unique and infinite, unique but *a priori* exposed to substitution, unique and yet general, interminable in spite of the urgency of the decision.
>
> (Derrida 1999a, 115)

This is the austere discipline of the decision which cannot simply exercise knowledge. If one knew unequivocally in advance what to do, there would be no decision but 'the application of a rule, the consequence of a premiss or of a matrix' (Derrida 1999b, 66). In the silence of its interruption of consecutive temporality, in its very anachrony, the decision must be hospitable to the unknowable and the transcendent, turning the decision-maker from host into hostage. Its strange logic traces out the indissociable heterogeneity of absolute and conditional hospitality, as the singularity of ethical infinity is, of necessity, converted into general measures or circumscribed pragmatic steps. And these perversions mask the concomitant risk, encapsulated in 'hostipitality', that the seemingly benevolent may transpose itself into the malign.

This irreducibility of the decision in its derailing of reassuring temporal sequences suggests revisiting the extreme case of a messianic 'hospitality without reserve' (Derrida 1994, 65). The context and rationale of such thinking are lucidly, if briefly, investigated in the *Adieu to Emanuel Levinas*, where Derrida contends that phenomenal existence, duly supported by '"real" qualities' or 'predicates', is not a prerequisite for hospitality (Derrida 1999a, 110-11). The other must simply be welcomed in its alterity, however troublingly *unheimlich* or uncanny. 'There would be no hospitality without the chance of spectrality,' Derrida insists, 'a hospitality offered to the *guest* as *ghost* or *Geist* or *Gast*' (ibid.: 110-12, especially 111). And, because spectrality at once exceeds ontological categories and deconstruction, it may impose orders (as does the ghost of Hamlet's father on the battlements of Elsinore) or give and refuse pardon (like God who is beyond essence). Derrida thus wistfully reflects that the spectral may arouse an ultimate hospitality in its guise as the Face of the Wholly Other (ibid.: 111). This is decisively saying *yes* to dead things whenever they turn up, *arrivants* whose links with their turbulent history dematerialise into the promise of a veiled future-yet-to-come (playing on '*avenir*' and '*à venir*'). Spectrality forebodes the pure event, a

> messianic opening to . . . the event that cannot be awaited *as such*, or recognised in advance therefore, to the event as the foreigner itself, to her or

to him for whom one must leave an empty place, always, in memory of the hope.

(Derrida 1994, 65)

The essays by Dale Townshend and Merle A. Williams in this collection venture directly into the domain of spectrality, whereas several other chapters are painfully haunted by ghosts of the past. Pardon and hope are not consistently the outcome, though; the orders imposed and events precipitated run the gamut of an aporetic hospitality juggling with the terrifying volatility of untrammelled possibility.

If there can be no hospitality without the risk and the prospect of spectrality, though, language is of central significance in its turn. As he brings *Totality and Infinity* to a close, Levinas argues that 'the essence of language is goodness, or again . . . the essence of language is friendship and hospitality' (Levinas 1969, 305). To apprehend the self from within, to produce an 'I', is already and by the same movement to turn towards the Other in extraversion and in the desire for expression. The purpose of language is construed as welcoming, ethical responsiveness, although Levinas will adapt and refine this position into his complex account of the Saying and the Said in *Otherwise than Being*. Nancy addresses these notions in quite a different, but equally hospitable, manner. For him, 'saying is corporeal', whereas what is said is incorporeal, exposing all bodies 'according to their being-with-one-another' (Nancy 2000, 84); they are (as he has taken care to explain) *amongst themselves* ['*entre eux*'] as origins, so that their disposition becomes a relation of meaning. In a single stride, he closes the gap between the animate and the inanimate by contending that 'language is the exposing of plural singularity' (ibid.). It gives the meaning 'of the world as being-with, the simultaneity of all presences that *are* with regard to one another, where no one is for oneself without being for others' (ibid.: 85). In this way, dialogue with the self cannot be distinguished from discourse with others in accordance with a self-consistent logic of temporal coexistence; this is also singular plural and aligned with the prevailing principles of hospitality. From Nancy's perspective, there can, furthermore, be no ultimate language, but only 'languages, words, voices, an originarily singular sharing of voices without which there would be no voice' (ibid.: 85). Humans are, in effect, granted no particular privilege; their task is 'to expose the world and its proper being-with-all-beings in the world' (ibid.). In an idiosyncratic modification of characteristically phenomenological practice, Nancy intertwines language with the meaning of the life-world.

In *Sharing the World*, Luce Irigaray underscores the regenerative capacity of fertile silence in accordance with her philosophy of letting-be. Yet she remains concerned about the communicative use of language in more conventional ways as well, combining awareness of a certain kind of singular plurality with sensitivity to difference:

> The way we talk, with and to one another, reflects or develops a manner of being in relation with oneself, with the world, with the other or others, to

which we must pay attention if we want to make hospitality that respects difference(s) between us possible.

(Irigaray 2013, 49)

So she recommends mutual verbal exchanges that rely on formulae of equivalence (such as 'we talk to one another') (Irigaray 2013, 49). In addition, she laments the alienation of an increasing 'remoteness' and indeed the 'forgetting' of 'self-affection' since the demise of ancient Greek culture. She draws attention to the erosion of the middle voice as a modality for conveying a comprehensive relation of the self to the self that was neither uniformly active nor passive, in addition to the disappearance of dual forms as a means of uniting different elements in harmonious, integrated function: hands or eyes, 'but also the two sexes or the two genders' (ibid.: 52-53). Here hospitality consists not so much in the interruption associated with Levinas or Derrida, but in the linguistic apprehension of subtle collaborations across seeming tensions, divisions or incompatibilities.

In her rich and penetrating *Derrida and Hospitality*, Judith Still makes a strong case for 'an openness of reading and writing, along with political openness (at the level of the State) and ethical openness between individuals' (Still 2013, 82). She suggests that absolute or pure hospitality to texts is both impossible and undesirable, because readers will inevitably choose to be selective in their citations, adoptions or interpretations – undiscriminating receptiveness could, in fact, amount to a type of insanity. Nonetheless, Still aptly contends that 'respectful and responsible readings are . . . modes of conditional hospitality' (Still 2013, 83), while outlining models for the kinds of intertextual guests she might elect to invite into her enquiry (ibid.: 82-84). In this process (ibid.: 83, 85-86), she cordially acknowledges Hillis Miller's pyrotechnic display in 'The Critic as Host' (1979), in which he cumulatively demonstrates the resources of deconstruction while performatively refuting allegations that this critical orientation is 'parasitical' on the 'obvious' or 'univocal' account of a text (Miller 1979, 217). This essay is also the *locus classicus* for the etymological derivations of 'host' and 'guest' (Miller 1979, 220-21; see 4–5 above), not to mention the notion of the 'parasite'. The Greek *parasitos* initially meant 'beside the grain' or food, an attractive image of hospitable conviviality. Later connotations of the word, however, shift the valence to hostipitality, since the guest comes to greedily exploit the host (ibid.: 220). Miller's conceptual archaeology tests the extent to which texts may be deemed to prey on one another, with poems putatively feeding off their predecessors or critical discourse consuming the lifeblood of literature. Nonetheless, he cannily unfolds a hospitable/hostipitable concatenation of negotiations among works in an unlimited series without any fixed beginning or end (ibid.: 225-26). In a not dissimilar fashion, 'metaphysics' is shown to be inhabited by the 'nihilism' that in narrow binary theory ought to be its incompatible other. Anticipating Derrida on the impassability of the aporia as a precondition for walking, Miller comments that

the place we inhabit, wherever we are, is always this in-between zone, place of host and parasite, neither inside nor outside . . . a region of the *Unheimlich*, which reforms itself wherever we are . . . in whatever text, in the most inclusive sense of the word, we happen to be living.

(ibid.: 231)

So the reversible semantics of host and guest is woven into the contingent fabric of language, as well as textuality and critical analysis in the broadest sense of those terms.

Both Miller and Still are clearly alive to the imbricated ethics and politics of textual responsiveness. Paola Zaccaria, who was deeply affected by the 'blistering wound inflicted upon hospitality' through the botched circumstances of the Albanian influx into Bari in 1991 (Zaccaria 2013, 168), tentatively proposes the figure of translation as a remedy. She suggests that the translator experiences the antinomies between the laws and *The* law of hospitality, serving at once as host in receiving the migrant's text and as guest in 'find[ing] refuge' in the text of another. Even if the resultant piece is written in one's own mother tongue, it is correspondingly traced by the tongue of the other – Zaccaria's diction anchors itself in the corporeality of expression as much as the innovation of creative language (ibid.: 175-76). Yet she foresees the potential concussion between translation and untranslatability if the guest speaks an unknown dialect, or has been silenced by trauma, or may even be an '"absolute arrivant", without any ID or visa' (ibid.: 180). Language and protean textuality become entrammelled in the (over-)determining characteristics of a hospitality rendered perilously exacting in its pure iteration, but shabbily inadequate – even shameful – when hedged with conditions.

Each of the ten chapters that follow is attuned in its own way to these conflicting imperatives. Reflecting a considered editorial choice, the essays are arranged in a roughly chronological order according to the period(s) in which the works discussed first appeared. This minimal, almost contingent, principle of ordering does not seek to imply some form of historical causality, although many of the essays are interested in the historical development of forms of hospitality and/or inhospitality. Rather, the intention is to keep editorial configuration to a minimum (just as there has been no intervention to alter tongues, voices, linguistic registers or stylistic hallmarks); the purpose is instead to facilitate multiply interweaving and heteroglossic conversations among the texts and their authors. These contributors have freely set the parameters of their hospitable engagements, issuing a wide spectrum of invitations and in some instances encouraging the prospect of textual visitation. Scholars in both the South and the North reflect searchingly and with empathy and insight on phenomena in their respective zones of experience and intellectual competence. Unrestricted border-crossing allows for multiple intellectual transitions which the aporias of hospitality conversely haunt with spectres of transgression, exclusion and alienation. The *being-with* of the volume occurs in the *between* of translation and untranslatability, the excess of pure hospitality and the unavoidable compromises of conditional welcome, the constraints of actuality and the unknowability of a not-yet foreclosed future. The north-south and south-south figures pattern the ensuing singular plural exchanges through irresistible attractions and repulsions that must nevertheless be understood, reappraised, transformed.

Donald R. Wehrs reads romances by Chrétien de Troyes, Wolfram von Eschenbach and Gottfried von Strassburg to take the measure of their inherent 'hermeneutical hospitality'. He investigates the extent to which such texts set up zones whose 'affective particularities' (Charles Altieri) must be fleshed out by audience responses. He shows how Romance connects hospitality to the agency of affect, within the context of cultural paradigm shifts towards a pious lay life in which heterosexual amorous experience can claim a legitimate place; a change in orientation from all-male cathedral schools to the court thus brings in its wake a concomitant shift in generic boundaries. The emergence of Romance is in part driven by reaction against a patristic and scholastic conceptualism inhospitable to the hermeneutic pluralism associated with the flesh and with the feminine. Romance hence stages narrative's hospitality to ethical notions that can be made concrete, literally incarnated in characters' actions and the associated trajectories (for instance, the quest or the trial), by contrast with the constraints of more cerebral conceptual structures. With these concerns in view, Wehrs's examination encompasses such apparently disparate models as contemporary neurobiology (cognitive hospitality to the affects of the other through 'mirror neurones') and medieval theological contexts of affective hospitality, whose ethical injunction is attentiveness to the good. Recognising the uncertainty of rules for regulating degrees of hospitality, Romance is seen to offer narrative models for calibrating and controlling the polarised risks of too little or too much empathetic receptiveness, just as today neurobiology describes different brain functions that counterbalance each other. The discussion ranges across the cultural and narrative theories used by many of the contributors to this volume, from pre-conceptual affective connection (Emmanuel Levinas and Julia Kristeva), as well as the culturalist 'structuring' of these linkages, to the notion of 'just distance' (Paul Ricoeur).

Dale Townshend's essay opens with two scenes of human and spectral hospitality in Sarah Waters's novel *The Little Stranger* (2009). This recurring double trope in the Gothic has become associated with a double order of hospitality that is staged as early as Shakespeare's *Macbeth*; the ordinary hospitality that is often subject to murderous violation is poised against the absolute hospitality rehearsed by Banquo's ghostly appearance at Macbeth's banqueting table. Townshend places the British Gothic within a long lineage that stretches from Macbeth to the contemporary Gothic. Because his narrative begins with Shakespeare's rehearsals of spectral hospitality, Townshend is able to create a narrative that is cognate with Derrida's complex explorations of the tensions within this very notion itself. On the one hand, an actually existing 'conditional' hospitality is always corrupted by a number of linguistic, logistical and practical problems that inevitably implicate it with its opposite: potential hostility towards the visitor and the possibility of the host's being taken 'hostage'. On the other hand, there emerges a hypothetical and impossible, but theoretically indispensable, 'absolute' hospitality whose unachievable status is the vital precondition for an ethics of hospitality that may remain consistently ethical, rather than sliding into the merely pragmatic.

For Townsend, the spectral hospitality that runs through the Gothic heritage is often located, although not without a striking degree of ambivalence, on the side of 'absolute' hospitality, given that it is a form of 'uninvited' 'visitation'. The guest as ghost, coming as a surprise, does not fall under the mastery of the host and may well take him hostage in a manner reminiscent of Levinas' Absolute Other, as evoked by Derrida in his notion of the unconditionality of true hospitality. The affects of terror and horror, which are associated with Gothic writing from Horace Walpole onwards, are typically provoked in an unprepared host by the appearance of an uninvited guest. Indeed, the Gothic novel transforms eighteenth-century fictional forms into frameworks for hosting Shakespearean ghosts, who prove recalcitrantly disruptive. So too, ghostly figures may be less welcomed into Gothic texts than exorcised by the narrative strategies adopted. This consistent ambivalence is to be found from Ann Radcliffe's *The Italian* (1797) (which stages a direct engagement with *Macbeth*) and Matthew Lewis's *The Monk* (1796) to Emily Brontë's *Wuthering Heights* (1847) and Bram Stoker's *Dracula* (1897). Then it duly appears in twentieth-century avatars of the Gothic, such as Robert Bloch's *Psycho* (1959) and Stephen King's *The Shining* (1977). Spanning the inventively shifting legacy of more than four centuries, hospitality vacillates between its conditional manifestation and absolute 'hosti/pita/lity', occupying the 'hiatus' or 'abyss' between the entangled terms.

Drawing on Theodor Adorno and Derrida, Mike Marais's piece commences by exploring the aporia of the home assumed by the act of welcoming. Hospitality is predicated upon the boundaries which make a home the homely into which the guest may be welcomed. Yet, by the same token, those boundaries render the guest an interloper, an intruder and a potential enemy to be combated or ejected. Inhospitality is inscribed in the very homeliness that enables – and thus disables – hospitality. True hospitality therefore necessitates the unhomeliness of the home that Adorno diagnosed during the final days of the Second World War. Wandering or vagrancy, a mode of travel that never brings you home, leaves home futural, anticipated but never attained, and thus never domesticated into the 'borderlines' that enable a hostipitality. Marais unfolds this complex of ideas by investigating Beckett's *Molloy* (1951), in which the protagonist Moran embarks upon an Abrahamic-Homeric wandering that takes him back to a home which has become unhomely or *unheimlich*. This wandering effectively makes Moran unrecognisable to his fellows, while his narrative of experience becomes equally foreign to those who receive it, including its readers. Marais duly poses the question: How are we as readers to relate, from within the reductive terms of home, to that which home seeks to exclude in order to constitute itself as home? Which linguistic codes can we implement so as to recognise what home renders unrecognisable from within its constitutive codes of recognition? In order to respond, the reader must reconstitute her or his own linguistic, semiotic or epistemological home as less homely. (These concerns resonate suggestively with those of Derrida, Levinas and Nancy, in addition to other theories and practices of linguistic hospitality explored by Merle A. Williams and Russell West-Pavlov in their chapters on Cixous and Scott respectively.) Marais claims that Beckett's *Molloy* is informed by an ethic of hospitality premised on a responsibility for those exclusions that enable community. This approach limits the limitations of home, opening it to a guest who has not already been identified and so remains perhaps unknowable, thereby making the place of welcome less a home than, in terms of Marais's pithy spatio-temporal paradox, a haunt.

Rebecca Fasselt's reading of Sol Plaatje's novel *Mhudi* (1930) considers a fictional evocation of the precolonial era in South Africa from a perspective prior to apartheid, highlighting the ways in which the text casts a critical gaze upon race relations before the Second World War. By implication, Fasselt's chapter also refracts that gaze across the fraught period of post-apartheid following its celebratory transitional honeymoon, particularly the second decade of democracy, when issues of hospitality and hostility began to overshadow the erstwhile utopia of the rainbow nation. At this juncture, Fasselt's preoccupations intersect in fascinating ways with David Watson's enquiry. Like Plaatje, who employs the genre of the historical novel to set up palimpsests that multiply historical horizons, so too Fasselt replicates the gesture of historiographical 'entanglement' in her own text. She suggests that Plaatje returns to the precolonial past, with its conflicts between the Barolong, the Matabele and the Boers, so as to escape the stifling binary of settler and native, black and white, in a manner that significantly calls to mind a decade of immigrant versus native conflicts in post-apartheid South Africa, where the fault lines lie between various African identities as much as between Black natives and white settlers (on this topic, see Sanders 2016). Plaatje's revisiting of the period of the *mfecane*, the great demographic and geopolitical upheaval in southern Africa in the 1840s, allows him to escape the prison-house of the nation and its simplistic narrative of European colonisation. In fact, *Mhudi* enacts a constant criss-crossing between the roles of guest and host, between power and powerlessness, possession and dispossession, hospitality and hostility.

Fasselt underscores Plaatje's cyclical notion of the switches between offers of hospitality and their withdrawal, culminating in a retreat into hostility between the potential partners. The transformation of the colonisers from guests into master-hosts is only the last of many such switches (but one that resonates across the colonial world, as shown in West-Pavlov's essay on Kim Scott's fictions of first contact in South-Western Australia). The idea of a cyclical pattern allows Plaatje to highlight multi-planar and multi-local temporalities, thereby displacing the hegemony of linear notions of historical teleology. This, in turn, enables him to make unruly, disruptive connections between past and present that Fasselt further co-opts in order to craft a utopian account of Plaatje's fiction, thus addressing the multifarious malaises of contemporary South Africa. Stressing the historical open-endedness of Plaatje's text, in contrast to those critics who see the author's vision as consummated by the birth of the new democratic order, Fasselt links Plaatje's temporalities to a tradition of the 'not yet' that runs from Gramsci and

Bloch through to postcolonial thinkers such as Ashcroft. These temporal intertwinings are themselves redolent of the syncopated temporalities informing the ethical realm of the decision, which paradoxically bridges absolute and conditional hospitality. An open-ended utopian spirit is borne out by several conflicting notions of hospitality that underpin the novel's ending, which is variously construed as pessimistic and hopeful, although as yet unrealised. Eschewing textual closure hence becomes a form of backward-looking intertextual hospitality that enables a forward-looking utopian hospitality, supplemented by a play of hospitalities and inhospitalities. These permutations finally sustain a hospitable gesture to us as readers – for we, today, will decide which of the available options may gain the upper hand. In the modus of hauntology and hospitable accommodation, Fasselt's chapter incisively explores the aporetic temporalities of specific practices and narratives of hospitality.

Jane Taylor's creative reflection examines the nexus of hospitality and personhood. She begins with the Enlightenment congealing of personhood, religion and place which both guarantees hospitality for the native and excludes the foreigner. Taylor acerbically draws links with South Africa's apartheid policy, which carved out ethnic enclaves imagined as foreign states within the state, effectively denying hospitality to its own citizens. These Bantustans amounted to pseudo-states designated as reservations of unproductive territory; this deceptive strategy gave pseudo-legality to a system of discrimination by inserting it into the framework of international law. Black South Africans, long foreigners in their own land, became *de jure* and not merely *de facto* strangers. This splitting of South African national personhood so as to relegate the black majority to the status of internal foreigners perverted the multiplicity that exists within the persona and between persons, endangering community by excising the other. The body politic, Taylor suggests, cannot exist without the foreign body (which, following Jean-Luc Nancy, she articulates as *l'intrus* ('the intruder') along lines that intersect with Dale Townshend's chapter). Yet, Taylor contends, such distortion of the body politic has somehow become a local norm to the extent that another category of unwanted guest was invented after the abolition of apartheid in order to replace the inhabitants of Bantustans. The intruder or burglar has become entrenched as a stock threat in the South African imaginary; this nightmare figure has now been elevated to transnational status: South Africa has the illegal African immigrant as its new other. Through an ingenious variation within her argument, Taylor plays with the relationship between consciousness and embodiment as a strategy for probing the self-other dichotomy. If John Locke's puzzle of two separate consciousnesses' inhabiting a single body leads him to the conclusion that personhood resides in consciousness, then a twentieth-century heart transplant demonstrates how a seemingly alien, donated organ can be assimilated into the body of an otherwise doomed person. Beliefs about foreignness and belonging are hence revealingly complicated, highlighting analogies between the person and the body politic, possession and hospitality. It is the gift, as interpreted by Marcel Mauss, that is seen as vital to sustaining human sociality.

In her chapter on the mourning of loss and the inter-implicated loss of mourning, Merle A. Williams explores the friendship between Hélène Cixous and Jacques Derrida as a space of hospitality, one that may embrace an entire lifetime, until the very last of the last days, at once encompassing and exceeding death. This relationship is shaped against the background of Cixous's doubly alienating experience of exile as a Jewish child under Vichy rule, and as a French girl in a colonial Algeria to which she could not and would not belong. After leaving to attend university in a thoroughly unwelcoming France, she finds repeatedly deferred hospitality fulfilled in her personal and professional association with Jacques Derrida. An intriguing counterpoint emerges in her belated forging of a bond with her inaccessible Algerian classmate, Zohra Drif, for years as resistant to closeness as Algeria itself, because seemingly never to be possessed. Yet it is Drif who facilitates Cixous's unexpected return to Algeria, to the scenes of her childhood and her father's grave – only for the geographical Algeria to elude her once again.

By contrast, the friendship with Derrida is mediated by language, with the burgeoning inventiveness of their multiple verbal, literary and philosophical exchanges coming to trace the inexhaustible possibilities of life and the shadowy unknowability of death. Sinuous linguistic webs entwine the obtrusive awareness of death – to be '*Vutsch*' in the German slang of Cixous's mother, the archetypal Eve, and '*fichu*' in the French register of Derrida's father – with the *fichu* as 'shawl' or as a 'veil' that conceals but may also reveal, separating while uniting the dead with the living. An irrepressible linguistic energy then appropriates the unveiling of the apocalypse, which finds affinities with the *histos* as fabric or the scarred skin of the dying Eve. Further connotations and echoes facilitate transformation into the *voile* (as Walter Benjamin's dream sail or an Islamic veil), then leading to the *tallit* or prayer shawl as a symbol of transcendent hospitality in and through prayer. These textual webs both hide and expose meaning, dispersing and generating it, doubling the ontology of existence with a Derridean 'hauntology' of the mutual infusion of death and life. The entire friendship between Derrida and Cixous revolves around issues of 'learning to live' – 'finally'. Williams's essay works as a performative act of hospitality; the reader is invited to enter a space of proto-philosophical, proto-poetic language, an opening to linguistic hospitality of the sort that Levinas might have imagined, since the pliant twists and turns of the argument follow the textualising logic of the hospitable interaction between Derrida and Cixous.

David Watson's chapter offers a reading of Atticus Lish's novel *Preparation for the Next Life* (2015) in order to track a contemporary shift in the modelling of narratives of migrancy. Whereas the governing trope of the tale of migration once mapped a curve from the familiar to the foreign (a story of alienation), the new paradigm becomes the increasing securitisation of migrancy, founded upon the identification of the migrant as a threat and culminating in the radical curtailment of hospitality. The element of transgression already identified as a facet of hospitality comes to dominate the entire paradigm, resulting in a transgression of the very norms of co-existence. This conceptual realignment has become terrifyingly topical with the interdiction on immigration for Muslims in the first week of Donald Trump's presidency, as well as his deployment of troops to protect the US-Mexican border in November 2018, to cite only a couple of examples in the headlines at the moment of writing. In the emergent paradigm analysed by Watson, security becomes a conditional form of hospitality that differentiates starkly between desirable and undesirable forms of migration; this procedure culminates in the production of inhospitality, understood not only as the abstract negation of hospitality but as an apparatus of affective and social forms of life to be inhabited and endured by the migrant. Freedom and mobility are conjoined and juxtaposed with an articulation of security that connects it with dispossession and immobility, which then intersect in the body of the migrant. Watson concludes by turning the excluded condition of the migrant into a continuum shared by dispossessed aliens and dispossessed citizens alike, therefore suggesting that forms of hospitality which are transversal to the nation-state and its zones of exclusion may offer innovative possibilities for political action.

The impetus towards sharing as propounded, for example, in the theories of Nancy and Irigaray, becomes even more compelling when its spills over the circumscribed borders of the human. Judith Still's essay on the hospitality offered by and to animals explores the ways in which this notion, traditionally thought in terms of relationships only between humans, may be unsettled when interactions are shifted to straddle the border between humans and the non-human, as represented in this context by animals. (The chapters by Townshend and Williams extend such border-crossing to the dead, while West-Pavlov's essay, questioning the very notion of death, shifts this boundary even farther to include the landscape as a whole). Still embarks incrementally on the disruption of customary demarcations in her reading of *Ladivine* (2013), a recent fiction by Marie NDiaye. First, she switches from the perspective of the welcoming or unwelcoming host, laden with obligations, to the position of the guest. Second, she moves the locus of (in)hospitality from Europe (which, especially since the refugee 'crisis' of 2015, has rather narcissistically imagined itself as bearing the burden of global hospitality) to an unspecified area in the global south, where the hosts are the Indigenous people and the guests European tourists, thus suggesting associations with the chapters by Fasselt and Taylor. Hospitality is bedevilled by a colonial past and a neocolonial present that render genuine forms of welcome almost impossible for both partners in the tourist transaction. Third, Still undertakes a final unsettlement of the not-quite isomorphic host-guest and hospitality-inhospitality borders by installing in the position of caring host not a human, but an animal. As it would seem, a dog shepherds or sympathises and empathises with the unwelcome guest. Still's essay does not resolve these questions, but in keeping with the putatively magical realist, or perhaps more appropriately metaphorical-literalist, tenor of NDiaye's fiction, leaves the dog as a textual figure without resettling the boundaries disturbed by the narrative. In a world where more and more borders are being closed, as David Watson's commentary demonstrates and as Donald Trump's draconian 2018 restrictions on immigration have corroborated, it is a salutary decision to leave borders open, even when they are intangibly aesthetic and philosophical in nature.

Following Judith Still's opening of the transspecies site of hospitality, Russell West-Pavlov's chapter continues this dynamic by dealing with hospitality between humans and the cosmos. Not ghosts, but the still-present and powerfully active Dreaming ancestors are embodied in Indigenous 'Country' and its landscape formations. The piece opens with questions about Australian Indigenous 'welcomes' to 'Country', or rituals of admission and acknowledgement of admission to Indigenous territory. Such welcomes have recently become common in a settler nation only now confronting its two-hundred-year history of invasion, genocidal and ecocidal subjugation and continuing managerial colonialism. The chapter discusses a number of instances of literary 'welcome protocols' to be found in the work of Western Australian Noongar writer Kim Scott, in particular the memoir *Kayang & Me* (co-authored with Scott's aunt, the Indigenous elder Hazel Brown; 2005), and the first-contact novel *That Deadman Dance* (2010). These narrative instantiations of welcome resonate with the linguistic manifestations of hospitality explored in many of the chapters in the volume. Linguistic-performative welcomes to Country work in two directions at once. They rehearse the equal personhood of humans and non-human actors, such as animals and places in the landscape. At the same time as they cast nature as alive, sentient and intentional (adopting the terminology of Brazilian anthropologist Viveiros de Castro), they also reveal nature as not singular and universal, but multiple, caught up in unceasing transformations. In this manner, welcomes to Country reveal the hospitality of the cosmos itself, which imposes infinite obligations upon all its inhabitants in a form of conditional hospitality. By the same token, however, these welcomes point to the infinite dynamism of the cosmos within itself, so that this conditional hospitality is also unconditionally absolute by virtue of the infinite generosity of cosmic creativity that it provides for those it welcomes. Australian Indigenous traditions accordingly reveal a mode of ultimate cosmic hospitality embodied in Country, exceeding and radicalising the terms of the debate as usually played out in the contemporary critical humanities.

Like several other contributors to this volume, Anthea Buys enquires about the hospitality that is generic to the work of art itself. How does a work of art (like a work of literature in the chapters by Wehrs, Townshend, Fasselt and Still) open itself to the outside world in a hospitable gesture? How indeed do artists welcome outsiders into the artistic spaces that art, in the age of the installation, has so often come to incorporate? How does art, as a space and not merely as an object, become what Nicholas Bourriaud in his *Relational Aesthetics* (Bourriaud 2002, 30) describes as a realm of convivial sociability? The question becomes all the more acute and over-determined for Buys, because the homes and indeed physical houses in her descriptions are the topic and the topos, the real site, of artistic installations dealing with hospitality, inhospitality and homelessness. The artists range from Constant Nieuwenhuys, who was active from the 1950s onwards, to Gordon Matta-Clark in the 1970s, Martha Rosler in the late 1980s and Theaster Gates in the late 2000s. Buys closely questions the underlying dynamics of their installations of hospitality, disclosing the artist's persisting mastery over the house even in the face of performative gestures of artistic conviviality. Citing Jacques Rancière's notion of 'policing', she claims that this mastery is isomorphic with a neutralisation of the putative political force of the aesthetic gesture. In this regard, the selected works of art express the vulnerability, openness or porosity of the home or house, as well as approaching a multipolar notion of hospitality. Matta-Clark's sliced or perforated houses illustrate the spatial embodiment of a less 'policed' hospitality, but not necessarily one that is more harmonious. Rather, this creation of shattered dwellings suggests that hospitality, if it is to be genuine, cannot exclude the possibility of conflict and hostility. These notions have been radicalised by later artist-activists, such as Rosler, who draws attention to the machinations of the real estate market in encouraging inhospitality. Yet again, the ambivalence of hostipitality, with its intermingling of welcome and transgression, is foregrounded, although this time by an aesthetic practice that draws attention to the imbrication of accommodation and rebuff in the governance and custodianship of both built and natural environments.

The essays in this collection present a palette of perspectives on hospitality, inhospitality and their ambivalent hybrid interconnections across a range of historical periods from the medieval, through the colonial, to the present. The different discussions range across the North and the South, but also across a variety of genres, particularly literary-linguistic forms. The heterogeneity of the chosen approaches serves as a timely reminder of the aptness of multiple, open-ended and complex understandings of these issues. Without engagements of this kind, we will find ourselves poorly equipped to confront the tensions, aporias and dilemmas of hospitality, as we take up residence in this turbulent, uncertain and perhaps even apocalyptic twenty-first century.

References

Bourriaud, Nicolas. 2002. *Relational Aesthetics*. Translated by Simon Pleasance and Fronza Woods, with Mathieu Copeland. Dijon: Les presses du réel.

Claviez, Thomas (ed.). 2013. *The Conditions of Hospitality: Ethics, Politics, and Aesthetics at the Threshold of the Possible*. New York: Fordham University Press.

Derrida, Jacques. 1994. *Specters of Marx: The State of the Debt, the Work of Mourning, and the New International*. Translated by Peggy Kamuf. Introduction by Bernd Magnus and Stephen Cullenberg. London and New York: Routledge.

———. 1999a. *Adieu to Emmanuel Levinas*. Translated by Pascale-Anne Brault and Michael Naas. Stanford, CA: Stanford University Press.

———. 1999b. 'Hospitality, Justice and Responsibility: A Dialogue with Jacques Derrida'. In *Questioning Ethics: Contemporary Debates in Philosophy*, edited by Richard Kearney and Mark Dooley, 65–83. London and New York: Routledge.

———. 2000a. 'Hostipitality', translated by Barry Stocker and Forbes Morlock. *Angelaki: Journal of the Theoretical Humanities* 5.3: 3–18.

———. 2000b. *Of Hospitality: Anne Dufourmantelle Invites Jacques Derrida to Respond*. Translated by Rachel Bowlby. Stanford, CA: Stanford University Press.

———. 2002. 'Hostipitality: Session of January 8, 1997'. In *Acts of Religion*, edited and introduced by Gil Anidjar, 356–420. London and New York: Routledge.

Dufourmantelle, Anne. 2013. 'Hospitality – Under Compassion and Violence'. In *The Conditions of Hospitality: Ethics, Politics, and Aesthetics on the Threshold of the Possible*, edited by Thomas Claviez, 13-23. New York: Fordham University Press.

IPCC [Intergovernmental Panel on Climate Change]. 2018. *Global Warming of 1.5°: An IPCC Special Report . . .* – Summary for Policy-Makers. www.ipcc.ch/pdf/special-reports/sr15/sr15_spm_final.pdf (accessed 24 November 2018).

Irigaray, Luce. 2008. *Sharing the World*. London and New York: Continuum.

———. 2013. 'Toward a Mutual Hospitality'. In *The Conditions of Hospitality: Ethics, Politics, and Aesthetics on the Threshold of the Possible*, edited by Thomas Claviez, 42-54. New York: Fordham University Press.

Levinas, Emmanuel. 1969. *Totality and Infinity: An Essay on Exteriority*. Translated by Alphonso Lingis. Pittsburgh, PA: Duquesne University Press.

———. 1998. *Otherwise than Being or Beyond Essence*. Translated by Alphonso Lingis. Pittsburgh, PA: Duquesne University Press.

Miller, J. Hillis. 1979. 'The Critic as Host'. In *Deconstruction and Criticism*, edited by Harold Bloom, Paul de Man, Jacques Derrida, Geoffrey H. Hartmann and J. Hillis Miller, 217-53. London and Henley: Routledge and Kegan Paul.

Nancy, Jean-Luc. 2000. 'Of Being Singular Plural'. In *Being Singular Plural*, translated by Robert B. Richardson and Anne O'Byrne. Stanford, CA: Stanford University Press.

Nealon, Jeffrey T. 2016. *Plant Theory: Biopower and Vegetable Life*. Stanford, CA: Stanford University Press.

Rigaud, Kanta Kumari, Alex de Sherbinin, Bryan Jones, et al. 2018. *Groundswell: Preparing for Internal Climate Migration*. Washington, DC: World Bank. https://openknowledge.worldbank.org/handle/10986/29461 (accessed 24 November 2018).

Sanders, Mark. 2016. *Learning Zulu: A Secret History of Language in South Africa*. Princeton, NJ: Princeton University Press.

Still, Judith. 2013. *Derrida and Hospitality: Theory and Practice*. Edinburgh: Edinburgh University Press.

UNHCR. 2011. *Global Trends Forced Displacement in 2011*. www.unhcr.org/statistics/country/4fd6f87f9/unhcr-global-trends-2011.html (accessed 24 November 2018).

———. 2014. *Global Trends Forced Displacement in 2014*. www.unhcr.org/556725e69.html (accessed 24 November 2018).

———. 2017. *Global Trends Forced Displacement in 2017*. www.unhcr.org/globaltrends2017/ (accessed 24 November 2018).

———. 2019. *Global Trends Forced Displacement in 2018*. Released 19 June 2019. www.unhcr.org/globaltrends2018/ (accessed 20 September 2019).

WMO [World Meteorological Organization]. 2018. *Greenhouse Gas Levels in Atmosphere Reach New Record*. Press Release Number 22112018, 20 November 2018. https://public.wmo.int/en/media/press-release/greenhouse-gas-levels-atmosphere-reach-new-record (accessed 24 November 2018).

Zaccaria, Paola. 2013. 'The Art and Poetics of Translation as Hospitality'. In *The Conditions of Hospitality: Ethics, Politics, and Aesthetics at the Threshold of the Possible*, edited by Thomas Claviez, 168-84. New York: Fordham University Press.

2
WELCOMING AND PLURALISM IN THE ROMANCES OF CHRÉTIEN, WOLFRAM AND GOTTFRIED

Donald R. Wehrs

In a 2014 essay, 'Appreciating Appreciation', Charles Altieri recalls Wittgenstein's distinction between 'acts of description that carry truth values and acts of description that display states of mind and feeling' (Altieri 2014, 45). Noting that many expressive actions 'strive to be recognised by their particularity rather than their argumentative capacity', Altieri argues that 'recognition of expressive particularity requires that audiences be willing and capable of fleshing out the possible significance of these actions by developing appropriate responses that engage and respect that particularity' (ibid.: 46-47). This kind of 'fleshing out', or affective, intellectual 'welcoming', is urged upon courtly audiences by the remarkable vernacular narrative poetry that flowered between Chrétien de Troyes' invention of Arthurian romance in the 1160s and Wolfram von Eschenbach's *Parzival* and Gottfried von Strassburg's *Tristan*, both *c.* 1210. Literary efforts to induce audiences to 'welcome' pluralistic, complicating textual nuances reflect a new 'hospitality' within Latin Christendom to the notion that affective sensations and susceptibilities intrinsic to embodied, sociable human life may bear ethical and religious significance (Fulton 2002; McNamer 2010). This 'hospitality' is evident in efforts to transmute Ciceronian-clerical ideals of male friendship into defences of heterosexual love, and to affirm ethical-pious sociality's presence within lay life (Jaeger 1999; Reddy 2012; Green 1994, especially 249-315).

Romance's interest in human affective experience and its possible authority and significance partakes of a broader twelfth-century questioning of Neoplatonic-Patristic metaphysics and hermeneutics. This questioning is prompted in part by the influence of Abelard's logic and ethics (Sturges 1991, 6-23; Vance 1987), in part by increased literacy generally (Haug 1997, especially 91-227; Stock 1983), and in part by shifts in the site of efforts to cultivate humanistic ethical-religious sociality from all-male cathedral schools to the mixed clerical and lay, male and female milieu of courts (Jaeger 1994; Kay 2001, 305; Kelly 1992, 15-31 and 117-21). Paradoxically, expanding high medieval literacy works against its consequence in antiquity. There, written 'standard versions' of Homer and Hesiod disclosed differences between archaic and classical Greek thought which were explained away by methods of interpreting traditional texts that divested textual surfaces of any 'inhospitable' resistance to the decoder's metaphysical, moral or theistic assumptions (Brisson 2004, 8).[1] Once refractory particularities came to be seen as unwanted guests, they were either consigned to invisibility or enfolded within larger, homogenising, totalising conceptual patterns (Struck 2004, 26-76; Lamberton 1986, 12-33).[2]

Moreover, if the mind is to be kept from hosting incorrect or dissonant content, affective experience must not be conceded its own capacity to discern significance. Epitomising early medieval piety, John Scottus Eriugena, in his ninth-century *Periphyseon*, distinguishes between a spiritual body, gendered male and governed by an understanding derived from *logos* or *ratio*, and a material body, gendered female and conveying an illegitimate exterior sense that may pervert or seduce inner sense (Moran 1989, 139-43). Eriugena suggests that attending to or welcoming disruptive, dissonant textual nuances is the equivalent of coming under the sway of seductive female voices (Otten 1991, 160-219; Moran 1989, 174-85; Carabine 2000, 93-107).

By contrast, contemporary philosophy associates ethics with welcoming discrete particulars whose irreducible substance and significance press upon us affective immediacies that, for Levinas, 'an-archically' disrupt the 'principles' composing conceptual and cultural worlds in which we are 'at home', *chez soi* (Levinas 1981, 99-102; Levinas 1969, 33, 36, 40). Receptivity to textual difference and interpretative pluralism, treated as extensions of welcoming strangers into one's home, indicates a willingness to listen to others, to attend to signification whose internal directionality may be distinct from our presuppositions and desires. Extending such hospitality, we encounter abidingly non-harmonised, aporetic dimensions of thought, the identification and amplification of which pre-occupies Derrida, and whose registering seems embedded within the sociality of language itself. As Levinas observes and Derrida reiterates, 'language *is* hospitality' (Derrida 2000, 135, emphasis in original; Levinas 1969, 64-77 and 204-12; Levinas 1981, 3-4, 34-38 and 45-51).

This is not an exclusively modern notion. Aristotle, defining words as 'symbols of affections of the soul' (Aristotle 1987, 12), makes language's hosting of affective immediacies the basis of its intelligibility. Emerging from what minds and bodies normatively '"suffer" or "undergo"' (Struck 2004, 61) in everyday living,[3] language elicits and speaks to pre-linguistic, pre-conceptual embodied susceptibilities. This is where Levinas locates ethical sensibility (Levinas 1969, 187-201 and 299-304; Levinas 1981, 61-97). It is also where contemporary neuroscience situates neural mirroring of others and somatic empathy (Klimecki and Singer 2013; Coplan and Goldie 2011; Iacoboni 2008). Clinical research in 2010 suggests that, on a neurophysiological level, a momentary empathic 'hosting' of another's somatic state *necessarily* unsettles forms of egocentric emotion processing, which determine that whatever is perceived to be of 'biological value' *for us* is felt *by us* to be good (Damasio 2010, 31-60). Indeed, involuntary bodily resonance with others recurrently disrupts 'inhospitable' prioritising of self over others, in-groups over out-groups (Singer 2006). There is, thus, a neurophysiological basis for the aporias that Derrida notes in the concept of hospitality, its 'unconditional or hyperbolic' dimension forcing us to 'straddle' selfless and 'biologic' modalities of the good (Derrida 2000, 137).[4] Just as witnessing or imagining another's action induces neural activity involved in performing the action, so brain areas that monitor our body states (the anterior cingulate cortex and the anterior insula) are engaged in registering another's body state (Klimecki and Singer 2013). Being so affected by others' somatic experience underlies our hearing 'unconditional' commands for 'hyperbolic' hospitality as not only intelligible and possible, but as something to which our deepest interiority, our heart's understanding, is felt to give involuntarily assent, or to remember as having been previously enjoined.

The theological basis of medieval hermeneutical hospitality to literary particularity

Within medieval contexts, however, where entertaining wrong ideas and feelings was considered a threat to salvation, their possible incitement and reinforcement by discordant or complicating textual nuances might well appear as dangers to eternal well-being, no less than to temporal interest. Still, unease with Neoplatonic-Patristic marginalising of scriptural surface details, building up during the early twelfth century (Sturges 1991, 13-16), was heightened by Abelard, whose radical rethinking of logic, metaphysics, ethics and grace entered into chivalric romance's innovative form and content (Vance 1987, 14-40; Kay 2001, 11-15). Retrieving anti-Platonic ontological implications in Aristotle's logic, Abelard rejects the notion that what is most real in an individual is what most adheres to an abstract form bestowing being (Marenbon 2013, 119; King 2004, 81). For Abelard, Constant Mews argues, 'When we speak of "this animal" or "that body", the *sententia*, or judgment, that we are making is about *singularia*, that which is unique, not some universal thing'; similarly, 'what matters with language is the sense or force of a proposition rather than individual words' (Mews 2005, 87). Brian Stock points out that '[i]n Abelard's view, a sentence . . . expresses the manner in which things relate to each other', so that words 'are the verbalizations of man's inner conceptions of reality' (Stock 1983, 384; also Guilfoy 2004; Abaelardus 1970). To hear or read another is to make oneself hospitable, at least provisionally, to another's individuated understandings (intellections) of images naturally resembling things in the world, which (as image, thing, or both) move affections of the soul (Stock 1983, 378; Guilfoy 2004, 202). Discourse communicates how a mind works *in particularised instances*, with images resembling things accorded conventional signs (Stock 1983, 382-83).

Spelling out the theological implications of such philosophy, Abelard makes valorisation of concrete particularity and pluralism central to a reformed, rational-ethical conception of Christianity.[5] For Abelard, 'the Holy Spirit is not simply the love of the Father and the Son but rather the love of God for creation'

(Mews 2005, 114; see also Marenbon 1997, 54-61; Abaelardus 1970, 297-551) and so divine love encompasses love for what is other (creation), embracing concern for the good of the other (and others), valorising plurality. Human nature and reason, born of that love, incline towards elemental desire for the good and ethical sense (Marenbon 1997, 216-50). In the *Theologia christiana* (*c.* mid-1120s), Abelard insists that the Holy Spirit's 'comforting' love articulates 'God's goodness to the world' and that 'Paul's comment about the *Invisibilia Dei* being revealed to the pagans supports the notion that righteousness (*justitia*) has its origin in natural law, not in any written law' (Mews 2005, 132, 134).[6] Reading Paul's *Invisibilia Dei* passage (Romans 1:20) as indicating that natural law bestows the perception of ethical significance and inclinations towards the good on *all* humans (Marenbon 1997, 64-69; Mews 2005, 186-95; Abaelardus 1970, 153-56 and 172-82), Abelard stresses how Christ's 'teaching us through word and example even to death . . . bind[s] us to himself through longing (*amor*) so that true love (*caritas*) would fear nothing for his sake' (Mews 2005, 189; see also Williams 2004; Marenbon 1997, 324-26). Being moved, affectively, by the moral beauty of others' words and actions, above all Christ's, brings bodily hospitality to *passiones* (*pathos*), which bears upon intentional consciousness in ways that increase its receptivity to moral, spiritual redemptive agencies.[7]

Distinguishing between 'a wrong will and consent to that wrong will in deliberate contempt of God' (Mews 2005, 220; Abelard 1971; Mann 2004), Abelard argues that suffering natural desire, as in desiring fruit from another's garden, need not in itself constitute sin. While the 'very nature of [human] infirmity' may 'compel' one 'to desire what he is not allowed to take', if one 'represses' rather than 'extinguish[es]' desire, one 'is not drawn to consent (*non trahitur ad consensum*)' and so 'does not incur sin' (Abelard 1971, 15). Moreover, the imperative to love others enjoins us to search out with imaginative sympathy the intentions consented to in actions, for 'there is no sin unless it is against conscience' (*peccatum non est nisi contra conscientiam*; ibid.: 26-27). Against the background of Paul's claim that conscience is the Law of the Gentiles, Abelard pointedly asks, 'For those who do not know Christ and therefore reject the Christian faith because they believe it to be contrary to God, what contempt of God have they in what they do for God's sake and therefore think they do well?' (ibid.: 57). What matters about an idea or action is not its absolute validity or rightness, but rather the intention or spirit, motivating or expressed by it, that is, whether it aspires (however mistakenly) to ethical-sociable piety.

This perspective allows the value of literary-rhetorical arts to be conceived not in terms of rightly picturing in fables pre-established theological dogmas and philosophical claims, but rather in terms of those arts' arousing within us forms of ethical-sociable pious intentionality and affections enjoined by the 'spirit' of both natural and divine law.[8] Notably, in a series of *Planctus* (verse lamentations), Abelard, as a poet, sought to depict Old Testament characters as affectively complex singularised individuals by placing them within 'a lyric world where the quality of feeling is what matters', a world where literary art moving affections of the soul acquires 'an authority all [its] own' (Wetherbee 2004). Chrétien brings that authority into vernacular poetry.

Chivalric romance and giving welcome to literary expressive particularity

Identifying in his first romance the *bele conjointure* (beautifully apt, sound, perceptive combination) of *matiere* (material, story) and *san* as his signature achievement, Chrétien implies that to brush aside complexly artful textual surfaces is to lack courtly liberality, sophistication, and wit. *San* indeed denotes wisdom, learning, and sense (*sens*), which may encompass an awareness of ultimate reality, or of courtly and practical life, or of intellect informed by sociable affections and humanising values (de Troyes 1987, line 14).[9] Listeners or readers attentive to what is expressively particular, Chrétien intimates, embark on 'adventures' in which imaginative writing, long thought of as a vehicle for illustrating received ideas,[10] engages the affections in ways that refine ethical-rational understanding of what matters most (which was, for the twelfth-century Anglo-Norman world, theological-political concerns).

In a groundbreaking study, K. Sarah-Jane Murray notes that *Erec et Enide* not only interweaves classical and Celtic literary material to create a new genre, but also draws upon the structure and themes of Martianus Capella's enormously influential late classical allegory, *The Marriage of Mercury and Philology* (c. 410-39) (Murray 2008, 173-215). Murray argues that in reconfiguring human, female Philology's relation to divine, male Mercury in terms of active reciprocity between a lady and her knight, Chrétien reimagines Martianus's Neoplatonic allegory of the mind's descent into matter as a marriage of learning and eloquence figured in terms of an imagined earthly (if idealised) marriage. He thus implicitly renegotiates poetry's 'marriage' with metaphysics.[11]

Positing a narrative world where knights are 'hardiz et conbatanz et fiers' ['brave and combative and fierce'] and ladies and maidens 'gentes et beles' ['noble and beautiful'] (31), Chrétien poses the question of how (male) self-protective and aggressive impulses might be turned away from a ferocity which undermines all those forms of courteous (female) 'welcoming' that sustain political, sociable, and biological life. Erec, a young heir to a throne serving an apprenticeship in knighthood at Arthur's court, witnesses the queen, Guinevere, who sends a maiden to inquire after the identity of an armoured knight accompanied by a dwarf and a maiden. After Guinevere's maid declares on the queen's behalf, 'a ce chevalier voel parler' ['I wish to speak to that knight'] (168), the dwarf strikes her with a whip. When Guinevere asks the unarmed Erec to reiterate a polite greeting, the dwarf strikes him with the same whip.

Female speech solicits sociality; Erec's attentiveness to what it asks, which is central to his civil sense of what is due to others (in Derrida's terms, to the juridico-political aspects of hospitality), places him in the maiden's role. But the knight's discourtesy, given conventional personification in the dwarf, treats what is outside or other merely as a threat or prey. Erec begins to find his own identity through adventures that prompt narrative equivalents of rhetorical *inventio* (the finding of *topoi* to support claims). He seeks permission from the queen to pursue the knight, to exact revenge, certainly, but also to bring to account a 'vilains' and 'outrageus' ['uncourtly and unprincipled'] (241) adversary, one for whom elite male combativeness is identical with boorish, small-minded anti-sociality, as symbolised by the dwarf's physique.[12] In seeking to enforce moderation upon qualities he shares, to make what is masculine 'greet' what is feminine with respect, Erec is led, by marvellous adventure, to Enide.

Coming upon a fortified town, he is received as a guest by an impoverished, elderly minor noble whose daughter, though hyperbolically beautiful (411-37), has no less admirable qualities of mind and heart. Erec recognises in Enide's kindness to her father and hospitality towards himself a good sense ('bien senee', 509) that her father also lauds (537-40). In chivalric romance, narrative causality 'discovers' a moral logic that connects metaphysical principles with socio-political experience. As he fights the discourteous knight, Erec looks towards Enide, and his strength increases: 'por s'amor et por sa biauté / a reprise molt grant fierté' ['because of her love and her beauty / he regained his great courage'] (915-16). His 'fierté', unlike the discourteous knight's, is strengthened by sociable affection. In bewildered defeat, the discourteous knight asks what he has done to incur Erec's wrath. Erec replies, 'Granz viltance est de ferir fame!' ['It is a vile thing to strike a woman!'] (1017). Separating knighthood from the 'viltance' of the dwarf's aggression should establish a 'true' courtliness, uniting hospitality's hyperbolic and juridico-political dimensions, in acknowledging that others, above all women, are more than plunder to be seized or obstacles to be swept away.

Chrétien's romance goes on to suggest that an inaugural welcoming into oneself of what is distinctive to another, figured in marriage, must be refined and concretely incarnated through overcoming a series of ordeals, depicted as chivalric adventures, that reform intentionality by enacting within wedded love increasing trust and reciprocity. As a final challenge, Erec is led to an enchanted garden where there are flowers all year, fruit cannot be removed, and no plants produce spice or medicine (5693-5718). The garden, suspending materiality's 'marriage' to time, enforces a stasis that denies Creation's fecundity. Erec encounters stakes bearing the heads of defeated knights and a horn no one has been able to sound.

Confronted with this uncanny realm, Enide need not speak, for Erec, well-knowing her heart (5787), addresses her apprehensions for him by declaring, not out of 'orguel' ['pride'] (5815), but from a wish 'conforter' ['to comfort'] (5816) her, that courage born of her love makes him confident against any opponent. Erec encounters a beautiful maiden and then a knight. The latter, viewing Erec's approach to the maiden as a threat to dispossess him of her, challenges him to a duel. Erec prevails, and the defeated knight, Maboagrain, describes how, in courting the maiden, he had promised to stay in the garden until some knight vanquished him. Not believing he could be overcome, she intended to keep him 'toz les jorz' ['all the days'] that he lived 'avoec li' ['with her'], effectively held 'an prison' ['in prison'] (6050-51). Reworking magical material from Welsh folklore, Chrétien presents the maiden and knight as analogues of Enide and Erec (indeed, the maiden is Enide's cousin). In them, however, erotic love has been perverted into possessive, tyrannical *cupiditas* (desire).

Only the defeat of the antisocial, egotistic impulses epitomised by each lover's imprisoning of the other can put psychic space in harmony with the larger cosmic-metaphysical orderings of being. Nature ceases to be alienated from time when Eric sounds the horn, releasing a joy ('joie', 6144) that penetrates and transforms the order of things. Just as Erec frees Maboagrain, so Enide seeks the maiden, hears her story and tells her own. Through Enide's words, emblematic of the romance itself, the lady 'se conforte' ['was consoled'] (6289), the sight of which makes Maboagrain happy. In providing 'comfort' for others, like Enide's words, and by implication Chrétien's poem, and by the forms of welcoming perfected in marital love, humans partake in the Holy Spirit's redemptive agency. Similarly, Chrétien's welcoming through his generically and culturally heterogeneous material in his innovatively new genre, the chivalric romance, and his inviting his audience to do the same, links the forms of hospitable intentionality cultivated by marital love with those elicited and honed by the literary arts. Moreover, 'joy' attesting to a non-egocentric affective resonance with another, as in Maboagrain's joy at seeing his lady being comforted, also applies to the audience's bearing towards Chrétien's characters, thus intimating that, by giving welcome to literary arts that bring us into non-egocentric affective resonance with imagined others, we may partake in a similarly diffusive joy.

Hospitality to the stranger and welcoming intellectual daring in Wolfram's *Parzival*

Wolfram follows Chrétien in thinking of poetic discovery (*inventio*) less in terms of finding *topoi* to serve argumentative intentions (*intentio*) (Kelly 1992, 32-67) than in terms of discerning the sense that emerges from adventurous poetic conjunctions. He likewise makes the effects of *intentio*'s receptivity to such sense central to his narrative's 'matter', and so to vernacular poetry's cultural, social value.[13] In German contexts, affirming that literary discourse and life in the lay world may be hospitable to effectual goodness accords with what D. H. Green calls a 'new secular ideal' championing courtly society's 'cultural independence' against clerical efforts to divest lay society of internally generated legitimacy and value (Green 1994, 275; see also 270-315). The papacy of Innocent III (1197-1216), coinciding with *Parzival*'s composition, tirelessly affiliated Catholic piety with armed conquest and coercively enforced orthodoxy (Claster 2009, 195-96, 211-12). This was epitomised by the fiasco of the Fourth Crusade (1198–1204), when Constantinople was pillaged instead of Jerusalem being recaptured. 'Crusading' as a term shifted from denoting efforts to regain Jerusalem to designating endeavours to subjugate by force all perceived opponents of papal authority or interests (Toch

1999). Moreover, assertions of papal supremacy and Latin ethnocentric insularity routinely went together (Watt 1999, 114-18, 126-45; Moore 1987).

Thus, in *Parzival's* prologue, a strong political-religious edge adheres to Wolfram's repudiation of aesthetic, moral and intellectual forms of mediocrity and cowardice. In declaring, 'Ist zwîvel herzen nâchgebûr, / daz muoz der sêle werden sûr' (1, 1-2) ['If inconstancy is the heart's neighbor, the soul will not fail to find it bitter' (3)],[14] Wolfram might appear to be starting, conventionally, from a maxim or *sententia*, but 'zwîvel,' whose semantic range runs from 'inconstancy' to religious despair (Haug 1997, 158; Schirok 2002, 74; Powell 2009, 84-85), opens up to interpretative ambiguities that, paradoxically, welcome a higher form of 'constancy' or loyalty – signified by the crucial word *triuwe* (also spelled *triwe*).[15] The next lines, 'gesmæhet unde gezieret / ist, swâ sich parrieret / unverzaget mannes muot / als agelstern varwe tuot' (1, 3–6) ['Blame and praise alike befall when a dauntless man's spirit is black-and-white-mixed like the magpie's plumage' (3)], are a famous crux,[16] for they exploit the semantic range of 'muot', which is translatable as 'courage' as well as 'spirit', to denote martial valour, intrepid spirit (dispositional or affective virtues), and moral/intellectual courage. Faith ('triuwe') counters the kinds of 'zwîvel' that make us inconstant to 'muot', to the courage or spirit appropriate for knights (and others) who are 'unverzaget' (1, 5), dauntless, fearless. Only the 'unverzaget', those undaunted in fidelity to an inner 'muot' made possible by trust in God's loving goodness, have courage enough to follow the example of the 'âventiure', here signifying not primarily Parzival's story but Wolfram's writing. Wolfram observes that his simile of the black-and-white-mixed plumage of the magpie is a 'vliegende bîspel' (1, 15) ['flying metaphor' (3)], apt to be 'gar ze snel' (1, 16) ['much too swift'] for 'tumben liuten', ['dull-witted people']; when they try to grasp it, it will dart away like a startled hare ('schellac hase', 1, 19). Poor listeners and readers resemble inept hunters. Dullness in cognitive *following* implies deficient welcoming of another's word, a withholding of trust akin to that of a knight refusing to follow his lord's lead into battle.

Wolfram asks his audience both for loyalty (*triwe*) and, as Haug notes, for *stæte* ('constancy') (Haug 1997, 162), qualities associated with religion, political allegiance and marital fidelity. The welcome he solicits, however, is not a demand for uncritical acceptance or blind deference. Because his poem's tales and lessons are 'nimmer des verzagent' (2, 9) ['never (without) courage' (4)], because they 'vliehent unde jagent' (2, 10) ['flee and hunt'], 'entwîchent unde kêrent' (2, 11) ['dart away and come back'], 'lasternt und êrent' (2, 12) ['reprove and honour'], one cannot follow their sense without exercising intellectual, moral and affective equivalents of knightly virtues. Daring to think on one's own and daring to host others' thoughts both work against becoming either 'versitzet' or 'vergêt' (2, 15), immobilised or aimlessly off-course. Without 'muot', one will shut out all that problematises conventional opinion; without 'triuwe', trust in God's goodness and by extension confidence in goodness within this life and other people, one will lack ethical-rational sociality. 'Muot' and 'triuwe' must work together dialogically.[17] But for Wolfram, behind dialogism (actively responsive understanding of another's words and welcoming of diverse speech genres, voices, and worldviews (Morson and Emerson 1990, 23-25, 54-56)) stands a trust or faith that, 'wed' to *muot*, disdains such faith as induces (or excuses) uncritical conformity.

Faith as trust/loyalty, for Wolfram, underlies an understanding of divine agency that both sanctifies marital love and enjoins hospitality irrespective of ethnic, racial, cultural and confessional difference. After years of fruitless warfare following his abjuring a God whom he views as having poorly rewarded his service, Parzival comes as an unknown stranger to the dwelling of a hermit, Trevrizent. Offering the knight hospitality, Trevrizent insists that, despite being a layman, he is well-read in scripture and so can affirm that one should be loyal ('getriwe', 462, 18) to God, because 'got selbe ein triuwe ist' (462, 19) ['God Himself is a faithful (One)']; He is truth ('wârheit', 462, 25), and so can be false 'an nieman' (462, 28) ['to no one']. Trevrizent's claim is a variant of Abelard's that God, being rational goodness itself, cannot do otherwise than He does, though this position was much contested in the generations before Wolfram, as John Marenbon notes (Marenbon 2013, 45-133). Trevrizent further argues that the incarnation proceeds from perfected *triuwe* as its logical consequence: 'er hât vil durch uns getân,/ sît sîn edel hôher art / durch uns ze menschen bilde wart' (462, 22-24) ['He did much for us when His noble, lofty nature took on, for our sakes, the likeness of man' (248)]. The reiteration of 'durch uns' underscores that *triuwe*'s essence lies in making others' good the principle – in the senses of both the origin and the rule – of its actions.

Sin, balking at offering others the 'hyperbolic' hospitality that perfected *triuwe* enjoins, instead incites bloodshed and so robs the earth of innocence or virginity. Nonetheless, earthly goodness abides, above all in maidens without falseness. Divine appreciation of maidenly purity is such that God makes Himself the child of the most exemplary of maidens (464, 23-26), an act through which 'er uns sippe lougent niht' (465, 5) ['(He) did not deny His kinship with us' (249)]. God extends *to all* people the ethical solicitude associated with kinship bonds. Devotion to other people's good, purified of the egocentric processing of emotion, indifferent to ethnicity, culture, race and class, as well as forgiving of previous injury, constitutes the 'erbarme' (465, 8) [pity or compassion] whose 'geselleschaft' [society or company] *is* God.[18] Wolfram stresses less coming to desire one's true good (Augustine's theme) than rather coming to host intentions of making others the focus of love and reparation, intentions God nurtures, models, and enables (as Abelard argues): 'nu kêret iwer gemüete, / daz er iu danke güete' (467, 9-10) ['Now turn your heart to Him, that He may acknowledge your goodness' (250)]. The proper turning of our 'gemüete' – or affective interiority – brings into us a particularised goodness ('güete') whose kindly, hospitable recognition by God yields the appreciation ('danke') of His extending to us protective grace.[19]

Emulating God's example enlarges human welcoming of others, as is dramatised by the Grail society's welcoming of Parzival's biracial, non-Christian half-brother.

While riding along, Parzival encounters a rich stranger ('rîche gaste', 735, 8), with whom he falls into single combat. Expressing goodwill towards them both, the narrator declares that their fighting puts at risk each man's 'freude, sælde, und êre' (742, 22) ['joy, salvation, and honor' (387)], since victory for either must bring about loss of all 'wertlîch freude' (742, 25) ['worldly joy']; it will ensure for the one who kills the other everlasting 'herzen riwe' (742, 26) ['heart's regret']. When Parzival, pressed in battle, shouts the name of his wife's kingdom, he is infused with such strength that he deals the heathen a blow sufficient to make his opponent stagger. This narrative sequences does not, however, attest to Christian courtly love's ability to conjure up a quantum of force greater than the quantum of force called forth by heathen courtly love. Instead, the strength given to Parzival paradoxically *helps* him by breaking his sword in two (744, 14-18). The sense ('sin') of this material ('mære') is that spiritual power is *not* something we can call forth and translate into physical force simply by enunciating the correct verbal formula.

His sword broken, Parzival finds himself in peril, but the heathen knight extends grace to him. By addressing Parzival as 'werlîcher man' (744, 29) and 'werlîcher helt' (745, 3), ['a brave/noble/worthy man and hero'], he shows his understanding that Parzival would have continued the fight without a sword, but he (the stranger) could have expected no gain in renown had he exploited this advantage. Generously declaring that Parzival would have prevailed had the sword not broken (745, 4-6), the stranger asks his name and identifies himself as Feirefiz, Parzival's half-brother (745, 26-30). Throughout this scene, Wolfram stresses that the initiative leading away from unwitting fratricide is all attributable to Feirefiz. In simple plot terms, Parzival is indebted to another's goodness for all that follows in the narrative, including his healing the Grail kingdom and being reunited with his wife.[20] Although Wolfram could have contrived the story so that Parzival extended a grace to which Feirefiz responded, he pointedly avoids this possibility.

Reconciled, they soon encounter Gawan, Parzival's cousin, who kisses Fierefiz, and then introduces his newly found kinsman to his female relatives, who likewise kiss the stranger. Parzival acknowledges to Gawan his brother's graciousness in throwing away his own sword: 'er vorhte et an mir sünde, / ê wir gerechenten ze künde' (759, 15-16) ['Even before we had worked out our kinship, he was afraid of committing a sin against me' (395)]. Wolfram stresses the causal sequence: literal kinship is discovered *as the result of* one person's fear ('vorhte') of sinning against another. Strikingly, the one whose fear of sin ('sünde', a theologically weighted term) triggers the flowering of gracious, reformative, moral community is not a Christian.[21] Fierefiz is soon introduced to Arthur and others, and the stranger ('gaste') always finds himself enveloped in the 'guoten willen' (765, 27) ['good will'] of having come among 'guoten friunden' (765, 29) ['good friends']. All this suggests that Wolfram conspicuously distances religious and racial bigotry from the ideal world he depicts.

Indeed, Fierefiz is similarly welcomed by the Grail society, even though it is an association of religious knights devoted to promoting Christianity, though by example rather than by violence. Moreover, the romance suggests that this hospitability is congruent with divine will. When Fierefiz asks about the source of the food and wine being served in the Grail castle, it becomes clear that, though a 'heiden' (810, 2), he is able to appreciate and partake in the Grail's fruits despite being unable to see the Grail itself. He does, however, see the beautiful Repanse de Schoye, whose name meaning 'Overflowing or Spreading of Joy', identifies her with the good brought forth into natural, material life by the Grail. In fact, he sees her with an eye so properly attuned to recognising what is rationally desirable that the emotional hold of his previous loves upon him begins to dissipate.[22] Without baptism, Fierefiz is still accorded respect and treated with kindness, even by a lay courtly community with a distinctly religious mission. Notably, conversion is not a requirement for friendship, and the Grail itself enacts ecumenical hospitality. Its food and wine are emblematic not just of the good things of the earth that in love God provides for his kin ('sippe'), all of humankind; in their Eucharistic resonances, these gifts further denote the comforts of divine loving-kindness, the gifts of the Holy Spirit. These are diffused to all within a community (notably hard to find) that is born of receptive participation in that very loving-kindness, although the source is visible to (fully understood by) only Christians.

Gottfried and transformative hospitality to others' love and art

Writing contemporaneously with Wolfram, Gottfried presents appreciative welcoming of what is good, including aesthetic appreciation, as an ethical-religious obligation: 'Der guote man swaz der in guot / und niwan der werlt ze guote tuot, / zwer daz iht anders wan in guot / vernemen wil, der missetuot' (5-8) ['We do wrong to receive otherwise than well what a good man does well-meaningly and solely for our good' (41)].[23] Anything less than receiving 'the good' with a proper spirit or understanding is not just wrongdoing (a 'missetuot'), but wrongdoing born of a perverted will (the act of one who wills to take – 'vernemen wil' – what is good as something bad). Gottfried hence describes the effect of Tristan and Isolde's love, as well as his poem's art, upon the best of souls and readers, in remarkably Eucharistic terms. Though Tristan and Isolde are dead, they still live, for wherever the tale is heard, their 'triuwe' – their 'triuwen reinekeit', their 'herzeliep' and 'herzeliet' (231-32) ['fidelity, loyal purity, heart's joy and heart's suffering'] – will become 'brot' (233) ['bread'] for all 'edelen herzen' ['noble hearts']. When one reads or hears Tristan and Isolde's story, one becomes a communicant of an invisible, spiritual society for whom their deaths are the 'brot' (240) ['bread'] of the living.

The radicalising of hospitality implicit in taking such a 'host' into one's heart may be glimpsed by looking at one narrative moment. Tristan and Isolde's love, the involuntary consequence of their unwittingly drinking a potion, is marked by a high degree of self-love until each forgoes the opportunity to escape this painful longing offered by the presence of a magical dog. Tristan sends the dog to Isolde, thus placing her good above his own; she divests the dog of its magic, for she would rather endure the pain her love inflicts than lose the identity that her love confers. In not wishing to be 'vro' (16399) ['happy' (256)] without Tristan's companionship, Isolde becomes a singularised holy paradox: 'diu getriuwe stæte senedærin' (16400) ['(t)his constant, faithful lover']. With her 'vröude unde ir leben' (16401) ['joy and her life'] given over, as she now clearly understands, to 'sene unde Tristande' (16402), Isolde overcomes the separation of self and other (her life and Tristan) that seems to doom humans to be vassals of *cupiditas*.[24]

Ironically, this shift from sexual obsession to emotional inseparability makes the lovers more, rather than less, vulnerable to public exposure. Because 'des herzen vriunt, daz ouge was / gewendet nach dem herzen ie' (16490-91) ['that friend of the heart, the eye, was ever turned toward the heart' (258)], Isolde and Tristan are often unable to disengage their looks from each other until their king, Mark, who is Isolde's husband and Tristan's uncle, 'envünde ie dar inne / den balsemen der minne' (16499-16500) ['had found Love's balm in them']. As a consequence, his heart is tormented by 'solhen zorn und solhen haz' (16510) ['such envy and hatred'] that his doubt ('zwivel', 16513) is overcome, but with the effect that 'leit und zorn' (16515) ['pain and anger'] make him lose 'sinne und maze' (16516) ['measure and reason'].

Mark is not incensed simply that another man has expropriated his sexual property, damaged his reputation or compromised his political position. What causes the death of his sense or reason ('ez was siner sinne ein tot', 16517) is that he shares Tristan's absolute valorisation of Isolde – 'wan ime was ie genote / niht dinges vor Isote / und was ie dar an stæte' (16521-23) ['he valued nothing above Isolde, and in this he never wavered']. Nonetheless, he can discern between the lovers an intimacy of soul, a joy of interconnectedness, that constitutes a bliss from which he is excluded. Whereas he had previously seemed strangely untouched by mere erotic pleasures, through seeing the interaction of Tristan and Isolde he has now come to discover the substantiality of a joy whose weight and texture was previously unregistered by him. In this respect, he oddly resembles a reader or auditor of the narrative of which he is a part.[25] Desperate to escape the pain accompanying the realisation that his wife is to him 'lieber dan sin lip' (16526) ['dearer . . . than life'], Mark fondly imagines that anger may drown affection. He no longer cares whether his suspicions of a sexual liaison are true or not (16533-34), for what he cannot help but see, rather than proof of technical adultery, drives him into 'blinden leide' (16535) ['blind agony'].

Summoning both his wife and his nephew before the court, Mark tells Isolde that he can see that her heart and eyes are bound to Tristan (16554-56). Still, he cannot revenge himself, though it is his right (and indeed political duty), for he loves them both too much to kill or harm them (16588-98). In a gesture of extraordinary generosity, Mark acknowledges their moral and ontological separateness from himself and his concerns. Perceiving them in their own terms, rather than in relation to himself, he banishes but also blesses them. Mark renounces his claims upon each so that they may live together the lives that they must live through and for one another: 'sit iuwer liebe so groz ist, / son wil ich iuch nach dirre vrist / beswæren noch betwingen / an keinen iuwern dingen' (16599-16602) ['Since your love is so great, from this hour I shall not vex or molest you in any of your concerns' (259)]; 'vart ir beidiu gote ergeben, / leitet liebe unde leben, / als iu ze muote geste' (16617-19) ['Go, the two of you, with God's protection. Live and love as you please . . .'].

While Gottfried depicts this sublime hospitality to the actuality of others' experience and their needs as fleeting, he shows Mark for a moment to be the ideal reader of Tristan and Isolde's love, as imagined in the prologue, someone who, moved by their example of self-forgetting devotion to each other, emulates it to the point of undergoing an inner transformation that may without exaggeration or blasphemy be likened to taking in the Eucharistic host. In learning to welcome such wondrous affective transformations, we ourselves become hospitable to the graces in literary art that, for Chrétien, Wolfram, and Gottfried, figure those of religion. Yet secular readers may view such transformations as engaging neuroanatomical processes which are registered in phenomenological consciousness as the hearing of absolute commands to unconditional hospitality, as described by Levinas and Derrida. Appreciating art's eliciting of such affectivity hardly undoes the aporias that Derrida notes in the notion of hospitality. What it does make plain, however, is that aesthetic appreciation, pluralistic intellectual welcoming and ethical responsiveness are all rooted in involuntary somatic resonances with others that momentarily, but recurrently, suspend otherwise structuring self/other or in-group/out-group differences; moreover, these imbricated reactions bear more than an analogical or adventitious relation to one another.

Notes

1 By contrast, oral discourse is open to continuous, often unconscious revision. See Vansina (1985).
2 The subordination of literary significance to philosophical regulation in classical culture is discussed in greater detail in Wehrs (2011, especially 521-45).
3 See also Modrak (2001). For Aristotelian entwinements of the ethical, affective, and intelligible, see Baracchi (2008) and Long (2004).
4 For the involuntary relation of embodied sociality to ethical sense, see Krueger (2008). On the ethical disruption of egocentric emotion processing, see Levinas (1969, 303), Levinas (1981, 3-4) and Levinas (1990, 9).
5 For the resistance of Abelard's contemporaries to his insistence that ethical rationality must regulate divine will, see Marenbon (2013, 45–87).
6 Marenbon notes that for Abelard there is 'a common measure between God's goodness and that of other things' (1997, 218).
7 The relation of this aspect of Abelard's thought to John of Salisbury's pluralistic political philosophy, as well as his sharing a defence of the liberal arts with Chrétien de Troyes, is discussed in Wehrs (2014).
8 On Chrétien's knowledge of Abelard's ethical thought, see Duggan (2001, 124, 134, 148); see also Kay (2001, 52).

9 All further references are drawn from this edition and will be cited parenthetically by line numbers in the text. All translations are Carroll's unless otherwise indicated. On the denotative and connotative range of *conjointure* and *san*, see Kelly (1992, 15-31, 117-21).
10 See especially the notion that fictions act as veils for conceptual-metaphysical truths in Macrobius (1952, 11-12). Isidore of Seville designates any narrative irreducible to such 'veiling' as mere fiction (*fabula*), that is, tales *contra naturam* (Isidore of Seville 1910, 44).
11 Different aspects of the relationship of Chrétien's romance to Martianus's allegory are explored in Wehrs (2019, 302–03).
12 Romance conventions for denoting inner moral qualities by outward appearances attest to inhospitable aspects of courtly society. However, where the genre's imagined worlds are concerned, judging by appearances is endorsed *only* if the outside is indeed an index of the inside (which is not always the case).
13 For the ways in which Chrétien, Wolfram and Gottfried separate poetic theory and practice from the mere reiteration of classical rhetorical treatises, see Haug (1997, especially 7-25, 153-227), as well as Schirok (2002) and Powell (2009).
14 All references from Wolfram's works are drawn from the Lachman (1926) edition and will be cited parenthetically by line numbers in the text. The English translation, unless otherwise indicated, is that of Helen M. Mustard and Charles E. Passage, and will be cited parenthetically by page numbers in the text.
15 On the religious, feudal, courtly and amorous valences of *triuwe*, see Kratz (1973, 460–61).
16 Schirok asks whether this posits a mixing together of qualities (good and bad) or a patterning of separate qualities, some consistently good, others consistently bad (2002, 74). For Powell, the second position is necessary (2009, 83) if Wolfram is to defend lay discourse's claim to 'Sinnfindung' (ibid.: 86) or a sense-discovery no less authoritative than didactic-homiletic clerical argument.
17 On dialogism in Wolfram, see Gross (1995).
18 In *Gemstones of Paradise*, G. Ronald Murphy, S.J. argues that God is presented as 'pure loyalty itself' (2006, 173).
19 I also discuss lines 467 and 9-10 briefly in a different context in Wehrs (2017, 427–28).
20 On Parzival's 'testiness' and 'touchiness' in contrast to Fierefiz's magnanimity, see Green (1982, 249); also Kratz (1973, 394-95, 571).
21 While Wolfram attributes to Muslims 'pagan' polytheistic ideas that reflect popular conventions of the time, the ecumenical sociality he portrays is predicated upon religious tolerance as well as shared secular chivalric norms. See Classen (2012, 155–57).
22 Murphy points out that 'Fierefiz implicitly recognise[s] the Trinitarian pattern of relatedness as he rejoices that the brothers recognised each other', doing so 'in words that are almost Pauline' (2006, 123; see also 752, 7-30). His amorous fixation on Repanse de Schoye similarly figures a pre-attunement to the 'spirit' of Christian revelation (ibid.: 125) that almost anticipates Thomas Aquinas's later argument that some may attain the benefits of the sacraments without receiving them visibly, since 'faith operat[es] out of affection . . . a loving feeling by which God performs an inner sanctification of the person' (ibid.: 124). Wolfram's 'almost literally anticipating Thomas's dictum' (ibid.) also closely resembles Abelard's reading of Paul's account of the 'conscience of the gentiles' showing 'the work of the law written in their hearts' (Romans 2:14-15).
23 All references are drawn from the 1967 edition (von Strassburg 1967b) and will be cited parenthetically by line number in the text. All translations unless otherwise indicated are from A. T. Hatto's translation and will be cited parenthetically by page number.
24 For a brief related discussion of this episode, see Wehrs (2017, 428).
25 Albrecht Classen insightfully explores proximities between Mark and the reader in 'König Marke in Gottfrieds von Strassburg *Tristan*' (1992).

References

Abaelardus, Petrus. 1970. *Opera*. Edited by Victor Cousin. Hildesheim and New York: Georg Olms Verlag.

Abelard, Peter. 1971. *Ethics*. Translated and edited by D. E. Luscombe. Oxford: Clarendon Press.

Altieri, Charles. 2014. 'Appreciating Appreciation'. In *Criticism after Critique: Aesthetics, Literature, and the Political*, edited by Jeffrey R. Di Leo, 45-65. New York: Palgrave Macmillan. https://doi.org/10.1057/9781137428776_4

Aristotle. 1987. *De interpretatione*. In *A New Aristotle Reader*, edited by J. L. Ackrill, 12–23. Princetin, NJ: Princeton University Press.

Baracchi, Claudia. 2008. *Aristotle's Ethics as First Philosophy*. Cambridge: Cambridge University Press.

Brisson, Luc. 2004. *How Philosophers Saved Myths: Allegorical Interpretation and Classical Mythology*. Translated by Catherine Tihanyi. Chicago: University of Chicago Press.

Carabine, Deidre. 2000. *John Scottus Eriugena*. New York: Oxford University Press.

Classen, Albrecht. 1992. 'König Marke in Gottfrieds von Strassburg *Tristan*: Versuch einer Apologie'. *Amsterdamer Beiträge zur älteren Germanistik* 35: 37-63.

———. 2012. 'Early Outreaches from Medieval Christendom to the Muslim East: Wolfram von Eschenbach, Ramon Llull and Nicholas of Cusa Explore Options to Communicate with Representatives of Arabic Islam: Tolerance in the Middle Ages?'. *Studia Neophilologica* 84.2: 151-65.

Claster, Jill N. 2009. *Sacred Violence: The European Crusades to the Middle East, 1095–1396*. Toronto: University of Toronto Press.

Coplan, Amy and Peter Goldie (eds.). 2011. *Empathy: Philosophical and Psychological Perspectives*. Oxford: Oxford University Press.

Damasio, Antonio R. 2010. *Self Comes to Mind: Constructing the Conscious Brain*. London: Vintage.

Derrida, Jacques. 2000. *Of Hospitality: Anne Dufourmantelle Invites Jacques Derrida to Respond*. Translated by Rachel Bowlby. Stanford, CA: Stanford University Press.

de Troyes, Chrétien. 1987. *Erec and Enide*. Edited and translated by Charleton W. Carroll. New York: Garland.

Duggan, Joseph J. 2001. *The Romances of Chrétien de Troyes*. New Haven, CT: Yale University Press.

Fulton, Rachel. 2002. *From Judgment to Passion: Devotion to Christ and the Virgin Mary, 800–1200*. New York: Columbia University Press.

Green, D. H. 1982. *The Art of Recognition in Wolfram's Parzival*. Cambridge: Cambridge University Press.

———. 1994. *Medieval Listening and Reading: The Primary Reception of German Literature 800–1300*. Cambridge: Cambridge University Press.

Gross, Arthur. 1995. *Romancing the Grail: Genre, Science, and Quest in Wolfram's 'Parzival'*. Ithaca, NY: Cornell University Press.

Guilfoy, Kevin. 2004. 'Mind and Cognition'. In *The Cambridge Companion to Abelard*, edited by Jeffrey E. Bowers and Kevin Guilfoy, 200-22. Cambridge: Cambridge University Press.

Haug, Walter. 1997. *Vernacular Literary Theory in the Middle Ages: The German Tradition 800–1300, in Its European Context*. Translated by Joanna M. Catling. Cambridge: Cambridge University Press.

Iacobini, Marco. 2008. *Mirroring People: The New Science of How We Connect with Others*. New York: Farrar, Straus and Giroux.

Isidore of Seville. 1910. *Etymologiae*. Edited by W. H. Lindsay. Oxford: Oxford University Press.
Jaeger, C. Stephen. 1994. *The Envy of Angels: Cathedral Schools and Social Ideals in Medieval Europe, 950–1200*. Philadelphia: University of Pennsylvania Press.
———. 1999. *Ennobling Love: In Search of a Lost Sensibility*. Philadelphia: University of Pennsylvania Press.
Kay, Sarah. 2001. *Courtly Contradictions: The Emergence of the Literary Object in the Twelfth Century*. Stanford, CA: Stanford University Press.
Kelly, Douglas. 1992. *The Art of Medieval French Romance*. Madison: University of Wisconsin Press.
King, Peter. 2004. 'Metaphysics'. In *The Cambridge Companion to Abelard*, edited by Jeffrey E. Bowers and Kevin Guilfoy, 65–125. Cambridge: Cambridge University Press.
Klimecki, Olga and Tania Singer. 2013. 'Empathy from the Perspective of Social Neuroscience'. In *The Cambridge Handbook of Human Affective Neuroscience*, edited by Jorge Armony and Patrik Vuilleumier, 533–49. Cambridge: Cambridge University Press.
Kratz, Henry. 1973. *Wolfram von Eschenbach's 'Parzival': An Attempt at a Total Evaluation*. Bern: Francke Verlag.
Krueger, Joel W. 2008. 'Levinasian Reflections on Somaticity and the Ethical Self'. *Inquiry* 51.6: 603–26.
Lachman, Karl (ed.). 1926. *Wolfram von Eschenbach*. 6th edn. Berlin und Leipzig: Walter de Gruyter.
Lamberton, Richard. 1986. *Homer the Theologian: Neoplatonist Allegorical Readings and the Growth of the Epic Tradition*. Berkeley: University of California Press.
Levinas, Emmanuel. 1969. *Totality and Infinity: An Essay on Exteriority*. Translated by Alphonso Lingis. Pittsburgh, PA: Duquesne University Press.
———. 1981. *Otherwise than Being or Being Essence*. Translated by Alphonso Lingis. Pittsburgh, PA: Duquesne University Press.
———. 1990. *Difficult Freedom: Essays on Judaism*. Translated by Seán Hand. Baltimore, MD: Johns Hopkins University Press.
Long, Christopher P. 2004. *The Ethics of Ontology: Rethinking the Aristotelian Legacy*. Albany: State University of New York Press.
Macrobius, Ambrosius Theodosius. 1952. *Commentary on the 'Dream of Scipio'*. Translated by William H. Stahl. New York: Columbia University Press.
Mann, William E. 2004. 'Ethics'. In *The Cambridge Companion to Abelard*, edited by Jeffrey E. Bowers and Kevin Guilfoy, 279–304. Cambridge: Cambridge University Press.
Marenbon, John. 1997. *The Philosophy of Peter Abelard*. Cambridge: Cambridge University Press.
———. 2013. *Abelard in Four Dimensions: A Twelfth-Century Philosopher in His Context and Ours*. Notre Dame, IN: Notre Dame University Press.
McNamer, Sarah. 2010. *Affective Meditation and the Invention of Medieval Compassion*. Philadelphia: University of Pennsylvania Press.
Mews, Constant J. 2005. *Abelard and Heloise*. Oxford: Oxford University Press.
Modrak, Deborah K. W. 2001. *Aristotle's Theory of Language and Meaning*. Cambridge: Cambridge University Press.
Moore, R. I. 1987. *The Formation of a Persecuting Society: Power and Deviance in Western Europe, 950–1250*. Oxford: Basil Blackwell.
Moran, Dermot. 1989. *The Philosophy of John Scottus Eriugena: A Study of Idealism in the Middle Ages*. Cambridge: Cambridge University Press.

Morson, Gary Saul and Caryl Emerson. 1990. *Mikhail Bakhtin: Creation of a Prosaics*. Stanford, CA: Stanford University Press.

Murphy, G. Ronald, S. J. 2006. *Gemstones of Paradise: The Holy Grail in Wolfram's 'Parzival'*. Oxford: Oxford University Press.

Murray, K. Sarah-Jane. 2008. *From Plato to Lancelot: A Preface to Chrétien de Troyes*. Syracuse, NY: Syracuse University Press.

Otten, Willemien. 1991. *The Anthropology of John Scottus Eriugena*. Leiden: Brill.

Powell, Morgan. 2009. 'Die *Tumben* und die *Wîsen*: Wolframs *Parzival* Prolog neu gedeutet'. *Beiträge zur Geschichte der deutschen Sprache und Literatur* 131.1: 50-90.

Reddy, William M. 2012. *The Making of Romantic Love: Longing and Sexuality in Europe, South Asia, and Japan, 900-1200 CE*. Chicago: University of Chicago Press.

Schirok, Bernd. 2002. 'Von "zusammengereihten Sprüchen" zum "literaturtheoretische[n] Konzep"': Wolfram's Programm im *Parzival*: Die spate Entdeckung, die Umsetzung und die Konsequenzen für die Interpretation'. In *Wolframstudien XVII: Wolfram von Eschenbach, Bilanzen und Perspektiven; Eichstätter Kolloquium 2000*, edited by Wolfgang Haubrichs, Eckart C. Lutz and Klaus Ridder, 63-94. Berlin: E. Schmidt.

Singer, Tania. 2006. 'The Neuronal Basis of Empathy and Mind Reading: Review of Literature and Implications for Future Research'. *Neuroscience and Behavioral Review* 30.6: 855-63.

Stock, Brian. 1983. *The Implications of Literacy: Written Language and Models of Interpretation in the Eleventh and Twelfth Centuries*. Princeton, NJ: Princeton University Press.

Struck, Peter T. 2004. *Birth of the Symbol: Ancient Readers at the Limits of their Texts*. Princeton, NJ: Princeton University Press.

Sturges, Robert S. 1991. *Medieval Interpretation: Models of Reading in Literary Narrative, 1100-1500*. Cardondale, IL: Southern Illinois University Press.

Toch, Michal. 1999. 'Welfs, Hohenstaufens, and Habsburgs'. In *The New Cambridge Medieval History: Volume V c. 1198-1300*, edited by David Abulafia, 375-404. Cambridge: Cambridge University Press.

Vance, Eugene. 1987. *From Topic to Tale: Logic and Narrativity in the Middle Ages*. Minneapolis: University of Minnesota Press.

Vansina, Jan. 1985. *Oral Tradition as History*. Madison: University of Wisconsin Press.

von Eschenbach, Wolfram. 1961. *Parzival*. Translated by Helen M. Mustard and Charles E. Passage. New York: Vintage.

von Strassburg, Gottfried. 1967a. *Tristan*. Edited by Gottfried Weber. Darmstadt: Wissenschaftliche Buchgesellschaft.

———. 1967b. *Tristan, with the 'Tristran' of Thomas*. Translated by A. T. Hatto. rev. ed. Harmondsworth, Middlesex: Penguin.

Watt, J. A. 1999. 'The Papacy'. In *The New Cambridge Medieval History: Volume V c. 1198-1300*, edited by David Abulafia, 105-63. Cambridge: Cambridge University Press.

Wehrs, Donald R. 2011. 'Placing Human Constants with Literary History: Generic Revision and Affective Sociality in *The Winter's Tale* and *The Tempest*'. *Poetics Today* 32.3: 521-91.

———. 2014. 'Emotional Significance and Predation's Uneasy Conscience in John of Salisbury and Chrétien's *Perceval*'. *Literature & Theology* 28.3: 284-98.

———. 2017. 'Narrative and Affect in Epic, Romance, and the Novel'. In *The Palgrave Handbook of Affect Studies and Textual Criticism*, edited by Donald R. Wehrs and Thomas Blake, 413-49. New York: Palgrave Macmillan.

———. 2019. 'Conceptual Blending and Genre Invention from Chrétien de Troyes to Cervantes and Shakespeare'. In *Secrets of Creativity: What Neuroscience, the Arts, and Our*

Minds Reveal, edited by Suzanne Balbantian and Paul M. Smith, 296–316. New York: Oxford University Press.

Wetherbee, Winthrop. 2004. 'Literary Works'. In *The Cambridge Companion to Abelard*, edited by Jeffrey E. Bowers and Kevin Guilfoy, 61-62. Cambridge: Cambridge University Press.

Williams, Thomas. 2004. 'Sin, Grace, and Redemption'. In *The Cambridge Companion to Abelard*, edited by Jeffrey E. Bowers and Kevin Guilfoy, 265-69. Cambridge: Cambridge University Press.

3
GUESTS, HOSTS, GHOSTS
Towards an ethics of gothic writing

Dale Townshend

> I suppose that every big hotel has got its ghosts.
> ~ Jack Torrance, in Stephen King, *The Shining* (King 2007, 290)
>
> There would be no hospitality without the chance of spectrality.
> ~ Jacques Derrida, *Adieu to Emmanuel Levinas* (Derrida 1999a, 111-12)

Like many a ghostly fiction before it, Sarah Waters's acclaimed Gothic novel, *The Little Stranger* (2009), turns upon the difference between two competing yet compatible conceptualisations of hospitality. Early in the narrative, the siblings Caroline and Roderick Ayres and their mother, Mrs Ayres, plan to throw a 'little gathering' at Hundreds Hall, their once grand but now somewhat run-down Georgian mansion (Waters 2010, 77), so as to welcome their new neighbours, Peter and Diana Baker-Hyde, to the district of rural Warwickshire. Their intentions are nothing if not hospitable. Caroline and her mother, having meticulously prepared the dilapidated interiors of the old Hall for the reception of the invited guests, anxiously welcome a group that comprises, among a number of other locals, the Baker-Hydes, their young daughter Gillian, Mrs Baker-Hyde's brother Mr Morley, and Dr Faraday, the novel's narrator. Roderick Ayres, however, the son who has served as the 'master of Hundreds' (84) ever since the death of his father several years earlier, has curiously absented himself from the evening's proceedings. Apparently refusing to play the role of gracious host, he has morosely holed himself up in his bedroom, occasioning a conspicuous absence at the heart of the scene that his mother implausibly attempts to explain away to her guests as the consequence of an old war injury. Nonetheless, the music-playing, drinking and conversation in the Saloon at Hundreds proceed until the convivial hum is abruptly ruptured by a 'tearing yelp', a shriek, and 'a single piercing note that sank at once to a thin, low, liquid wail' (97); while playing quietly in the corner of the room, Gillian, the Baker-Hyde's young daughter, has been savaged by Gyp, the Ayres's hitherto good-natured Labrador. Punctured by so sudden and unforeseen an act of violence, the scene of hospitality rapidly dissipates in a confusion of embarrassed apology, terse exchange and hasty departure.

As subsequent developments in the plot reveal, Roderick has not, in fact, absented himself from the party on the grounds of his anti-social nature alone. Rather, he has been detained by the 'little stranger' of the novel's title, the host and master locked into a ghostly scene of hospitality that is far more challenging, more dangerous and altogether more 'radical' than that at work in the party that Mrs Ayres throws to welcome the newcomers. A law unto itself, the strange and uninvited guest holds Roderick hostage while throwing all 'ordinary' laws of hospitality into utter disarray: '"Most days it doesn't come at all"', he explains, '"But it likes to surprise me, to catch me out. It's just like a sly, spiteful child. It sets traps for me"' (165). Understandably, he is ineradicably altered by this, the first of many encounters with the strange and malevolent spectral energy in Hundreds Hall. Though once 'Lord of the Manor' (193) and the 'master of the estate and its servants' (198), Roderick sees out the remainder of his life in a mental asylum in Birmingham, a pale, unrecognisable spectre of the man that he once was, a veritable stranger to himself. Not insignificantly, however, the initial actions of this 'malevolent thing' (164) or 'vicious presence' (165) temporally coincide with the party in the Saloon. Though Roderick's room is separated from the rest of the house by a number of interior walls, he comes to realise with a mounting sense of horror that Gillian Baker-Hyde 'must have been bitten at just about the time he had been calling out at that vicious presence in his room to leave him alone' (165). Although, from this moment onwards, he keeps to his room in an attempt at localising the 'infection' (165), these precautions prove futile in the face of a violent and disturbing energy that will not be spatially contained, and which, shortly afterwards, begins to wreak destruction throughout the rest of the house. The two conceptualisations of hospitality offered in Waters's novel - the welcome party in the Saloon and the ghostly visitation in Roderick's room, the former ordinary and commonplace, the latter spectral and disruptive - seem to be intimately linked, even inseparable; the dog-attack that ends the dinner-party, it is clear, is a manifestation of the same spectral force or energy that comes to terrorise the household at large.

As I wish to argue in this chapter, Waters's pointed contrasting of two scenes of hospitality in *The Little Stranger* invites consideration through the perspectives on hospitality presented in the later work of Jacques Derrida, a preoccupation that, while implicit in his negotiation of an ethics of spectrality in *Specters of Marx* (1993; trans. 1994), is explicitly addressed in such publications of the late 1990s and early 2000s as *Adieu to Emmanuel Levinas* (1995; trans. 1999), *Of Hospitality* (1997; trans. 2000), *On Cosmopolitanism and Forgiveness* (1997; trans. 2001) and a number of anthologised essays and published interviews. Well beyond *The Little Stranger*, I argue, the Gothic literary aesthetic is a mode that is fundamentally preoccupied with notions of hospitality, a consideration that situates Waters's novel in a literary tradition going at least as far back as the late eighteenth century, when writers habitually appropriated the two 'versions' or 'orders' of hospitality offered up in Shakespeare's *Macbeth* as the source for their narratives: the rules of 'ordinary' hospitality that are notoriously subject to bloody, murderous violation at Macbeth's castle, and the Law of absolute hospitality that is figured in the play with the arrival of the ghost of Banquo at Macbeth's banqueting table in Act III, scene iv. Behind its characteristic concerns with uninvited guests, murderous hosts and the manifold haunted spaces of hospitality, I claim, we might identify in the Gothic an ethics of hospitality that is consonant with Derrida's own, one situated, as it is for Derrida, in the aporia between two equally impossible possibilities: 'ordinary', 'commonplace' or 'conditional' hospitality, on the one hand, and 'radical', 'absolute', 'unconditional' or 'hyperbolical' hospitality on the other.[1]

Between violence and impossibility

Derrida's approach to the 'problem' of hospitality proceeds by way of a tentative sketching out of the difference between two orders, distinguishing 'ordinary' hospitality from 'radical' hospitality, the 'conditional' from the 'unconditional', the 'commonplace' from the 'hyperbolical' as he proceeds. According to 'traditional' or 'ordinary' understandings of the term, the host invites a stranger across a threshold so as to extend to him/her the offer of hospitality, in the fashion of the Ayres family inviting the Baker-Hydes to the welcome party at Hundreds Hall in *The Little Stranger*, or, to take Derrida's more political example from *Of Hospitality*, in the manner in which a nation or state extends the 'right' of hospitality to a stranger or foreigner (such as an immigrant or refugee from another country), offering him or her there the promise of protection, asylum, succour, safety and comfort. Indeed, that this form of hospitality answers to notions of the political and its attendant laws (in the plural) is emphasised by Derrida in *Adieu to Emmanuel Levinas*, a work in which he locates this particular conceptualisation of 'ordinary' hospitality in Immanuel Kant's discussion of the grounds of the political peace of the nation-state in his Third Definitive Article, 'Cosmopolitan Right Shall be Limited to Conditions of Universal Hospitality,' from *To Perpetual Peace: A Philosophical Sketch* (1795). In contrast with his appropriation of *Hamlet* in *Specters of Marx*, Derrida's work on hospitality does not make creative, illustrative recourse to Shakespearean example or precedent. Nonetheless, it is difficult not to be reminded of *Macbeth*, particularly those gestures in which Macbeth and his Lady invite their guest Duncan across the threshold of their castle in an act of apparent hospitality. Graciously accepting their invitation, Duncan duly regards Macbeth as 'mine host' (I.vi.29) and Lady Macbeth as the 'fair and noble hostess' (I.vi.23), roles that both parties self-consciously perform for much of the action. To invite strangers or foreigners across a threshold so as to welcome them into a home or nation is to engage in an act of hospitality in the political, ordinary or commonplace sense of the term.

From the moment of this initiating gesture, however, this mode of 'ordinary' hospitality, Derrida contends, is compromised by an inescapable violence that is bound up in the problems inherent in language itself. For, when he is invited, welcomed and addressed in a tongue that, by definition, is not his own, the foreigner becomes subject to a language that is 'imposed on him by the master of the house, the host, the king, the lord, the authorities, the nation, the State, the father, etc.' (Derrida 2000b, 15). Violence inheres in traditional notions of hospitality in other respects, too, for in choosing, selecting and discriminating between those to whom hospitality may or may not be extended – in logistical terms alone, it is never possible simply to admit everyone – the host enacts a form of sovereignty that is, at its heart, exclusionary (ibid.: 55). Again, the hospitality extended to the unsuspecting Duncan in *Macbeth* is revealing: though he expects to pass the night in Macbeth's castle in peace, he is brutally murdered in his sleep, falling victim at this moment, we might say, to the inescapable violence that lurks beneath the surface of any hospitable act. In Shakespeare's play as in Derrida, 'ordinary' hospitality is a gesture that is founded in hostility as if by a certain tragic inevitability. Derrida foregrounds these more unsettling aspects of hospitality through a characteristic turn towards etymology: the Latin noun *hostis*, from which the English term 'host' derives, means both 'foreigner' or 'stranger' and 'enemy' simultaneously. The act of hospitality is thus troubled by the hostility of a stranger-as-enemy at its heart, a preoccupation that Derrida sums up through his coining of the neologism 'hostipitality': the scene of hospitality has always already been infiltrated by the hostility of the enemy.[2]

If both parties are to commit to it at all, ordinary hospitality and the laws that govern it require that both the host and the guest, the welcoming country and the stranger, be identifiable through, and answerable to, the workings of a proper name. But it is in this very dependence on names that hospitality excludes as a possible guest that which Derrida (following the work of Emmanuel Levinas) terms the absolute other. Under these conditions, hospitality is not, nor ever can be, 'offered to an anonymous new arrival and someone who has neither name, nor patronym, nor family, nor social status, and who is therefore treated not as a foreigner but as another barbarian' (Derrida 2000b, 25). In the face of the absolute other, these problems of language are only exacerbated; as Derrida argues, the proper name, its use and attribution may only ever misrepresent, silence and violently obscure the singularity and anonymity of the other. Consequently, where the absolute other is concerned, the question of hospitality ('What is your name?') becomes tantamount to a torturous interrogation.

Yet it is precisely towards the field of the absolute other that Derrida's ethical system is oriented. If, in the earlier *Specters of Marx*, the ethical gesture resides in offering to the ghostly messiah 'without messianism' or 'content' that which Derrida terms a 'hospitality without reserve' (Derrida 1994, 65), ethics in his work more explicitly devoted to hospitality consists in offering to the absolute other an 'absolute or unconditional hospitality' in a form that in all senses 'breaks with hospitality in the ordinary sense, with conditional hospitality, with the right to or pact of hospitality' (Derrida 2000b, 25). The Shakespearean point of reference, of course, is the unexpected arrival of the ghost of Banquo during the banqueting scene, the point at which the drama opens onto a scene of hospitality that is far more disturbing, radical and extraordinary than that figured in the Macbeths' hosting of Duncan: ['*The GHOST of BANQUO enters, and sits in MACBETH's place*']. If hospitality in the ordinary sense is a political gesture epitomised by Kant's *Perpetual Peace*, so hospitality in this second, more challenging sense is for Derrida to be found in Levinas's *Totality and Infinity*, a text that, even if it does not always make use of the term, 'bequeaths to us an immense treatise *of hospitality*' (Derrida 1999a, 21). While ordinary hospitality consists of so many laws (in the plural), radical hospitality directed towards the absolute other answers only to one singular Law: the absolute Law that is an ethical obligation towards, and responsibility for, the other.[3] Thus, if ordinary hospitality is founded upon the violence of the question, absolute hospitality ought to be characterised by a 'double effacement': the 'effacement of the question' ('What is your name?') and of the name itself (Derrida 2000b, 28). Silence would seem to be the inescapable consequence, for to question and to name, Derrida contends, presupposes a subjective 'who' that might respond as such. Radical hospitality, by contrast, extends the offer of hospitality towards an absolute other that is neither capable of being, nor is ever likely to be, the subject of language, law and the proper name.

Unable to name his guest or even to ask a question, the host within this scheme of radical hospitality foregoes the sense of mastery – the mastery of both his self and his domicile – that is crucial to the functioning of hospitality in the ordinary sense of the word, that is, the mastery and self-possession that Derrida sums up in the word 'ipseity' (Derrida 2000b, 53–55). Macbeth's reactions to the arrival of the uninvited guest illustrate this particularly well: slipping into his seat and taking his place at the table, Banquo's ghost, so Lady Macbeth observes, leaves the host 'quite unmann'd in folly' with a pale visage that is 'blanch'd with fear' (III.iv.115). As is also the case with Roderick Ayres in *The Little Stranger*, the host within the field of radical hospitality forfeits the 'sovereignty of oneself over one's home' that is crucial to hospitality in the 'classic sense' (Derrida 2000b, 59). He becomes a mere guest, a ghost, a veritable 'stranger' to himself. With the host becoming hostage, so the guest becomes a parasite, the correlative of the word 'host' in another, more disturbing sense, a 'little stranger' or spectral guest who, in Derrida's phrasing, 'is wrong, illegitimate, clandestine, liable to expulsion or arrest' (Derrida 2000b, 61).[4]

Indeed, it is in his determination to unsettle the 'ipseity' or 'mastery' of the 'host' that Derrida most distinguishes his account of radical hospitality from the idealism of Kant: according to a certain 'implacable law of hospitality', the mastery of the host is never more than an illusion, for he, too, only ever occupies his home as if he were 'already a *guest* in his own home' (Derrida 1999a, 42). In part, Derrida's argument here is based upon the radical undecidability at play in the modern French word '*hôte*' itself: deriving ultimately from the Old French 'oste'/'hoste', 'hôte' can mean either 'host' (in the masculine) or 'guest' (in the feminine). Signifying both meanings simultaneously, *hôte* can be translated as *either* 'guest' *or* 'host' only through an act of violence. This equivocation is by no means restricted to the French. In English, too, the words 'guest' and 'host' are etymologically linked, stemming, as they do, from the same Indo-European root, **ghosti-s* (guest, stranger), a manifestation of Derridean *différance* that J. Hillis Miller has exploited to ingenious effect in 'The Critic as Host' (Miller 1979).

At first glance, hospitality in this hypothetical or radical sense seems to be as far removed from hospitality in the ordinary or commonplace sense as conceivably possible. While ordinary hospitality its bound up in rights, limits and conditions, absolute or 'pure' hospitality for Derrida is wholly unconditional: emphatically 'without conditions,' this is a hospitality that, contra Kant, is offered to the newcomer 'even if he is not a citizen' (Derrida 1999b, 70). While ordinary hospitality requires that the guest make some return either directly or through a payment in kind, radical hospitality forfeits all relations of reciprocity, for, as Derrida cautions, '[i]f I inscribe the gesture of hospitality within a circle in which the guest should give back to the host, then it is not hospitality but conditional hospitality' (Derrida 1999b, 69). While the one is conditional and reciprocal, the other imposes no bounds. And yet, upon closer consideration, the two orders seem more alike than utterly distinct from one another. Disarming the host's ability to 'host', his mastery, his power to name, to question and to select who – or even what – is admitted to his home, radical hospitality is as fraught with difficulty as the 'ordinary' hospitality with which it is rhetorically juxtaposed. Unravelling the 'ipseity' that is central to any act of 'ordinary' hospitality, the absolute other turns hosts into hostages and guests into parasites, repeating the violence of 'hostipitality' on the figure of the one who receives and welcomes him. Thus, as ethical as this stance might be in principle, an undiscriminating, non-violent 'openness' to the absolute other remains, for Derrida, ultimately unachievable; in a move that is cognate with this theorist's work on mourning and forgiveness elsewhere, Derrida consistently figures radical, absolute hospitality under the sign of 'impossibility'.

Certainly, the emphasis that Derrida, following Levinas, places upon infinity seems to suggest as much, for however ethical our intentions, infinite hospitality, a hospitality without reserve or limits in time, space and numerical calculation, can never be practically achieved as such. Consequently, while it encapsulates Derrida's ethical position, the claim that absolute hospitality 'is granted upon the welcoming of the idea of infinity, and thus of the unconditional' only serves to underscore its unachievability (Derrida 1999a, 48). However, as *Adieu to Emmanuel Levinas* reminds us, it is precisely the impossibility of sustaining a silent, non-conditional and limitless opening towards the other that grounds the ethical relation. To render it in any sense possible, realisable or achievable would simultaneously be to risk the chance of perverting the field of ethics into a confined, limited and circumscribed system, one that, in the end, turns out to be as violent and threatening towards the absolute other as hospitality in its ordinary sense (Derrida 1999a, 35). The field of pure ethics must always exceed its actualisation if it is to remain ethical at all.

Gothic hospitalities

As Colin Davis has noted, Derrida consistently approaches Levinas's figure of absolute alterity through the figure of the ghost (Davis 2007). The links between an ethics of hospitality, spectrality and absolute alterity become particularly clear in *Adieu to Emmanuel Levinas*, in which Derrida argues that, like the host who, as a guest in his own home, has been 'stripped of every ontological predicate', the absolute other is never 'reducible to its actual predicate, to what one might define or thematise about it' (Derrida 1999a, 111). Rather, the Levinasian other, in Derrida's reading, is 'naked, bared of every property', this 'nudity' its 'infinitely exposed vulnerability: its skin' (ibid.). In turn, it is this 'absence of determinable properties, of concrete predicates, of empirical visibility' in and of the other that gives its face what Derrida describes as 'a spectral aura' (ibid.): according to 'a profound necessity', he suggests, the other bears 'at least the face or figure of a spirit or phantom (*Geist, ghost*)' (ibid.). Though lacking in ontological presence, the ghost is never simply 'absent'; rather, as Derrida insists throughout his *oeuvre*, the ghost exceeds and calls into question some of the most cherished ontological oppositions of Western metaphysics, including those between absence and presence, being and nothingness, life and death. Capable of giving pardon and orders in the fashion of the ghost of old Hamlet in Shakespeare's play, the spectre, in this sense, is 'God without being, God uncontaminated by being', thus fulfilling Levinas's definition of the Face of the Wholly Other (Derrida 1999a, 112). Recalling the pose advocated in relation to the *arrivant* in *Specters of Marx*, Derrida claims in *Adieu to Emmanuel Levinas* that hospitality in part consists of adopting an attitude of welcome towards the guest as ghost – an attitude of receptiveness that never pauses to reflect on the form that she/he/it might assume. Conceived as a Levinasian other, the guest becomes a ghost; consequently, Derrida in an evocative turn of phrase asserts that '[t]here would be no hospitality without the chance of spectrality' (Derrida 1999a, 111–12). Although the word 'ghost' derives not from **ghosti-s* but from a different Indo-European root, **gheiz-d* (shocked, aghast, confused), Derrida exploits the aural and orthographic proximities between *Gast* and *Gastgeber*, the modern German words for 'guest' and 'host' respectively, as well as notions of the ghostly: '*Host* or *guest* [in English], *Gastgeber* or *Gast*, the *hôte* would be not only a hostage. It would have, according to a profound necessity, at least the face or figure of a spirit or phantom (*Geist, ghost*)' (Derrida 1999a, 111).

To wait without waiting, to await without a 'horizon of anticipation' the arrival of a ghostly visitor that, in a moment of absolute surprise, unsettles the host to the point of 'madness' (Derrida 2000a, 362): there is, indeed, something inherently Gothic about Derrida's programme of radical hospitality. Well beyond the metaphors of ghostliness, Derrida's ethics of hospitality seems to rely upon a number of emotional affects that, ever since the late eighteenth century, we have come to associate specifically with the Gothic aesthetic, the supernatural literature of horror and terror that arose in Britain with the publication of Horace Walpole's

The Castle of Otranto in late 1764. In principle, of course, the arrival of the other ought always to be met with a smile (Derrida 2002, 358). Compromised by any trace of anger, sadness or obligation on the host's side, the field of radical hospitality should ideally be characterised by a certain degree of mirth, that 'happy' and 'joyous' scene of laughter, smiles and also, conceivably, tears (of joy, of deliverance) to which Derrida so poetically refers (Derrida 2002, 359). However, that these responses are difficult to sustain in reaction to what is likely to be the ghostly other's abrupt and unsettling arrival only serves further to underline the impossibility of absolute hospitality. For if the visitation of the other ought always to remain of the order of the 'unforeseen, unforeseeable [*imprévu, imprévisible*], unpredictable, unexpected and unpredictable, unwarranted [*inattendu*]' (Derrida 2002, 381), it follows that such an arrival is more likely to be met with shock and disruption than smiles, mirth and laughter. As Derrida puts it, if one is to say 'yes' to the uninvited visitor, if one is indeed 'to let oneself be swept by the coming of the wholly other' who is always unexpected and absolutely unforeseen and unforeseeable, one has to lay oneself open to the possibility of a certain discomfort (Derrida 2002, 361). In itself, unconditional hospitality is 'terrible' and 'unbearable' insofar as it breaks with relations of reciprocity, suspends the host's powers of identification and unsettles his mastery (Derrida 1999b, 70). More than this, unconditional hospitality always hovers precariously on the brink of horror and terror since, in refusing to discriminate between those who are and those who are not to be admitted, it always includes within itself the possibility of entertaining a guest that is demonic in nature (Derrida 1999b, 71). The ghostly other, that is, might well take the form of a malevolent spirit, as it does in *The Little Stranger*; yet if absolute hospitality is to be 'absolute' in any meaningful sense, it must remain open to the possibility of entertaining pure evil. A system of ghostliness that is generative of certain 'terrible', 'unbearable' and madness-inducing responses, radical hospitality is potentially Gothic in its effects and affects.

The effulgence of the Gothic in the later eighteenth century coincided historically with the rise of a pervasive political ideology that was structured around the Kantian theme of Universal Hospitality. Following the increasingly anti-clerical turn of events in revolutionary France, and in 1792 the imposition of a new civic oath that required all members of the clergy to swear allegiance to revolutionary principles upon the pain of exile to Guiana, French Catholic clerics fled the country for Britain and other parts of continental Europe in large numbers (Purves 2009, 32). By September 1792, Maria Purves points out, some 1,500 French priests had entered England, with numbers rising to around 5,000 in little more than a year (ibid.). Seizing the opportunity to express his distaste for the Revolution as much as his humanitarian concern for the plight of the French émigrés, Edmund Burke anonymously published his 'Case of the Suffering Clergy of France' in *The Times* on 18 September 1792, articulating a nationwide appeal to Protestant Britons to extend the possibility of refuge, comfort and asylum to the Catholic other: 'They are here under the sacred protection of hospitality – Englishmen, who cherish the virtue of hospitality, and who do not wish an hard and scanty construction of its laws, will not think it enough that such Guests are in safety from the violence of their own countrymen, while they perish from our neglect' (Burke 1792, 3). Burke was not alone in these concerns. Frances Burney, for example, expressed a rousing call for the extension of national hospitality towards the persecuted French clergy in her *Brief Reflections Relative to the Emigrant French Clergy* (1793), while John Moir rephrased the largely secular views of Burke and Burney in more orthodox Christian terms in his *Hospitality: A Discourse Occasioned by Reading His Majesty's Letter in Behalf of the Emigrant French Clergy* (1793). Similar views were expressed by Hannah More as well as preached from several pulpits across the country. In these and other forums, eighteenth-century Britons were frequently urged to engage and extend a national English or 'Gothic' tradition of hospitality towards French-Catholic others.

And yet, when situated beside such national calls to action, early Gothic writing seems to be the most inhospitable of literary modes; notoriously anti-Catholic in orientation, the Gothic offers the Catholic other anything but a hospitable place of refuge.[5] Instead, the Gothic at its most characteristic is given over to the spectacular exposure and punishment of Catholic indiscretion, not least in the cruel, torturous deaths of Father Ambrosio and the Prioress of St Clare in Matthew Lewis's *The Monk; A Romance* (1796). While Burke, Burney and other advocates of the Catholic cause put their sentimental descriptions of the violence that revolutionaries had aroused against Catholics to work in the interest of evoking British sympathies, Gothic writing stages and exacerbates this violence as a means of punishing and expelling the foreign other, the Catholic Priest, Abbess or Father who, it is feared, poses a threat to everything that the nation cherishes about itself. Gothic fiction of the 1790s, we might say, systematically infringes the cultural and political 'laws' on hospitality towards the Catholic other with which it was contemporary.

Well beyond its treatment of Catholics, early Gothic fiction often depends upon the staged violation of the code and practice of hospitality in its ordinary sense, an aspect of the mode, I would suggest, that derives more often than not from appropriations of Shakespeare's *Macbeth*. In Ann Radcliffe's *The Italian* (1797), for instance, the heroine Ellena di Rosalba is abducted from the chapel of San Sebastian and taken to the ruined house of Spalatro (the accomplice of the arch-villain Father Schedoni), which is remotely situated somewhere on the Italian coast. In a climactic scene epigraphically framed by Macbeth's words from the closing lines of Act I – 'I am settled, and bend up / Each corporal agent to this terrible feat' (I.vii.80-81) - Schedoni and Spalatro intend to put into action their plan to execute Ellena while she sleeps. The dialogue that ensues between the executioners directly replays that between Macbeth and his Lady concerning their plan to kill the slumbering Duncan. '"The bloody hand is always before me!"' the anxious Spalatro exclaims as he tries to communicate his guilt-induced visions to Schedoni (Radcliffe 1968, 230). Dismissing Spalatro's fears as mere folly, Schedoni's reply echoes Lady Macbeth's questioning of her husband's masculine revolve during the banquet scene: "'[W]here is this frenzy of fear to end? To what are these visions, painted in blood, to lead? I thought I was talking with a man, but find I am speaking only to a baby, possessed with his nurse's dreams!'" (230). However, Schedoni too will come to experience the wavering resolve of a Macbeth when, dagger poised above the breast of the slumbering heroine, he misrecognises her as his child and fails to carry through the assassination. The tension at this point in Radcliffe's narrative derives from Shakespeare's bloody violation of the laws of hospitality in *Macbeth*.

As though it has encountered in hospitality traces of the same 'hostipitality' identified by Derrida, early Gothic fiction turns to negotiate hospitality in another, more radical sense. Here too, though, the Gothic consistently suggests that the gesture of radical hospitality, an undiscriminating openness to the arrival of an uninvited spectral guest, is beset by all manner of insurmountable difficulties. If the ghost is indeed a figure of absolute otherness, its unannounced and unexpected arrival is registered in the Gothic as an experience of unbearable terror, to the extent that the spectre can never be permanently welcomed in the Gothic text, but must rather be subjected to a hasty and robust strategy of exorcism. Again, Lewis's *The Monk* epitomises this process. Framed by an epigraph taken from Macbeth's response to the appearance of Banquo's ghost, the second volume recounts the story of the ghost of the Bleeding Nun, the apparition of one Beatrice las Cisternas that, as local legend has it, returns to haunt the Castle of Lindenberg in Germany on the 5th of May of every fifth year. Seeking to escape her imprisonment in the Castle so that she may rendezvous and elope with her lover Don Raymond, the young heroine Agnes proposes to disguise herself as the ghost of the Bleeding Nun on the approaching night of its return. With the plan going disastrously awry, Don Raymond is left in the embrace not of his lover but of the ghostly arms of the Bleeding Nun herself, a spectral figure of otherness that, in a reworking of Gottfried August Bürger's ballad 'Lenore' (1774), unveils herself before the unsuspecting suitor in a moment of absolute, unspeakable horror (Lewis 2004, 155). Unseen by anyone other than Raymond, she is an unwelcome and uninvited guest that, like the ghost of Banquo, 'unmans' the startled host and reduces him to his 'second infancy' (157). Although the ghost is eventually laid to rest through a combination of proper burial and the occult rituals of the Wandering Jew, Lewis's inset tale foregrounds the impossibility of hospitality in its absolute or radical sense; the unanticipated arrival of an uninvited spectral guest is likely to occasion the experience of unbearable terror, the charge of which can be dissipated only by a magical act of expulsion.

Ordinary hospitality results in bloodshed and radical hospitality ends in exorcism. Yet the early Gothic assumes its ethical potential precisely through its tireless vacillation between the two orders of hospitality, the ordinary and the spectral, that it finds realised in Shakespeare's *Macbeth*. I shall return to this paradox later, but for the moment it is worth turning to some of the key Gothic fictions of the nineteenth century in order to consider how later writers extended the earlier tradition's preoccupations with hospitality in both its ordinary and absolute senses, often founding narratives in the complex place of indecision between them. Emily Brontë's *Wuthering Heights* (1847), for instance, constantly juxtaposes the commonplace welcoming of strangers across thresholds with scenes of hospitality towards ghostly or spectral visitors. '"I don't keep accommodations for visitors [*sic*]"', Heathcliff brusquely replies when, detained at the Heights owing to the inclement turn in the weather, Lockwood requires of him a night's lodging. '"Guests are so exceedingly rare in this house"', he continues, '"that I and my dogs, I am willing to own, hardly know how to receive them"' (Brontë 2009, 5). Such pointed displays of inhospitality, however, are contrasted with the gestures of unlimited, unconditional and absolute hospitality that Heathcliff offers to the ghost of Cathy. '"'Come in! come in!"', he sobs at the open window, "Cathy, do come. Oh do – *once* more! Oh! my heart's darling, hear me *this* time – Catherine, at last!"' (24). As he reneges on the human, so his gestures towards the field of the ghostly become more exaggerated. However, when the spectral guest eventually arrives, this results in the host's loss of mastery to the point of an eclipse of subjectivity and death.

While the ghosts of Victorian Gothic are central to the mode's preoccupations, it is, of course, primarily through the figure of the vampire that nineteenth-century writers explored notions of hospitality, hostility and literal or symbolic forms of parasitism. Here too, the narrative interplay between two opposing but interlinked orders of hospitality is paramount. In Sheridan Le Fanu's 'Carmilla' (1871–1872), for instance, the laws of ordinary hospitality at the Austrian castle of Laura and her father are mobilised with the unexpected arrival of a beautiful young woman, who is involved in a carriage accident in the nearby woods when apparently travelling with her mother. Sympathetic to her plight, Laura and her father act in accordance with the codes 'which hospitality indicated' (Le Fanu 1970, 20), bidding their guest 'welcome'; Laura expresses 'how much pleasure her accidental arrival had given us all, and especially what a happiness it was to me' (20). With her curious habits and demands, however, it soon becomes clear that this guest is anything but ordinary. But, as Le Fanu's text is keen to emphasise, she is more than merely a 'bad' guest; in refusing to disclose her full name, her familial origins or the country from which she originates, this stranger is a figure of absolute alterity that opens up the scene of hospitality at the castle to something far more extreme and unsettling. Frustrating the nominal identification upon which the act of ordinary hospitality depends, this unfathomable guest is known by a plurality of names, including Carmilla, Marcia Karnstein, Millarca and Mircalla, Countess Karnstein. Her ever-changing physicality is equally resistant to classification, as she mutates from a beautiful young woman into 'a monstrous cat' (37), 'a beast in a cage' (37), a 'black creature' (67) and a dark shapeless form across the narrative. '"The precautions of nervous people are infectious"', Laura observes, as she too begins to manifest the guest's strange behaviours (37). In reality, this guest is a blood-sucking vampire, exploiting Laura's position as 'host' in a much more sinister sense, for as a parasite she will feed upon her host. '"I live in your warm life, and you shall die – die, sweetly die into mine'" (25), Carmilla sweetly croons, as Laura becomes languid, melancholy and as pale as a ghost. The host has been taken hostage, the practice of hospitality perverted into a dangerous, parasitic hostility between host and guest. Like *The Monk*, Le Fanu's narrative ends on a note of expulsion. Eventually tied to, and identified with, one single proper name, Mircalla, Countess Karnstein is traced back to her tomb in the ruined Chapel of Karnstein; following ritualised, magical prayers of delivery and exorcism, the 'perfidious and beautiful guest' is killed (70) by a stake through the heart, her body decapitated and burned. While it continues to throw the patriarchal structures of language, nationality, subjectivity and desire into disarray, the narrative suggests that the absolute other may not comfortably or easily become the subject of any act of hospitality.

Similar assumptions are set in place during the final moments of Bram Stoker's *Dracula* (1897), in which the vampiric Count is finally defeated by the wily Crew of Light after a tense game of hide-and-seek. Stoker's novel derives its force, in part, from a concerted interrogation of received conceptualisations of hospitality, illustrating the ease with which the positions of 'guest' and 'host' constantly shift and change place while amplifying the 'hostility' by which all acts of hospitality in the novel seem to be characterised. It is through the subject-position of 'guest' that the vampire achieves his most deadly effects in Stoker's fiction: as vampire mythology has it, Dracula may only cross the threshold of the bourgeois home and psyche once he has been invited in, either deliberately (in the invocations of the delusional Renfield) or unwittingly (through the carelessness of Lucy and Mina). Even though his hosts are reluctant to acknowledge it, in England the Transylvanian stranger always plays the role of the invited guest; as in 'Carmilla', though, the vampiric guest in *Dracula* rapidly turns parasitic upon its hosts, rendering their blood-drained bodies and selves almost indistinguishable from ghosts. Though Dracula ends his life as a guest, it is as a host, we remember, that he first sets out, not least in the fragment 'Dracula's Guest', the deleted first chapter of Stoker's novel that was posthumously published in 1914. '"Welcome to my house!"' the Count disingenuously proclaims as Jonathan Harker first enters the castle, '"Enter freely. Go safely; and leave something of the happiness you bring!"' (Stoker 1998, 46). Although Harker is at this moment struck by the 'light and warmth and the Count's courteous welcome' (47), he is, in effect, little more than the 'prisoner' that he later acknowledges himself as being (57). Despite appearances to the contrary, hostility has already infiltrated the guest/host relation as the host holds the guest hostage. When Dracula reveals to Jonathan the cold and inhospitable reaches beyond the castle door, taunting him with a paraphrase of Alexander Pope's translation of the *Odyssey* that reads '"Welcome the coming, speed the parting guest"' (81), hospitality is revealed for what it is: little more than a quotable poetic adage that thinly masks a system of more violent and bloodthirsty intent.

Thus the two poles or orders of hospitality come to structure and determine much Gothic writing of the Victorian and Edwardian periods. With the publication of Wilkie Collins's *The Haunted Hotel: A Mystery of Modern Venice* in 1878, the Gothic is relocated to the hospitable spaces of nineteenth-century modernity, in this instance a Venetian Palace-turned-Hotel that is haunted by the ghostly head of a man who was once murdered there. Ordinary hospitality in the novella is troubled, compromised and threatened by a spectral death's-head that not only vexes the comfort of the hotel's other occupants, but whose anterior presence in the hotel also makes the host and proprietor himself a guest. While the inhabitants of hotels and inns continue to pay for their food and lodgings, the forms of hospitality that they enjoy there can only ever be bound by conditional relations of reciprocity and exchange.

The late nineteenth- and early twentieth-century ghost story, too, often details the horrors and terrors attendant upon the arrival of an uninvited, spectral guest, as if to stress the impossibility of hospitality in its absolute, unconditional sense. In the short fictions of writers such as M. R. James and Algernon Blackwood, these encounters with spectres often take place in spaces of 'ordinary' hospitality, such as the Globe Inn, the seaside guesthouse in James's '"Oh, Whistle, and I'll Come to You, My Lad"', or the spectral room in the Golden Lion Hotel in 'Number 13' from *Ghost Stories of an Antiquary* (1904). Further examples include the hotel room in the mountains that is haunted by the ghost of a suicide in Algernon Blackwood's 'The Occupant of the Room' (1909), as well as the hired rooms and apartments that feature in some of the stories collected in Blackwood's *The Empty House, and Other Ghost Stories* (1906) and *The Listener, and Other Stories* (1907). Edith Nesbit in her turn puts the haunted spaces of hospitality to particularly horrific use in her story of the throat-slitting ghost that appears in the shaving mirror in a room of 'a certain commercial hotel' (Nesbit 2006, 211) in the story 'Number 17' (1910), while in May Sinclair's 'Where Their Fire Is Not Quenched' from *Uncanny Stories* (1923), the ghosts of two unfaithful lovers return incessantly to the Hotel Saint Pierre, occupying the very room (Number 107) in which they once spent an unfulfilling holiday when alive. Undercutting the presumed 'homeliness' of hotel rooms, inns, hired lodgings and rented accommodation with a sense of the 'unhomely', these and other ghost stories in this tradition render hospitality a thoroughly uncanny affair: hospitality in its ordinary sense – the welcoming and entertainment of guests – is by no means the simple matter that it first appears to be. At the very least, it is always violently excluding of a ghostly guest who cannot or does not pay, whose name, because it is often nameless, has not been entered on any hotel register, but who nonetheless inhabits the room. The uninvited, unseen guest in these stories displaces the scene of hospitality into a different register; yet the entertaining of ghostly visitors – the extension of absolute hospitality towards a spectral other – is a gesture so fraught with discomfort that it is impossible to achieve anywhere but in the *frissons* of the ghost story.

Three key fictions of the twentieth century reaffirm the tireless shuttling between hospitality in the ordinary and the absolute senses that, as I have argued, has been characteristic of the Gothic mode since the late eighteenth century.

Drawing upon the Gothic tendency to render abbeys, convents, hotels, inns and other conventional spaces of hospitality as sites of horror and danger, Robert Bloch's *Psycho* (1959) transports Gothic convention to a remote American motel. Arriving at the Bates Motel on that fateful stormy night, Mary Crane is surprised to discover conversation, food and other gestures of welcome. '"And thanks for the hospitality"' (Bloch 2013, 35), she cheerfully calls out to Norman, her seemingly kind and thoughtful host, as she makes her way from the kitchen of the adjoining house to her lodgings. This comment only amplifies the horror of the scene in which, shortly afterwards, Norman brutally murders her, a bloody violation of the laws of hospitality immortalised in the iconic shower scene in Alfred Hitchcock's 1960 filmic version of Bloch's novel. A replaying of *Macbeth* this undoubtedly is, for as in Shakespeare's play, this murder has been masterminded, or so the delusional Norman believes, by his mother, an avatar of the redoubtable Lady Macbeth. As his psychosis intensifies, so the 'unsex'd' Norman seems to become his mother, washing his own hands as if to cleanse himself of guilt, and musing to himself, '"A regular Lady Macbeth. Shakespeare had known a lot about psychology"' (96).

William Peter Blatty's *The Exorcist* (1971) explores the impossibility of hospitality in its absolute sense through a powerful and disturbing account of demonic possession. Invaded by a malevolent spirit, the twelve-year-old Regan MacNeil plays host against her will to an unwanted and uninvited spectral guest. To open oneself up to the absolute other, the fiction implies, is to court the dangers of possession. As life-threatening as it is impossible, Regan's act of radical hospitality has to be counteracted by a system of faith and an act of exorcism in which the Host, here the bread that is also the body of Christ, plays a significant role. As concretised in the title of John Ajvide Lindqvist's more recent vampire fiction, the modern Gothic often cautions readers to 'Let the Right One In', cultivating an attitude towards strangers that, though seemingly sensible, is always in danger of excluding the absolute other from the ethical field. As Derrida reminds us, an ethics of hospitality ought always to remain open to the possibility of entertaining pure evil: 'For unconditional hospitality to take place you have to accept the risk of the other coming and destroying the place, initiating a revolution, stealing everything, or killing everyone' (Derrida 1999b, 71). Modern Gothic repeatedly explores the horrors and terrors attendant upon this position. Stephen King's *The Shining* (1977) brings commonplace and radical hospitality to bear in the story of Jack Torrance, a man who, like Blatty's Regan, is possessed by the spirit of the past, although in one of modernity's hospitable spaces, the isolated Overlook Hotel. In King's novel, Jack's unquestioning openness towards the other results in violence, alcoholism, attempted homicide and an irreversible descent into madness. At the Overlook Hotel, ordinary hospitality is constantly disrupted by the ghosts of those guests who have previously lived and died there: the murdered daughters of the former landlord Grady, the ghostly revellers in the Ball Room, the bloated body of the suicide in the bathroom of Room 217. As Jack observes, '"I suppose that every big hotel has got its ghosts"' (King 2007, 290), sounding a note that chimes aptly with Derrida's account of the centrality of ghosts to any ethical encounter. The young, supernaturally gifted Danny's predicament in the novel lies in his ability to see the failure and impossibility of hospitality in both senses, a failure and impossibility that for him clearly spell violence, murder, suicide and bloodshed.

The step towards hospitality

In this way, examples proliferate across the Gothic tradition. Caught between limitation, exclusion and violence, on the one hand, and ghostly impossibility on the other, Gothic textuality tirelessly returns to explore two orders of hospitality that are cognate with those outlined in Jacques Derrida's own 'Gothic' reflections on the subject. Finding solutions to the problem of hospitality in neither term, the Gothic consistently points to that difficult, paradoxical 'hiatus' (Derrida 1999a, 20) or 'abyss' (Derrida 2001, 54) between them. For neither ordinary nor radical hospitality, Derrida shows, can exist without its counterpart. Although the laws of ordinary hospitality can only ever 'pervert' the Law of pure hospitality, they remain necessary if absolute hospitality is to have any purchase beyond the realm of pure philosophical abstraction (Derrida 2001, 22-23). By the same token, ordinary hospitality requires hospitality in its absolute sense as an ethical ideal towards which it may aspire, for '[i]t is a question of knowing how to transform and improve the law, and of knowing if this improvement is possible within an historical space' (Derrida 2001, 22-23). As such, ordinary and absolute hospitality in the Gothic are 'irreconcilable' yet 'indissociable' (Derrida 2001, 45) entities, notions that are at once 'contradictory, antimonic, *and* inseparable' (Derrida 2000b, 81). Though the one is problematic and the other impossible, both poles are necessary in what can only ever be a step 'towards' an ethics of hospitality.

This is the step that that Gothic has always already taken. Playing on the doubleness of the French word '*pas*' as both 'step' and a negative adverb in the French phrase '*pas d'hospitalité*', Derrida claims that to take a step in the direction of hospitality is also to cancel out the terms of its existence (Derrida 2000b, 75-77). Even as we offer political, ordinary or commonplace hospitality to a stranger according to certain culturally codified laws, we fall foul of the absolute Law of hospitality that is pure ethics itself; similarly, even as we heed this absolute Law, we risk violating and infringing the cultural laws on which ordinary hospitality is based. Gothic writing works in, and through, similar complexities: figuring ordinary hospitality as an act of violence and absolute hospitality as an experience of the impossible, it returns its readers to the restless, aporetic space of ethics between them. For, as the sheer persistence of the scenes, themes and spaces of hospitality in the Gothic suggests, to remain inactive and altogether to ignore the call to hospitality is no alternative at all. Rather, an ethics of hospitality in the Gothic resides in a Derridean aporia, 'the non-road, the barred way, the non-passage' (Derrida 2000a, 13) that, however fraught the journey, remains the only way forward. 'For me', Derrida maintains, the aporia of the non-way 'is not simply paralysis' but the very 'condition of walking: if there was no *aporia* we wouldn't walk, we wouldn't find our way; path-breaking implies *aporia*. This impossibility to find one's way is the condition of ethics' (Derrida 1999b, 73). To offer hospitality even as we cancel it out, to take the step of hospitality even as, in this very gesture, we acknowledge each step's perverting effects: a Gothic ethics of hospitality is implicated in the 'non-dialectizable [*non-dialectisable*] tension' (Derrida 2002, 362) or 'insoluble antinomy' between the Law of absolute hospitality and its multiple conditions and laws (Derrida 2000b, 77).

Notes

1 For an alternative reading of hospitality in the Gothic, one that deploys Derridean insights but does not locate the ethics of hospitality in the impasse between the 'ordinary' and the 'radical', see Watkiss (2012).
2 Elaborating upon the notion of 'hostipitality' in his essay of the same name, Derrida claims that, like the English word 'hospitality', the German term '*Hospitalität*' is 'a word of Latin origin, of a troubled and troubling origin, a word which carries its own contradiction incorporated into it, a Latin word which allows itself to be parasitised by its opposite, "hostility", the undesirable guest [hôte] which it harbors as the self-contradiction in its own body' (Derrida 2000a, 3).
3 Ultimately, though, Derrida continues, the ethics of absolute hospitality remains as heterogeneous to notions of law as pure Justice itself: 'Just hospitality', Derrida reasons, 'breaks with hospitality by right'; while it is not necessarily opposed to this version, 'it is as strangely heterogeneous to it as justice is heterogeneous to the law to which it is as yet so close, from which in truth it is indissociable' (Derrida 2000b, 25-27).
4 Despite my conflation of the 'stranger' and Levinas's absolute other in this reading of *The Little Stranger*, it is important to bear in mind that, in designating the other as a stranger, one has already, in a sense, limited and circumscribed its otherness by defining and conceptualising it in relation to the structures of family, nation, state and citizenship. As Derrida contends in 'Hostipitality', 'if one determines the other as stranger, one is already introducing the circles of conditionality that are family, nation, state, and citizenship' (Derrida 2000a, 8). The other, by contrast, might well exceed these structures: 'Perhaps there is an other who is still more foreign than the one whose foreignness cannot be restricted to foreignness in relation to language, family, or citizenship' (Derrida 2000a, 8).
5 The anti-Catholic nature of the Gothic has long been a subject of scholarship in the field; for a recent and comprehensive account, see Diane Long Hoeveler (2014).

References

Blackwood, Algernon. 1906. *The Empty House, and Other Ghost Stories*. London: Eveleigh Nash.
———. 1907. *The Listener, and Other Stories*. London: Eveleigh Nash.
Blatty, William Peter. 2007 [1971]. *The Exorcist*. London: Corgi Books.
Bloch, Robert. 2013 [1959]. *Psycho*. London: Robert Hale Limited.
Brontë, Emily. 2009 [1847]. *Wuthering Heights*. Edited by Ian Jack. Introduction and Notes by Helen Small. Oxford World's Classics. Oxford and New York: Oxford University Press.
Bürger, Gottfried August. 1774. 'Lenore'. *Göttinger Musenalmanach A MDCCLXXIV*, 214–26.
[Burke, Edmund]. 1792. 'Case of the Suffering Clergy of France'. *The Times*, September 18: 3.

Burney, Frances. 1793. *Brief Reflections Relative to the Emigrant French Clergy: Earnestly Submitted to the Humane Consideration of the Ladies of Great Britain*. London: Printed by T. Davison, for Thomas Cadell.
Collins, Wilkie. 2003 [1878]. *The Haunted Hotel: A Mystery of Modern Venice*. New York: Dover Publications, Inc.
Davis, Colin. 2007. *Haunted Subjects: Deconstruction, Psychoanalysis and the Return of the Dead*. Houndmills: Palgrave Macmillan.
Derrida, Jacques. 1994 [1993]. *Specters of Marx: The State of the Debt, the Work of Mourning, and the New International*. Translated by Peggy Kamuf. Introduction by Bernd Magnus and Stephen Cullenberg. London and New York: Routledge.
———. 1999a. *Adieu to Emmanuel Levinas*. Translated by Pascale-Anne Brault and Michael Naas. Stanford, CA: Stanford University Press.
———. 1999b. 'Hospitality, Justice and Responsibility: A Dialogue with Jacques Derrida'. In *Questioning Ethics: Contemporary Debates in Philosophy*, edited by Richard Kearney and Mark Dooley, 65-83. London and New York: Routledge.
———. 2000a. 'Hostipitality', translated by Barry Stocker and Forbes Morlock. *Angelaki: Journal of the Theoretical Humanities* 5.3: 3-18.
———. 2000b [1997]. *Of Hospitality: Anne Dufourmantelle Invites Jacques Derrida to Respond*. Translated by Rachel Bowlby. Stanford, CA: Stanford University Press.
———. 2001 [1997]. *On Cosmopolitanism and Forgiveness*. Edited by Simon Critchley and Richard Kearney. London and New York: Routledge.
———. 2002. 'Hostipitality: Session of January 8, 1997'. In *Acts of Religion*, edited and introduced by Gil Anidjar, 358-420. New York and London: Routledge.
Hitchcock, Alfred (dir). 1960. *Psycho*. Paramount Pictures.
Hoeveler, Diane Long. 2014. *The Gothic Ideology: Religious Hysteria and Anti-Catholicism in British Popular Fiction, 1780–1880*. Cardiff: University of Wales Press.
James, M. R. 2017 [1904]. *Ghost Stories of an Antiquary*. London: William Collins.
Kant, Immanuel. 2003 [1795]. *To Perpetual Peace: A Philosophical Sketch*. Translated by Ted Humphrey. Indianapolis, IN: Hackett Publishing Company.
King, Stephen. 2007 [1977]. *The Shining*. London: Hodder and Stoughton.
Le Fanu, Joseph Sheridan. 1970. *Vampire Lovers and Other Stories*. London: Fontana Books.
Levinas, Emmanuel. 1969 [1961]. *Totality and Infinity: An Essay on Exteriority*. Translated by Alphonso Lingis. Pittsburg, PA: Duquesne University Press.
Lewis, Matthew Gregory. 2004 [1796]. *The Monk: A Romance*. Edited by D. L. Macdonald and Kathleen Scherf. Peterborough, Ontario: Broadview Press.
Lindqvist, John Ajvide. 2007 [2004]. *Let the Right One In*. London: Quercus.
Miller, J. Hillis. 1979. 'The Critic as Host'. In *Deconstruction and Criticism*, edited by Harold Bloom, Paul de Man, Jacques Derrida, Geoffrey H. Hartman and J. Hillis Miller, 217–53. London and Henley: Routledge & Kegan Paul.
Moir, John. 1793. *Hospitality: A Discourse Occasioned by Reading His Majesty's Letter in Behalf of the Emigrant French Clergy*. London: Sold by Mr. Rivington.
Nesbit, Edith. 2006 [1910]. 'Number 17'. In *The Powers of Darkness: Tales of Terror*, 209–16. Ware: Wordsworth.
Purves, Maria. 2009. *The Gothic and Catholicism: Religion, Cultural Exchange and the Popular Novel, 1785–1829*. Cardiff: University of Wales Press.
Radcliffe, Ann. 1968 [1797]. *The Italian: Or, the Confessional of the Black Penitents*. Edited by Frederick Garber. Oxford World's Classics. Oxford: Oxford University Press.
Shakespeare, William. 1951 [*c*. 1606]. *Macbeth*. Edited by Kenneth Muir. The Arden Shakespeare. London and New York: Routledge.
Sinclair, May. 1923. *Uncanny Stories*. London: Hutchinson and Co.

Stoker, Bram. 1998 [1897]. *Dracula*. Edited by Glennis Byron. Peterborough, Ontario: Broadview Press.
Walpole, Horace. 2014 [1764]. *The Castle of Otranto*. Edited by Nick Groom. Oxford World's Classics. Oxford: Oxford University Press.
Waters, Sarah. 2010 [2009]. *The Little Stranger*. London: Virago Press.
Watkiss, Joanne. 2012. '"Welcome the Coming, Speed the Parting Guest": Hospitality and the Gothic'. In *A New Companion to the Gothic*, edited by David Punter, 523–34. Oxford: Blackwell Publishing.

4

'A WANDERING TO FIND HOME'

Samuel Beckett's *Molloy* and the unhomeliness of home

Mike Marais

One year before the end of World War II, Theodor Adorno declared that '[t]he house is past' or gone ['*Das Haus ist vergangen*'] (Adorno 1991, 39). The 'immanent development of technology', culminating in the 'bombings of European cities, as well as the labour and concentration camps', had decided the 'fate of houses' (ibid.). For Adorno, the idea of the house, and with it belonging, is ethically suspect in the context of the mass destruction attendant on fascism with its sentimental and nostalgic desire for homeliness. Given the incipient violence inherent in homeliness, homelessness becomes an ethical imperative. Hence he concludes that 'it is part of morality not to be at home in one's home' (ibid.). While he does not say as much, it is nevertheless clear enough that Adorno's profound suspicion of homeliness is related to his criticism of identifying thought's tendency to reduce otherness by integrating it into the known and familiar (see, for instance, Adorno 1973, 144-51). Indeed, it is this form of thought's transformative violence, its subsumption of the individual and specific under the universal, that renders the home homely. One may speculate that one reason for Adorno's admiration of Samuel Beckett's writing is that it not only offers a sustained critique of notions of homeliness, but does so by thinking beyond the identity principle. In the process, novels like *Molloy* exemplify Adorno's argument that the aesthetic is able to reveal the non-identity of objects with thought: 'Aesthetic identity is meant to assist the non-identical in its struggle against the repressive identification compulsion that rules the outside world' (Adorno 1984, 6).

As Adorno well understood, part of the problem with homeliness is its territorialism, and hence its ascription of boundaries between insider and outsider. Indeed, the gesture of hospitality, which is called for by the territoriality of home and belonging, inevitably positions the guest as an outsider and therefore as a potential enemy. In *Adieu to Emmanuel Levinas*, for instance, Jacques Derrida remarks that

> [t]o dare to say welcome is perhaps to insinuate that one is at home here, . . . and that at home one receives, invites, or offers hospitality, thus appropriating for oneself a place to *welcome* . . . the other, or, worse, *welcoming* the other in order to appropriate for oneself a place and then speak the language of hospitality.
>
> (Derrida 1999, 15-16)

In this understanding, hospitality is always incipiently hostile (see Derrida 2000, 45), a mechanism that enables the political, which, as Carl Schmitt argues, depends on the potential enemy – that is, 'the other, the stranger', with whom 'conflicts . . . are possible' (Schmitt 1996, 27).

For hospitality to become more hospitable, and therefore less conditional, the host would have to question his or her sense of being at home, of belonging, and thereby render home unhomely, that is, both familiar and strange. Elsewhere, Derrida, drawing on Sigmund Freud's (1955 [1919]) observation that the word *unheimlich* ambivalently signifies an estrangement within the familiar, states that this term, while speaking to the stranger, 'is not unfamiliar', that 'it provides a place, in a troubling way, for a form of welcome in itself that recalls the haunt as much as the home' (Derrida 1997, 58). For a welcome to be more welcoming, it must proceed from a home that constantly makes itself unhomely. It must emanate from a place which questions, and so defers, the differences that enable home. The host who welcomes the other person from such a home would be in the process of becoming, if not homeless, less at home.

If it were continually to be rendered unhomely, home would not be *vergangen* but futural in nature. It would be always yet to come. In this essay, I develop this idea through a consideration of the tropes of travel and vagrancy in Samuel Beckett's *Molloy*. Although it was published more than six decades ago, this novel provides a profound meditation on the unhomeliness of home that still contributes to our understanding of the ways in which the limits of hospitality may be limited. The basic proposition that informs my argument is that the vagrant is a person without a place, and that Beckett uses this figure, who troubles identifying thought because he or she is unrecognisable from the perspective of home, to reflect on the possibility of reducing home's territoriality, thus rendering the hospitality that proceeds from it less conditional.

★★★

The difference between travel and vagrancy is determined by the ways in which these activities position themselves relative to home. A traveller travels from a place called home to a foreign destination, afterwards returning home. Home is both his or her origin and *telos*. It is the final destination, the fixed coordinate in terms of which everything else is placed and located. Travel thus involves a movement of return which, being recuperative and even appropriative, is not only physical but also epistemological in nature. The traveller reduces the strangeness encountered by domesticating it, by understanding it in the terms of home, and thereby rendering it familiar. In the process, both a personal identity and that of home are affirmed.

Travel's movement of return is what distinguishes it from wandering and, indeed, vagrancy, both of which are potentially movements without end. The vagrant constantly moves into the unknown and unpredicted, without ever returning home. Accordingly, his or her wandering into and in the unknown is ateleological and not mediated by any one community's codes of recognition, which are necessarily informed by notions of familiarity that are normative in nature. After all, if community constitutes itself differentially, the forms of identification, and therefore the codes of recognition that it makes available to its members, must also be premised on difference.[1] In particular, they are premised on the difference between inside and outside, and therefore on the presence of the outsider and potential enemy. Being of no fixed address, the vagrant cannot share the conceptions of familiarity and strangeness, known and unknown, that ground community's sense of the homeliness of home.

For Beckett, one is always travelling to, rather than from, home. Life, as the eponym of *Murphy* puts it, is a 'wandering to find home' (Beckett 2009, 4). Through this assertion, the novel suggests that travel, in the absence of a point of departure and an attainable destination, while not totally aimless, becomes a form of wandering. One is on a road – which is more non-place than place – to a destination that one can never finally reach and therefore appropriate for oneself as a place. Such wandering is also a prominent feature of Beckett's *Molloy*, which contains many allusions to archetypal travellers such as Odysseus, Abraham, Christ, Everyman, and Christian. Rubin Rabinovitz observes that Molloy, like Odysseus, was once a sailor, that he mentions the Aegean, his Homeric ancestor's black boat, and, in an allusion to Circe, the herb moly (Rabinovitz 1979, 25). Moreover, the novel contains a scene that alludes to Odysseus's return home to Ithaca. The theme of wandering and exile that is introduced by these allusions is also reinforced by references to Abraham: in this regard, Rabinovitz notes that the voice heard by Molloy recalls God's instruction to Abraham to relocate to Canaan (ibid.: 26); and David Hayman points out that the scenes in which Moran and his son depart for Ballyba echo the story of Abraham and Isaac (Hayman 1970, 141). Despite these allusions, the second part of the novel, rather than depicting a journey that culminates in some form of self- or spiritual enlightenment, charts an anti-*Bildung* of sorts, a process of self-dissolution, in which Moran loses control of self and outside world, undergoing a process of becoming vagrant.

Moran's narrative opens with him enjoying the peace, stability, and security of home:

> All was still. . . . From my neighbours' chimneys the smoke rose straight and blue. None but tranquil sounds, the clicking of mallet and ball, a rake on

pebbles, a distant lawn-mower, the bell of my beloved church. And birds of course, blackbird and thrush, their song sadly dying, vanquished by the heat. . . . Contentedly I inhaled the scent of my lemon-verbena.

(Beckett 2006b, 88)

As this intentionally hackneyed, and therefore parodic, description of domestic bliss suggests, Moran is, to use his own description of himself, 'a creature of his house' (109). Importantly, his experience of the homeliness of home includes epistemological security and the control of self through reason. For instance, he describes himself as having a 'methodical mind' and prides himself on being 'master of himself', on being able to rein 'back his thoughts within the limits of the calculable' (93, 104, 108, 109). He is a seeker, that is, someone who is 'paid to seek' (106), and therefore a kind of detective who engages in 'enquiry' (93). As is usually the case with the conventional detective figure in literature, he is thus a version of the knowing subject, a rational agent who is master of his own destiny (see Kenner 1988, 35).

Molloy is a novel about visits and visitations. Moran's enjoyment of home is interrupted by a visit from Gabar, who tells him that he and his son are to undertake a mission to find Molloy. The details of this mission are, at best, nebulous; despite saying that Molloy is 'no stranger to him' (107), Moran is able to provide only the following description of him:

> He panted. . . .
>
> Even in open country he seemed to be charging through a jungle. . . . In spite of this he advanced but slowly. He swayed, to and fro, like a bear.
>
> He rolled his head, uttering incomprehensible words.
>
> He was massive and hulking, to the point of misshapenness. And, without being black, of a dark colour. . . .
>
> I had no clue to his age. . . .
>
> I had no information as to his face. I assumed it was hirsute, craggy and grimacing. Nothing justified my doing so.
>
> (108-9)

It would seem that Molloy is both strange and familiar. He is uncanny, and the uncanny, as Nicholas Royle contends, 'cannot be pinned down or controlled' (Royle 2003, 15). Molloy exceeds the 'limits of the calculable'. From Moran's perspective, which is that of home, he is unrecognisable, unknowable and, as the disjointed, contradictory, almost aleatory nature of the portrayal implies, beyond the compass of words.

Moran fares no better in describing the destination of his journey, that is, Ballyba, 'the Molloy country' (Beckett 2006b, 129). Although he attempts a description, he immediately questions it: 'I wonder if I was not confusing it with some other place' (129). It follows that he leaves home with little advance knowledge, and therefore expectation, of what it is that he is supposed to achieve, where he is going, and whom it is that he is seeking. This much is emphasised by the following account of his preparations:

> It was then the unheard of sight was seen of Moran making ready to go without knowing where he was going, having consulted neither map nor timetable, considered neither itinerary nor halts, heedless of the weather outlook, with only the vaguest notion of the outfit he would need, the time the expedition was likely to take, the money he would require and even the very nature of the work to be done and consequently the means to be employed.
> (118)

In itself, Moran's rambling and elliptical report emphasises his journey's vagrant nature. While he does finally reach Ballyba, it is only by accident and without his having realised that he has done so (152). Ultimately, his report is more about his dissolution than about the journey he undertakes. It is about the 'great changes' he has 'suffered' and his 'growing resignation to being dispossessed of self' (143). The seeker, which is to say the rational subject, ultimately forfeits his subjectivity and with it any sense of a *telos* and destination. Lying in a makeshift shelter in Ballyba, within sight of Bally, his putative destination, he finds that his 'unfailing pastime,' namely himself, is 'far now' from his 'thoughts' (156). Crucially, this passive state follows his inarticulate encounter with a shepherd, in the course of which it becomes clear that his disintegration has left him on the very margins of language: 'I looked about me again incapable of speech. I did not know how I would ever be able to break this silence' (153). Evidently, the dissolution that Moran undergoes involves a loss of the ability to occupy a subject position in language. Even though the narrating self who attempts to describe this experience uses the word 'I', his experiencing self is unable to do so. In conventional first-person narratives, as F. K. Stanzel has shown (Stanzel 1984, 113), there is continuity between the experiencing I and the narrating I: the former undergoes a formation or *Bildung* and, at the end of the novel, which is the point of retrospection from which the narrative proceeds, becomes the narrating I. In Beckett's novel, there is no such continuity, nor any teleological progression from ignorance to knowledge that invests the self with coherence and unity. Instead, there is a radical disjuncture between the experiencing self, who is no longer an I, and the narrating self, who is an I, and therefore unable to know or identify his former self from the position in language and culture from which he writes.

In the time of which the narrating I tries to speak, which is a time out of language, culture, history – and therefore immemorial – Moran the erstwhile seeker has become a waiter. The search, in the absence of a subject who is able to act and therefore seek and find, has become a very particular kind of waiting. Moran waits without expectation. That is, he waits for he knows not what – a 'situation' akin to 'the turd waiting for the flush' (156). The kind of waiting involved is non-intentional, since it happens in the absence of a subject which can direct its consciousness towards an object and thereby constitute it. Moran, the seeker, has become 'incurious', an experience that is described by Molloy in the first of the novel's two narratives: 'For to know nothing is nothing, not to want to know anything likewise, but to be beyond knowing anything, to know you are beyond knowing anything, that is when peace enters in, to the soul of the incurious seeker' (58–59). Because Moran is not located in and by the subject positions inscribed in and by language, his waiting is not informed by society's codes of recognition and he can therefore expect nothing that a subject could recognise. To use Derrida's term, he has become unconditionally hospitable, and is therefore open '*to who or what turns up*, before any determination, before any anticipation, before any identification' (Derrida 2000, 77).

What does turn up is himself, or more precisely, the self that had been displaced by the subject positions that Moran had previously occupied in language and culture. In other words, what arrives is what would be unrecognisable from the perspective of the subject that seeks. The spectral self that turns up is the one that had been displaced by the seeking subject, while its arrival is the displacement of that subject. From his position of retrospection, the narrating I describes this displacement: 'And what I saw was more like a crumbling, a frenzied collapsing of all that had always protected me from all I was always condemned to be' (Beckett 2006b, 143). Tellingly, though, Moran, the narrating I, cannot describe his experiencing self's visitor, just as he cannot describe Molloy. If he were to describe this subjectless self, he would be able to do so only in language that failed to describe Molloy. In effect, the alterior, uncanny self that Moran encounters is Molloy. As Fred Miller Robinson puts it, Moran's journey is in search of 'this tramp self within himself' (Robinson 1981, 344). However, it does not follow that these two characters are simply interchangeable: it is Moran the waiter, rather than Moran the seeker or narrating I, who is Molloy's doppelgänger. Ultimately, then, Moran does encounter Molloy, but only in losing the ability to seek and find him. That is, his loss of the ability to seek and find enables the event of Molloy's visit. The added irony is that what he had sought had always been within him.

★★★

Instead of the standard travel narrative in which the traveller assimilates the unknown into the known, thereby consolidating the epistemological authority of home together with a sense of self, Moran's report thus describes a journey in which the subject is unsettled by his encounter with an otherness that cannot be understood from within home's structures of knowledge and which is therefore refractory to identifying thought. Interestingly, Emmanuel Levinas's understanding of hospitality hinges on a movement without return from self to other. Rather than recuperating the other from within and into culture's structures of knowledge, the self is unhomed and sacrifices itself to the other. In explaining this movement, Levinas uses the metaphor of travel, comparing Abraham's departure from his homeland to Odysseus's return home: 'To the myth of Ulysses returning to Ithaca, we would like to oppose the story of Abraham leaving his homeland forever for a still unknown land and even forbidding his son to be brought back to its point of departure' (Levinas 1986, 348). In the case of Abraham, one has what Alphonso Lingis calls a movement of 'infinition', that is, a movement whose dehiscence precludes the possibility of foreclosing on the unknown by relating it to the known, which is exactly what happens in the assimilative 'movement of Being' (Lingis 1998, xxxviii, xix, xxii).

Like Abraham's journey, Moran's moves towards otherness and is therefore ostensibly exterior in its trajectory. Unlike Abraham's, however, his journey troubles the distinction between interior and exterior because it leads to an encounter with the other within the self – an other which, as his narration indicates, insists on coming into being. Tellingly in this regard, Moran's attempt to recount the story of his experience, to establish in language a relation of correlation with his former, alterior self, stages the failure of the recuperative movement of Being by foregrounding the irreducible difference of the experiencing self to the narrating I. From his position in language and culture, Moran cannot identify, and thus conceptually master, his former self. If, as Nicholas Royle tells us, the uncanny 'has to do with a sense of ourselves as double, split, at odds with ourselves' (Royle 2003, 6), then Moran's narration of his narrative performs his bifurcation, his sense that he is not who he had thought he was, and that the familiar is therefore also strange.

Because it inclines towards both the Abrahamic and the Odyssean, the journey that Moran undertakes in *Molloy* departs quite radically from the kind described in standard travel narratives. And it is because both these movements stall that one finds, in Moran's narrative, a homecoming which is nonetheless not a return to the point from which he departed. Like Odysseus, he goes back home, that is, to his house in 'the Moran country' and, as his retrospective narration indicates, once again says I (Beckett 2006b, 127). Accordingly, the movement that characterises his journey (and, indeed, his narrative) is not quite an irreversible one of infinition. Neither is it a recuperative movement of Being, though. The home to which he returns has become *unheimlich*: his bees and hens are dead, his housekeeper has left, and he himself soon abandons the house to live in the garden, a decision recalling the makeshift shelters that he and his son construct in their wanderings, one of which he comes to think of as 'my little house' (142). By the end of the novel, he is clearly no longer 'a creature of his house' (109). Home is no longer homely. Yet he is still there. He is both at home and an outsider.

If Moran's house has become unhomely, it is because his encounter with the unknown has altered his conception of self. While he may again say 'I', like the narrator of *The Unnamable* (Beckett 2006c [1953]), he does so 'unbelieving' (285), and indeed frequently switches to the third person. Moran's sense of self-possession or -mastery, as well as of the familiarity of home, has been mediated by his encounter with that which home seeks to exclude, but which, ironically, is nevertheless already inside it. It follows that home is now also a haunt, and that he, in his own words, is 'haunted and possessed by chimeras' (109).

Moran's narration proceeds from this unsettled, ambivalent, and indeterminate position. In fact, he tells his story because of his sense of the unhomeliness of home. As Royle observes, the uncanny is 'bound up with a compulsion to tell' (12). Moran tells his story because he is possessed by an otherness that is both familiar and strange, proximate and distant. By implication, he writes under the inspiration of that which home seeks to exclude. Significantly, in this connection, he listens to a 'voice' that advises him on how 'to endure the long anguish of vagrancy and freedom' (Beckett 2006b, 27). Well before the end of the novel, the narrating I mentions this voice and reflects that its advice may mean that he will 'one day be banished' from his house and 'from the absurd comforts of . . . home where all is snug and neat' and where his 'enemies' cannot 'reach' him (127). Moran thus writes not only because Youdi, his superior, requires a report on his mission, but also because he is heeding the authority of the voice to which he listens (170). Indeed, on the last page of the novel, he admits as much when he says that the voice 'told me to write the report' (170). On the one hand, then, Moran must obey Youdi's instruction to go home and to write from home; on the other hand, he must obey the voice's instruction to leave home and to write from a vagrant position which is precisely not a position. He is required to be both Odysseus and Abraham.

Although 'within' him (126), the authoritative voice is 'ambiguous' (126) and does 'not use the words that Moran had been taught when he was little and that he in turn had taught to his little one' (169–70). Presumably, then, the voice is linked to his former, alterior self, who is beyond, or at best, on the margins of, language. Like this alterior self, the voice cannot be located, placed, and so positioned and identified, in the language of home. In responding to this alterity, Moran is thus responding to an authority beyond language and social forms. His writing is a response to that which exceeds writing; he 'follows' this authority, to use his own word (126). He writes to bear witness to what exceeds social forms and to what these forms try to elide. Alternatively put, his writing seeks to testify to the limitlessness that the limits of social forms necessarily delimit, and which constantly threatens to interrupt them.

If the alterior voice to which he listens is 'within' him, the corollary must be that he is the involuntary host of a radical otherness, and that his act of writing is a gesture of unconditional hospitality towards it, which, however, is constantly rendered conditional by the medium in which it is extended. What starts as a movement of infinition becomes a movement of Being. Although Moran writes to respond to the excess of language, to make a home for it, he does so in language. Accordingly, his 'following' of the voice in his writing is not an act that could ever be completed. It is endless, which is to say vagrant, in nature. The rift between Moran, the narrating I, and his experiencing self foregrounds precisely the ateleological nature of the form of following here involved by performing the self's otherness to itself. While Moran, the narrating I, responds to his former self, seeking to address it in his writing, he cannot do so. He can neither (in a generous movement of infinition) give himself to this alterior self, nor (in an assimilative movement of Being) recuperate it from his subject position in language and culture. And because he cannot complete the movement of Being, the self that is already inside him is always still to come. It is yet to be identified, recognised, and so welcomed.

Through his writing, Moran is thus required to follow something that is not a recognisable object of and for consciousness. His writing is a following of what he already bears within himself. In a sense, he follows that by which he is being followed, pursues that by which he is pursued, possessed, and haunted. This much is made clear at the very beginning of his report, in his account of Gabar's visit which (it will be remembered) interrupts his enjoyment of the homeliness of home. The fact that Gabar is a messenger, and that his name is related to Gabriel (see Hamilton 2005, 334), associates him with the angel-messenger who, in the Bible, announces to Mary that the Holy Ghost will visit itself upon her (see *Authorised King James Version*, Luke 1:31–35). Shortly after Gabar's visit, while Moran is lying on his bed, he is tellingly paid a second visit, which is, however, also a visitation. This visit takes the form of an 'apparition' of Molloy (Beckett 2006b, 109), which the narrating I tries, but fails, to describe in the passage previously cited.[2] Just as tellingly, after Gabar's visit, Moran encounters a neighbour who asks him whether he has 'seen a ghost' (93). When he finally embarks on his search for Molloy, it is 12 p.m., the witching hour. The implication is that he follows Molloy because he has already been possessed by him; therefore his following is a haunting and a persecution. In his house, he has been visited by a ghost – and ghosts do not respect the boundaries between inside and outside, past and future.

A further implication is that Moran's following is a servitude. By following, through his writing, the alterior, unrecognisable voice inside him, he *attends* to it; as the various senses and history of this word suggest, he takes care of it, watches over it, ministers to it, listens to it, directs his ears to it, waits upon it, accompanies it (see 'attend', *Oxford English Dictionary Online*). In the novel, the references to the voice to which Moran listens bring about a shift in emphasis from the visibility and recognisability of the visitor (a word that derives from the Latin *visitare*, 'to go to see', and *videre*, 'to see') to the invisibility of a guest, who can only be listened to attentively, without expectation. Not to expect – the etymological sense of this verb is 'to look out for' – is not to seek to see, and so to recognise, the visitor. It is to listen, to attend, a state in which the self does not reduce the other to an intentional object for consciousness. Attention, as Blanchot maintains, 'is waiting: not the effort . . . or the mobilization of knowledge around something with which one might concern oneself' (Blanchot 1995, 121)

One finds in *Molloy* an irreducible tension between attentionality and intentionality. Despite his attentiveness, Moran is located in language and can only follow the voice in language, which entails trying to render it recognisable, an object for consciousness. Because he cannot locate and accommodate the voice in language, his responsibility to and for this alterior force is without end. In the novel, the motif of lameness suggests the interminable nature of his responsibility. Moran's lameness develops on the evening of the day on which he is visited by Gabar and Molloy; the condition worsens progressively until he is finally reduced to immobility in his shelter outside Bally. Before this occurs, though, the aporetic nature of his pursuit is further metaphorised by the bicycle with which he seeks to continue his futile following. The purport of the metaphor is clear enough: he must follow something, yet lacks the wherewithal and the means with which to follow it. So too it is with his writing: he must follow in language what exceeds language. Accordingly, the task of following can never be discharged. Through his writing, Molloy thus both waits on and waits for this radical alterity.

My argument is that there is an ethic of hospitality at work in Beckett's conception of waiting and following in *Molloy*. Although the text's focus is ostensibly the self's concern with its own otherness rather than its obligation to the otherness of the other person, what is at issue is nonetheless a form of responsibility that derives from an encounter with an alterity that cannot be recognised from within community's structures of recognition. As already proposed, the narrating I ceaselessly tries to tell a story about a spectral self which is proximate yet unrecognisable, and therefore also distant, from a position in community and language. If this strangely familiar, and therefore uncanny, self is unrecognisable to the narrating I, it must also be unrecognisable to other members of the community in and by which home is located. Exactly this is intimated in the scene describing the second visit that Moran is paid in his shelter outside Bally. His unexpected visitor is again Gabar, who conveys Youdi's message that he is to return home. Moran, who does not 'recognize this far-off voice', responds to Gabar's arrival and to this order by asking him 'You recognize me?', and then again 'Do you recognize me?' (157). The suggestion is that Gabar, who as the emissary of Youdi is associated with home and community, cannot possibly recognise the stranger that Moran has become. Moran should be as unrecognisable to Gabar as Molloy is to Moran. If the latter is becoming vagrant through being unsettled by his encounter with the stranger within himself, it should follow that he will be unrecognisable, or at the very least barely recognisable, from the perspective of home. Indeed, the vagrant, as Jacques-Alain Miller notes in a discussion of Jeremy Bentham and panopticism, is without a place and unidentifiable. He or she is invisible in society, which, being panoptical, seeks to render all visible, identifiable, recognisable, and therefore categorisable (Miller 1987, 17). In resisting such placement, the vagrant obviously resists the kind of calculative thinking to which Moran once subscribed, and to which Gabar still subscribes.

On encountering Moran, Gabar interestingly addresses him by his name, and then responds to his question by again using his name, 'Ah Moran', followed by 'what a man!' (Beckett 2006b, 158). Gabar identifies, recognises, and places Moran as 'Moran' and 'a man'. Notwithstanding its emphasis on the naming of the unnameable and therefore the reduction of its alterity, the exchange between these two characters presupposes the covert presence of a third party – the reader of the novel – who is able to detect the irony inherent in Gabar's reply to Moran's question. The reader cannot but realize that Gabar responds to Moran, the seeker, the subject, rather than to the subjectless waiter who exceeds the identity that is posited by this name and, indeed, the noun 'man'. In engaging with this exchange, the reader is aware of a misidentification, a misrecognition. She or he is conscious, or becomes conscious, of an alterity that cannot be named and contained by the proper noun 'Moran' and the common noun 'man'. If linguistic reason is what distinguishes 'man' from other animals, as has been argued for centuries, then Moran cannot be a man. Whatever he is exceeds, and so questions, the opposition between 'man' and animal. In this scene, the reader therefore becomes aware of a radical disjunction, indeed an infinite distance, between the words 'Moran', 'man' and what they claim to name, thus encountering their ironic inability to signify adequately. In terms of Adorno's argument against identifying thought, the reader appreciates in realising the word's inadequacy that concepts do not 'exhaust the thing conceived', that they leave a 'remainder' and, consequently, that 'all concepts refer to nonconceptualities' (Adorno 1984, 5, 11).

My argument is not that in this novel Beckett attempts to represent being in the absence of identifying thought. After all, the reader reads not what Moran experiences, but his record of an experience that he did not experience as a subject. Through its emphasis on Moran's linguistic and conceptual estrangement from the experience of which he tries to write, the novel acknowledges its own implication in identifying thought, while at the same time gesturing towards, and therefore not seeking to identify, a world without identifying thought. The text evokes what its own implication in language, discourse, and thought denies. In so doing, it exemplifies Adorno's thesis that art has a 'twofold essence': although in the world, its relationship to the non-conceptual divorces it from the world, the language of subsumption, identifying thought and, very importantly, itself. It is both 'an autonomous entity and a social fact' (ibid.: 8), estranged from history yet unable to take up a position outside it.

By means of its 'twofold essence', which enables it to distance itself from itself, Beckett's *Molloy* not only exposes the limits of identifying thought but also places the reader in relation to that which such thought fails to exhaust. For instance, the scene in which Gabar identifies Moran requires the reader to relate to the remainder left by this identification, which is also the remainder that Moran follows through his narration. The reader must relate to the excess of Moran's narration, and must do so from home, from within the language in which she or he reads. Through ironising identifying thought, then, the novel effectively burdens the reader with the question of hospitality that it has broached. How is she or he to relate to that which exceeds the text and its medium without reducing its alterity? If the reader were to be confronted with this question through involvement in reading the novel, his or her home would already have become less homely and could no longer simply be a place from which to welcome someone, duly recognising that person as an outsider, and in the process identifying the place from which the language of hospitality is spoken as a home and a territory. Were this to happen, the reader's reading of the novel would follow Moran's writing in its following of the unrecognisable voice that speaks to him from within. The reader would thus be waiting on and for this alterity, and would therefore have assumed responsibility for it.

In conveying to the reader a sense of the excess of Moran's narrative, Beckett's *Molloy* points to the alterity that remains after the negations of identifying thought. The novel's preoccupation with this ineliminable remainder is ultimately a preoccupation with what Levinas terms the *il y a*, that is, the 'there is' or not nothing that consciousness would encounter in the absence of a controlling subject (Levinas 1978, 58). In this impersonal, neutral situation, which resonates with the form of being that Moran experiences in his shelter outside Bally, and which exceeds and so inspires his narration, Being is detached from beings that control it. It is, to use Levinas's word, the incessant 'murmur' (ibid.: 59) of the not nothing of the *il y a* that Moran follows and, by extension, that Beckett follows. While Shane Weller maintains that in his writing Beckett tries to escape the absolute alterity of the *il y a* (Weller 2006, 12–13), the metaphor of following in *Molloy* quite self-consciously indicates that the writer is haunted by, and must therefore pursue, this irreducible alterity. Rather than trying to escape it, the novel seeks to place itself in relation to the ineliminable not nothing, and thereby to affect the reader in such a way that she or he too is affected by it. What this text shows is that the constant murmur of the 'there is' interrupts the subject, renders the home unhomely, questions the conceptual violence of identifying thought, and in the process opens a path to the ethical.

★★★

My argument, then, is that *Molloy* is informed by an ethic of hospitality that is premised on a responsibility for the exclusions that enable community. If this is so, the charge of solipsism that is so often levelled at Beckett's writing[3] – and which is probably related to the critical tendency in the mid-twentieth century to read its preoccupation with the self's search for itself from a Cartesian perspective – is simply misplaced in the case of this novel, which foregrounds the notion of home and, by extension, community. After all, solipsism is predicated on the assumption that the subject is autonomous, that the individual is knowable, and therefore at home with itself. While the focus of *Molloy* is most certainly the individual, this is an individual who is located in community rather than being autonomous. For Beckett, the self encounters itself as a subject only in an intersubjective world. It is surely for this reason that Adorno, in one of the marginalia in his copy of *The Unnamable*, notes that 'B[eckett]'s novels are the critique of solipsism' (Adorno 2010, 172). For its identity, the self relies on the subject positions, and therefore the forms of identification and codes of recognition that community makes available to its members and which are (as I have argued) produced by the differential process through which community establishes and conserves itself. Since it is this exclusionary movement that ultimately determines what constitutes a recognisable subject, Beckett's concern with the self's unrecognisability to itself is always already a concern with community. *Molloy* shows not merely that community's insider depends on the existence of an outsider, but that the former, in being estranged from himself by language and the codes that govern recognition, is in fact also an outsider of sorts. Moran's search for Molloy, the stranger, is a search for a self that has been excluded and rendered unrecognisable by community's forms and language. The question of how to respond to community's exclusions, which is the question of hospitality, is thus foregrounded in this novel, despite its apparent preoccupation with the self's relationship with itself.

With particular reference to the motifs of waiting and following, I have shown that this novel's obsession with the excess of community's forms of identification and recognition destabilises, without erasing, the distinction between inside and outside, endlessly deferring the principal difference on which community and notions of belonging are premised. Home becomes less homely because it is haunted by that which it seeks to exclude. This does not mean, however, that the house is *vergangen*. As the narrating I reflecting on his experiencing self's return home, Moran wonders whether he could have wondered whether the home to which he was returning was a 'ruin':

> I forged my way . . . towards what I would have called my ruin if I could have conceived what I had left to be ruined. Perhaps I have conceived it since, perhaps I have not done conceiving it, it takes time, one is bound to in time.
> (Beckett 2006b, 159–60)

Although he uses the word 'ruin', the house that Moran finds on his return is not quite gone. As I have argued, he is unsettled, out of place at home, talks of 'clearing out' (169), of leaving, but is nevertheless still there, albeit not inside the house. He is neither at home nor not at home. By extension, he is becoming vagrant, and therefore not yet vagrant. If home is a ruin, it is one that is still habitable. Very significantly, as I have already indicated, Moran is now able to refer to the 'absurd comforts' of his house. Evidently, he feels no nostalgia for the homeliness of the home that he once thought he had possessed. If there is any nostalgia in the novel, it is orientated to the future, to the home that is yet to come. Rather than being gone or in the past, the house is incomplete because it has yet to become a home to that which it excludes, but on whose exclusion it relies for its existence. Its incompletion, however, necessarily points to the possibility of completion, to the possibility of a future in which it may be complete. Paradoxically, then, the novel's erosion of the difference between inside and outside, rendering home incomplete, enables a gesturing towards the possibility of the very completion that the deferral of a final point of difference between inside and outside precludes. Even as it locates home in the future, the novel's ending thus suggests that this future will always be still to come, that the *telos* of home will always be yet to be attained. If Moran is becoming vagrant, he is 'wandering to find home'. While he has a *telos*, he is wandering, rather than journeying, towards it. At work in the novel's conception of futurity, then, is an ateleological teleology.

Molloy is very much a novel about change – particularly the change that Moran and his home undergo – and it is therefore about community's conceptions of time and futurity. Early in this chapter, I cited the idyllic description of home that Moran provides at the beginning of his narrative. A striking feature of this description is its suggestion that home is static and timeless. For Moran, the birdsong and church bells have always sounded as they do in the narrating I's description; it is his sense of their endless repetition that makes these 'sounds' so 'tranquil' and reassuring. In part, home's familiarity and homeliness are produced by suspending time and thereby overcoming it. From the perspective of home, if thus conceived, the future can only ever repeat the present. In seeking to perpetuate itself, home forecloses on the future and thereby attempts to reduce it to a version of the present. By contrast, at the end of the novel, home is conceived as incomplete, and therefore as being able to hold itself open to the future. Precisely because the boundary that it draws between outside and inside has become permeable, the home described can accommodate change, and can therefore become other than it is. Since this home is unhomely or uncanny, it is, to use Royle's description of the unfamiliar, 'never fixed, but constantly altering' (Royle 2003, 5). The corollary is that the home of the future may well be unrecognisable from the perspective of the home of the present, just as the home at the end of the novel is unrecognisable from the perspective of the home at the beginning of Moran's narrative. Instead of being expected, then, the home of the future can only be awaited without expectation or with reduced expectation. In fact, this hospitable comportment to the future is articulated in Moran's admission that he knows 'scarcely any better where' he is 'going' and 'what awaits' him than he did on the night of his departure for 'the Molloy country' (Beckett 2006b, 127).

In terms of this stance towards the future, Moran is interchangeable with Malone in *Malone Dies* (Beckett 2006a) and with the narrator of *The Unnamable*. (Beckett 2006c). For all three characters, home is not *vergangen* but still to come, and always in a form that is unidentifiable from the present. Yet the trilogy nonetheless endorses Adorno's assertion that 'it is part of morality not to be at home in one's home'. Only from a spectral home whose origin is located in the future can the future be contemplated as a future, rather than being reduced to what Derrida in *Specters of Marx* calls a 'future present' (Derrida 1994, 48, 81). Here and elsewhere, Derrida suggests that hospitality, far from being a possibility open to a subject who acts, is a disruptive event that demands one live with the kind of uncertainty that is inevitably elided by attempts at thinking of futurity in terms of self-identity. Beckett's trilogy expresses the possibility of such a disruptive event.

Acknowledgement

I hereby acknowledge the financial support of the National Research Foundation of South Africa in writing this essay.

Notes

1 Judith Butler refers to 'the differential operation of norms of recognition' (2004, 44). She adds that '[t]he "I" who cannot come into being without a "you" is also fundamentally dependent on a set of norms of recognition that originated neither with the "I" nor with the "you"' (Butler 2004, 45).
2 I am indebted to Jessica Marais for drawing my attention to this visit.

3 Russell Smith's comment is one of the more recent examples of this commonplace of criticism: 'Many of Beckett's characters are implacably committed to a solipsistic withdrawal from the world and any other human beings who happen to inhabit it' (Smith 2008, 1).

References

Adorno, Theodor W. 1973 [1966]. *Negative Dialectics*. Translated by E. B. Ashton. London: Routledge and Kegan Paul.
———. 1984 [1966]. *Aesthetic Theory*. Translated by C. Lenhardt. Edited by Gretel Adorno and Rolf Tiedemann. London: Routledge and Kegan Paul.
———. 1991 [1951]. *Minima Moralia: Reflections from Damaged Life*. Translated by E. F. N. Jephcott. London: Verso.
———. 2010 [1994]. 'Notes on Beckett', translated by Dirk van Hulle and Shane Weller. *Journal of Beckett Studies* 19.2: 157-78.
'Attend'. *Oxford English Dictionary Online* (accessed 14 May 2015).
Authorised King James Version of the Holy Bible. n.d. London: Collins.
Beckett, Samuel. 2006a [1951]. *Malone Dies*. In *Samuel Beckett: The Grove Centenary Edition*. Vol. 2, translated by Patrick Bowles and Samuel Beckett and edited by Paul Auster, 171–281. New York: Grove.
———. 2006b [1951]. *Molloy*. In *Samuel Beckett: The Grove Centenary Edition*. Vol. 2, translated by Patrick Bowles and Samuel Beckett and edited by Paul Auster, 1–170. New York: Grove.
———. 2006c [1953]. *The Unnamable*. In *Samuel Beckett: The Grove Centenary Edition*. Vol. 2, translated by Samuel Beckett and edited by Paul Auster, 283-407. New York: Grove.
———. 2009. *Murphy*. London: Faber.
Blanchot, Maurice. 1995 [1969]. *The Infinite Conversation*. Translated by Susan Hanson. Minneapolis: University of Minnesota Press.
Butler, Judith. 2004. *Precarious Life: The Powers of Mourning and Violence*. London and New York: Verso.
Derrida, Jacques. 1994. *Specters of Marx: The State of the Debt, the Work of Mourning, and the New International*. Translated by Peggy Kamuf. Introduction by Bernd Magnus and Stephen Cullenberg. New York: Routledge.
———. 1997 [1994]. *The Politics of Friendship*. Translated by George Collins. London: Verso.
———. 1999 [1997]. *Adieu to Emmanuel Levinas*. Translated by Pascale-Anne Brault and Michael Naas. Stanford, CA: Stanford University Press.
———. 2000 [1997]. *Of Hospitality: Anne Dufourmantelle Invites Jacques Derrida to Respond*. Translated by Rachel Bowlby. Stanford, CA: Stanford University Press.
Freud, Sigmund. 1955 [1919]. 'The Uncanny'. In *The Standard Edition of the Complete Psychological Works of Sigmund Freud*. Vol. 17, translated by James Strachey, 218-52. London: Hogarth Press.
Hamilton, Geoff. 2005. 'Annihilating All That's Made: Beckett's *Molloy* and the Pastoral Tradition'. *Samuel Beckett Today/Aujourd'hui* 15: 325-39.
Hayman, David. 1970. '*Molloy* or the Quest for Meaninglessness: A Global Interpretation'. In *Samuel Beckett Now: Critical Approaches to His Novels, Poetry, and Plays*, edited by Melvin J. Friedman, 129-56. Chicago: University of Chicago Press.
Kenner, Hugh. 1988. 'The Trilogy'. In *Modern Critical Interpretations: Samuel Beckett's 'Molloy', 'Malone Dies', 'The Unnamable'*, edited by Harold Bloom, 31-50. New York: Chelsea House.

Levinas, Emmanuel. 1978 [1947]. *Existence and Existents*. Translated by Alphonso Lingis. The Hague: Martinus Nijhoff.

———. 1986 [1949]. 'The Trace of the Other'. In *Deconstruction in Context*, translated by Alphonso Lingis and edited by Mark Taylor, 345–59. Chicago: University of Chicago Press.

Lingis, Alphonso. 1998 [1974]. 'Introduction'. In *Otherwise than Being or Beyond Essence*, by Emmanuel Levinas, xvii–xlv. Pittsburgh, PA: Duquesne University Press.

Miller, Jacques-Alain. 1987 [1975]. 'Jeremy Bentham's Panoptic Device', translated by Richard Miller. *October* 41: 3–29.

Rabinovitz, Rubin. 2015 [1979]. '"Molloy" and the Archetypal Traveller'. *Journal of Beckett Studies* 5: 25–44. Web (accessed 11 August 2015).

Robinson, Fred Miller. 1981. '"An Art of Superior Tramps": Beckett and Giacometti'. *Centennial Review* 25.4: 331–44.

Royle, Nicholas. 2003. *The Uncanny*. Manchester: Manchester University Press.

Schmitt, Carl. 1996 [1932]. *The Concept of the Political*. Translated by George Schwab. Chicago: University of Chicago Press.

Smith, Russell. 2008. 'Introduction: Beckett's Ethical Undoing'. In *Beckett and Ethics*, edited by Russell Smith, 1–20. London: Continuum.

Stanzel, F. K. 1984 [1979]. *A Theory of Narrative*. Translated by Charlotte Goedsche. Cambridge: Cambridge University Press.

Weller, Shane. 2006. *Beckett, Literature, and the Ethics of Alterity*. Houndmills: Palgrave Macmillan.

5

DEFYING CLOSURE

Hospitality, colonialism and mobility beyond the limits of the nation in Sol Plaatje's *Mhudi*

Rebecca Fasselt

Hospitality, according to Jacques Derrida, is 'not only . . . a culture . . . but there is no culture that is not also a culture of hospitality' (Derrida 2002, 361). While certain elements of hospitality appear universal, the laws and practices of hospitality differ from one cultural setting to another and change across time (Rosello 2001, viii). Hospitality, as Avril Bell emphasises, 'in all cases . . . encompasses a complex and power-laden set of relations between people and place' (Bell 2010, 240). But these power relations are always highly context-dependent and, particularly in the postcolonial context, have to be carefully placed in relation to past violations of hospitality during the time of colonial oppression.

In this chapter, I read Sol Plaatje's historical novel *Mhudi* (1930), which is considered the first novel by an African author to be written in English (Couzens 1975), through the lens of hospitality by bringing into conversation local and Western writings on the concept. Hospitality, I argue, lies at the very heart of Plaatje's multi-layered engagement with the South African past, present and future in *Mhudi*. Published in 1930 after the formation of the South African Union in 1910, the novel uses its historical setting in the 1830s to critique the government at the time of writing and, particularly, the passing of the 1913 Natives' Land Act.[1] The Act, as Plaatje puts it in *Native Life in South Africa* (1916), made 'the South African native . . . not actually a slave, but a pariah in the land of his birth' (Plaatje 2007, 21), and thus constituted an act of gross inhospitality against which Plaatje envisions 'an alternative, more hospitable, South African future' (Steiner 2014, 12).

Ever since the work regained critical interest in the 1970s as part of a wave of revisionism in historical and literary studies (Couzens 1975; Couzens and Gray 1978; Willan 1984), it has been read as an historical novel that rewrites colonial and apartheid historiography from the point of view of the Barolong (Couzens 1975; Green 2006) and, more generally, as a text that – like other works of historical fiction of the time – engages 'with the processes of social, political and cultural retrieval and reconstruction' (Peterson 2012, 305). Rather than ascribing historical prominence to the 'Great Trek' as in Afrikaner nationalist mythology (Marks and Trapido 1987), the novel stages multiple hospitable relations and their abuses among various southern African communities during the time of the *mfecane* (loosely translated as 'scattering' or 'crushing') – the displacement, forced migration and resettlement that took place across the southern African region in the early nineteenth century (Hamilton 1995).

Similarly to common theorisations of hospitality such as those by Derrida, Plaatje propels us to imagine the notion as open and fluid, with intertwined rather than dichotomous host/guest identities and shifting power relations, while at the same time displaying an acute awareness of the constant risks involved in the hospitable encounter. What distinguishes his idea of hospitality from that of Derrida and others, however, is his engagement with the colonial violations of hospitality that made South Africa an 'inhospitable native land' (Plaatje 1996b, 362), depriving black people of their identities as hosts, relegating them to a state of 'nonbeing' (Fanon 1986, 10) and, ultimately, destroying the practice of hospitality itself. I will draw on work by Black Consciousness philosopher Steve Biko, who was influenced by Plaatje's 'commitment to a diverse understanding of nationhood' (Gordon 2008a, 193), to illustrate local specificities of the workings of hospitality in *Mhudi*.

A number of scholars have suggested that Plaatje's vision of a hospitable future for all South Africans in the novel has been actualised with the country's transition to democracy (Johnson 1994; Chennells 1997). In these accounts, black people have finally become part of a new, inclusive, non-racial discourse of national hospitality. In contrast to these readings, which align Plaatje's fictional rendition of hospitality with post-apartheid national ideology, I suggest that Plaatje's idea of hospitality foregrounds movement rather than *telos* and is infused with a utopian vision of a more hospitable future. While critics such as Michael Green (2006) and Tina Steiner (2014) have highlighted the novel's profound investment in the future as well as a broad cosmopolitan vision of the nation, I argue that Plaatje's idea of hospitality as a deferred utopian possibility gestures beyond the confines of the national, and is intricately linked to transnational mobility and migration.

This discussion begins by providing a background to Biko's understanding of the violations of hospitality in the colonial context and then examines the depiction of pastoral hospitality in *Mhudi*, arguing that the novel adopts an anti-pastoral mode that undermines the idea of precolonial harmony and open-door hospitality. Next, I will show that the novel portrays intergroup hospitality among the Barolong, the Matabele and the Boers as a continuous cycle of gestures towards, and violations of, welcome. To these unstable manifestations I will juxtapose exceptional individual exchanges of hospitality that momentarily suspend the hierarchical design inherent in any relation of hospitality, while eventually lapsing back into an asymmetrical configuration. The last section will trace the manner in which *Mhudi* defies readings that endorse historical closure in favour of embracing a postcolonial utopianism founded on incessant movement and renewal.

Colonial abuses of hospitality, as interpreted by Biko

In his reflections on the National Party's 'homeland' politics, Biko foregrounds the violations of hospitality by the settler-colonisers and the apartheid regime. Adopting the voice of South Africa's black majority population (i.e., in the understanding of Black Consciousness, including all those 'who are by law or tradition politically, economically and socially discriminated against as a group in South African society' (Biko 2004, 53)), he writes:

> Our kindness has been misused and our hospitality turned against us. Whereas whites were mere guests to us on their arrival in this country they have now pushed us out to a 13% corner of the land and are acting as bad hosts in the rest of the country.
>
> (ibid.: 95)

Hospitality here becomes a metaphor to comment on the power relationship between 'settlers' and 'natives' played out through the question of land. To follow Biko's claims, the multiple forms of dispossession that marked colonialism and apartheid can be read as a history of inhospitality towards black people. Notwithstanding their initial 'guest status', the Dutch – and later the English – settler-colonisers ruthlessly exploited the hospitality of their hosts. For Biko, hospitality therefore constitutes a risky and precarious undertaking that may go fatally wrong, with the host ultimately losing her/his home as a consequence of the usurping behaviour of the (coloniser-)guest. The very extension of a gesture of welcome, Biko seems to suggest, can easily destroy hospitality in such a manner that the host becomes hostage to the guest.

These reflections are highly expressive both of the intrinsic risk of a 'breakdown of hospitality' (Still 2010, 20) and of the intricate connection between hospitality and hostility noted by Derrida and others (Derrida 2000a, 3; McNulty 2007, xii). Central to the 'breakdown of hospitality' for Biko, however, is not only the violent acquisition of the hosts' home and land, but the concomitant taking hostage of the hosts' minds, 'the most potent weapon in the hands of the oppressor' (Biko 2004, 74).

Foregrounding in the South African context what Gideon Baker elsewhere calls the 'host-harming history of hospitality' (Baker 2010, 23), Biko's understanding of hospitality in the colonial and apartheid setting diverges from many of the scholarly readings of the term (Derrida 2000b; Rosello 2001). While the hostility intrinsic to the hospitable relation has been intricately tied to the host in these accounts, Biko locates the violence leading to the abuse of hospitality in the guest. In contrast to Derrida's dynamic interplay between 'conditional hospitality' and 'unconditional hospitality' (Derrida 2000b) that is free of any reciprocity and open to the radically unknown, therefore breaking the laws of political/economic relations, hospitality for Biko is rooted in a self-conscious acknowledgement of reciprocity.

This relationship of reciprocity, however, cannot emanate from an adoption of, or integration into, white scripts of hospitality (Biko 2004, 101). Illustrating his critique of white liberalism with reference to interracial hosting, Biko notes that

> the black-white circles are almost always a creation of white liberals. As a testimony to their claim of complete identification with the blacks, they call a few 'intelligent and articulate' blacks to 'come around for tea at home', where all present ask each other the same old hackneyed question 'how can we bring about change in South Africa?'
>
> (ibid.: 23)

Opening their homes here becomes a means for white liberals to absolve themselves of complicity in apartheid's injustices. Hospitality untainted by an ideology of white supremacy can be achieved in Black Consciousness philosophy only by resetting the table 'in true African style' (ibid.: 75). Black people are effectively barred from enjoying 'true' hospitality in the white home, since they have been conditioned during colonialism and apartheid to internalise the values of the white guest-masters (ibid.: 31).

Echoing Frantz Fanon's 'zone of nonbeing' (Fanon 1986, 10) or status as 'the wretched of the earth' (*les damnés de la terre*) (Fanon 1967), Biko observes that black people in South Africa have been reduced to an 'empty shell' (Biko 2004, 31). As Nelson Maldonado-Torres explains, the '*damné* . . . has non-ontological resistance in the eyes of the dominant group. . . . The *damné* exists in the mode of not-being there' (Maldonado-Torres 2007, 257). Drawing on Emile Benveniste's observations on the etymological relatedness between *damné* and *donner* ('to give'), he further explains that the '*damné* is literally the subject who cannot give because what he or she has has been taken from him or her' (ibid.: 258). For Biko, the prerequisite for a more hospitable society is thus the reconstitution of black people as 'givers' through a hosting of the self in a way that makes 'the black man[2] [sic] see himself as a being, entire in himself' (Biko 2004, 74). According to Nigel Gibson,

> eschewing white liberal humanism, Black Consciousness's claim to authenticity and self-determination would have to come endogenously. This was the act of negativity that for Biko was a self-determination as *a prerequisite to mutual reciprocity*.
>
> (Gibson 2016, 11–12)

Biko, as an African existentialist philosopher (Gordon 2008a), prioritises ontology over ethics in the relation of hospitality owing to the violent politics of inhospitality practised by the apartheid regime. Commenting on the problematic relation between ethics and politics for Fanon and Biko, Lewis R. Gordon maintains that to 'assert the ethical, consequently had the effect of presupposing the inherent justice of the political situation when it was circumstance itself that was being brought into question' (Gordon 2008b, 88–89). The history of colonialism thus necessitates 'political intervention for ethical life' (ibid.: 89). Biko's 'intervention for ethical life' and, by extension, a more hospitable society, lies in a reconstruction of the black self, not only for herself or himself, but for the entire country: 'In time we shall be in a position to bestow upon South Africa the greatest gift possible – a more human face' (Biko 2004, 108). Black Consciousness philosophy, in this sense, is 'the identity of the self-for-the-self and for humanity' (Sithole 2016, 109). Since hospitality can be characterised as a 'form of gift' (Rosello 2001, viii), Black Consciousness as a philosophy of liberation and 'gift-giving' also contains an inbuilt ethic of hospitality. This ethic of hospitality, at least at a rhetorical level, however, largely pertained to the liberation of the 'black man'. Foregrounding racial solidarity, Black Consciousness eschewed other oppressive forces such as gender, class, age, sexual orientation (Gqola 2001, 136). As Daniel R. Magaziner notes, '[on] the one hand, Black Consciousness welcomed women into its ranks and leaderships, while on the other its language seemingly precluded women's participation as full and equal partners in the liberating project' (2011, 46).

In my view, Plaatje shares a similar orientation. *Mhudi* addresses abuses of hospitality by settlers regarding the question of land. In the introduction to the Quagga Press edition, Tim Couzens observes that '[t]he novel . . . is a moral attack on the descendants of those who were welcomed to the land and helped by their hosts to drive off those who threatened it' (Couzens 1975, 14). Staging multiple hospitable exchanges among various population groups during the *mfecane*, the text complicates any straightforward binary design at multiple levels of hospitality – pastoral, intergroup, individual and (trans)national. In contrast to Biko's gendered and masculine language of hospitality, Plaatje's project foregrounds, rather than eclipses, women in hospitable relations.

Untainted pastoral hospitality?

The trope of pristine nature and a life of harmonious togetherness in precolonial Africa, spoiled by the corrupting influence of colonialism, tends to suffuse much African literature, particularly writing of the so-called first generation (Caminero-Santangelo 2011). Its primary function, according to Byron Caminero-Santangelo, is to produce a counter-narrative: 'The effect [is] to create stories challenging imperial representations in which Africa is defined by negation . . . and in which the coming of the heroic European conqueror represents the advent of a proper ordering of (wild) nature' (ibid.: 148). As an example of the 'authentic essence' of precolonial life, one may refer to the practice of hospitality, which is often proclaimed as a fundamental trait of the traditional African homestead (Driver 2009, 18). Such linkages of hospitality with rural communities living close to nature are common across the world, and usually map hospitality as a quality and practice that has come increasingly under threat (Jelloun 1999, 37–38).

Mhudi similarly juxtaposes an idyllic, pastoral setting of hospitality to a later breakdown of hospitable relations. Couzens, for instance, reads *Mhudi* as a literary precursor of Chinua Achebe's *Things Fall Apart* (1958), contending that Plaatje's text foreshadows key themes of Achebe's novel. It 'portrays a traditional society at a crucial stage of transition. Throughout the novel [Plaatje] hints at the qualities of traditional life which seem to make it more attractive than the life of its usurpers. One of these qualities is hospitality' (Couzens 1975, 6). *Mhudi* opens with the narrator's depiction of the everyday life of the Bechuana living in the areas between 'Central Transvaal' and the 'Kalahari Desert' in the eighteenth century (Plaatje 1996a, 13). Reciprocal hospitality that has not yet been disrupted by colonial oppression appears as a primary contributing factor to the community's success. The peasants assist one another on their farms in exchange for a feast at the end of the day. During a communal day of thatching a dwelling,

> the guests might receive an invitation from a peasant who had a stockade to erect at a third homestead on a subsequent day; and great would be the expectation of the fat bullock to be slaughtered by the good man, to say nothing of the good things to be prepared by the kind hostess. Thus a month's job would be accomplished in a day.
>
> (14–15)[3]

It is not only reciprocal intragroup hospitality that characterises Plaatje's portrayal of precolonial life. The Qoranna Chief Massouw, who warmly welcomes the novel's main protagonists Mhudi and Ra-Thaga, embraces an ethics of welcome towards anyone who may arrive on his doorstep:

> Let it be understood that every person in my dominion, whether a Bldi [Barolong], a Hottentot, a Griqua or anything else, is one of us. My home is his home, my lands are his lands, my cattle are his cattle, and my law is his shield.
>
> (61–62)

This understanding of his own dominion through interrelationality recalls the saying '*Ke motho ka ba bangoe*' ('Through others I am somebody' (Plaatje 1916, 171)) that Plaatje lists in his *Sechuana Proverbs*. Embedded in the southern African ethic of *botho* (*ubuntu*), the newly arrived guest becomes 'one of us' by enabling the host to claim the very identity of host. Although the Qoranna community is founded on a hierarchical structure, with Chief Massouw as its head, he can hold this position only through his relation with others. As the proverb suggests, '*Kgosi ke kgosi ka morafe*' ('A chief is a chief by the grace of his tribe') (ibid.).

Although Plaatje invokes the pastoral genre in African literature through his depiction of an interrelational ethic of hospitality, he is well aware of its problematic aspects.[4] Thus he at the same time mocks the tradition by adopting an anti-pastoral mode that unmasks 'the distance between reality and the pastoral convention' (Gifford 1999, 128). The narrative voice states that

> [t]hese peasants were content to live their monotonous lives and thought nought of their overseas kinsmen who were making history on the plantations

and harbours of Virginia and Mississippi at that time; nor did they know or care about the relations of the Hottentots and the Boers at Capetown nearer their home.

(Plaatje 1996a, 14)

Drawing attention to the coexistence of very different – and predominantly inhospitable – inter-human relations within different geographical contexts, the narrative voice deflates the pastoral ideal of unsullied hospitality. In this sense, the novel exposes the limitations of the pastoral, where it takes the form of an almost 'timeless', 'Eden-like world' (Couzens 1996, 160). In contrast to Couzens, who reads the arrival of the Matabele as the introduction of 'historical time' (ibid.: 160) – thus incidentally invoking a linear conception of time – my perception is that Plaatje locates the hospitable practices in question within a plurality of temporalities.

Unstable intergroup hospitalities

Plaatje does not focus primarily on interracial hospitality, which begins to feature only in Chapter 10 with the arrival of the Voortrekkers. As Couzens notes,

[t]he introduction of the whites into the novel one-third of the way through is simply the introduction of a third force which is no more important or valuable than the two forces [Barolong and Matabele] already existing.

(Couzens 1971, 190–91)

For the main part of the novel, Plaatje is concerned with Matabele-Barolong interrelations. In this way, the novel also defies reading as a mere subversion of colonial narratives. Initially, the Matabele are portrayed as violent intruders, as shown in their frequent comparison to wild animals. In terms of hospitality, they are represented as lurid usurpers, destroying the pastoral lives of the Barolong: 'Upon these peaceful regions over one hundred years ago there descended one Mzilikazi, king of a ferocious tribe called the Matabele, a powerful usurper of determined character who by his own sword proclaimed himself ruler over all the land' (Plaatje 1996a, 15). The Matabele, in a manoeuvre that resembles conditional hospitality in its national guise, begin to collect taxes from the Barolong; so the state instituted by the conqueror imposes rules on those who want to be granted welcome in its territory.

Yet with the introduction of the Matabele Commander-in-Chief Gubuza, who questions what he regards as the hyperbolic celebration of his people's slaughter of the Barolong, Plaatje forecloses a one-dimensional reading of the Matabele. Gubuza openly interrogates the behaviour of the Matabele tax collector whose killing by the Barolong has sparked a war, asking: 'Did Bhoya simply deliver his message or did he violate Barolong rights in any way?' (Plaatje 1996a, 39). In this sense, Gubuza is represented as a potentially even-handed 'host' of the Barolong, a position that undermines simple justifications for the near extermination of the enemy. In this episode, as J. M. Phelps points out, Plaatje proceeds 'not only to expose the limitations of the narrow nationalism which fuels the autocratic power of Mzilikazi, but, more cogently, to reveal how autocracy disrupts the body politic by fostering the autocratic ambitions of others' (Phelps 1993, 51). Plaatje thus lays bare the restrictions and dangers of a national hospitality that allows violent measures to uphold the sovereignty of the nation.

Moreover, Plaatje's use of multiple focalisers and large sections narrated in the direct speech of both the Barolong and Matabele characters revises the early image of the Matabele, as given through chapters and passages focalised through the Barolong. Likewise, he portrays hospitality as a practice of all groups in the novel. Among the Matabele, too, hospitality is considered a high virtue, and King Mzilikazi frequently praises 'the stately way' in which his favourite wife, Queen Umnandi, 'received court guests' (Plaatje 1996a, 72). According to Green, 'Plaatje is concerned to demonstrate that the Barolong view of the Matabele as driven simply by an unmotivated bloodlust stands in as much need of correction as do the white versions of history that see all black warfare in similar terms' (Green 2006, 39).

In Chapter 10, the arriving Voortrekkers become guests of the Barolong, with whose help and collaboration the latter are finally able to overthrow King Mzilikazi's Matabele army. The enactment of hospitality between these two groups initially seems free of prejudice and, at least from the side of the Barolong, infused with goodwill and a curiosity to learn from the other. They initially inform the Boers that 'the country round about was wide and there was plenty of land for all' (Plaatje 1996a, 66). Again, in accord with the ethics of intersubjective constitution and mutuality advocated by the Qoranna chief, the Barolong embrace an ethic of sharing. The narrative voice emphasises their lavish hospitality when they '[r]egale the Boers with meat and milk and corn-mash' (ibid.: 67). Even after their near-extinction at the hands of the Matabele, the Barolong retain the code of welcoming guests.

Yet the hospitable encounter between the two groups also appears conflictual and racialised, and thus characterised by uneasy power relations as well as a lack of reciprocity. At various times, it verges on hostility. One day, Ra-Thaga is almost attacked by one of the Boers for drinking water out of a vessel in the Boer settlement. He learns only later that 'Boers at their own homes never allow black people to drink out of their vessels' (ibid.: 127), thus revealing the asymmetrical nature of interracial hospitality that Biko criticises. Embedded within a discourse of racial superiority, hospitality here amounts to an economic transaction or pact, given that De Villiers assures Ra-Thaga that 'no Morolong could be hurt by the Boers while they enjoyed Barolong hospitality' (ibid.: 127). What unites the two groups is mainly their joint view of the Matabele as their enemy. Ra-Thaga's private experience of repudiation and inhospitality is thus homologous to a larger political discourse about hospitality adopted by the Boer community towards other groups.

This instability in the hospitable relationship between the Boers and the Barolong is further underscored by Plaatje's portrayal of the Boers' treatment of their 'Hottentot slaves'. The frequent violence meted out to the slaves dramatises the breakdown and violation of hospitality in the colonial context. Like Biko, Plaatje foregrounds what Baker's analysis of colonialism with respect to hospitality terms 'the usurping violence of guests rather than the assimilating violence of hosts' (Baker 2011, 32). For the Boers' former hosts, the Cape San communities, have been turned into their slaves and stripped of their humanity in a process that has enacted the collapse of hospitality. Echoing Biko's observations on the breakdown of hospitality in the colonial context, Baker notes:

> To abuse hospitality by claiming the host's habitation as one's own is . . . actually worse than abuse since it pushes hospitality beyond its limits – in phenomenological terms, it denies to the host one's (temporary) presence as a guest by which his host-status, and hospitality itself, is first established. . . . The incipient colonialist not only appropriates land, but destroys the hospitality relation itself and with it the possibility of human sociability.
>
> (ibid.: 58)

By introducing these episodes, Plaatje interrogates the Boers' future role as guests of the Barolong and issues an implicit warning that the same destiny may await them. In anticipation of Biko, he perceives hospitality as a personal, political and social practice that is defined by asymmetrical power relations in which the erstwhile coloniser-guest violently assumes the position of host and master.

Similarly, the offer of the Voortrekker leader Potgieter to the Barolong in the event of a victory over the Matabele appears disingenuous and devoid of the ideals of reciprocal hospitality. It is this incident that foreshadows the grave violations of hospitality through the introduction of the Natives' Land Act that Plaatje experienced during the time of writing his novel. Potgieter's 'word of honour' that 'they would make a just division of their spoil by keeping all the land for the Boers and handing over the captured cattle to the Barolong' (Plaatje 1996a, 118) violates the contract of hospitality between the two groups. Chief Tauana of the Ra-Tshidi immediately identifies the offer as '"an absurd bargain!"' (ibid.) and makes his participation conditional on the return of his fathers' land. Plaatje, it seems, suggests that in the colonial setting even contractual modes of hospitality cannot guarantee the life and physical integrity of the host. This question, as posed by Paul K. Saint-Amour in a different context, also lies at the heart of the novel's engagement with individual exchanges of hospitality: 'How can absolute hospitality [as formulated by Derrida] be thought when colonialism has resignified hospitality *tout court*, underscoring the historical proximity of visitation and occupation, guest and invader?' (Saint-Amour 2007, 111). The thinking of hospitality in *Mhudi* becomes possible only in exceptional individual moments of welcome grounded in mutual recognition that suspends the characteristics of host and guest as distinct roles or as a practice of the 'to come' which is imagined from the vantage point of mobility, in a similar fashion to Biko's gift of hospitality.

Exceptional individual moments of welcome

Even Ra-Thaga and De Villiers's friendship, which stands out as an encouraging example among the generally tainted or compromised hospitable interactions, is not entirely free of the burden of contractual hospitality.[5] The narrative voice highlights that '[t]here was one special bond of fellow-feeling between them, namely their mutual aversion to the Matabele' (Plaatje 1996a, 92). Yet their hospitable relation, I suggest, is exceptional inasmuch as it is grounded in an attempt to learn each other's language. Both men prove to be 'very diligent and persevering and, having ample opportunities for practice, they both made very good progress' (ibid.: 92). Their dedication indicates that their language exchange goes considerably beyond the superficialities of merely conventional greetings.

As Still comments in relation to the modern nation-state's hospitality to migrants: '[t]he question of language is critical – forcing the other to speak my language even as they ask for asylum is hardly hospitable' (Still 2010, 19). In contemporary migration politics and practices, it is usually the hosts who impose their language on the arriving stranger. By contrast, in the colonial setting that Biko and Plaatje address, the initial guests force their language on colonised peoples, claiming a position of cultural and linguistic superiority. Seeing the other's language as a bridge towards understanding and intercultural exchange (Steiner 2014, 19; Sanders 2002, 52), the two men in Plaatje's novel conversely acknowledge the supremacy of neither host nor guest. Interracial hosting here is unfettered from the white scripts of hospitality that govern the white liberal home which Biko critiques. In refraining from imposing their own hegemony, the two men embrace a model of reciprocal hosting, forging new forms of social association that seem foundational to any future politics of hospitality. Language and translation in *Mhudi* thus demarcate the critical space of intercultural hospitality. Plaatje reworks the conventional terms of hospitality by finding a momentary point of balance where, to use Baker's words, the 'tension between hospitality as *both* a right of hosts and of strangers' (Baker 2013, 9) is abrogated. For Derrida, absolute hospitality can only be non-reciprocal, with the guest arriving without invitation and without being expected to offer recompense in any form. Plaatje temporarily holds in abeyance clear role allocations of host or guest to either man, suggesting that it is only from these moments of non-distinction that new languages of hospitality can arise.

These moments of harmonious hosting, however, are designed as fleeting points of equilibrium that are necessarily unsettled over time. For hospitality is always a precarious balancing act between the interests of host and guest. This becomes manifest when De Villiers expresses his deep sense of gratitude and feeling of obligation to Ra-Thaga (Plaatje 1996a, 132). He promises to make Ra-Thaga his 'right-hand man' (132) in the event that Potgieter should appoint him as captain after the victory. However, the transitory moment of mutuality soon gives way to the standard colonial hierarchy in which Ra-Thaga is demoted to the role of assistant. When Ra-Thaga recommends that De Villiers should consider Annetje as a wife, De Villiers responds: '"Man, Ra-Thaga, I always told you that you had a brown skin over a white heart'" (133). 'For a stranger to be made less threatening', Cynthia Schoolar Williams observes, 'he must be moved along a continuum from feared outsider to accepted member of the community, even if temporarily' (Williams 2014, 23). Again, the novel shows that the point of balance in a hospitable relationship can only ever be a glimpse into a hospitable future that is forever suspended.

Mhudi's relationship with the Boers displays similar – if not still more dramatic – ambiguities. While the narrative voice repeatedly comments on Mhudi's negative perception of the Boers, resulting from their violent treatment of their slaves, she acknowledges the exceptionally humane qualities of De Villiers and Annetje. Annetje appears to her as an 'angel' (Plaatje 1996a, 137) when she appeals on behalf of a young slave who is beaten without reason. In contrast to the linguistic hospitality of the men, the two women do not speak each other's language. Moreover, Annetje's love for Mhudi appears compromised and imbedded in colonial hierarchies: 'Annetje too had fallen in love with Mhudi. She said if she lived to have little ones of her own surely they would be proud to have for an ayah such a noble mosadi as Mhudi' (154). Steiner aptly notes that

> Plaatje's mixing of languages juxtaposes 'ayah' and 'mosadi' (Setswana for 'woman') in such a way as to emphasise the words' non-equivalence. . . . ['Ayah'] is thus a term steeped in the legacy of the British Empire and connotes a servile relationship.
> (Steiner 2014, 19; see also Chrisman 1997, 68)

The inability to speak each other's language forecloses the emergence of mutual reciprocity in Biko's terms and deprives Mhudi of a self that is not defined through a relation of servitude to whites. Narrating momentary hospitality between the two men (while portraying Mhudi and Annetje's interactions as dominated by ambivalences and contradictions), also allows Plaatje to question the common association between femininity and hospitality that renders women as 'natural' hosts (Aristarkhova 2012, 168). In the novel, the mutual hosting through language appears to be a more primary parameter within hospitable relations than an 'idealized feminine' that according to Aristarkhova (ibid.: 170) characterises Derrida's formulation of hospitality.

This does not imply, however, that women are portrayed as absent, silenced or de-materialised hosts without agency. The novel goes beyond a mere focus on individual interracial friendships by including the sisterly relation between the Matabele Queen Umnandi and Mhudi. The women start calling each other '"Matabele sister"' (Plaatje 1996a, 139) and '"[my] Mlolweni sister"' (ibid.: 140) respectively and are inscribed as key reconciliatory figures between the two ethnic groups. Mhudi's final words to Umnandi bespeak their role as peacemakers: '"Urge him [Mzilikazi], even as I would urge all men of my acquaintance, to gather more sense and cease warring against their kind. Depart in peace, my sister"' (ibid.: 140). One may claim that women are framed merely as 'mothers of their nations' who provide the fertile ground for more hospitable future relations between men.[6] Yet Plaatje's rendition of the maternal is more complex, even though he praises motherhood in *Native Life* 'as the historic role of African women' (Hughes 2016, 184). Heather Hughes maintains that '[i]t would be simplistic . . . to treat his argument as an assertion of men's control over women's reproductive duty', stressing that women themselves perceived motherhood as a 'source of empowerment' (ibid.: 164–65). In *Mhudi*, Umnandi and Mhudi's roles as potential 'mothers of the nation' are not conceived as 'the first home' that is 'pre-given' (Aristarkhova 2012, 177). The repetition of the agentive verb 'urge' in the quotation from the novel demonstrates Plaatje's emphasis on women as initiators of hospitality, committed to 'doing' rather than 'being'. Moreover, these articulations take place in a moment of transition and mobility, rather than in the stasis of the home. Unfettering his concept from an antithetical designation of mobility to those performing and receiving hospitality, Plaatje shows that hosting can take place from a position of imminent migration. The novel thus outlines hospitality as a practice through which power relations are in constant flux, directly linking hosting to mobility.

Hospitality beyond the nation

Critical scholarship on *Mhudi*, particularly material written at the time of the transition to democratic government in South Africa during the 1990s, positions Plaatje's novel as a foundational narrative of the 'new' South Africa and infers that the vision of hospitality embraced in the text has now found historical actualisation. In an article for the *Sunday Independent*, Andries Walter Oliphant recalls Plaatje's influential comment on the detrimental implications of the Natives' Land Act for black people in South Africa. He ponders how Plaatje might have written about election day, suggesting this possible response: '"Waking on the morning of April 27, 1994, black South Africans, if not exactly masters, found themselves free in the land of their birth". [Plaatje's] . . . own role in this is now fully recognised' (Oliphant 1997, 22). While not unequivocal hosts and masters in the new South Africa, black South Africans, Oliphant implies, have finally broken the fetters of an abused 'hosthood'. David Johnson goes a step further: '[T]he community Plaatje tentatively imagined in literary discourse in *Mhudi* over seventy years ago', he argues, 'is now being realised in political discourse in Mandela's speeches' (Johnson 1994, 351). Similarly, Anthony Chennells proposes that reading *Mhudi* from the vantage point of incipient democracy is more satisfactory than during apartheid: '[T]he satisfaction derives in part from the victory of the African National Congress in the South African elections which, for the moment at least, stabilises the narrative of South African history as comedy' (Chennells 1997, 55–56).

Chennells pertinently draws attention to the novel's multivocity. His equation of the plurality of voices in *Mhudi* with the voice of the newly elected party, however, is steeped in the assumption, at times adopted by postcolonial critics, of an unequivocal 'split between a monologic, authoritative colonial vision and a subversive, dialogic postcolonial hybridity' (Caminero-Santangelo 2005, 13). He contends: 'A victory for a party organised by blacks will be, of its very nature, the voice of the many displacing a single voice since no voice, including white voices, is silenced' (Chennells 1997, 56–57). Understandably, these readings of the novel in the 'new' South Africa participate in the national euphoria of the early 1990s. Lulled by the promises of the new democratic dispensation, these accounts, however, occlude prominent ideas contained in Plaatje's narrative, most notably the novel's conception of time. Textual references to the cyclical reappearance of Halley's Comet, which in the novel heralds the defeat of the Matabele, serve to undermine these readings of the text in terms of historical closure.

Green, by contrast, uncovers the problematic issues inherent in these 'end-of history' readings: 'In as much as *Mhudi* calls up the history of the nation, then, this is . . . a *future* history' (Green 2006, 42). If the novel's concept of hospitality were to have come alive with the demise of the apartheid regime, how should we read the text today? The very open-endedness of the narrative points beyond the national euphoria or the honeymoon moment in South Africa's young democracy. In this sense, the novel's vision has not lost currency with the arrival of a sense of post-apartheid disillusionment in the 2000s, an attitude that continues to characterise the present. Its resistance to finality and simultaneous embrace of a hospitable discourse of the 'not-yet' mirrors Achille Mbembe's Gramscian characterisation of South Africa's continuing in-between status as 'still caught in this interval, between an intractable present and an irrecoverable past' (Mbembe 2012, n.p.). Earlier modes of welcoming others have an unbroken bearing on the novel's present and future vision of hospitality. Plaatje's text figures hospitality within a zone of transition in which the right to hospitality of the stranger/traveller is increasingly replaced by state laws that demarcate zones of welcome/rejection, culminating in the Natives' Land Act of 1913 and, a few decades later, the National Party's segregationist laws. This transitional zone contains within it a layering of multiple earlier and future practices of hospitality that stretch towards and capture the contemporary moment.

The text's tenacious adherence to a Blochian not-yet allows for a reading through Bill Ashcroft's notion of 'postcolonial utopianism'. This form of utopianism, Ashcroft argues,

> is grounded in a continual process, a difficult and even paradoxical process of emancipation without teleology, a cyclic 'return' to the future. The present is the crucial site of the continual motion by which the new comes into being. In such transformative conceptions of utopian hope the 'not-yet' is always a possibility emerging from the past.
>
> (Ashcroft 2013, 99)

The utopian element of *Mhudi* lies essentially in its vision of hospitality as a social and political practice. This utopian import is illustrated in the novel's ambiguous ending, which stages three conflicting visions of hospitality.

The first vision may be read as an exemplification of abused hospitality in Biko's terms. This is expressed in Matabele Chief Mzilikazi's retelling of the story of

'Zungu of old' to his people after their defeat by an alliance of the Barolong, the Griquas and the Voortrekkers – a moment that predicts the continuation of war and the breakdown of the hospitable relationship between the Boers and the Barolong. Zungu's attempt at taming a lion's whelp in the expectation that it will serve him as a 'useful mastiff' (Plaatje 1996a, 147) goes fatally wrong, despite his feeding it milk from his own cows. Upon returning home one day, he finds that the young lion has eaten his children and wives, and he himself is almost lacerated by the animal. In the king's view, hospitality is thus a fundamentally perilous and imprudent gesture. Mzilikazi employs the story as an allegory to prophesy a similar abuse of the hospitality that the Barolong have afforded to the Voortrekkers, saying that the 'Bechuana [i.e. the Barolong] are fools to think that these unnatural *Kiwas* (white men) will return their so-called friendship with honest friendship' (ibid.). He further envisages their dispossession of their lands and in due course their complete enslavement by the Voortrekkers. Mzilikazi says:

> 'They will despoil them of the very lands they have rendered unsafe for us; they will entice the Bechuana youth to war and the chase, only to use them as pack-oxen; yea, they will refuse to share with them the spoils of victory'.
> (ibid.)

Embracing the cyclical model of history espoused in the novel, King Mzilikazi predicts that the Barolong will suffer the same fate as the San peoples of the Cape. The violation of relations of hospitality, the king seems to imply, will eventually lead to a disavowal of the Barolong's humanity.

The second vision of hospitality at first appears more optimistic. The Matabele, having lost their land and many of their men, decide to travel northwards. The narrative voice describes them as 'a hopeful nation', 'travelling persistently towards the land of promise to found new Matabeleland' (ibid.: 149). The king settles with his nation at Bulawayo, where the reunion with his beloved favourite wife Umnandi takes place. The narrative voice summarises the nation's future as follows:

> In the course of a prosperous life during which the Matabele grew in power and affluence, Umnandi's son extended the awe-inspiring sway of his government to distant territories of the hinterland; and when at length he succeeded his father as Matabele king, he wielded a yet greater power than that of his renowned father.
> (ibid.: 152)

Chennells observes a fundamental change in the narrative portrayal of the Matabele towards the end of the novel. The focus on the domestic realm, familial bonds and procreation in his judgement shows that 'the nation turns from hierarchy, obedience and death to reciprocity, love and regeneration as the sources of its new identity' (Chennells 1997, 40). Chennells reads the Matabele strand of the narrative in terms of a linear progression from a tyrannical striving for power to family bliss that becomes a synecdoche for the newfound nation in a space removed from the influence of colonialism. Yet this sense of national self-realisation, Chennels concedes, can work only against the backdrop of a textual silence: the later invasion of the territory by Cecil John Rhodes, of which Plaatje's readers were undoubtedly aware.

Compounding extra-textual events, a closer look at the text itself reveals that the novel does not envision the destiny of the Matabele as a linear development. The expressions 'sway' and 'wielded a yet greater power' in the quoted passage seem to imply that Mzilikazi's son may use the same or even harsher methods than his father to exercise and secure his dominance. The final image of the Matabele in the novel, therefore, rather than encoding nationalist fulfilment, highlights the tension between the utopian promise of peace, unity and hospitality, on the one hand, and the ideology of nation-building, on the other. Hospitable discourse, the story suggests, is frequently interrupted by the closures that accompany national ideologies. Uncompromised hospitality in Plaatje's narrative vision, therefore, must lie beyond the confines of the nation. Moreover, *Mhudi* proposes that the overthrow of the Matabele was foreshadowed by the appearance of Halley's Comet in 1935. This link between the Matabele's destiny and the comet (which re-emerges approximately every 75 years) implies that the Matabele's new 'land of promise' (Plaatje 1996a, 149) may yet again be taken away from them.

To these pessimistic and compromised projections of the future, Plaatje opposes Ra-Thaga's optimistic final promise to Mhudi. The closing chapter named 'A Contented Homecoming' (ibid.: 153) narrates how the couple, having been given an old wagon by De Villiers, embark on their journey towards Thaba Ncho, 'where a warm welcome was awaiting them' (ibid.: 157). Not only do they seem certain of a hospitable reception, but the contrast to their former life of uncertainty and danger is underlined even more strongly. Ra-Thaga assures Mhudi that he will never again leave her: "'I have had my revenge and ought to be satisfied; from henceforth, I shall have no ears for the call of war or the chase, my ears shall be open to only one call – the call of your voice'" (ibid.). (The Lovedale edition includes 'the call of the Chief' (Plaatje 1989, 200) in addition to Mhudi's voice.)[7] In relation to Mzilikazi's storytelling, this invocation of a private idyll appears somewhat unsettling. Commenting on these contradictions, Phaswane Mpe observes that the novel 'seems to oscillate between hope and, on a subtextual level at least, despair over the possibility of ever achieving that which is clearly so desirable: peace and justice' (Mpe 1996, 88).

Given that the novel ends before Mhudi and Ra-Thaga's journey is completed – before they reach their destination of presumed welcome – hospitality essentially becomes a matter of futurity: a not-yet-realised but possible future actuality. This is not to be understood in terms of Derrida's openness towards the radically unknown (Derrida 2000b, 25), as the couple clearly have in mind their place of arrival and look forward to the reunion with their children. Rather, the ending reveals a firm belief in a future beyond the violent history of hospitality in the South African context, a future that in Biko's sense is brought about through the gift of the 'self' in the interests of humanity. Whether the outcome will ultimately be more hospitable or equally marked by betrayal remains undecided.

Written a century after the events described, at a time when new laws restricting hospitality for the majority population had just been introduced through the Natives' Land Act, *Mhudi* imagines a more hospitable future for South Africa by resorting to the past. These entangled temporalities and practices of hospitality make up the utopian texture of the novel. For as Ashcroft notes,

> [m]emory refers to a past *that has never been present* not only because the present is a continual flow, but because memory invokes a past that must be *projected*, so to speak into the future – not only the future of its recalling, but the future of the realm of the possibility itself.
>
> (Ashcroft 2013, 100)

Plaatje's textual merging of pastoral and private practices with the political laws of hospitality thus draws attention to what Still terms the '*intertextual quality*' of hospitality (Still 2010, 27). Plaatje emphasises that hospitality is not a fixed cultural practice, but a multitude of heterogeneous practices that always contain reverberations of previous hospitalities. Hospitality is constantly altered by those participating in it, those who draw on various enactments and formulations of the notion to redefine and adjust it to their contemporary context. Troubling our conventional classificatory grids of time, Plaatje's 1930 novel marks a transitional moment in which past conceptions of welcome are contemporaneous with present and future imaginings.

All three of the scenarios that I have addressed resist a narrative impulse towards closure, demonstrating that *Mhudi* vehemently opposes the restrictive politics of hospitality that were aligned with the Union government of Plaatje's time. Indeed, the final image of Mhudi and Ra-Thaga's journey is one of being in transition (see Chrisman 1997, 203). The novel's inclusion of multiple spaces transcends the confines of the South African nation today (as it does in present-day Zimbabwe and the United States (see the earlier reference to slavery)), and most prominently its final image of transit makes it a compelling plea for the embrace of mobility and migration. Moving hospitality away from rootedness and stasis, Plaatje imagines not only a *future* history of the nation (Green 2006) or a cosmopolitan nation that embraces both humans and the land (Steiner 2014), but a future history that lies beyond the limits of the nation. The novel's hospitable vision of the future is of critical importance particularly in the present South African context, where hospitality is still denied to a large number of South Africans who feel economically marginalised, as well as (im)migrants and refugees from other parts of Africa who have repeatedly been subjected to violence in recent years. If Plaatje were alive in contemporary South Africa, he would remind us of the long history of intra-African hospitality and appeal to us to reciprocate the hospitable gestures that South Africans have received in the past. In response to a letter 'under the auspices of the African National Congress to compass the expulsion from the Union of all

Blantyre Natives [migrants from present-day Malawi]', he wrote in 1928 that '[t]he time will come when more of my own relatives will find life intolerable in "a white man's country" and migrate to Central Africa, where some of them are already; in that case, a Blantyre retaliation may prove very uncomfortable' (Plaatje 1996b, 362; see also Remmington 2016). Reading *Mhudi* today equally reminds us of Plaatje's mandate to fight inhospitable (state) ideologies and to keep open the possibility for the development of new languages of hospitality that are cognisant of colonial legacies, while embracing mobility and migration.

Notes

1. The Act legislated that black farmers on land owned by whites should become wage labourers or move to 'native areas' that initially constituted a mere 7% of the country's land; the African land reserves were increased to 13% in the Native Trust and Land Act of 1936. Beinart and Delius call the Act a 'template but not a turning point', arguing that 'land alienation was neither the major intention nor the outcome of the Act' (Beinart and Delius 2015, 24). While conceding that 'the application of the Natives' Land Act was uneven and [that] it took decades for its effects to be felt around the country', Dlamini points out that 'there is no escaping the fact that the Act was tainted – however temporary its initial status and however soft its power – by a type of race-thinking against which Plaatje rebelled' (Dlamini 2016, 208).
2. As Magaziner argues, 'women had a definite place in this [the late 1960s and early 70s] era's organisations, but they sometimes had to earn it by being more defiant (more "manly") than men. And even as women such as [Mamphela] Ramphele earned great repute, by the mid-1970s women's abilities to be vocal equals was being undermined' (2010, 235). See also, Gqola (2001), MacQueen (2009) and Driver (1990).
3. While the reference to 'the kind hostess' here invokes traditional gendered notions of space and seems to position hospitality as foundational of 'the feminine', the novel repudiates the frequently established connection between hospitality and sexual difference (see Aristarkhova 2012).
4. In his reflection on African cultural concepts, Biko similarly praises the open-door hospitality in 'traditional African culture' (Biko 2004, 46), without conceiving 'culture' as static.
5. For a discussion of the link between friendship and hospitality, see Still (2010, Chapter 3).
6. For Couzens (1977, 18) and Gray (1979, 181), Mhudi represents the 'Mother Africa' trope that is frequently found in first- and second-generation African writing. Myrtle Hooper (1992), by contrast, provides a more nuanced reading of Mhudi, who is hardly defined through childrearing and domesticity.
7. For a groundbreaking revaluation of the relationship between the two editions, see Willan (2015).

References

Achebe, Chinua. 1958. *Things Fall Apart*. London: William Heinemann.
Aristarkhova, Irina. 2012. 'Hospitality and the Maternal'. *Hypatia* 27.1: 163–81.
Ashcroft, Bill. 2013. 'African Futures: The Necessity of Utopia'. *International Journal of African Renaissance Studies* 8.1: 94–114.
Baker, Gideon. 2010. 'The Spectre of Montezuma: Hospitality and Haunting'. *Millennium: Journal of International Studies* 39.1: 23–42.
———. 2011. *Politicising Ethics in International Relations: Cosmopolitanism as Hospitality*. London: Routledge.
———. 2013. 'Introduction'. In *Hospitality and World Politics*, edited by Gideon Baker, 1–20. New York: Palgrave Macmillan.

Beinart, William and Peter Delius. 2015. 'The Natives' Land Act of 2013: A Template But Not a Turning Point'. In *Land Divided, Land Restored: Land Reform in South Africa for the Twenty-First Century*, edited by Ben Cousins and Cherryl Walker, 24–40. Johannesburg: Jacana.

Bell, Avril. 2010. 'Being "at Home" in the Nation: Hospitality and Sovereignty in Talk about Immigration'. *Ethnicities* 10.2: 236–56.

Biko, Steve. 2004 [1978]. *I Write What I Like*. Oxford: Heinemann.

Caminero-Santangelo, Byron. 2005. *African Fiction and Joseph Conrad: Reading Postcolonial Intertextuality*. Albany: State University of New York Press.

———. 2011. 'Shifting the Center: A Tradition of Environmental Literary Discourse from Africa'. In *Environmental Criticism for the Twenty-First Century*, edited by Stephanie LeMenager, Teresa Shewry and Ken Hiltner, 148–62. New York: Routledge.

Chennells, Anthony. 1997. 'Plotting South African History: Narrative in Sol Plaatje's "Mhudi"'. *English in Africa* 24.1: 37–58.

Chrisman, Laura. 1997. 'Fathering the Black Nation of South Africa: Gender and Generation in Sol Plaatje's *Native Life in South Africa* and *Mhudi*'. *Social Dynamics* 23.2: 57–73.

Couzens, Tim. 1971. 'The Dark Side of the World: Sol Plaatje's "Mhudi"'. *English Studies in Africa* 14.2: 187–203.

———. 1975. 'Introduction'. In *Mhudi*, by Sol Plaatje, 1–15. Johannesburg: Quagga Press.

———. 1977. 'Introduction'. In *Mhudi*, by Sol Plaatje, 1–20. London: Heinemann.

———. 1996. 'Supplementary Material and Commentary'. In *Mhudi*, by Sol Plaatje, 159–90. Cape Town: Francolin.

Couzens, Tim and Stephen Gray. 1978. 'Printers' and Other Devils: The Texts of Sol T. Plaatje's *Mhudi*'. *Research in African Literatures* 9.2: 198–215.

Derrida, Jacques. 2000a. 'Hostipitality', translated by Barry Stocker and Forbes Morlock. *Angelaki: Journal of the Theoretical Humanities* 5.3: 3–18.

———. 2000b. *Of Hospitality: Anne Dufourmantelle Invites Jacques Derrida to Respond*. Translated by Rachel Bowlby. Stanford, CA: Stanford Unversity Press.

———. 2002. *Acts of Religion*. Edited and introduced by Gil Anidjar. New York and London: Routledge.

Dlamini, Jacob. 2016. 'Land and Belonging: On the Tomb Ya Ga Solomon Plaatje'. In *Sol Plaatje's 'Native Life in South Africa': Past and Present*, edited by Janet Remmington, Brian Willan and Bhekizizwe Peterson, 196–210. Johannesburg: Wits University Press.

Driver, Dorothy. 1990. '"M'a Ngoana O Tsoare Thipa ka Bohaleng" – The Child's Mother Grabs the Sharp End of the Knife: Women as Mothers, Women as Writers'. In *Rendering Things Visible: Essays on South African Literary Culture*, edited by Martin Trump, 223–55. Johannesburg: Ravan Press.

———. 2009. '"On These Premises I Am the Government": Njabulo Ndebele's *The Cry of Winnie Mandela* and the Reconstructions of Gender and Nation'. In *Africa Writing Europe: Opposition, Juxtaposition, Entanglement*, edited by Maria Olaussen and Christina Angelfors, 1–38. Amsterdam: Rodopi.

Fanon, Frantz. 1967. *The Wretched of the Earth*. Translated by Constance Farrington. London: Penguin.

———. 1986. *Black Skin, White Mask*. Translated by Charles Lam Markmann. London: Pluto Press.

Gibson, Nigel. 2016. 'The Specter of Fanon: The Student Movements and the Rationality of Revolt in South Africa'. *Social Identities*. Online 23.5: 1–21.

Gifford, Terry. 1999. *The Pastoral*. New York: Routledge.

Gordon, Lewis R. 2008a. *An Introduction to Africana Philosophy*. Cambridge: Cambridge University Press.

———. 2008b. 'A Phenomenology of Biko's Black Consciousness'. In *Biko Lives! Contesting the Legacies of Steve Biko*, edited by Andile Mngxitama, Amanda Alexander and Nigel C. Gibson, 83–93. New York: Palgrave Macmillan.

Gqola, Pumla. 2001. 'Contradictory Locations: Blackwomen and the Discourse of the Black Consciousness Movement (BCM) in South Africa'. *Meridians* 2.1: 130–52.

Gray, Stephen. 1979. *South African Literature: An Introduction*. Cape Town: Philips.

Green, Michael. 2006. 'Generic Instability and the National Project: History, Nation, and Form in Sol T. Plaatje's *Mhudi*'. *Research in African Literatures* 37.4: 34–47.

Hamilton, Carolyn. 1995. *The Mfecane Aftermath: Reconstructive Debates in Southern African History*. Johannesburg: Wits University Press.

Hooper, Myrtle. 1992. 'Rewriting History: The "Feminism" of *Mhudi*'. *English Studies in Africa* 35.1: 68–79.

Hughes, Heather. 2016. 'Women and Society in *Native Life in South Africa*: Roles and Ruptures'. In *Sol Plaatje's 'Native Life in South Africa': Past and Present*, edited by Janet Remmington, Brian Willan and Bhekizizwe Peterson, 158–74. Johannesburg: Wits University Press.

Jelloun, Tahar Ben. 1999. *French Hospitality: Racism and North African Immigrants*. Translated by Barbara Bray. New York: Columbia University Press.

Johnson, David. 1994. 'Literature for the Rainbow Nation: The Case of Sol Plaatje's *Mhudi*'. *Journal of Literary Studies* 10.3/4: 345–58.

MacQueen, Ian. 2009. 'Categories of Struggle: Reassessing Black Consciousness in South Africa through Gender, 1967–1976'. In *Paths to Gender: European Historical Perspectives on Women and Men*, edited by Carla Salvaterra and Berteke Waaldijk, 260–70. Pisa: Plus-Pisa University Press.

Magaziner, Daniel R. 2010. *The Law and the Prophets: Black Consciousness in South Africa, 1968–1977*. Athens: Ohio University Press.

———. 2011. 'Pieces of a (Wo)man: Feminism, Gender and Adulthood in Black Consciousness, 1968–1977'. *Journal of Southern African Studies* 37.1: 45–61.

Maldonado-Torres, Nelson. 2007. 'On the Coloniality of Being: Contributions to the Development of a Concept'. *Cultural Studies* 21.2–3: 240–70.

Marks, Shula and Stanley Trapido. 1987. 'The Politics of Race, Class and Nationalism'. In *The Politics of Race, Class and Nationalism in Twentieth-Century South Africa*, edited by Shula Marks and Stanley Trapido, 10–70. London: Longman.

Mbembe, Achille. 2012. 'Rule of Property versus Rule of the Poor'. *Mail & Guardian*, 15 June. www.mg.co.za/article/2012-06-15-rule-of-property-versus-rule-of-the-poor/ (accessed 20 May 2016).

McNulty, Tracy. 2007. *The Hostess: Hospitality, Femininity, and the Expropriation of Identity*. Minneapolis: University of Minnesota Press.

Mpe, Phaswane. 1996. '"Naturally These Stories Lost Nothing by Repetition": Plaatje's Mediation of Oral History in *Mhudi*'. *Current Writing* 8.1: 75–89.

Oliphant, Andries Walter. 1997. 'Plaatje's Writing Opens a Window on the Lost Heritage of So Many South Africans'. *Sunday Independent*, 18 May: 22.

Peterson, Bhekizizwe. 2012. 'Black Writers and the Historical Novel: 1910–1948'. In *The Cambridge History of South African Literature*, edited by David Attwell and Derek Attridge, 291–307. Cambridge: Cambridge University Press.

Phelps, J. M. 1993. 'Sol Plaatje's *Mhudi* and Democratic Government'. *English Studies in Africa* 36.1: 47–56.

Plaatje, Sol T. 1916. *Sechuana Proverbs with Literal Translations and Their European Equivalents. Diane tsa secoana le maele a sekgooa a dumalanang naco*. London: K. Paul, Trench, Trubner & Co.

———. 1989 [1930]. *Mhudi*. Johannesburg: AD Donker.
———. 1996a. *Mhudi*. Cape Town: Francolin.
———. 1996b. *Selected Writings*. Edited by Brian Willan. Johannesburg: Wits University Press.
———. 2007 [1916]. *Native Life in South Africa*. Northlands: Picador Africa.
Remmington, Janet. 2016. 'Going Places: *Native Life in South Africa* and the Politics of Mobility'. In *Sol Plaatje's 'Native Life in South Africa': Past and Present*, edited by Janet Remmington, Brian Willan and Bhekizizwe Peterson, 54–80. Johannesburg: Wits University Press.
Rosello, Mireille. 2001. *Postcolonial Hospitality: The Immigrant as Guest*. Stanford, CA: Stanford University Press.
Saint-Amour, Paul K. 2007. '"Christmas Yet to Come": Hospitality, Futurity, the Carol, and "The Dead"'. *Representations* 98.1: 93–117.
Sanders, Mark. 2002. *Complicities: The Intellectual and Apartheid*. Durham, NC: Duke University Press.
Sithole, Tendayi. 2016. *Decolonial Meditations of Black Consciousness*. London: Lexington Books.
Steiner, Tina. 2014. 'Traversing Social Landscapes: Sol Plaatje's *Mhudi* and the Question of Community'. *English in Africa* 41.3: 7–26.
Still, Judith. 2010. *Derrida and Hospitality: Theory and Practice*. Edinburgh: Edinburgh University Press.
Willan, Brian. 1984. *Sol Plaatje: A Biography*. Johannesburg: Ravan Press.
———. 2015. 'What "Other Devils"? The Texts of Sol T. Plaatje's *Mhudi* Revisited'. *Journal of Southern African Studies* 41.6: 1331–47.
Williams, Cynthia Schoolar. 2014. *Hospitality and the Transatlantic Imagination, 1815–1835*. New York: Palgrave Macmillan.

6

HOME IS WHERE THE HEART IS

A creative and theoretical reflection

Jane Taylor

Preamble

Journey – a day's work, a day's travel, a day's length.

(Late middle ages)

Old French

How to begin considering 'hospitality' from the twenty-first century, within the great tornado of human event that seems to have broken every promise ever made about defending the guest or honouring the host? We have looked aghast at travellers who have been impelled to sink or swim on their own. For all that *The Med* has been domesticated as a utopian tourist destination, the Mediterranean was, in 2017, described as the most deadly sea in the world.[1] It is perhaps grimly appropriate that the image so readily presented to me as I began writing this piece should have arisen from recent scenes of threat on the Mediterranean.

And thus the literal and the metaphoric fall in upon one another.

These pages will follow a logic premised on the tension within representational complexity. I will consider hospitality variously, sometimes as a conceit, sometimes literally. Vehicle and tenor cannot be anchored. Much of my argument is grounded in distinctly Western, Protestant traditions, as I engage the lineages of thought about the stranger that have informed recent European accounts of cultural crisis around person and territory. While it has been several decades since scholars and social theorists began to draw attention to the increasingly desperate situation of dislocated populations globally, it was only in the past few years that the phenomenon was effectively characterised as a 'European crisis'. In 2015 Angela Merkel granted refugee status to a million or more people in flight from North Africa.

The complex causes and effects of these events are not the subject of this chapter, although that necessarily influences my thinking. I am interested in considering what these events can tell us about 'hospitality', and by implication what such considerations have to say about the recent histories of 'hospitality' within Southern Africa, once the continent's region of hypothesised refuge from war.

Hospitality is a minimal obligation if we seek to engage in human society. In other words, our complex of demeanours towards hospitality delimits and enables the protocols of our sociality as humans. It is, in this sense, a 'total social fact'. (Here I invoke Marcel Mauss, who wrote so compellingly of 'the gift' as a total social fact.[2] Gifts, he explained, 'are at once legal, economic, religious, aesthetic, morphological and so on' (Mauss 1966, 76-77). The 'total social fact', much like the Althusserian conception of ideology, is a ubiquitous medium that we inhabit, while it is transparent and invisible to us.)

Hospitality in contemporary settings, one might hope to suggest, is the safeguard against slavery. It is slavery's antithesis, in that the practice as well as the concept of hospitality provides for and sustains a notionally free and mobile agent. As the epigraph at the head of this chapter makes evident, 'journey' is the old French word for 'a day's term; a day's labour; a day's travel'. The rise of the 'journeyman' had signalled a change in the mode of production, with serfs, slaves and indentured labour ultimately being replaced by travelling workers who pursued employment for a day's wages where they could find it.

It is with some sense of ghastly horror that we have become aware of the return to practices of slavery in regions across the globe, in domestic as well as industrial circumstances. We 'learn', as if we did not already know, that many migrant persons are effectively captive, having had their passports and agency stripped from them by traffickers, or at the site of employment. Such persons of course have few citizenship rights, and are subject to vilification and abuse.[3] Here is manifest the inverse relation between hospitality and slavery in the contemporary setting of globalisation.

In consequence of my Western education, I of course first learned about the principles of hospitality in relation to Greek ideals. *Xenia*, I grasped, was the founding principle of sociality, arising from the obligation (and privilege) of hospitality. In the past decade, that principle of *xenia* has most frequently come back to my mind as its negative, through its failure, because of the vehement and vicious outbreaks of xenophobia in my country. South Africa has in recent years become (or perhaps just more manifestly is) a place of hostility towards the alien, with communities of refugees, migrants and foreign workers subjected to periodic outbursts of violent attack. Two of the most potent determinants of discrimination, *race* and *foreignness*, serve at times as distinct conceptual fields, at times they function as one roughly unified conceptual terrain. It is grotesque, given the history of race in this country, that many of the most vehement attacks are directed at intra-African migrants, visitors from across this continent.

Go. Die.

The cry against the foreigner has been 'go home, or die here'. In 2008 a surge of hostility burst out in furious attacks against vulnerable visitors, many of whom had fled just such brutality in their previous countries of residence. There are alternatives to extermination. Assimilation is one such option.

I

Hospitality has a complex history and is embedded in a cluster of ideas. It necessarily implies a distinction between inside and outside, between hosts and guests. In recent history, 'nation' has provided the terrain upon which the limits of membership have been defined. The requirements for membership are generally determined by a regional power. Modern Western conceptions of 'nation' are usually understood to have gathered value in the late eighteenth and nineteenth centuries, particularly through the influence of Herder. His was a largely linguistic orientation, and his *Treatise on the Origin of Language* (1772) locates identity as a formation arising through language. His is a kind of culturalist ('ethnographic') thinking that strikes a current reader as surprisingly relativist. He understands worldview and value to arise from the language through which one is moulded. Being is, in such terms, belonging. Culture is acquired, not innate, and it is only through the hospitality of one's own language milieu that identity becomes stabilised. Herder's thought had an immense impact on the emergence of a proto-German personhood associated with a particular style of literature, costume and music. Religion arises as secondary to culture, and Herder was of the opinion that Germans had capitulated to a unifying Christianity at some cost to their culture.

Yet the compulsion to submit to a dominant regional orthodoxy was tested within the religious field substantially earlier, as a political effect of the Reformation in the Germanic states.[4] For Protestant regions in Germany after the Peace of Augsburg (GHDI 1555), the principle of *cuius regio, eius* religio (literally: 'Whose region, his religion') became operative, and citizens either had to follow the doctrines of their Prince or relocate. Faith and nation were co-emerging. (The long future of that set of determinations would cast its pall over succeeding generations.) Furthermore, the Peace of Augsburg had made accommodation only for Lutheranism and did not acknowledge such Reform movements as Calvinism, which remained subject to heresy charges. Calvin, too, increasingly invested in the policing of boundaries, was a fierce antagonist of individuals whom he deemed heretics.[5]

During the past century, the terms of hospitality have been defined in often contradictory ways. Within many contemporary contexts, there has been an inherited legacy of legitimated cultural and religious pugilism despite an avowed multiculturalism. In tandem with an acknowledgment of complexity, there has been increasingly diminished defence of minority rights. To be 'at home' is a benefit made available as a reward for conformism and for normativity.

II

In the South African instance, the household has been divided against itself.

During the past decade of xenophobic assaults in South Africa, it has been the merchant who is so often the subject of attack. Simmel, in his celebrated essay on 'The Stranger' (originally published in 1908) suggests that the trader *is* the exemplary stranger, characterised as the one who is landless (Simmel 1971, 144–45). It is significant then to recall that in South Africa (as indeed in most postcolonial contexts) the trader does not enter into a region where Indigenous communities have possession of place, nor do settler communities have moral claims of ownership. As a result of the colonial history of displacement and land-theft, Simmel's model becomes skewed. Grimly, neither the stranger nor the host is at home. 'Dispossession' *is* in many ways the postcolonial condition. Moreover, it has increasingly come to define the displacement of persons across the globe.

Nonetheless, Simmel's model in some respects evokes conceptions of continuity and place which situate the stranger. Lingering in landlessness, the native pines for place. Perhaps Simmel needs to be rethought to take account of the circumstances of a transforming global reality that acknowledges the post-colony. Zygmunt Bauman's examination of the question provides key insights here:

> In the native world-view, the essence of the stranger is homelessness. Unlike an alien or a foreigner, the stranger is not simply a newcomer, a person temporarily out of place. He is an *eternal wanderer*, homeless always and everywhere, without hope of ever 'arriving'.
>
> (Bauman 1991, 79)

The novelist J. M. Coetzee has done some of the fundamental rethinking of landlessness through an oblique instrument, his novel *Disgrace*. This, of all his novels, has had an immense impact on local discourses about representation, and it is well to recall that representation lies at the heart of Coetzee's questioning of power. He attends to reading habits, demonstrating how choice and action are captive in various ways to modes of reading. Coetzee allows his readers to chase themselves into blind alleys in *Disgrace* because we read naively, taking the text as the world.

There are several hermeneutic snares in the novel. A significant example for this discussion arises in relation to one of the central protagonists, Lucy Lurie. She is, we are told, reading *The Mystery of Edwin Drood*, a novel that was left unfinished at the time of Charles Dickens's death in 1870. Why is this enigmatic text her choice? For Coetzee there is surely no sharper index of sensibility than one's preferred reading.

Is the unfinished novel not the shape of the post-colonial 'plot'? Coetzee is likely to have found Frank Kermode's *The Sense of an Ending* resonating within him while he was parsing the value of this idea for his own novel. Moreover, *Edwin Drood* thematises postcoloniality and dispossession. Two of the central characters, twins, are Neville and Helena Landless. In Coetzee's *Disgrace*, Petrus, a key figure in the second half of the novel, is himself 'landless'. The combination of violence and intrigue is staged through various mechanisms for the recovery of property rights. Lucy Lurie is brutally raped. Yet in much of European law, rape is historically classified as a property theft (although there is a long-standing tradition of literary and creative critique that challenges this formulation). *Disgrace* stages possible strategies for recovery – or for reparation – after sexual and property violations: through sexual liaison, through theft, through reproduction, through political pragmatism, through the law.

Coetzee's novel is certainly an interrogation of what may or may not be narratively possible. The opening section is unsympathetic in its treatment of the 'confessional imperative' of the university hearing in which David Lurie is 'urged' to seek forgiveness for his sexual liaison with a student.

The 'campus novel' first half of the narrative is effectively left unresolved, with David Lurie relocating in order to extract himself from the context of his university, and so that another kind of narrative may unfold in a frontier region associated with the wars of conquest in the Eastern Cape. Here, presumably, a different kind of resolution may be possible, may be necessary? Lurie's 'act of possession' within the sexualised context of the university pedagogy is – in a way – measured against the act of possession identified with settler colonialism.

Ownership remains unresolved at the end of the novel. Lucy is pregnant – and in such terms, a host. Yet she will submit herself to living as a visitor on what had been her own land in exchange for Petrus's oversight and protection for her child. The rapist and father of the child is the brother-in-law of Petrus, Pollux. Pollux's mythological inheritance is not that of the Western classics; and he himself may not be aware that he is named after one of a pair of twins born to Leda, a mortal who in Greek mythology had been seduced by Zeus in the guise of a swan. In choosing this name, Coetzee may well be invoking the complexities of the colonial legacy. A kind of nominalism is activated by the name, yet it also registers that such inheritances, while often carried as cultural memes, may be activated for some, and not others, in a discursive field of power because of the educational exclusions of the apartheid schooling system.

Is the pregnant body a 'host' of a kind? If so, then Lucy's refusal to seek legal redress after her violation averts the ending away from the law and into rather a dark pragmatics of hospitality. There is a kind of negotiation between Petrus (with his pressing claim to land ownership) and Lucy (the expectant mother). The biological fathers, David Lurie and Pollux, are in a sense irrelevant to the settlement.

Earlier I implied that Coetzee inserts *Edwin Drood* into the novel in order to reveal how the naïve reader assumes that he is writing about history, while so often, it turns out, he is writing about texts. Yet of course, there is history to reckon with.

III

Under the auspices of apartheid, several territories within the South African state had been resolved into so-called 'self-governing' homelands. In order to strip most black South Africans of their vote and their rights to residence, a number of ethnicities were elaborated (deploying a spectrum of ethnographic studies generated by apartheid universities, anthropologists and artists, who elaborated 'tribal' representations that would become the dubious supports for prosthetic identities). The so-called Bantustans or homelands were effectively 'native reserves' given the status of isolated states. These were marooned within the surrounding South Africa. They were usually accorded no political recognition by the international community; indeed these regions suffered from seriously damaging isolation and economic abandonment. So, for example, black South Africans whose home language was Ndebele, were given political citizenship in KwaNdebele and stripped of citizenship within the larger polity of South Africa.

That mechanism provided the great alibi of the apartheid state, because the majority black population of the country was thereby denied the vote within South Africa, the country in which they worked and dwelt for the bulk of the year. The Bantustans, moreover, were generally located in regions without viable infrastructure or resources. In a profoundly cynical manipulation of ethnicities, habitus and geography, apartheid engineers had conjured a geo-political instrument deemed to have 'solved' the problem of majority rights, while possessing the regions with rich mining industries and urban development. Black African citizens were re-designated, often based on language use, as citizens of some hypothetical ethnicity and its spurious 'homeland' (a kind of ancestral territory in one of several regions of undeveloped countryside.) 'Customary practices' were recovered, discovered, invented; in order to consolidate the boundaries of community, culinary practices, decorative arts, musical and narrative traditions, beliefs, and bio-medical regimes were enforced and reinforced, all such notions 'grounded' in separateness. The national body was tribalised and territorialised as part of an imperative upon which white modernity was premised.[6] African and white modernities were, apparently, irreconcilable. The whitened cities advanced, ascending upward in high-rise developments and spreading out horizontally in suburban sprawls, while black labour, hyperbolically modern, yet stripped of humanity, provided a force of surrogate masculinity underground in the pursuit of mineral wealth.

The heart was ripped from persons and persons were torn from the heart. The apartheid state instituted curfews, passbooks and violent regimes of law to manage the ebb and flow of persons who, no longer citizens in the South African state, were still deployed as labour units working on the mines, in construction or in heavy industry. African women were frequently deployed to work as nannies raising white babies, or were relegated to tough situations from nursing to prostitution.

Remarkably, in 1990, after several years of bitter and acrimonious internal conflict or even civil war, as well as a deadly border war with neighbouring states, the antagonists in this strife turned to negotiation. Was it possible to begin again to imagine a hypothesised national body healed, a reconciled South African state, with the stranded organs once again stitched back into the whole?

IV

There is a rather remarkable series of thought experiments in Locke's *Essay concerning Human Understanding* that informs my thinking about hospitality, community, persons and peoples. Locke's own empiricism persistently worries his own empirical question.

> Could we suppose two distinct incommunicable consciousnesses acting the same Body, the one constantly by Day, the other by Night; and on the other side the same consciousness acting by Intervals two distinct Bodies: I ask in the first case, whether the *Day* and the *Night-man* would not be two as distinct Persons, as *Socrates* and *Plato*; and whether in the second case, there would not be one Person in two distinct Bodies; as much as one Man is the same in two distinct clothings.
>
> (Locke 1975, 344)

The puzzle, in Locke's famous chapter 'Of Identity and Diversity' (in Book II of his *Essay*), is this: in what does personhood consist? The challenge to the common sense presumption that body and consciousness are one thing is surprisingly confounding. Locke first invites us to imagine two consciousnesses inhabiting one body, alternately by day and by night; then he asks us to turn to the idea of one consciousness inhabiting two bodies. Through this modelling of the problem, he resolves (as he has clearly set out to do) that personhood resides in consciousness. Even in the West, then, the apparently natural assumption that an individual person is located in a non-contradictory way within a single body is not simply the easy gift of the Enlightenment.

'Self-fashioning', as initially mooted in relation to early modern times, is not so much about the invention of an individual self through imaginative brio and ambition, I would suggest.[7] Rather, the very 'fashioning' of self as a concept is at the same time steadily worked through a combative and tormented series of experiments in dismemberment, discipline and inquisition, as the systems of internal and external authority (king, conscience and the Church of Rome) are incrementally shifted. If my conscience is at odds with my king? A torment. My king at odds with my priest? A torment. Locke set out to define the locus of the self in consciousness, and this increasingly seemed consonant with conscience. As he would note in *A Letter concerning Toleration*, 'every one is orthodox to himself' (Locke 1796, 5).

Here we have a particular modelling of the compound and contradictory subject, since the 'subject' of politics is being distilled through competing national, ecclesiastical and imperial interests, on one hand, and conscience, on the other. The politics of hospitality is increasingly a politics of exclusion. It is worth recalling, as I note previously, that in the sixteenth century the Augsburg Treaty resolved that one's faith was determined by one's geopolitical location. Charles V had granted that anyone living within a principality that did not advocate his or her own faith was free to leave. Preserving the peace required this dispensation.

> His Imperial Majesty, and We, and the electors, princes, and estates of the Holy Empire will not make war upon any estate of the empire on account of the Augsburg Confession and the doctrine, religion, and faith of the same,

nor injure nor do violence to those estates that hold it. . . . Nor shall We, through mandate or in any other way, trouble or disparage them, but shall let them quietly and peacefully enjoy their religion . . . and ceremonies, as well as their possessions, real and personal property, lands, people, dominions, governments, honors, and rights. Further, a complete peace within the disputed Christian religion shall be attained only by Christian, friendly, and peaceful means through his Imperial and Royal Majesties, the honorable princes, and by threat of punishment for breach of the Public Peace.

(GHDI)

It is difficult to read this gestural latitudinarianism from the perspective of the twenty-first century.

During the upheaval of the Reformation, many of the parameters of hospitality were radically altered, as attitudes to 'dissent' became vehement and disagreement about matters of belief increasingly lethal. John Calvin was integrally involved in heretic hunting. Locke's conception of toleration, while it begins to embrace new modes of membership, inclusion and exclusion, is itself circumscribed in scope. 'Non-conformism' is to become a new idea, the limits of which will have to be tested.

Much of what is at stake during this upheaval is a transformation in attitudes to semiotics and symbol, in addition to the metaphorics of the sacramental 'host'. It is worth dwelling for a moment on the complex etymologies associated with that term. For the Romans, the *hostia* was an offering or a sacrifice, but the term was also used on occasion for the vanquished enemy, who might be given up in sacrifice to the gods. It seems that this latter concept sometimes became the word for 'victim' in Ovid and other writers. In Indo-European traditions, 'ghost' is associated with the stranger and the guest; this rather uncanny conjunction resolves itself into a complex mélange of entangled meanings, one of which entails the complex of body and spirit.[8]

V

In 1636, the Great Charter of Charles I granted the Reader in Anatomy at Oxford University the right to demand, for the purposes of anatomical dissection, the body of any person executed *within* 21 miles of the city (Mitchell et al. 2011, 92). It had previously been a requirement that the cadavers were sourced from Oxford itself. Some two hundred years earlier, in Bologna, the statute on dissections had stipulated that the corpse was to come from at least 30 miles *outside* of that city (Ferrari 1984, 54).

Substantial medical, cosmological, theological and legal variables are clearly at play in these two legislative rulings, bearing in mind the two-hundred-year difference between a European and an English university context. It is difficult to speculate on the meaning of such distinctions; however the rulings do assert one absolute truth: that *neither* legislation, whether about proximity or distance, was natural or given. Both practices – the exogamous garnering of corpses, or the endogamous, are surely culturally specific and defined.

(In 'The Stranger', George Simmel notes that it had been the practice in certain Italian cities to recruit 'their judges from outside, because no native was free from entanglement in family interests and factionalism' (1971, 404). This is inherently interesting, but quite how that might inflect any interpretation of medical research is beyond the scope of this chapter.)

The protocols pertaining to the early modern anatomy may strike a modern sensibility as enigmatic, allegorical. What can be read from these injunctions against the anatomising of the insider, of the outsider? What are the rights and obligations of belonging?

It was in light of these provocations that I read the opening lines of Jean Luc Nancy's '*L'Intrus*'/'The Intruder'. The text begins as follows:

> *The intruder [l'intrus]* enters by force, through surprise of ruse, in any case without the right and without having first been admitted. There must be something of the *intrus* in the *stranger*; otherwise the stranger would lose its strangeness: if he already has the right to enter and remain, if he is awaited and received without any part of him being unexpected or unwelcome, he is no longer the *intrus*, nor is he any longer the stranger.
>
> (Nancy 2002, 1, my emphasis)

These meditations agitate the reader to an uneasy disquiet: we are vulnerable; our window latches will not hold; will the electric fence be repaired by tonight? The intruder is a figure much described in South African fantasias where he – the housebreaker is almost exclusively male – is associated with acts of brutal violence, physical assault and rape. The notorious trial of the Paralympic runner Oscar Pistorius fed on this psychic trope. His alibi in a globally disseminated trial for his shooting of his fiancée was that he had fired his gun in a panicked reaction to a suspected housebreaking.[9] In this way, the house-breaker, the border-hopper, the smuggler have proliferated in popular discourses and aesthetic representations. Both realities and phantoms have been bred from the soil of colonial conflict.

In France too, which is the setting for Nancy's paper, the new right with its own discourses on xenophobia, not to mention its mythos of a pure French identity and personhood, has attempted to mobilise an increasingly generalised European anxiety about immigration.[10] The political context makes it all but impossible to consider the longitudinal demonstration of hospitality as a cultural good. As Nancy notes, it is at times a matter of discomfort, this *hospitality*:

> the stranger's coming will not cease being a disturbance and perturbation of intimacy. . . . Receiving the stranger must then also necessarily entail experiencing his intrusion. Most often one does not wish to admit this: the theme of the *intrus*, in itself, intrudes on our moral correctness. . . . Hence the theme of the *intrus* is inextricable from the truth of the stranger.
>
> (Nancy 2002, 2)

Yet Nancy's paper and its subject matter take a *swerve*: his meditation on the intruder arises from an elsewhere that is as close to the self as it is possible to imagine: from the very heart of the matter, the source of the self, the core of his being.

> I, therefore, received the heart of another, now nearly ten years ago. It was a transplant, grafted on. My own heart (as you've gathered, it is entirely a matter of the 'proper', of being one, or one's 'own' – or else it is not in the least and, properly speaking, there is nothing to understand, no mystery, not even a question: rather, as the doctors prefer to say, there is the simple necessity [*la simple évidence*] of a transplantation) – my own heart in fact was worn out, for reasons that have never been clear. Thus to live, it was necessary to receive another's, an other heart. . . . My heart was becoming my own foreigner.
>
> (Nancy 2002, 3–4)

This is the fact of the matter: the matter of fact. Nancy received a transplanted heart. A vital organ, made available through a donation, came to settle inside him. That stranger became the utmost of him; for without it, he had no being. Having almost been lost, he became found. Redeemed. The stranger had necessarily moved in; and was cohabiting with him, having taken up shop as a permanent resident.

And here I undertake a similar *swerve* in the terms of my discussion in order to abstract my thoughts from the all but overwhelming exigencies of the current world-historical reality, the catastrophe/the crisis/the tragedy of refugees in the redefined and redefining global Europe. This strategy enables me to consider the significance of Nancy's meditation on the transplant that sustains him, even while (in the back of my mind) I am aware of the shifting discourses about the 'border', the foreigner and the visitor as intruder.

Some ten years ago I wrote a novel about the first medically credible human heart transplant. The surgery had taken place in Cape Town on 3 December 1967. I have an interest in bio-medical history: that certainly is part of what engaged me when I turned to consider these events. Moreover, I wanted to understand the transplant in light of a particular set of historical circumstances that defined the end of the twentieth century in South Africa. In 1996, the country had initiated the Truth and Reconciliation Commission (TRC), a series of public hearings aimed at consolidating information about the human rights violations perpetrated during the apartheid era. The Commission was established by the 'Promotion of National Unity and Reconciliation Act', Number 34 of 1995. Something in that formulation suggests that South Africans were engaging in a process of reorienting the self in relation to the self. 'Are we as a nation pre-disposed to a change of heart?', I asked myself. Had South Africa in 1967 engaged in an allegorical anticipation of the monumental political transformation that would take place in the 1990s?

It seemed to me almost incomprehensible that Mr Darvall had been asked to make his daughter's heart available to save the life of a stranger. That act had seemed to me a violence when I read of the circumstance. Denise Darvall and her mother were both struck down by a drunk driver in a speeding car. Mrs Darvall was killed immediately, but Denise lingered. Her father, traumatised and in a state of shocked grief, was persuaded to be the first: for the first time, to make his daughter's heart available for transplantation. How striking, that the victim here was being asked to make yet another sacrifice in order to make sustained life possible. The complexity of the allegorical field began to take on the texture of the uncanny.

The transplanted heart is anything *but* at home in the recipient body. Intense and regularly monitored regimes of management are necessary to block the rejection of the organ. Sandoz, the generics division of the Swiss pharmaceuticals company Novartis, had encouraged its staff, when travelling on holiday, always to return with a small sample of the local (foreign) soil in a plastic bag. One such small package arrived from Norway; it contained a fungus with marvellous immunosuppression properties. This became the basis of cyclosporine, a wonder-drug that has been pivotal in the advancement of transplant surgeries. Our tolerance of invasive organs is a possibility not because the host has become more accommodating; rather, through collaborative effort, we have discovered how to manage our innate inclination to reject and destroy the intruder amongst us.

A particular order of thought seems necessary if we are to reflect on hospitality in generative terms. At some level, what is entailed is a reconsideration of the complexity of the inter-; the intra-; trans-; supra-; bi-; post-. Thus it seems productive to turn to another text by Nancy, and another of his meditations on hospitality, on living with the heart of another inside of oneself – living with the heart of another as oneself, in fact. The extract comes from *Being Singular Plural:*

> In order for the human to be discovered, and in order for the phrase 'human meaning' to acquire some meaning, everything that has ever laid claim to the truth about the nature, essence, or end of 'man' must be undone. In other words, nothing must remain of what, under the title of meaning, related the earth [*la terre*] and the human to a specifiable horizon. Again, it is Nietzsche who said that we are now 'on the horizon of the infinite': that is, we are now at the point where 'there is no more "land"'.
>
> (Nancy 2000, xi)

Once more, I turn back to Mauss, and the 'total social fact'. The gift is what will sustain our sociality. Hospitality is the gift we have the obligation to give and the right to expect.

Notes

1 This is the assessment of the International Organization for Migration (IOM's Global Migration Data Analysis Centre, 2017).
2 The notion of the 'social fact' was actually conceived by Emile Durkheim, Mauss's uncle and occasional collaborator.
3 The artist Walid Raad has in the past several years engaged in very visible assaults against the practices of slavery associated with the development of 'faux' art museums on Saadiyat Island in Abu Dhabi. Glamorous venues that are indebted to the celebrity of global

cultural centres, such as the Louvre and the Guggenheim Museums, are being built using these brand names, yet deploying enslaved migrant workers. Together with a furious collective, *52 Weeks of Gulf Labor*, Raad engaged in the event *Occupy Guggenheim* in order to alert complicit cultural elites in the West to their collusion with sordid and violent people trafficking.
4 There is an emerging menace within this conflation of place, faith, and power. Recently, Alain Badiou has characterised the conflation of state and identitarianism as an inheritance of the Pauline appeal to a universalism premised on conversion (Badiou 2003, 57).
5 Nonetheless, there is a strand of thought that runs from the eighteenth century through sentimental literature and Romanticism, celebrating the exotic as long as it remains foreign. By the nineteenth century, the infiltration of the colonial other into the metropole is figured in Arthur Conan Doyle's Sherlock Holmes stories as a poison entering the system (Doyle 2001). Foreigners are frequently treated with suspicion in such texts, although the traffic in (somewhat magical) commodities is welcomed.
6 While not wholly analogous, it is worth recalling the precedent established by the Augsburg Settlement of 1555, cited previously.
7 Stephen Greenblatt's *Renaissance Self-Fashioning* posits that early modern subjects of talent (from Sir Thomas More to Shakespeare) prove to be almost endlessly inventive agents, shaping themselves in relation to shifting fault lines as state and church are battered against each other (Greenblatt 1980).
8 This is not the context for a detailed scrutiny of such ideas, but some of this history can be tracked through Lewis Ramshorn (from the German text by Francis Lieber) in his *Dictionary of Latin Synonyms* (Ramshorn 1841).
9 In 2009, the theatre director Brett Bailey constructed a site-specific work at the South African National Arts Festival that deployed a similar motif. *The Terminal/Blood Diamonds* was composed of several *tableaux vivants,* one of which staged a masked housebreaker entering through a domestic window while a woman lay asleep in her bed. Again, Mark Gevisser's *Lost and Found in Johannesburg* gives an account of the violence against his guests and himself during a dinner in his home.
10 It is impossible within the scope of this short piece to begin to examine the impact of the continuing dilemma concerning migrancy and refuge across the Mediterranean and Europe.

References

Badiou, Alain. 2003. *Saint Paul: The Foundations of Universalism*. Translated by Ray Brassier. Stanford, CA: Stanford University Press.
Bailey, Brett. 2009. 'Site-specific Work at the South African National Arts Festival': *The Terminal/Blood Diamonds, Tableaux Vivants.*
Bauman, Zygmunt. 1991. *Modernity and Ambivalence*. Ithaca, NY: Cornell University Press.
Coetzee, J. M. 1999. *Disgrace*. London: Secker and Warburg.
Dickens, Charles. 2002. *The Mystery of Edwin Drood* (Unfinished). Edited by David Paroissien. Harmondsworth, Middlesex: Penguin.
Doyle, Arthur Conan. 2001 [1890]. *The Sign of the Four*. Edited by Ed Glinert. Harmondsworth, Middlesex: Penguin.
Ferrari, Giovanna. 1984. 'Public Anatomy Lessons and the Carnival: The Anatomy Theatre of Bologna'. *Past and Present* 117.1: 50–106.
Gevisser, Mark. 2014. *Lost and Found in Johannesburg*. New York: Farrar, Straus and Giroux.
GHDI [German History in Documents and Images]. 'The Religious Peace of Augsburg (September 25, 1555)'. In *From the Reformation to the Thirty Years War, 1500–1648*, edited by Thomas A. Brady, Jr. and Ellen Yutzy Glebe. http://germanhistorydocs.ghi-dc.org/sub_document.cfm?document_id=4386 (accessed 22 January 2018).

Greenblatt, Stephen. 1980. *Renaissance Self-Fashioning*. Chicago: University of Chicago Press.
Herder, Johann Gottfried. 2012 [1772]. *Treatise on the Origin of Language*. Edited and translated by Michael N. Forster. Cambridge: Cambridge University Press, 2002. Online edition 2012.
International Organization for Migration (IOM's Global Migration Data Analysis Centre, Geneva). 2017. www.dw.com>mediterranean-worlds-deadliest-border-for-migrants-says-un/a41525468 (accessed 22 January 2018).
Kermode, Frank. 1967. *The Sense of an Ending*. Oxford: Oxford University Press.
Locke, John. 1796. *A Letter concerning Toleration*. Edited by J. Cockin. Huddersfield: J. Brook.
———. 1975. *An Essay Concerning Human Understanding*. Edited by Peter H. Nidditch. Oxford: Clarendon Press.
Mauss, Marcel. 1966. *The Gift*. London: Cohen &West.
Mitchell, P. D., C. Boston, et al. 2011. 'The Study of Anatomy in England from 1700 to the Early 20th Century'. *Journal of Anatomy* 219.2: 91–99.
Nancy, Jean-Luc. 2000. *Being Singular Plural*. Translated by Robert D. Richardson and Anne O'Byrne. Stanford, CA: Stanford University Press.
———. 2002 [2000]. '*L'Intrus*'. Translated by Susan Hanson. *New Centennial Review* 2.3: 1–14.
Raad, Walid. 2016. *Occupy Guggenheim Arts Intervention*. New York: Guggenheim Museum (ongoing).
Ramshorn, Lewis. 1841. *Dictionary of Latin Synonyms*. Boston: Charles C. Little and James Brown.
Simmel, Georg. 1971 [1908]. 'The Stranger'. In *Georg Simmel: On Individuality and Social Forms: Selected Writings*, edited by Donald N. Levine, 143–49. Chicago and London: University of Chicago Press.

7

HÉLÈNE CIXOUS'S MOURNING OF LOSS AND THE LOSS OF MOURNING

From Algerian apprehensions to *Hyperdream* – and beyond

Merle A. Williams

> *You can always lose more . . .*
>
> (Cixous 2009a, 10)

> *The whole time I was living in Algeria I would dream of one day arriving in Algeria, I would have done anything to get there . . .*
>
> (Cixous 2006, 3)

The plight of Antigone and Ismene in Sophocles's *Oedipus at Colonos* prompts an extended digression in Jacques Derrida's reflections on hospitality. Oedipus, the outlaw, has bound his host Theseus by a terrible oath not to reveal his place of burial, thus turning the host-king into a cunningly constrained, morally submissive hostage. Yet this transgression of the principles of a freely offered hospitality breeds further transgression in the daughters of Oedipus, who resist their father and their host, chafing against an enforced failure of hospitality to the at once loved and hated dead. Antigone, in particular, finds herself burdened with 'an interminable mourning, an infinite mourning . . . beyond any possible work of mourning. The only possible mourning is the impossible mourning'. Railing in her distress, she demands a compounded impossibility of her father: that a dead, blind man should see her tears, even in the recessiveness of her most private self-awareness. (Derrida 2000, 115). She is in mourning for the very process of mourning itself (ibid.: 111).

Such a darkened vision, which is also a vision of darkness, contrasts sharply with Hélène Cixous's generous hospitality in 'wager[ing]' her 'life on life', although, paradoxically, this endeavour too entails an interminable, ineluctable mourning (Derrida 2006, xiii). In *H.C. for Life, That Is to Say . . .*, Derrida pays moving tribute to a dear friend and cherished colleague by insisting that she is on 'the side of life against death, for life without death, beyond a death whose test and threat are none the less endured, in mourning even in the life blood and breath, in the soul of writing'. By contrast, he 'feels [himself] drawn *to the side* of death' (Derrida 2006, xiii). In his epilogue to the volume, Derrida elaborates that he is 'and [remains] for life *convaincu de mort* (both *convicted* and *convinced* of death); *convicted*, that is to say at fault and accused, found guilty, imprisoned or jailed after a verdict, here a death sentence, but also *convinced*, convinced by the truth of death, of a true speech (*veridictum*), of a verdict as regards death' (ibid.: 158). He can 'manage to believe' Cixous only when she speaks in the subjunctive mood of '*would that I might*' (ibid.: 158, 4).

This sustained, life-enhancing and life-contesting debate lies at the core of a warmly hospitable friendship consistently characterised by mutually respectful receptiveness and harmony in difference. The association found its roots in Cixous's first sighting of Derrida when the young scholar was interrogating notions of death before a distinguished academic panel in defence of his doctoral thesis for the *aggregation de philosophie*. In *H.C. for Life* (Derrida 2006, 5), he describes the moment when his back was significantly turned to Cixous, whom he had never met. She reciprocates with her impression of an inadvertently enacted primal scene in the imaginatively reconfigured biographical *Portrait of Jacques Derrida as a Young Jewish Saint* (Cixous 2004, 5–6). And their passionate engagement continued for a lifetime, or until death. In *Hyperdream*, which includes a plangent elegy for Derrida, Cixous lovingly captures the nuance of his thought and speech:

> I'm always having to call you back, to remind you of death he would say, in the end I'm always having to remind you that that on my side we die too fast, while you on your side live too fast.
>
> (Cixous 2009a, 89)

For years Cixous had listened acutely to the timbre of Derrida's 'telephone voice' as it created a remote privacy in intimacy through its disembodiment. She had tried to meet the demands of loyal responsiveness by judiciously agreeing with or contradicting his views, working to 'balance his own life forces against his own death forces' (ibid.: 94). Then she came to realise that the lines of interaction had, in effect, been ambivalently drawn until the early 1990s: she had been '*begg[ing] the question*', not quite believing what Derrida both desired her to embrace and to repudiate. It was only belatedly, if not at the last, that she had committed to playing for her own team (ibid.: 96).

Cixous's unique mode of hospitality to 'what death has in store deep within life itself' (Derrida 2006, xiii) requires a rite of passage through the strangely dislocated spatio-temporality of the *entredeux* or the 'in-between'. This transition 'evicts us from ourselves' because we are almost, if not entirely, dead, yet not ready for the process of reliving (Cixous 1997, 9). The interruption of this passage precipitates instability and uncertainty, opening the way for a radical reassessment of human experience. For Cixous, reintegration is achieved primarily through writing and through dreams. In *Hyperdream*, as a vivid illustration, she seeks to negotiate the recent death of Derrida in the light of the newly diagnosed terminal illness of her mother Eve, who has developed a virulent form of skin cancer. As she spreads ointment on her mother's back, she '*go[es] on living*', simultaneously disoriented and intensely aware. Her index finger writes its mythical tale of anguish and loss, in which the burst boils are described as cyclopean eyes and 'little cadaverised jellyfish' – *meduses*, in French. Love and pity combine in touching and being touched by the canvas of her mother's skin, which bears testimony to a watershed perception in Cixous's history, just as it declares what can so easily happen to the living (Cixous 2009a, 11). Mother and daughter have entered 'the regime of the "last times"' in the sense of the 'ultimate', the 'last last' or the eschatological, as well as the 'lately' or those which have 'just happened'. The difference is that the ultimate period has no fixed date (ibid.: 6). The excoriating ritual of anointing Eve is refracted through Cixous's longing to cross beyond the immediate into the reassuring consolation of her dead friend. For this she needs a dream, hence the title of her allusively crafted fictional autobiography, *Hyperdream*. As Catherine MacGillivray suggests in her introduction to *FirstDays of the Year*, Cixous's singular kind of writing often becomes an 'edge pursuit: a pursuit of the edge, practiced on the edge; an edgy pushing at edges in an effort to feel and fall over them' (MacGillivray 1998, xx–xxi). Writing 'on board the dream' (Cixous 1991, 106) becomes a dream-writing that opens doors or makes them vanish, crossing or erasing borders through a hospitality to otherness that concomitantly empowers the self for metamorphosis. Time itself is distended and reconfigured, absence infuses presence with an uncanny resonance of transient reprieve from loss.

To situate *Hyperdream* in its poetic-philosophical context, Cixous's *oeuvre* is redolent of losses calling for retrospective appraisal and haunted absences yearning towards the qualified fulfilment of textualisation. She is readily attuned to displacement and marginalisation. In 'My Algeriance, in Other Words: To Depart Not to Arrive from Algeria', Cixous notes that her 'history is held between a double contradictory memory' (Cixous 2005, 127–28). Her mother and grandmother were Jewish refugees from Nazi Germany, perversely saved by their qualification for French citizenship because their once native Strasbourg had become a French possession after the First World War. They were therefore entitled to invoke the most fundamental requirements for a wilfully attenuated conditional hospitality: a 'familial or genealogical right applying to more than one generation' and the accountability derived from 'nameable identities' or 'proper names' (Derrida 2000, 23). Her father's family, by contrast, were Jews of Spanish origin, resident in Algeria; they were all deprived of French citizenship under the Vichy government between 1940 and 1942, as even minimalist pretences of hospitality turned to outright hostility and stigmatisation. Cixous's father was prevented from practising medicine, while she and her brother were excluded from the state school system (ibid.: 127–28). Linguistically, too, she was at once cosmopolitan (more probably, merely polyglot) and rootless, with one parent fluent in French and the other in German, while sometimes 'jumping through Spanish and English' (ibid.: 137). At the age of ten, her father provided her with teachers in Arabic and Hebrew (ibid.: 137), although this arrangement ceased abruptly with Georges Cixous's premature death. '*I felt perfectly at home, nowhere*', his daughter writes (ibid.: 128), perhaps the ultimate irony of nomadic hospitality in pervasive inhospitality.

Yet Cixous's bitter familiarity with anti-Semitism equally sharpened her sensitivity to the harsh colonial repression of the local Algerian population. This vivid awareness is crystallised in her long-delayed 'Letter to Zohra Drif', which was first published in English translation in 1998. As a pupil at the staunchly French-Catholic Lycée Fromentin, she moved in an oppressive atmosphere of 'Algeria without Algerians'. At the age of eleven, Cixous heard one girl telling another who had refused to lend her an eraser not to be 'a Jew'; this rebuke was decoded as 'don't be stingy' (Cixous 2003, 85). A couple of years later, three Muslim girls – including Zohra Drif – joined the class. Cixous watched them unperceived, but with a sense of aching longing for their confident sense of belonging through their easy connectedness to Algerian life; 'with them I made sense to myself. I called to them in silence and without hope'. In 1955 she left North Africa, only to discover in a French newspaper in January 1957 that Zohra Drif had gone into hiding in the Casbah (ibid.: 87). Drif had joined the FLN (the National Liberation Front) and been recruited to plant bombs in the French quarter of Algiers, thus sharing responsibility for the explosion that killed three people and injured many others at the popular Milk Bar.[1] Events had overtaken Cixous's aspiration, framing her unfinished message as a 'photograph of [her] soul' and underscoring her 'extreme Algerian impotence' (ibid.: 88). For her there was simply no prospect of participating in the liberation struggle. In 'My Algeriance', she expresses her fraught reflections rather differently. She acknowledges that she could not lose Algeria, because she had 'never had it'; nonetheless, she had identified passionately with 'its rage at being wounded, amputated, humiliated' by relentless colonial impositions (Cixous 2005, 137).

In *Reveries of the Wild Woman* (another fictionalised autobiography), the emblematic figures of the Bike and the Dog reverberate at the heart of Cixous's unwilling alienation from an Algeria that seems repeatedly to close against her wavering advances. For four years, which assume the hazy guise of a pre-adolescent eternity, the young Cixous (as first person narrator) and her brother dream of receiving a bike that will enable them to explore the alluring terrain surrounding Algiers; it embodies the promise of freedom and discovery. As this modest, yet overwhelming, tragic-comedy unfolds, the 'bike-awaiters' turn into 'champion ghost cyclists', mercilessly 'racked by their need' to escape the confinement of home (Cixous 2006, 13). This consuming near-parody of Lacanian desire is punctured when their resolutely sensible, economical and Germanic mother presents them with a girl's bike, on the grounds that both can ride it. The enormity of this slight to masculinity is registered by Cixous's brother, whose assumed privileges as coloniser embroil him in a state of constant warfare with the local Arab boys. The gift of the Bike is reviled as '*the definitive crime*', an amputation of 'something definitive' and 'a basic act of death' (ibid.: 17). The insult of this symbolic castration is heightened because Eve is assumed to be the only '*Jewish woman in history*' capable of giving her son a woman's bicycle as a bar mitzvah present, thus crassly nullifying his achievement of manhood (see ibid.: 18).[2] Cixous comes achingly close to losing her brother when he runs away as a reprisal, only to return ignominiously defeated by the absence of welcome from the local boys. She actually loses Algeria, retreating into escapist, if omnivorous, reading that becomes a substitute for experiencing earth and sky. Her first attempt at riding the bicycle in the Clos Salembier had provoked an assault with a vegetable crate that dramatically terminated all further forays.

    The story of the Dog retraces the debacle of the Bike. Now a gift from her father (rather than her too-literal-minded mother) is humorously evoked as a failed Annunciation, since the proto-Derridean *arrivant* is patently incapable of initiating an unforeseeable future of pure, transformative event; bathetically, 'the Dog who was once the king and son of God is slowly descending into disinheritance, a flop of a life locked up in the cage' (ibid.: 29). He has failed to fill the gap left by the long-awaited baby which is never born to the family. Far from cleansing guilt, the Dog drives an acutely sensitive Cixous to evasion and moral self-aversion in consequence of his imprisoned misery. 'Am I Jewish, the Dog wondered I say. . . . But what does Jewish mean wondered the Dog, and Arab and dog, friend, brother, enemy, Papa, liberty nothing exists save injustice and brutality' (ibid.: 44). 'Too late and in part', it comes to be understood that Fips the Dog is Job. 'He is plagued' and 'god was well hidden'. Georges Cixous, 'the father who was mother[,] is dead, and now the pestilence and sores' (ibid.: 46). A universe seemingly devoid of justice, compassion and vestigial hospitality engenders this arid incapacity for mourning – not even the mourning of mourning, congealing loss into scarcely endured, random deprivation.

    Reveries of the Wild Woman in its turn tracks the double isolation of the Cixous family, whose members incur condescension from the French because they are Jewish, and resentment from the Arabs because they are deemed to be French. When the dashing father offers a lift uphill to two young Arab hitchhikers, the fierce identity politics and racism of anti-colonial revolutionary ferment are thrown into confusion. The doctor's pro-Arab symbolic act inspires mutual professions of brotherhood in both French and Arabic. His awkwardly compromising Jewishness has, of course, passed undetected (ibid.: 24-25). Yet this seemingly iconic moment of 'arriving in Algeria' is promptly debunked in retrospect by Cixous's brother. He claims that the two passengers were, in fact, old men in gandouras, waiting at a tram stop at the top of the hill (ibid.: 26).[3] The account is permeated by Cixous's bruised consciousness of multiple Algerian resistances to her reaching for acceptance, although this perspective is refracted through her partly willed failure to extend hospitable accommodations to the country of her birth. Playing the sceptical critic, her brother comments, 'I don't get the fragrance of the Algerian soil in this book' (ibid.: 47). Nonetheless, the story explores the romance of Oran with its Barbary figs, water vendors and old Jewish ritual slaughterer, who spares a pigeon because its lifetime mate has managed to escape (ibid.: 77-79). These vignettes are poised against the sordid violence of the Clos Salembier, where a young Arab 'mashes' his opponent's face with 'a stone as big as a fist' while 'howling big sobs' (ibid.: 43). Algeria doubly – almost irretrievably – lost because never possessed (yet evocatively remembered), Algeria dreamt unexpectedly after decades, is conjured from oblivion and transformed in a fine network of conflicting stresses. Perverse Algeria, apprehended through the continued frustration of openly empowering relationships, becomes on recollection a country poignant with delicate psychic intimations.

In this frequently paradoxical milieu, two episodes involving veils become revealing, not least because in 1998 Cixous and Derrida were to co-publish a volume entitled *Veils* (Cixous 2001; Derrida 2001b) as a contribution to the expanding intertext of their scholarly friendship. In the first incident, the nine-year-old Cixous spots a Moorish doll in an arcade window in Oran: 'the adorable creature . . . fills [her] with a desire absolutely deaf to commentary, to any calculation to reason, it is the *vital creature* suddenly I want it, I must have it, it is Her' (Cixous 2006, 75). She cannot resist the 'delicate face veil', the haik, silver clasp and anklets; she wants 'the hidden face' amid the splendour of its accoutrements. Her father, now king rather than god, is adamant in his refusal, tempting the child to commit parricide within the enclosed space of the car. Wanting the doll amounts to wanting Algeria in its tantalising withdrawals and flashes of gorgeous exposure. Cixous can scarcely forgive the beloved Georges – 'all the rest is disguise', or veiled (ibid.: 76). The overwhelming turbulence of these emotions anticipates Cixous's lonely contemplation of Zohra Drif and the other Muslim girls in her class, powerfully prefiguring an eviscerated Algeriance and enduring atopia. The second shocking occurrence takes place during a ride on a Ferris wheel, again in Oran. A man leans forward to hug a girl who dodges away from him, catching her veil in the moving machinery. When the wheel can finally be stopped, the body wrapped in the veil has been sliced in half before falling to the ground, to the appalled relief of the hypnotised spectators. Cixous feels guilty at having lived this grotesque experience as intensely as if it were her own, yet she is not dead. 'Since that accident something inside [her] is veiled to [her]' (ibid.: 82). These events cast loss and death in an alternative, perversely apocalyptic perspective. The latent violence of Algeria infuses consciousness and particularly the unconscious, instituting isolation, anguish and mourning as modalities of being. Arrival is scarcely comprehensible, even at the limit of the optative mood.

The loneliness of the self-defined exile or refugee, whose losses seem irreparable, is woven throughout the central section of *Hyperdream*, together with motifs of recollection, dreaming and death. The focal point here is not the emasculating Bike, the Dog as false Messiah, or even an unattainable Moorish Ur-femininity, but – disconcertingly, pathetically, ridiculously – Walter Benjamin's bed. In the period 'before-the-death-of Mummy', Eve as surrogate primal mother reverts to frenetic, humorous reminiscence. She describes the purchase of a metal bed-frame with springs or a *sommier* from Benjamin, who is unsentimentally pictured as a polite intellectual with glasses.[4] The concierge nearly disposes of this '*dead-loss piece of junk*' to a peddler, but it is subsequently recovered (Cixous 2006, 55–56). If Eve is pragmatically satisfied with the prolonged use-value of her acquisition, Cixous feels tantalised by her lack of knowledge about the bed on which her brother has slept for so many years. She is reluctant to consider it merely another mass-produced and 'soulless' commodity, especially against the background of Benjamin's landmark essay on 'The Work of Art in the Age of Mechanical Reproduction' (1970, 219–53). The cheap bed clearly lacks authenticity in Benjamin's terms, an essence that is at once uniquely identifiable and transmissible across a historical trajectory. So Cixous searches for a substitute 'aura' to locate the humble bed within an aesthetic and personal tradition that will hospitably contextualise it (see Benjamin 1970, 223). Under this impulse, she longs for it to speak to her as do dumb fairy-tale objects or creatures that have been brought to expression by human sympathy (Cixous 2009a, 55–56). Regret for the battered object and for the lonely existence of its nomadic owner calls to mind the death of her friend Derrida, who coined the *seroteamavi* effect in his 1995 essay on 'A Silkworm of One's Own'. This becomes a 'formula for Regret', 'a feeling of chagrin in a state of ghostliness', which responds to the 'nameless melancholy' of typically human suffering (Cixous 2009a, 61).

In 'A Silkworm of One's Own', Derrida fancifully figures his flights to three major South American cities as 'go[ing] off to the ends of the earth like a mortally wounded animal' 'before it's too late' (Derrida 2001a, 21). He wrestles with the notion of a mysterious verdict without established logical or judicial truth, woven modestly in diminution or *decrescendo* through the attempt to understand oneself (ibid.: 21-23). He tentatively moots some kind of 'return to life that's not a resurrection' (ibid.: 22), but the pressing issue emerges as that 'unknown verdict for an indeterminable fault' as a way of initiating a new era. Yet belatedness and loss loom inescapably, even at the ends of the earth where temporary hospitality provides no secure refuge. Derrida's proof text is drawn from Augustine's *Confessions* (Augustine 2016, Book 10, Chapter 27): 'sero te amavi, pulchritudo tam antiqua et tam nova' – 'So late have I loved thee, beauty so ancient and so new'. Whether the self-reproach is addressed to Christ or to God, 'so late' merges into its apparently inseparable other, 'too late'. And both become entrammelled in Derrida's favourite future perfect tense; because it is '*already* late', Augustine 'will have loved'. 'Late', Derrida argues, 'evaluates, desires, regrets, accuses, complains – and sighs for the verdict', postponing the time for loving. As Augustine admits, 'mecum eras, et tecum non eram' – 'You were with me and I was not with you' (Derrida 2001a, 33). Cixous detects Derrida's genius in spanning from ancient sensibility to a pain that is emblematic of the modern world (Cixous 2009a, 61-62). For forty-four years, she has been unable to empathise with Benjamin's impoverished sojourn in Paris during his enforced wanderings or to guess at his thoughts while lying on the bed. She has inadvertently betrayed his losses by not being with him, although the fiendishly uncomfortable bed has been all too insistently with her brother. She has lost the books she might have written under the inspiration of the neglected *sommier* with its imaginatively reconstituted aura. She has even lost a segment of Eve's early Parisian biography, now whimsically tossed off in the strident hilarity of garrulous old age. And Derrida's 'indeterminable fault', which generically encompasses 'all the perjuries in the world, blasphemies, profanations, sacrileges', knits together persecution and racism, prejudice and lovelessness: the flight of

Walter Benjamin and Eve Klein (later Cixous) from Nazi Germany, Hélène Cixous's departure from Algeria without arriving in a hospitable France, the seething aggression of the Clos Salembier, pointless anti-Semitism, a threatened body cut in two while wrapped in its veil.

Returning to the mundane, which is haunted by these far-reaching ethical and political faults, the loss of the bed's individual history is replayed in Cixous's misplacing her volume of Benjamin's letters, which should have remained with her in plain view. A newly acquired copy proves largely silent about the *sommier*, although it records Benjamin's sweaty struggle to carry it down seven floors to the concierge in the middle of an elevator strike. This ignominious process, followed by the 'massive migration of some rags' to which Benjamin is attached, precipitates '*the disappearance* of a very fine pen, for me irreplaceable. A true disaster' (Cixous 2009a, 69). Reflecting that '*one only loses what one can't replace*' (ibid.: 69), Cixous in her turn laments the vanishing of her precious nightgown from a New York hotel. She paints the theft as tantamount to stealing her skin, thus fusing her treatment of her mother's wounds and the loss of Benjamin's pen with a deeper anxiety: 'Will I ever write again . . . how to interpret the sign . . .?' (ibid.: 69) The imagined Benjamin wonders whether he will ever be himself again; Cixous tries to gauge what he might have produced if the bed had never been sold to her mother (ibid.: 70). It is scarcely surprising that such a latent fear of writer's block in an unpredictable future should point to the prophetic potential of the unconscious and of dreaming.

If the bed is a *sommier*, language itself invites associations with sleeping, 'snoozing', dreaming. A 'French foreign word' or *Fremdwort*, comments Eve; like Benjamin she is a mother-tongue German speaker – and, practical as ever, she prefers the comfort of the traditional stuffed horsehair mattress on a board (ibid.: 67). Yet Cixous, who has made her transient home in resolutely unmaking and remaking the French language, can stretch out within the generative linguistic ambit of foreignness. Such apparently alien dream-work stirs the memory of a German writing in French (despite the disappearance of his treasured pen) and an Algerian-born-Frenchman addressing Germans. In this fashion, a curious entanglement of inhospitable uprooting, loss, death, dreaming and figuration ensues yet again. In September 2001, Jacques Derrida delivered an address entitled '*Fichus*' in recognition of the award of the Theodor W. Adorno Prize in Frankfurt. Adorno was born on 11th September, while Derrida and Benjamin share a birthday of 15th July, the date on which a substantial section of *Hyperdream* was written. Under pressure of these coincidences, a landscape of alienation and deprivation, suffering and dream-writing explodes. The sinister fascination of the destruction of the Twin Towers in New York on 9/11 transmutes itself through a flexible patterning of images into Eve's cancer-eaten body as a burnt out tower (see Cixous 2009a, 19), which in turn morphs into Montaigne's beloved Martello tower near Bordeaux, the crystallisation for Cixous of expansive, genially astute and multifarious writing (see 29–33). There is no specific citation in *Hyperdream*, but Montaigne's *First Booke* of *Essayes* includes a Ciceronian piece entitled 'That to Philosophise is to learne how to Die'.

The reader is calmly counselled 'to stand and combat [death] with a resolute minde' (Montaigne 1893, 30).

In '*Fichus*', Derrida examines sleep as a suggestive reflection of the prospect of death. He constructs his speech 'with the ghostly or *unheimlich*, uncanny gestures of a sleepwalker . . . *as if* . . . dreaming' in order to catch a dream that Benjamin outlines to Gretel Adorno. Recorded in French, this dream of an isolated refugee in an internment camp is about 'changing a poem into a *fichu*', while in German it concerns 'making a scarf out of a poem' (Derrida 2005, 165). There is an oblique reference to an earlier letter to Gretel Adorno, in which Benjamin replies to her husband's 'slightly authoritarian and paternal criticisms' concerning the relationship between 'dream figures' and 'the "dialectical image"' (ibid.: 174). An old straw or panama hat with a crack in the crown, which Benjamin had inherited from his father, appears in the long narrative. Most engaging, though, is the 'graphical element' of the letter *d*. From the upper stroke of the *d* emanates 'an intense aspiration towards spirituality' carried by a little billowing sail with a blue border' (ibid.: 174). If the sail resembles the *fichu* as a scarf or small shawl for a woman's head and shoulders, it metonymically arouses an alternative adjectival signification. 'One day in September 1970, seeing his death approaching, my sick father said to me "I'm *fichu*"' – lost, condemned, done for' (ibid.: 173).

Derrida speculates on the conceivable denotations and connotations of the letter *d*, which, of course, is his father's and his own initial. It might stand for Detlev Holz, one of Benjamin's political pseudonyms, or the 'Detlef' with which he sometimes signed family letters; alternatively, it might represent Dr Dausse, who once treated Benjamin for malaria (ibid.: 175). Yet again, it might signal 'Dora', Benjamin's first wife, bearing in mind that this word is Greek for 'skin that has been scorched, scratched, or worked over'. A more usual etymology from *doron*, however, is 'gift of the gods', as in '*Theodor* Adorno' (ibid.: 176, 203: n. 23). If the possible implications are rather too freely translated from the French-German circuit into English, *d* clearly announces 'death'. Benjamin committed suicide about a year after sending his letter to Gretel Adorno.

Uncannily, '*Fichus*' and *Hyperdream* rotate around and interpenetrate each other. Cixous covers her mother's Medusa-scorched skin with the semiotics of hopeless palliation in response to the perceived gift of death, a verbal formulation that in the present reading mimics Derrida's *The Gift of Death*, a profound meditation on the force of ethical responsibility in the face of often precarious life and its extinction. In parallel, he (like Cixous) treads a familial path in '*Fichus*', following in his father's footsteps and living-dying what it means to be *fichu*. He knows that death always wins in the end. This is why Cixous must search for him in her *hyperdream*. Moreover, in *Prismen* Adorno praises Benjamin for '*over[coming]*the dream without *betraying* it' in his approach to surrealism and related movements, since he for '*the last time*' joined 'mysticism and enlightenment' 'in the form of the paradox of the impossible possibility' (Derrida 2005, 168).[5] For Derrida, 'the possibility of the impossible can only be dreamed'. At the same time, Adorno's motto 'for all the "last times of [his life]"' (Derrida 2005, 168) shades into Cixous's distinction between the 'latest' (or most recent) times and 'last times'. Lastly – but not for the last time – Derrida meditates on his past and prospective work, highlighting his abiding interest in language and literature, an interest shared with Adorno, and one which has the capacity to 'critically decenter' academic philosophy' (ibid.: 179-80). This is at least one of Cixous's aspirations too, especially in a text such as *Hyperdream*.

Hyperdream powerfully encapsulates the work of mourning, with this crucial phrase again strategically echoing the title given to an English collection of Derrida's moving eulogies and memorial essays compiled in 2001. Cixous's novel, from its perspective, unflinchingly contemplates the loss of her close friend (now himself the subject of loving recollection), as well as the imminent death of her mother. If Adorno foregrounds the 'impossible possibility' of Benjamin's uniting the transcendent receptiveness of 'mysticism' with the rational scope of 'enlightenment', then Derrida pursues Heidegger's analysis of death as the 'possibility of impossibility' where *Dasein* anticipates itself (Derrida 1993, 66-71). As *Dasein* 'stands before itself' trembling, it must confront the possibility 'of no longer being able to be there' in order to be itself as temporally destined to the world (ibid.: 66-68). Derrida's radically meticulous interpretation of *Being and Time* constitutes the plural logics of the aporia *par excellence*, magisterially combining and simultaneously eroding all explanations in terms of 'closed borders', 'permeable limits' and 'impossible antinomies' (ibid.: 20-21), liminal terms which subtly call to mind the tensions between the pragmatic laws of conditional hospitality and the absolute Law of unqualified welcome. Yet this attunement to possibilities of impossibility is as palpably personal as it is a teasing theoretical speculation. In her punningly entitled *Insister of Jacques Derrida*, Cixous at once playfully and movingly celebrates her dead friend by re-enacting the sinuosities of his philosophical enquiry. At one point, she dramatises herself asking her mother for linguistic clarification of a crucial pair of German antonyms. Eve replies that '*das ist unmöglich*, it's impossible, it's not at all possible a hundred per cent. *Das ist möglich*, it's possible, not 100% out of a hundred' (Cixous 2007, 76). The exchange continues to sway back and forth, as Eve finds her penchant for scientific precision challenged.

> – *Es ist ja unmöglich*: so it's impossible. It's a word that allows several possibilities, you see. Es könnte möglich sein, neh? It could be possible, huh? . . . It's not possible. *Das Wort ist wirklich unmöglich*.
>
> (ibid.: 77)

So Eve gives up on this really impossible, too 'elastic' word. However, these perplexities are Derrida's element. Writing on a rainy Wednesday, Cixous's inner ear hears his voice pronouncing a signature sentence at a public gathering: 'Comment voulez-vous que je meure?' Derrida is musing on his lot or fate, but what can such a sentence possibly mean? 'How do you want me to die? / How can I be expected to die? / How ever can I die?' Or perhaps 'How is it possible for me to die?' (Cixous 2009a, 139). The speaker seems to be in love with himself and weeping for himself, yet weeping also for the love of self and the other whose 'tint of a desire for death' is 'tinted with a desire for life' (ibid.: 81-82). *Sero me et te amavi.* So late, too late, will I have loved myself and you. Does one die too fast or live too fast? The debate swirls through the elastically shifting intertext of Derrida and Cixous, which is equally the locus of a magnificently hospitable friendship without limits, yet shaped by singular identities that find themselves in acceptingly resisting each other.

Through her hyperdreaming, Cixous grapples in her own fashion with such persistent impossibilities, although she wills to make them possible-impossible. She slips across boundaries, seeing invisible doors, crossing to the other side – Derrida's side in death – and bringing him spectrally back to life. In following this route, she remains true to Derrida's perhaps disconcerting insight in his farewell tribute to the late Emmanuel Levinas: 'There would be no hospitality without the chance of spectrality'. Hospitality cannot be confined to accommodating phenomenal existence or qualities, but must be offered unstintingly 'to the *guest* as *ghost* or *Geist* or *Gast*' – although *Gast* is, strictly speaking, derived from a different etymology (Derrida 1999, 111-12). So Derrida is induced to appear as a *revenant*, the longed-for ghost which '*begins by coming back*', fusing his first manifestation with the force of the last time that so intensely preoccupies Cixous (Derrida 1994, 10-11). Nonetheless, these transitions burden her with feeling abandoned for extended periods of uneventfulness to a blank, alien world that is devoid of any response. She struggles immensely before she manages to achieve a fleeting reward. 'When *all is lost* I say to my brother, then and only then, when you are on your last legs [as the twin towers of the body], *fichu*, that's when salvation may turn up' (Cixous 2009a, 139). She has *at last* met her 'friend J.D. again' on 'leave' from the realm she denominates the 'hospital', playing on the notions of an institution for treating the sick, a dwelling place and the site of transcendent hospitality. Her encounter is attended by an 'off-white straw boater'; this becomes a monstrously magical hat, like the hat in Benjamin's dream, after passing through the form of her late father's panama hat, a semblance which her brother might just have turned 'into Papa's presence' (ibid.: 140-41). Through these visionary strategies and techniques, Cixous converses once more with the vulnerable shade of J.D., entering the space-time of 'our most intimate foreignness', as she calls it in *Three Steps on the Ladder of Writing* (Cixous 1993, 63). Refugees from both sectors of the mortal divide are granted haunting temporary reunions, while their crossings rely on the unfathomable contaminations of both the unconscious and the poetic imagination.

In *So Close*, published a year after *Hyperdream*, the intermediate zone encroaches on a (not quite) lost Algeria, when Cixous returns briefly under the healing patronage of Zohra Drif, with whom she has formed her long desired bond almost too late. After the liberation of Algeria, Drif had belatedly found recognition of both her suffering and her exacting political principles; she was elected to the Senate, also becoming an influential activist in postcolonial contexts across the globe. Cixous's visit to the haunts of the dead takes place in a critically qualified communion with her friend and particularly under the shadow of Eve's still impending death, which in significant measure motivates its conception. The entire enterprise, in practice, becomes a kind of Derridean *hauntology*, imbued as it is with 'discourse of the end' or 'discourse about the end'. As Derrida slyly suggests, such eschatologies can be comprehended (in the multivocal sense of the word) only 'incomprehensibly' (Derrida 1994, 10). Cixous's search for the Derrida family home assumes surreal qualities as she repeatedly circles the cemetery and, tauntingly, a garish contemporary pizzeria with the somnambulistic sense that the house is not where she knows it ought to be. Help arrives only at her 'last chance', when the oldest resident of the neighbourhood explains that she has been passing 'in front of [Derrida's] door' with her 'back turned' (Cixous 2009b, 132–33), thus reversing their relative positions at their first encounter. Even on discovery, the door remains closed, its threshold physically uncrossable. Here the liberating fluidity of dream logic is stymied by the lumpish rigidity of physical principles and social mores in the waking world.

The promise of the panama hat as a forerunner of her father's presence is equivocally fulfilled when Cixous locates his grave after a subsequent dreamlike succession of failures, misdirections and baulked attempts. Georges Cixous is buried near the landmark of a cypress tree or *cyprès*, which homophonically brings his daughter *si près* or 'so close' to her beloved parent; yet 'so close' is as ambivalent as 'too late'. Throughout her past, especially in her childhood, she had found him 'too big, too heavy, too dead' (Cixous 2009b, 152) He now appears 'small' and 'simple', with his immortality assured. In their aloneness together, her father's tomb assumes the contours of a surrogate body as Cixous's sinks into a reverie to match his own seemingly timeless musings. After being warmly invited into their former apartment in Oran, she hurries to a public scribe to draft a letter for Georges. The local Ovid, Hassan Naso (rather than ancient Rome's Publius Ovidius Naso), is also a master of metamorphoses. On the machine 'grafted to his bent knees' he types in capitals: 'LOVE IS STRONG LIKE DEATH, IF YOU ARE IN A FOREIGN LAND, THE FOREIGNER IS YOURS, YOU KNOW WHERE TO FIND ME' (ibid.: 141). The narrative doubles back into the spatio-temporality of 'intimate foreignness', while touching implicitly on Derrida's '*Comment voulez-vous que je meure?*' The answer is an ambiguously speaking silence, although Cixous now sees 'everything from the other side, as in the beyond-life, beyond-memory' (ibid.: 154). *So Close/Si près* is traced by the elusive absent presence of Georges. After completing this work, Cixous realises that the geographical Algeria has again denied her the reassurance of a stable welcome. Its imaginary counterpart becomes her 'hyperfunerary stele' or the tomb that 'keeps [her] in dreams, summing [her] up' in a poignant *hauntology* that displaces ontology (Cixous 2009b, 160; Derrida 1994, 10).

The Cixous of *Hyperdream* eschews facile consolations and reconciliations with equal force. 'Having descended with [Derrida] into the labyrinth', she admonishes herself that 'I can only ever find myself lost. . . . I never find save to lose, according to a law not my own but which, in my friend's tragic logic . . . creates a synonymy between finding and losing' (Cixous 2009a, 160). To 'remain faithful' to Derrida, she must become unfaithful, countering his disbelief in 'leaves' from the hospital with the strength of her own belief in order to persuade him against his will to accept what he wants both to endorse and reject (ibid.). Derrida may indeed have been *fichu* – lost, done for – just as the redoubtable Eve proleptically declares in equivalent German slang that she too is *Vutsch*, done for or *fichu* (ibid.: 160-61). At once because and in spite of these translinguistic gymnastics, though, there remains the texture of Benjamin's *fichu*, which transmutes itself into the *histos* of woven cloth or canvas, an analogue in its turn of scratched, scorched skin. This is the text of Derrida's 'Plato's Pharmacy' that the critic cannot read without touching, thus risking 'getting a few fingers caught' in 'the addition of some new thread' (Derrida 1981, 65, 63). Beyond this, the skin-*histos*-text is Benjamin's blue-trimmed sail of the letter *d*, which becomes caught up and interwoven with the diminishing proto-Penelopean web of *Veils*. In a near-despairing translator's note on the sheer homophonic and homonymic ingenuity of Derrida's response to Cixous's dramatisation of the post-operative unveiling of her myopic vision in 'Savoir', Geoffrey Bennington explains that *voiles* is the plural of *voile* as both 'a veil' (masculine) and 'a sail' (feminine) (Bennington in Derrida 2001a, 93). Derrida has become weary both of the dauntless philosophical quest for the verdict as *veridictum* or 'true statement' and the apocalyptic imaginary that trades in 'tearing, bursting, lifting, folding [or] unfolding' veils (Derrida 2001a, 41), always bearing in mind that the literal meaning of the Greek 'apocalypse' is 'unveiling'. He wants the absolutely unforeseeable decision to come from elsewhere, from the other in its otherness as a vivid enactment of the risky Law of pure hospitality. This train of poetic exploration leads him away from the veil, tentatively past the sail, to the shawl – not exactly a *fichu* but the *tallit* or Jewish prayer shawl. Moreover, it must be acknowledged that a *tallit* is sometimes striped in blue, not unlike Benjamin's hopefully suggestive *d*-sail (see ibid.: 43).

Derrida's *tallit*, nonetheless, is pure white, a gift from his grandfather Moses who derives his name from the recipient of the Law on Mount Sinai, a Law that repeatedly enjoins hospitality to the familiar Biblical characters of the widow (like Eve), the orphan (like the Cixous children after their father's death) and the stranger (like the rebuffed young Hélène in the Clos Salembier). This unique shawl must always be passed down the male line in a family. It comes to carry two principal associations. The first is blessing and loving inclusion, as when Derrida and his brother sheltered beneath their father's *tallit* to receive his benediction on the Day of Atonement. The second association is death, for a man is buried in his *tallit* (ibid.: 45). The permissible materials for making a *tallit* include silk and wool; if linen is used, the fringes must be sewn onto leather patches (ibid.: 67–68). The guiding principle in Derrida's understanding is that 'the tallith must be something living taken from something living worn by something living' (ibid.: 69). More precisely, it has been taken from something dead which was once living, and serves to bury the dead when they too cease to live (ibid.: 69). Wool and leather recall ancient animal sacrifice or the Hebrew *korban* which means 'approach', a 'coming together'. If there is any 'truth' of the *tallit*, then, it is not linked to revelation or unveiling. Rather, the singular gift of the Law, combined with prayer instead of sacrifice, provides an 'unterminated and perhaps interminable sublimation, the coming together of the infinite coming together in the orison of prayer' (ibid.: 70) – possibly an ultimate form of pure hospitality? This is why one can never get rid of a *tallit* (ibid.: 71). It reframes the relationship between life and death through a performative event of transcendence that outflanks both apocalyptic expectation and the philosophical verdict by engaging to approach the absolutely other. Derrida's imaginative figure for the practical-metaphysical genesis of a *tallit* is the silkworm that also lends his essay its title: 'A Silkworm of One's Own'. Before reaching the age of bar mitzvah and earning the right to wear a *tallit*, he had kept silkworms and watched their metamorphosis with fascination. The caterpillars would weave their cocoons out of their own bodies, secreting and enveloping themselves in the very silk that they became. This projection of their being outside of themselves also entailed the preparation of a shroud. In due course, though, the cocoon would soften to release the moth's wings, '*a moment of awakening as much as of birth . . . the moment at which the unforeseeable reappropriation took place, the return to itself of the silkworm*' (ibid.: 91). The rhythm pulses from creative life to death to life in transcendent free flight, like the traditionally hospitable orison of *tallit*-enveloped prayer, not unlike the escape of Cixous's pigeon from the grip of the Oran slaughterer's hand.

In *H.C. for Life*, Derrida ponders, half humorously and half regretfully, on the *tallit* which he cannot give to his dear friend Cixous on account of her gender (Derrida 2006, 158). Yet she already has her own *tallit*, although she has apparently forgotten about it. Derrida harks back to her first published collection of short stories, *Le Prénom de Dieu* [*The Forename of God*] (1967), in which a narrator plots the acquisition of a *tallit* bequeathed to her by her father through the impersonation of her brothers. The silk of the *tallit's* fringes conceals her name; 'I need only have taken hold of it and God would have woven me and all silence would have become voice' (as quoted in Derrida 2006, 156). There is a prescient anticipation of the unconstrained 'approach' engendered by prayer in 'A Silkworm of One's Own'. In the penultimate story, '*La Baleine de Jonas*', the Master himself falls silent and the seemingly androgynous disciple wraps him-/herself in silk (like a *tallit*), sitting 'in front of God's mouth, with the book opened in front of me'. This first person narrator reflects that 'God dreams us and in His dream He kills us and eats us. . . . His dream feeds on our billions of dreams. All dream so that God dreamexists' (as quoted in Derrida 2006, 157). Derrida glosses this passage by arguing that the existence of God is proven more surely by dreams than by 'onto-theologico-philosophical proofs'. God can be said to dream because He is dreamt by human beings with the intense 'pleading power' of the subjunctive mood and at 'infinite speed', so that distinctions between virtuality and actuality, 'the desire of the phantasm' and reality are eroded (ibid.: 157). The emphasis here is psychoanalytic and somewhat sceptical. Nonetheless, the ambiguously generative and potentially destructive power of transcendence is seen to create and to be created by us in the fertile projections of an active unconscious yearning for what Benjamin shyly terms 'spirituality'. The special powers of the *tallit* and the dream impregnate the dynamics of life and death, as well as the inevitable loss that repeatedly threatens meaningful existence. As Derrida wryly observes in his *Politics of Friendship*, 'Surviving – that is the other name of mourning whose possibility is never to be awaited. For one does not survive without mourning' (Derrida 1997, 13).

Even when Derrida and Cixous are not engaged in direct intertextual exchange, the plangent resonances of their mutually sustaining dialogue echo across their writing. In his Exordium to *Specters of Marx*, Derrida confesses '"I would like to learn to live. Finally". Finally what' (Derrida 1994, xviii). His reply to this rhetorical question turned statement is that 'learning to live', if such a project is still feasible, 'can happen only between life and death'; it 'can only *maintain itself* with some ghost, can only *talk with or about* some ghost [s'entretenir *de quelque fantôme*]. So it would be necessary to learn spirits' (ibid.: xviii). The focus of his book is justice and the haunting afterlives of Marxism, yet he has implicitly foreseen the role in which Cixous will cast him in *Hyperdream*. He has already prepared for her sketch of their fictional encounter in the space-time of 'our most intimate foreignness'. And he has urged extravagant hospitality to the mysterious guest as ghost, *Geist* or *Gast*, the *revenant*-cum-*arrivant* who fuses first with last, while opening the strange vista of an unpredictable future:

> Let us say yes *to who or what turns up*, before any determination, before any anticipation . . . whether it has to do with a foreigner . . . or divine creature, a living or dead thing, male or female.
>
> (Derrida 2000, 77)

Learning to live (finally) is inseparable from learning to die, from touching the spiritual and embracing mourning as the ambivalent tax of a transient survival.

For Cixous, the mourning of loss is poetically changed into the loss of mourning with the force of a double genitive. In one sense, mourning is overcome through dream-work, the promise of Derrida's brief revivifying 'leave' from the obscurity of death against debilitating counter-intuitions. In another reading, mourning imbricates perpetually painful loss from within the fabric of living. These ideas are encapsulated in a paragraph that functions as the epigraph to *Hyperdream*, introducing the aporetically charged 'last days' of Cixous's mother Eve, the original Biblical mother. With the disruptive intensity of a contrived pun on the French word *tuer*, Eve is conceived at once as 'being time' and 'killing time', 'tiring time to death' as she moves inevitably towards an alternative dimension of transcendence.

> It was before the end, *tu es le temps*, you are time, killing time, I thought, the time before the end. Never before had I seen such finished splendour. Suddenly, I was warned that I was approaching the point, I saw I could see life glow. It was everywhere. Its dying embers flickered.
>
> (Cixous 2009a, 3)

This fleetingly vulnerable vision of glory is aligned with Cixous's conception of survival as *survie/sur-vie* or abundant excess, 'life piled on life' as Tennyson describes it in 'Ulysses' (Tennyson 1974, 1–24), just to enhance the ring of mythological allusions. Writing, in effect, translates life into rich, poetically inflected mythic prose. This interpretation is mirrored in a secret of Cixous's fiction that Derrida mischievously discloses to the uninitiated after rereading *Illa* (1980). If Algeria has frequently figured as 'paradise lost', because Cixous's brother perceives 'everything we lose' as 'paradisiac', while she recognises the 'hell of paradise' (Cixous 2006, 69), then Algiers boasts its own fallen Eden in the botanical garden called the Jardin d'Essais (Derrida 2006, 151). Under the spell of disillusionment, it may be construed as the *jardin décès* or a death garden, fostering those carnivorous plants whose indifferent voracity first shocked and warned Cixous as a child (Cixous 2009b, 134). Yet a subtle homophonic metamorphosis or metaphrase will redirect this proper name 'to the origin of being, to the sudden emergence of "it is" [*c'est*] and of the *Esse* [Being, essence]' (Derrida 2006, 151). This phonological inventiveness is tied into another aural pun, here on *H.C.* – *c'est* – who is the champion of and activist for life, Derrida's affectionately dedicated friend for the span of his mortality or 'for life'. Her tireless capability for mourning through transfiguring dream-writing becomes the measure of her hospitality to the fecund middle passage between death and life, which celebrates life in the 'glow' of its 'finished splendour'.

Notes

1. As translator of Cixous's *So Close* (first published in French in 2009), Peggy Kamuf provides a useful note on the *lycée* system in Algeria, as well as Drif's role in the savage war for Algerian independence from France (in Cixous 2009b, 162-63). Judith Still offers a searching investigation of the Frenchalgeria (*Algériefrançaise*) of Cixous and Derrida in *Derrida and Hospitality: Theory and Practice* (Still 2013, 143-71).
2. In *Portrait of Jacques Derrida as a Young Jewish Saint*, Cixous includes a wry recollection of her brother's bar mitzvah as yet another symptom of the pervasive Algerian attenuation of any meaningful ties. 'My bar mitzvah! hoots my brother, what a joke'. Asked to recite one of the core prayers of Jewish liturgy, he repeats a few words followed by 'Blahblah'; nonetheless, he is considered to have performed competently in front of the 'shitty little synagogue maybe pretty'. On his way home with his grandmother from Oran, he says 'with my ritual subtlety risen from the depths of my rage: I hope we're having ham for lunch' (Cixous 2004, 116).
3. Compare Still's discussion of this encounter (Still 2013, 168-71).
4. Beverley Bie Brahic comments at some length on the difficulty of finding an English translation of *sommier* that will both provide an accurate description of the object and capture the multiply shaded nuances of the French term (Cixous 2009a, 165).
5. See also Adorno's 'A Portrait of Walter Benjamin' in the English translation entitled *Prisms* (Adorno 1997, 240), where the wording of these complex philosophical relationships is slightly different.

References

Adorno, Theodor W. 1997. 'A Portrait of Walter Benjamin'. In *Prisms*, translated by Samuel and Shierry Weber, 227–40. Cambridge, MA: MIT Press.

Augustine. 2016. *Confessions, Volume II: Books 9–13*. Translated by Carolyn J.-B. Hammond. Loeb Classical Library, 27. Cambridge, MA: Harvard University Press.

Benjamin, Walter. 1970. 'The Work of Art in the Age of Mechanical Reproduction'. In *Illuminations: Essays & Reflections*, translated by Hannah Arendt, 219-53. London: Jonathan Cape.

Cixous, Hélène. 1967. *Le Prénom de Dieu*. Paris: Éditions Grasset.

———. 1980. *Illa*. Paris. Éditions des Femmes.

———. 1991. *'Coming to Writing' and Other Essays*. Translated by Sarah Cornell et al. Cambridge, MA: Harvard University Press.

———. 1993. *Three Steps on the Ladder of Writing*. Translated by Sarah Cornell and Susan Sellers. New York: Columbia University Press.

———. 1997. *Rootprints: Memory and Life Writing*. Translated by Eric Prenowitz. London and New York: Routledge.

———. 2001. '*Savoir*'. In *Veils*, translated by Geoffrey Bennington, 3–16. Stanford, CA: Stanford University Press.

———. 2003. 'Letter to Zohra Drif', translated by Eric Prenowitz. *College Literature* 30.1: 82-90.

———. 2004. *Portrait of Jacques Derrida as a Young Jewish Saint*. Translated by Beverley Bie Brahic. New York: Columbia University Press.

———. 2005. 'My Algeriance, in Other Words: To Depart Not to Arrive from Algeria'. In *Stigmata: Escaping Texts*, with a foreword by Jacques Derrida and a new preface by the author, 126-41. London: Routledge Classics.

———. 2006. *Reveries of the Wild Woman*. Translated by Beverley Bie Brahic. Evanston, IL: Northwestern University Press.

———. 2007. *Insister of Jacques Derrida*. Translated by Peggy Kamuf. Edinburgh: Edinburgh University Press.

———. 2009a. *Hyperdream*. Translated by Beverley Bie Brahic. Cambridge: Polity Press.

———. 2009b. *So Close*. Translated by Peggy Kamuf. Cambridge: Polity Press.

Derrida, Jacques. 1981. 'Plato's Pharmacy'. In *Dissemination*, translated by Barbara Johnson, 63-171. London: Athlone Press.

———. 1993. *Aporias*. Translated by Thomas Dutoit. Stanford, CA: Stanford University Press.

———. 1994. *Specters of Marx: The State of the Debt, the Work of Mourning, and the New International*. Translated by Peggy Kamuf. Introduction by Bernd Magnus and Stephen Cullenberg. New York and London: Routledge.

———. 1995. *The Gift of Death*. Translated by David Wills. Chicago and London: University of Chicago Press.

———. 1997. *Politics of Friendship*. Translated by George Collins. London and New York: Verso.

———. 1999. *Adieu to Emmanuel Levinas*. Translated by Pascale-Anne Brault and Michael Naas. Stanford, CA: Stanford University Press.

———. 2000. *Of Hospitality: Anne Dufourmantelle Invites Jacques Derrida to Respond*. Translated by Rachel Bowlby. Stanford, CA: Stanford University Press.

———. 2001a. 'A Silkworm of One's Own: Points of View Stitched on the Other Veil'. In *Veils*, translated by Geoffrey Bennington, 17-108. Stanford, CA: Stanford University Press.

———. 2001b. *The Work of Mourning*. Edited and translated by Pascale-Anne Brault and Michael Naas. Chicago and London: University of Chicago Press.

———. 2005. '*Fichus*: An Address'. In *Paper Machine*, translated by Rachel Bowlby, 164-81 and 202-3. Stanford, CA: Stanford University Press.

———. 2006. *H.C. for Life, That Is to Say* . . . . Translated by Laurent Milesi and Stefan Herbrechter. Stanford, CA: Stanford University Press.
Heidegger, Martin. 1978. *Being and Time*. Translated by John Macquarrie and Edward Robinson. Oxford: Basil Blackwell.
MacGillivray, Catherine A. F. 1998. 'Translator's Preface: Translating Hélène Cixous's Book of Days'. In *FirstDays of the Year, Hélène Cixous*, translated by Catherine A. F. MacGillivray, vii–xxiii. Minneapolis: University of Minnesota Press.
Montaigne, Michael Lord of. 1893. *The Essayes*. Translated by John Florio and introduced by Henry Morley. London: George Routledge and Sons.
Still, Judith. 2013. *Derrida and Hospitality: Theory and Practice*. Edinburgh: Edinburgh University Press.
Tennyson, Alfred. 1974. 'Ulysses'. In *'In Memoriam', 'Maud' and Other Poems*, edited by John D. Jump, 44-45. London and Melbourne: Dent.

8

INHOSPITABLE LIFE

Security and migrancy in Atticus Lish's *Preparation for the Next Life*

David Watson

In *The Figure of the Migrant*, Thomas Nail argues that the 'twenty-first century will be the century of the migrant' (Nail 2015, 1). According to the United Nations Development Program (UNDP), there are more than one billion international and internal migrants in the world today, as well as many who are undocumented or irregular (UNDP 2009, 21-23). The increase in human mobility has drawn attention to the political, environmental and economic instabilities – what Saskia Sassen refers to as the 'complex modes of expulsion' (Sassen 2014, 1) – that dislocate populations. Such mobility has, furthermore, reshaped the political landscape and ignited volatile debates about integration, assimilation, statelessness, human rights and xenophobia. But as recent developments in the United States and globally have shown, the story of migration in the twenty-first century is indissociable from its securitisation, with the performative attribution of discourses of danger to the migrant frequently determining how migrancy appears within geopolitical and literary imaginaries. Focusing on Atticus Lish's debut novel *Preparation for the Next Life*, I argue that this text explores how questions about security have become constitutive of contemporary migrant experience. Linking security to issues concerning hospitality, mobility, dispossession and the figuring of the migrant as a detainable form of life, Lish's novel does not merely explore the contemporary politics of migration; it also suggests how such migrant narratives may be reshaped by modes of security governance and rule.

First published in 2015, Lish's novel (which won the PEN/Faulkner Award for Fiction) appeared after fundamental transformations had taken place in how the United States viewed migration. Supplanting security threats associated with the Cold War, the migrant was propelled to the centre of security thinking after the attacks in New York City and Washington DC on September 11, 2001. In the United States, the newly constituted Department of Homeland Security (DHS) subsumed the defunct Immigration and Naturalization Service, declaring that it would 'verify and process the entry of people in order to prevent the entrance of contraband, unauthorized aliens, and potential terrorists' (DHS 2002, 22). Bundling together within its policy statements terrorism, drug and sex trafficking, arms dealing and undocumented migration, the DHS appeared to make no distinction among these projected threats to the newly drawn configuration of the homeland security state; in 2003 the body announced a ten-year strategy to guarantee 'national security by ensuring the departure from the United States of all removable aliens' (DHS 2003, ii). Although this strategy proved to be unsuccessful, the responses by the DHS to the events of September 11, 2001 hastened the transformation of the United States into what Daniel Kanstroom calls a 'deportation nation' (Kanstroom 2012) within which the deportation and indefinite detention of undocumented migrants are normalised practices, while the homeland's borders are militarised and vigilantly protected (Miller 2014). Thus, the increase in migratory flows that appears to have made the migrant the exemplary figure of the present has occurred, together with the inflation of the threats presented by this figure, resulting in the securitisation of '"immigration" in general as an utterly decisive site in the ostensible War on Terror' (De Genova 2007, 424).

The Donald Trump presidency, which began in 2017, should be understood in relation to this long history of the securitisation of the figure of the migrant. Published prior to the advent of this presidency, *Preparation for the Next Life* likewise takes as its backdrop this reconfiguration of migrancy as a security concern, thereby positioning itself implicitly in relation to a global transformation in how migrancy is viewed, and explicitly with respect to how this transformation has affected a contemporary politics of hospitality. After all, the securitisation of migration in the United States is hardly unique to its practices and, indeed, asks to be viewed from a transnational, if not global, perspective. The figure of the migrant has become central to a global security assemblage since the end of the Cold War and a concomitant waning of national sovereignty under globalisation (Huysmans and Squire 2009, 169). The 'militarization of the European borderscape' (Vaughan-Williams 2015, 20) that Nick Vaughan-Williams has identified not only resembles developments in the United States but also, for instance, in Australia, where during recent decades questions concerning migration have become 'politicized and securitized' (Curley 2016, 202). But it is not simply a matter of different states adopting similar policies or utilising the same practices and technologies – walls, drone surveillance, detention centres, biometric data, whole-body scanning and algorithmic profiling – to regulate and curb the flow of migrants. In the first instance, contemporary security enclosures cannot be understood straightforwardly in terms of a return to the sovereign nation-state form. 'The new walls', Wendy Brown notes, 'are built to regulate, rather than impede flows' (Brown 2010, 104) by accelerating some forms of global circulation – capital, consumer goods, labour forces – while obstructing others. In addition, what appears to be a state-based form of security is managed by a 'transnational field of professionals in the management of unease' (Bigo 2002, 64), including governmental and non-governmental agencies, as well as consultants, corporations and private security firms. Moreover, the work of securing borders is articulated transnationally; borders have become less lines of inclusion and exclusion, girding nation-states, than contracting and expanding zones within which mobility and movement are securitised (Mezzadra and Neilson 2013, viii). For instance, the policing of the US border is not restricted to the hundred-mile zone stretching inland from the coastal and land borders that the US Border Patrol takes as its jurisdiction, but extends to the 'virtual borders of its "national interest" and the edges of its ever-expanding military-surveillance grid' (Miller 2014, 197), with airports in other countries frequently serving as a frontline in the war on irregular migration. Within contemporary security discourse, the migrant acts increasingly as a point of convergence for national and international security interests, as well as the actions of state and non-state actors, while the securitised zone through which the migrant moves has been expanded well beyond the official border zones of nations such as the United States.

This global shift towards identifying the often precarious migrant with the dangerous referent object of contemporary security discourse presents a problem for a politics of hospitality, as Lish explores in *Preparation for the Next Life*. As Seyla Benhabib reminds us, such a politics addresses itself to 'the boundaries of the polity', where what is at stake is 'regulating relations among members, strangers and bounded communities' (Benhabib 2006, 22). What relation of hospitality is possible when the stranger, the migrant, appears in view not just as a figure politicised by the inclusionary and exclusionary claims of the nation-state, but as a securitised figure who is to be deported, detained or prevented from entering the polity? Ash Amin offers a sobering answer: a security and risk-driven society is 'less accommodating in its selections of the subjects that count, indeed aggressive in its interventions to excise the destabilising outside and the stranger who calls' (Amin 2013, n.p.). For Amin, anxieties about potential catastrophes and threats have become normalised, shaping contemporary social relationships even while social bonds grow more impersonal. The migrant – but also the minority or the dissident – pays a steep price for this normalisation of insecurity as the governing logic of neoliberal life (Evans 2013, 2). The migrant is securitised, while movement – its forms, practices, scales, technologies, politics and material contexts (Blunt 2007, 684) – is increasingly regulated, that is to say 'organized around both the desire and ability to determine who is permitted to enter what sorts of spaces' (Kotef 2015, 1). Who may enter the nation-state? What patterns of movement are abnormal and suggest a potential security threat? How to manage the unwelcome stranger, the securitised migrant? Such questions appear to organise and produce the state of normality characteristic of contemporary migrancy.

While it is clear that the antithetical relation between security and hospitality is constitutive of the contemporary politics of migration, it is less clear whether this tension has informed critical discussions of contemporary migrant narratives, or whether such discussions enable us to make sense of texts such as *Preparation for the Next Life*. Consider, for instance, Caren Irr's genealogy of migrant narratives in which she argues that the 'twenty-first-century migration novel is moving from the discrete geography of nations to the overlapping and virtual spaces of communication technologies' (Irr 2014, 26). For her, the contemporary media infrastructure provides a potent allegory for twenty-first-century multi-directional global flows and suggests a mode of migrant writing that serves as an alternative to the earlier 'traumatic migration novel' (ibid.: 25), which depicted immigration and attempts at cultural assimilation under the sign of trauma. But the securitisation of the migrant indicates a migration narrative irreducible to the smooth flow of data across the globe or the traumatic passage between different cultures.

While the versions of the migrant narrative that Irr identifies may be understood as privileging either cultural similarities or differences, literary works like Lish's novel have been suggestive of a shift from the cultural to the political, in particular the politics of security, in making sense of migration. Rather than reading Lish's novel in the light of recent critical discussions of migrant narratives, it may be more productive to situate it in relation to recent literary works from the United States that have begun to trace the impact of contemporary security politics on migrants and migration. For instance, in Susan Choi's *A Person of Interest*, a Maths professor, Dr Lee, who has migrated to the United States from a repressive Asian country, is considered as a person of interest by the Federal Bureau of Investigation after a package bomb explodes at his department. During the course of the novel, the reader discovers that the culprit is a domestic terrorist based on Ted Kaczynski, the infamous Unabomber, who went to graduate school with Choi's father. In the novel, Lee's status as a migrant is intimately connected with his being targeted by the investigation. He has internalised the affective deportment marking him as a suspect – 'the immigrant's sense of hopeless illegitimacy and impending exposure' (Choi 2009, 6). His performance of the affects and postures associated with being placed under scrutiny and surveillance draws the attention of an FBI investigator. Also concerned with the conditions under which the migrant becomes a suspect, Dave Eggers's non-fictional *Zeitoun* relates how Abduhlrahman Zeitoun, originally from Syria, is incarcerated by the DHS in New Orleans in the wake of Hurricane Katrina. Zeitoun's incarceration is justified by using the most basic performatives of securitisation: 'You guys are al Qaeda' (Eggers 2009, 212) and, again, 'You guys are terrorists. You're Taliban' (ibid.: 222). Through these modes of address, the guards and soldiers reposition Zeitoun and his companions within a security framework which renders them detainable, potential threats, stripped of legal protection. *Zeitoun* begins with a depiction of an increasingly transnational America, but reaches a climax by unveiling its contingencies: 'Innocents would be suspected. Innocents would be imprisoned' (ibid.: 263). As in *A Person of Interest*, the securitisation of the figure of the migrant contorts the story of migration within an increasingly cosmopolitan globe into one with darker political vectors.

It may very well be that Lish's *Preparation for the Next Life* offers the most thoroughgoing examination of the politics of migration that we have thus far encountered within contemporary US fiction. It certainly deepens and intensifies Eggers's and Choi's engagements with the securitised migrant by locating this figure firmly within the variegated landscape of contemporary politics. In an online interview with PEN America, Lish links the novel directly to his disenchantment with twenty-first-century American politics, even while indicating the variety of reasons for this disenchantment:

> I am against censorship; I believe that far too many things are declared to be 'secret' or to have a bearing on 'national security' when no harm would be done if they were made public. I also oppose the Patriot Act, American torture, and the special category of 'enemy noncombatant' whereby someone can be deprived of protections as a POW under the Geneva Convention. I oppose the extrajudicial imprisonment of detainees at Guantanamo Bay. I oppose the War on Terror and the War on Drugs. It makes me uneasy to consider quite how many prisons and prisoners the US has. The private prison industry and its lobby disturb me greatly. The criminalization of illegal alien status following 9/11 is a disturbing trend; immigration detainees – whole families – are the fastest growing population, maybe the largest population, in our prisons, along with persons detained for drug offenses. America has been a great place for me to live so far, and yet I recognize that this is because I've been lucky. This country has authoritarian tendencies.
>
> (PEN America 2017, n.p.)

Lish's agonistic rhetoric spells out for us the social and political horizons of *Preparation for the Next Life*. In his account, the rise of the national security state, the conduct of the war on terror, the growth of the US prison industrial complex and the ongoing securitisation and detention of migrants are interlinked and intertwined with one another, and form part of the authoritarian narrative of contemporary politics.

The burden of articulating this complex network of disparate yet interrelated developments is divided in the novel between its three principal characters, from whose perspectives the events in the narrative are focalised: Zou Lei, Brad Skinner and Jimmy Murphy. Each character's narrative networks the novel's plot into the various concerns that Lish identifies in the PEN America interview. Zou Lei is the daughter of a Han soldier from Northwest China and a Uighur woman, belonging to an Indigenous Muslim ethnic minority living primarily in the Xinjiang Autonomous Region in China, which also borders such nations as Kyrgyzstan, Afghanistan and Kazakhstan. Zou Lei enters the United States as an undocumented migrant, crossing over from Mexico before she is arrested in a warrantless immigration sweep in Connecticut, a state forming part of the country's hundred-mile border zone. Released from detention on her own recognisance, she attempts to disappear into the migrant community in Queens, where she meets Brad Skinner. Raised in a West Virginian trailer park, Skinner is the traumatised veteran of three tours of duty in Iraq, two of them in consequence of the involuntary extension of his service; he has finally been discharged after a mortar round explosion left him physically and psychologically scarred. Zou Lei and Skinner's love relationship develops in the public spaces and work areas of the multi-ethnic, largely disenfranchised world of Flatbush, Brooklyn, but also in the basement room he rents from the Irish Murphy family. Jimmy Murphy, an unemployed construction worker who has lost his union status, returns home after a prison stint for his third 'Driving under the Influence' offence, a stint that has resulted in his contracting HIV. Zou Lei and Skinner's fruitless attempts at marriage and legalising her status in the United States are derailed by a violent encounter with Jimmy, which ultimately finds the two men dead. Zou Lei flees, drifting south to Phoenix, Arizona, where the novel concludes by leaving her as nomadic as in its opening pages.

A paradigmatic instance of the novel's engagement with questions concerning hospitality and security occurs in a conversation between Zou Lei and Tesha Noor, an Uzbek from Afghanistan. Tesha now runs a grocery store after migrating to the United States in 1999, the same year as the so-called July Offensive by the Taliban in which the militia attempted to seize control of the whole of Afghanistan. The conversation takes place in Tesha's grocery store, which has a front window sporting both a poster listing the ninety-nine names of Allah and a leaflet from the New York Police Department indicating what 'number to call' (Lish 2015, 317) in a case of suspected terrorist activities. Tesha's family is from Bukhara in Uzbekistan, which is separated from Afghanistan by a 'heavily fortified border with . . . concrete barriers and electrified fences' (ibid.), but linked by a mountain range to the Northwest Chinese region Zou Lei identifies as home. Once, the novel tells us, this territory was traversed by 'tribal nomadic herdsman who did not recognize the borders between nations' (16), but then the 'Chinese closed the border' (ibid.). Tesha's story of being separated from his family in Bukhara adds another fortified border to the history of enclosures in the region. Moreover, the regulation of movement in that area, the novel suggests, results in the curtailment of hospitality, which takes, after all, the mobility of people as its condition of possibility. So Tesha and Zou Lei reflect nostalgically on the hospitality of the Uighur before the closing of the border, as well as their generous 'treatment of guests' (318): 'Even if he has nothing, he is generous', observes Tesha of Uighur hosts. To this Zou Lei responds, 'Yeah, because if you are my guest, I will protect you. You are in my house. You are safe' (ibid.). Borders and the regulation of movements curb the possibilities for this kind of hospitality, but, as the conversation soon illustrates, this contraction is repeating itself within the United States. With the NYPD leaflet pasted in his window, Tesha narrates to Zou Lei that since his arrival in the United States he has witnessed how 'America is going down' (319). 'It's Homeland Security' (319), he tells her, for American Muslims are vanishing; they are being detained without trial by the DHS and deported to the Middle East, with families being separated in the process. While the novel invites us to draw parallels between this treatment of American Muslims and migrants more generally, Zou Lei and Tesha's conversation prompts us to engage with depictions of a situation offering no guarantee of hospitality, since security interests and the regulation of mobility have deprived migrants across the globe of protection and safety.

How should this curtailment of hospitality in the name of security be understood? Zou Lei and Tesha do not inhabit a global landscape of ceaseless, uninterrupted flows. Their conversation gestures towards traumatic encounters that have less to do with departing from a nation of origin and trying to inhabit a new culture, though those factors surely play their part, than with living under the pressure of a juridical and political order within which they are securitised as detainable and deportable forms of life. Rather than turning towards the two modes Irr takes as paradigmatic of contemporary migrant narratives or resorting to a narrative that takes culture as a central problematic within migrancy, let me suggest that there are two perspectives from which to approach this conversation: one would focus on the attenuation of hospitality brought about by the intensified security assemblage working on migrants; the other would single out for consideration the affective experiences and forms of social life produced for the migrant by this attenuation. The first would take as its starting point a politics of hospitality attentive to how borders and modes of belonging are regulated; the second would begin from the perspective of the migrant, asking what experiences of inhospitality contemporary security assemblage produce. These lines of inquiry intersect and modulate each other in important ways, of course; running them together enables us to resist capturing the migrant within a narrative that is solely the property of the nation-state, of its inclusions or exclusions, its forms of hospitality and modes of security. The problem here, as Nail puts it, 'is that the migrant has been predominantly understood from the perspective of states' (4), with the history and experiences of migrancy itself occluded by the investment of thinking in how to accommodate or regulate the stranger. This investment, as I will shortly discuss, is part of the story told by *Preparation for the Next Life*, but the same holds true for the experiences of mobility and inhospitality constituting part of the narrative of migrancy.

From the perspective of a politics of hospitality, the conversation between Zou Lei and Tesha identifies the United States with a conditional form of hospitality, which, as Jacques Derrida explains 'belongs to the order of laws, rules, and norms – whether ethical, juridical, or political – at a national or international level' (Derrida 2005, 173). Unlike its unconditional counterpart, conditional hospitality secures itself through various technologies of governance by setting limits to and regulating the flow of people (Honig 2009, 116). That is as much as to say that showing hospitality towards some people and particular kinds of populations becomes possible because the nation-state inoculates itself against the inflow of other, unwanted and presumably dangerous strangers. In the conversation between Zou Lei and Tesha, the name 'Homeland Security' condenses metonymically the governmental assemblage that restricts hospitality and mobility, and yet this assemblage too makes migrancy of a particular kind possible by producing a conditional form of hospitality. It is this delimited form of hospitality that is to be found in the September 2002 edition of *The National Security Strategy of the United States of America*'s policy document:

> In a globalized world, events beyond America's borders have a greater impact inside them. Our society must be open to people, ideas, and goods from across the globe. The characteristics we most cherish – our freedom, our cities, our systems of movement, and modern life – are vulnerable to terrorism.
> (US National Security Council 2002, 31)

The concluding rhetorical appeal to vulnerability serves to delimit the vision of an open society offered in the previous sentence, securitising thereby its promise of hospitality, yet keeping in place the imperative to partake in the global flow of people, cognitive labour, consumer goods and capital.

The stakes of this type of conditional hospitality, which is intimately linked to security discourse, can be clarified by turning to Michel Foucault's discussion of security in his lectures delivered at the Collège de France in 1977 and 1978. The lecture series on the *dispositif* of security, published under the title *Security, Territory, Population*, puts this *dispositif* in relation to questions of discipline and punishment, liberalism, risk and biopolitics. The lectures, as Michael Dillon notes, open the way for supplementing geopolitical security discourses, which are oriented primarily towards the defence of the sovereign state, with a biopolitics of security. Elaborating on Foucault, Dillon argues that a biopolitical form of security 'secures by instantiating a general economy of the contingent throughout all the processes of circulation which impinge upon the promotion of the re-productive powers and potentials of Life as species being' (Dillon 2015, 45). Working on the population understood as a statistical entity, rather than the people or the individual citizen, this mode of security concerns itself with the management of contingent events and risks so as to secure the processes of circulation necessary, in the classic formulation of biopolitics, for making life live. In this sense, a biopolitics of security is, in the first instance, not concerned with 'setting limits, frontiers' but with 'permitting, guaranteeing, ensuring circulations: of people, of goods, of the air' (Foucault 2009, 51). Security, from this perspective, works to enable freedom of circulation through the management of contingencies and risks, thereby rendering 'freedom . . . nothing else but the correlative of the deployment of apparatuses of security' (ibid.: 48). Returning us to questions directly concerning contemporary migrancy and its securitisation, Louise Amoore argues that within a biopolitical framework security is not a matter of blocking or interrupting circulatory flows, but of harnessing their contingencies through risk-calculations. 'In effect', she notes, 'the raison d'être of the contemporary risk calculus is to differentiate the good and the bad in movement, to deploy the details of differential norms and qualities of mobility in order to make a security decision possible' (Amoore 2013, 73). By tracking and analysing movements, as well as calculating their riskiness, the contemporary security assemblage differentiates between mobilities that should be acted upon and regulated, and those that should be left alone or even stimulated. Sorting between movements that should be allowed or disallowed, security emerges here as a means of regulating and structuring the limits of hospitality, joining mobility itself as co-constitutive of a conditional form of hospitality that consequently finds itself open to the interventions of a security assemblage geared towards ensuring a contingent form of free circulation. Security and hospitality, much like security and freedom, blur into each other in this biopolitical formulation, making it difficult, even impossible, to determine where the one ends and the other begins.

The co-implication of security and conditional hospitality shapes and produces the juridical and political environment inhabited by Zou Lei and Tesha. But from the perspective of the irregular migrant or the suspected security threat, what is encountered is, in the first instance, not a conditional form of hospitality as such. Appropriately, the possibility of hospitality is projected into the past by Zou Lei and Tesha's conversation, and associated with a nostalgia-imbued open territorial arrangement they have never fully experienced or inhabited. Such an inflection of the possibility for hospitality by the past reveals the present, in turn, to be evacuated of forms of governance or a public sphere that would extend them hospitality rather than viewing them as potential threats or detainable migrants. To put this otherwise: the state's relationship towards them is one of inhospitality, which may suggest that the security assemblage brought to bear on migrants today should be understood in terms of the production of inhospitality. As *Preparation for the Next Life* makes clear, the inhospitality produced by security is not simply the negation of hospitality, that is, its absence; it also denotes the social and affective forms of life inhabited by the migrant.

What form does inhospitality take? What form of life does living with inhospitality produce for the migrant? When Zou Lei and Tesha's conversation veers towards a discussion of the contingencies faced by migrant communities, contingencies that include threats of detention and deportation, they begin to suggest how the workings of a security assemblage reproduce affects of insecurity within everyday life. The insecurity associated with the life of the migrant in the novel is clearly marked in a passage where Zou Lei is released from detention and attempts to disappear into New York:

> She was never going to get arrested again. She was going to stay where everybody was illegal just like her and get lost in the crowd and keep her head down. Forget living like an American. It was enough to be free and on the street. She'd rather take the scams, the tuberculosis, the overcrowding. She knew how to get by. On the street, she watched the undercovers. The paper carried stories of deportations, secret detentions, prisoner abuse. A Morristown cabdriver of Syrian ancestry was thought to be held in the Metropolitan Detention Center in Brooklyn. The Federal Bureau of Prisons had a list of detainees, but not all its detainees were on the list. A lawyer hired by the family said a person cannot simply vanish.
> Zou Lei stopped reading and started doing sit-ups.
> I'll be fast, she thought. They'll never get me.
> All she needed was to make some money. Pay her rent. Eat shishkawap. The fresh air was free.
>
> (Lish 2015, 50)

While the passage gestures towards an idea of freedom predicated on the free circulation of people and goods, even 'air', the basic problem here concerns the foreclosure of Zou Lei's dream of 'living like an American'. This dream is hinted at several times in the novel: in China, she is told stories by her mother of 'a place better than any other' (19) where nobody suffers deprivation and everyone is free.

Later, while working at a factory where she, like the other Uighur women, is treated as an 'illegal immigrant' in her own country by 'Taiwanese bosses' (27), she is told to go to America if she 'wanted heaven' (28). To remain within the United States, Zou Lei has to forego the possibility of becoming American, or rather, of living in any direct relation with a community or state that can be understood as American. Here, the state is reclassified as a national security state, which is to be evaded to avoid deportation and detention – the risks of being dispossessed of an everyday life. Unmoored in a shifting sea of other migrants, Zou Lei surrenders herself instead to the everyday contingencies of migrant life concerning food, security and health in the name of maintaining and sustaining an ordinary life.

Laying claim then to an invisibility from the state, an opaqueness that makes her difficult to police and track, Zou Lei abandons herself to the potential deprivations of life within a migrant community that the state has already abandoned except as a milieu to be securitised. This community, in itself, offers no guarantee concerning her survival and freedom. In fact, there is no community as such, only a series of potential threats to her health and money, which nonetheless appear minor in comparison with accounts of detention, deportation and abuse by the national security state. Ultimately, it seems that all she can set against threats to her freedom is her body itself, her mobile body: we encounter her frequently in the novel running through the city, 'migrating along the backdrop of the buildings with parapets connected together like one great fortress wall' (45). 'Freedom. Up to the self' (179), she reflects later on, suggesting that migrancy for her demands an individualised form of self-reliance, rather than a community, hospitality or political mediation. Ironically, in the novel, Foucault's connection of freedom with the circulation of the population is transformed into an equation of freedom with the rapid movements of a singular body training itself to evade capture and danger – for Zou Lei, the minimal degree of mobility required for her own survival.

It is instructive to juxtapose the previous passage with Lish's depiction of Zou Lei's incarceration in the detention centre. The continuous, individualised mobility Zou Lei connects with freedom contrasts sharply with the feeling of stasis associated with her detention, a fungible stasis she is told the authorities can extend indefinitely (13). But what links the two scenes in the novel is the association Lish makes between security, the national security state, and dispossession. The threat Zou Lei faces in New York is that she will be forced to give up the life she makes for herself due to her undocumented status. When she is arrested earlier in a migration sweep, she is first divested of her possessions, while in the detention centre the absence of clocks makes her lose her sense of time, leaving her feeling that there 'was nothing at all except . . . her and the other females, in the loud, dirty sealed room' (9). Stripped of legal protections and denied bail, she is instructed that the prison staff 'could help themselves to more of your life. All you had to do was give someone a reason' (11). This threat of violent dispossession at once depicts her in terms of a liberal conception of personhood as property, a form of possessive individualism, and suggests that she can be dispossessed of this inalienable property at the whims of the prison guards. As it turns out, a self, deprived of personhood, resides at the heart of the detention centre:

> They showed her what was going on on the top tier, in the cell that no one ever came out of. They had a project they'd been working on. It was a woman lying in a bunk. The deputies gave her to us. We take care of her. Right after 9/11 they put her in a cell with like fifteen guys. She was in Al Qaida for real. I don't know how they could get it up because she's so nasty. Look at her. She's old. Zou Lei looked at the woman. She couldn't tell if she was breathing. They told her she was Lebanese, a mom. . . . Dried feces on the walls. Her feet were black, hair tangled wild over her face, going gray, going white. They threw wet toilet paper at her. Used tampons. A black girl screamed at her. Ugh. You stink so bad! And ran out cackling.
>
> (Lish 2015, 14)

The perhaps inescapable aporia we encounter in this passage revolves around its figuration of the self as property. On the one hand, the woman in the cell is rendered the property of another, with the guards claiming her and then passing her around like goods to the other inmates. On the other hand, having others lay claim to her body and life is a form of dispossession, divesting her of her ownership of herself. The figure of the self as a form of property underwrites both the expropriations the woman undergoes as well as our sense of the intolerability of the violence to which she has been subjected, of its transgression against her personhood. This violence, metonymically presented by images of human waste and the phasing of her hair colour from grey to white, dispossesses her twice over: first she becomes the possession of another, then she is divested of traces of human life, leaving it unclear whether she is alive or already dead. It would be a mistake, however, to read this figuration of the woman in the cell as already dead as the central point of this passage. In the passage, she is displayed to Zou Lei, with this display playing a role in the administration and securing of the inmates. 'This is how regimes of violence control people', Brad Evans and Henry Giroux argue; they 'individualize fear and insecurity. . . . Fear of punishment, of being killed, tortured, or reduced to the mere level of survival has become the government's weapon of choice' (Evans and Giroux 2015, n.p.). The woman in the cell provides evidence of the threat faced by Zou Lei – they 'could help themselves to more of your life' (Lish 2015, 11) – thereby at once confirming the invasive nature of the power to which Zou Lei is subjected and framing her as a figure who can be dispossessed of a claim to her own life, as well as expropriated to the brink of mere survival and beyond.

In reckoning with the problem of giving narrative form to migrancy, *Preparation for the Next Life* can be seen to engage the figure of the migrant, Zou Lei, via two contrastive vectors. The first associates her with a perpetual mobility, linked within the novel to the exigencies of survival and freedom. The second, which appears to arise from a desire to calculate the costs of her securitisation as an illegal migrant, associates her with the threat of dispossession: she faces the risk of being deprived of her freedom and possessions, but ultimately also of herself and her life-world. We can begin to make sense of Lish's engagement with migrancy by turning, first, to Hagar Kotef's account of movement, in which he makes the point that corporeal liberty, or freedom, means nothing more than 'the liberty to move without external impediments' (Kotef 2015, 67). Zou Lei invests her body itself with the task of delivering this freedom, thus setting it against a 'regime of movement, which drains movement into a security hazard to be tightly managed', what Kotef describes as a 'securitization of liberty' (Kotef 2015, 20). This securitisation is identical with what Lish depicts as the threat of dispossession.

A recent dialogue between Judith Butler and Athena Athanasiou on the subject of dispossession is useful for clarifying its link to securitisation. Early in their conversation, Athanasiou identifies a mode of dispossession that she describes in the following terms:

> [B]eing dispossessed refers to processes and ideologies by which persons are disowned and abjected by normative and normalizing powers that define cultural intelligibility and that regulate the distribution of vulnerability: loss of land and community; ownership of one's living body by another person, as in histories of slavery; subjection to military, imperial, and economic violence; poverty, securitarian regimes.
>
> (Athanasiou and Butler 2013, n.p.)

With a history stretching from land seizures to that of 'eviscerating' for 'certain subjects, communities, or populations . . . the conditions of possibility for life and the "human" itself' (Athanasiou and Butler 2013, n.p.), the violent logic of dispossession secures certain forms of life by displacing and rendering others vulnerable, thereby enacting in effect what Kotef calls a 'a securitization of freedom of movement' (Kotef 2015, 20). Connecting dispossession directly to the contemporary management of migrancy, Butler describes the regulation of unwelcome migrants as operating according to a double-logic: populations are restricted to inhabiting a territory of which they have already been dispossessed by social and political forms of violence, and simultaneously denied entry, for instance, to European metropoles because they are 'presumed to belong to another land' (Athanasiou and Butler 2013, n.p.) and are understood as threatening these communities. This double deprivation produces immobile populations which belong 'to no land' – in many respects the ideal form of population envisaged by the securitisation of migrancy. In *Preparation for the Next Life*, the two contrastive logics I have outlined here, within which freedom and mobility are co-joined and juxtaposed with an articulation of security that links it with dispossession and immobility, are embodied by Zou Lei. Her body itself brings together the promise of a realised freedom and the threat of being deprived of the conditions of possibility for making life live.

Instances of dispossession and mobility continue throughout *Preparation for the Next Life* to characterise Zou Lei's experience of her securitised environment. The persistent association with movement in the novel is that of flight, of fleeing to retain a degree of freedom. This impulse is apparent in her relation to governmental authorities. When Skinner proposes to marry her to resolve questions around her legal status, an immigration lawyer informs Zou Lei that she could be forced to return to China, even though she no longer has a passport, and would then have to reapply to return to the United States. Inquiries about obtaining a marriage license similarly result in her learning that she could be arrested because of her undocumented status, even though this is exactly the issue she is attempting to resolve. The impasses and blockages she encounters lead to a by now familiar impulse: 'She wanted to reject every solution that involved going through a government office'; she reflects, 'she wished she could reduce everything to the simple physical test of running away' (Lish 2015, 345). Ultimately, however, it is not from the government she flees. Alone in Skinner's room, Zou Lei is attacked by Jimmy Murphy, who bursts into the basement bedroom and flings her onto the bed. She runs, first 'barefoot in the street' (381), and then after deciding to 'keep going until the world ended or she ended' (384), she walks through the night, covering 'thirty miles, maybe more' (409). Skinner's death as a result of Jimmy's attack on her leaves her adrift. Heading south she finds herself in the Arizona desert, 'a greater desert than any she has previously known . . . she kept going across it in the nomadic way that was natural to her. If she expected to see anything, it was the graves of other migrants' (413). At the end of the novel, Zou Lei's trajectory intersects with that of undocumented migrants who cross over the US-Mexico border, a primary site for the continuing militarisation and securitisation of border areas. Her movements serve also as a tributary to the nomadic flows that borders seek to regulate but which, for Zou Lei at least, belong to a much longer history than that of national borders. With Zou Lei's movements suggestive of an entire history of migrancy in various parts of the world, it is appropriate that the perpetual movement of the nomad morphs here into a reference to 'the graves of other migrants', thereby yoking together for the reader the extreme forms of experiencing mobility and dispossession that the novel associates with migrancy.

Between Zou Lei's arrival in New York and her flight from Jimmy Murphy, much of the novel is dedicated to narrating the unfolding romance between her and Skinner. The relationship often appears to function as a displaced version of the hospitality the novel resolutely refuses to identify with the state or community, with this difference at its most apparent when Skinner suggests that if Zou Lei were to be arrested by Homeland Security, he would 'burn the fucking flag of this fucking country and wipe my ass with the ashes' (246). For Zou Lei, Skinner seems to be associated with the promise of safety and the potential for feeling at home: fleeing from Murphy, she imagines that she would run to Skinner's door, he 'would open the door with his eyes worried and when he saw her, his eyes would relax in that instant and the weight would fall off his heart. She imagined the relief and joy of embracing him in the doorway' (393). But her conditional, optative narration frames this scene of hospitality as a purely virtual account of the future. The obvious unreality of this proleptic narrative is suggestive of the deficiencies and absence of possibilities inhering in her actual life-world rather than the new possibilities associated with Skinner. Moreover, throughout the novel, she is haunted by the insecurity of her position as an irregular migrant. In one scene she dreams about US Immigration and Customs Enforcement agents coming to Chinatown 'in the new white Homeland Security trucks . . . checking all the workers with biometric scanners' (179). Predictably, her anxieties about Homeland Security circle around the unnamed Lebanese woman locked in the cell: 'What if someone locked her up again just because he thought it was his job?' she wonders, adding in terror, 'And then she saw the cell' (345). The woman locked in the cell prefigures for Zou Lei one of her own potential futures, their encounter proleptically mediating for her and readers the risks associated with her undocumented status.

What is striking about this strand in the novel's narrative is that it intersects with and modulates the narrative of Skinner and Zou Lei's relationship, rather than standing in opposition to it. She accuses him of treating her like a 'garbage person . . . because I'm Muslim people, immigrant' (331), suggesting that Skinner views her as disposable for the same reasons as she and other migrant populations have been securitised within the US. Moreover, on the morning of Jimmy Murphy's attack and after Skinner has left her, she imagines that she is locked in his basement room, wondering to herself, 'What if this was an isolation cell and you were never going to leave it?' (380). Strikingly, the threat looming in these moments within the novel is that of deprivation: Zou Lei is afraid of Skinner's taking away her freedom of movement and her claim to humanity. In other words, what occurs in her relation towards the security assemblage within the United States is reinscribed as a potential risk within her personal relationship. The novel resists divorcing the private from the social and political, instead treating the private and public as potentially homologous: the same threat of dispossession seems to circulate between Zou Lei's relationship with Skinner and her relation to the national security state, hinting at an equivalence between the two. This particular marriage of the private and public is never fully consummated within the novel – it is Jimmy Murphy, not Skinner, who fulfils the structural role of Homeland Security by threatening Zou Lei. Yet the novel does resist cordoning off a private sphere for this relationship, thus allowing it to act as a substitute for a politics of hospitality that would induct Zou Lei into American life. In the same manner as movement – what the novel calls the 'nomadic way' – provides a recurring pattern for depicting Zou Lei's experience as a migrant, the threat of dispossession saturates her life and the pages of the novel, providing a logic for imagining the precarious position of the migrant within the contemporary United States.

In a final twist, the novel leaves us uncertain whether Zou Lei's experience of inhospitality belongs only to her, or is shared, although in a different key, by Skinner and Jimmy Murphy. Early in the novel, as a prelude to his first encounter with Zou Lei, Skinner boards a randomly chosen subway train, riding it through parts of New York he has never before visited, going (as he puts it) 'all the way to the end' (71). With the novel emphasising Skinner's mobility, as it does Zou Lei's, it also shows him sharing her anxieties about forms of life that are dispossessed of humanity: fearing that his war experiences have stripped him of his capacity to care for other people, he reflects that the human body has becomes for him an assemblage of dehumanised functions because 'he had seen those functions turned inside out by high explosives' (204). Moreover, at a crucial juncture within the novel, Skinner becomes dislocated, with his war memories and New York bleeding into each other, blurring into a generalised theatre of war within which vehicles on the freeway appear from the overpass to be targets of opportunity: 'Imagine if this was Iraq right now', he thinks, 'You'd be lighting up all these cars' (206). The Iraq war effort provides him with the coordinates by which to establish his own position:

> past Manhattan . . . was his unit in the barracks, the guys in Warrior Transition, in the group rooms where their wheelchairs were placed in formation . . . out there, if you kept going and going, eventually was the war.
>
> (206)

Orienting himself in relation to the military infrastructure and the ongoing war in Iraq, Skinner, like Zou Lei, is expropriated from anything resembling a home or community.

Jimmy Murphy was once a 'union man . . . going down into the ground for the City' (160). Imprisoned, Jimmy falls in with a white supremacist prison gang, his 'family . . . monitoring the other races' (179). Like Zou Lei, his experience of prison is one of stasis; no matter how much he sleeps, 'it was still the same calendar day' (173). Returning to New York, he views it from the racialised perspective by which he was interpellated in prison, noting 'Mexican voices' (307), streets filled with shops run by and for immigrants, migrant Asian women working in the sex industry. He violently assaults one of them. 'What he was doing', the novel tells us, 'sounded like a boxer hitting a heavy bag' (310). The novel does not invite us to sympathise with Jimmy's violent racism, but the point I am moving towards is that there are striking similarities within its representational framework in the depiction of Zou Lei, Skinner, and Jimmy. The migrant, the returning soldier and the former prisoner – all figures intimately connected with the political concerns Lish raises in his interview with PEN America – share a sense of dislocation, of life as something that can be deprived of its value and humanity, and, perhaps overall, a sense of being dispossessed of a habitable and hospitable world.

Identifying, like Lish, commonalities in the experiences of the citizen and the migrant, Gregory Feldman recently suggested in *We Are All Migrants* that rather than taking citizenship as a normative category, it is in fact migrancy that is constitutive of modern experience. Understanding migrant-hood to refer to the inability to shape, politically or otherwise, the society within which one finds oneself, Feldman argues that 'in today's world people face common conditions of existence for a life experience proverbially understood as that of the "migrant": rootless, uncertain, atomized, disempowered' (Feldman 2015, 4). Dispossessed of the possibility 'to constitute themselves so that they can directly negotiate the basis of their coexistence with others' (ibid.: 11), citizens and migrants alike suffer in Feldman's account from a deprivation he associates with migrant-hood. The resonances between the experiences of Zou Lei, Skinner and Murphy similarly invite us to search for the equivalences between them, the moments when the migrant and the citizen – the illegal alien, the traumatised soldier and the violently racist convict – can be aggregated together and situated within a commonly shared problematic and existence, the instances where the instructions shaping their lives – the DHS, the military, the carceral system – emerge as perhaps unevenly related but contiguous systems of deprivation. Perhaps one such common condition is best approached through a conversation between Zou Lei and a mullah she encounters at a mosque where she goes for a free meal. He describes God to her as a host welcoming and sheltering guests, before pointing to a sign over the doorway of the mosque, which reads in both Arabic and English 'Preparation for the Next Life' (324). Before her departure, Zou Lei remarks, 'I have a long way home' (325). Rather than accepting the implied invitation, she thus transforms it into an injunction of sorts, a proclamation announcing an open-ended delay in the arrival home or the welcoming of the stranger, one which relegates hospitality to an indefinitely deferred next life. Understood in this fashion, the 'next life' appears as the temporal equivalent of Athanasiou and Butler's 'no land', articulating together with it the dispossessive, securitising logic that seeks to make the life of the migrant inhospitable. But the bleak irony with which *Preparation for the Next Life* leaves us is that Jimmy and Skinner, as well as Zou Lei, could have remarked, 'I have a long way home'.

References

Amin, Ash. 2013. *Land of Strangers*. Kindle edition. Cambridge: Polity Press.
Amoore, Louise. 2013. *The Politics of Possibility: Risk and Security beyond Probability*. Durham, NC: Duke University Press.
Athanasiou, Athena and Judith Butler. 2013. *Dispossession: The Performative in the Political*. Kindle edition. Cambridge: Polity Press.
Benhabib, Seyla. 2006. *Another Cosmopolitanism: Hospitality, Sovereignty, and Democratic Iterations*. New York: Oxford University Press.
Bigo, Didier. 2002. 'Security and Immigration: Towards a Critique of the Governmentality of Unease'. *Alternatives* 27: 63-92.
Blunt, Alison. 2007. 'Cultural Geographies of Migration: Mobility, Transnationality and Diaspora'. *Progress in Human Geography* 31: 684-94.
Brown, Wendy. 2010. *Walled States, Waning Sovereignty*. New York: Zone Books.
Choi, Susan. 2009. *A Person of Interest*. New York: Penguin.
Curley, Melissa. 2016. 'Australia's Response to Asylum Seekers and Refugees'. In *An Introduction to Non-Traditional Security Studies: A Transnational Approach*, edited by Mely Caballero-Anthony, 201-9. London: Sage.
De Genova, Nicholas. 2007. 'The Production of Culprits: From Deportability to Detainability in the Aftermath of "Homeland Security"'. *Citizenship Studies* 11.5: 421-48.
Derrida, Jacques. 2005. *Rogues: Two Essays on Reason*. Translated by Pascale-Anne Brault and Michael Naas. Stanford, CA: Stanford University Press.
Dillon, Michael. 2015. *Biopolitics of Security: A Political Analytic of Finitude*. London: Routledge.
Eggers, Dave. 2009. *Zeitoun*. New York: Vintage.
Evans, Brad. 2013. *Neoliberal Terror*. Cambridge: Polity Press.

Evans, Bard and Henry A. Giroux. 2015. *Disposable Futures: The Seduction of Violence in the Age of Spectacle*. Kindle edition. San Francisco: City Lights Books.

Feldman, Gregory. 2015. *We Are All Migrants: Political Action and the Ubiquitous Condition of Migrant-hood*. Stanford, CA: Stanford University Press.

Foucault, Michel. 2009. *Security, Territory, Population: Lectures at the Collège de France 1977–1978*. Vol. 4. Edited by Michel Senellart. Translated by Graham Burchell. London: Macmillan.

Honig, Bonnie. 2009. *Emergency Politics: Paradox, Law, Democracy*. Princeton, NJ: Princeton University Press.

Huysmans, Jef and Vicki Squire. 2009. 'Migration and Security'. In *The Routledge Handbook of Security Studies*, edited by Myriam Dunn Cavelty, Victor Mauer and Thierry Balzacq, 169-79. London: Routledge.

Irr, Caren. 2014. *Toward the Geopolitical Novel: U.S. Fiction in the Twenty-First Century*. New York: Columbia University Press.

Kanstroom, Daniel. 2012. 'Deportation Nation'. *The New York Times*, 30 August. www.nytimes.com/2012/08/31/opinion/deportation-nation.html (accessed 3 April 2016).

Kotef, Hagar. 2015. *Movement and the Ordering of Freedom: On Liberal Governance of Mobility*. Durham, NC: Duke University Press.

Lish, Atticus. 2015. *Preparation for the Next Life*. London: Oneworld Publications.

Mezzadra, Sandro and Brett Neilson. 2013. *Border as Method, or, The Multiplication of Labour*. Durham, NC: Duke University Press.

Miller, Todd. 2014. *Border Patrol Nation: Dispatches from the Front Lines of Homeland Security*. San Francisco: City Light Books.

Nail, Thomas. 2015. *The Figure of the Migrant*. Stanford, CA: Stanford University Press.

PEN America. 2017. 'The PEN Ten with Atticus Lish'. *Pen.org*, 11 December. www.pen.org/the-pen-ten-with-atticus-lish/ (accessed 27 April 2016).

Sassen, Saskia. 2014. *Expulsions: Brutality and Complexity in the Global Economy*. Cambridge, MA: Harvard University Press.

United Nations Development Program. 2009. *Overcoming Barriers: Human Mobility and Development*. www.un.org/en/development/desa/population/events/pdf/8/UNDP_OHDR_Klugmann.pdf (accessed 2 April 2016).

US Department of Homeland Security (DHS). 2002. *National Strategy for Homeland Security*. www.dhs.gov/sites/default/files/publications/nat-strat-hls-2002.pdf (accessed 2 April 2016).

———. 2003. *Endgame: Office of Detention and Removal Strategic Plan, 2003–2012: Detention and Removal Strategy for a Secure Homeland*. www.hsdl.org/?view&did=470051 (accessed 3 April 2016).

US National Security Council. 2002. *The National Security Strategy of the United States of America*, September 2002. https://history.defense.gov/Portals/70/Documents/nss/nss2002.pdf?ver=2014-06-25-121337-027 (accessed 2 April 2016).

Vaughan-Williams, Nick. 2015. *Europe's Border Crisis: Biopolitical Security and Beyond*. Oxford: Oxford University Press.

9

BEING A GUEST

From uneasy tourism to welcoming dogs in Marie NDiaye's *Ladivine*

Judith Still

Introduction to hospitality, animals and NDiaye

In this chapter I shall examine the question of hospitality from the perspective of being a guest: first as an uncomfortable European visitor in a strange land, and then, more radically and more optimistically, as the recipient of, or rather participant in, animal hospitality. I shall start with Jacques Derrida and Luce Irigaray and then move to *Ladivine*, a long novel by Marie NDiaye, which raises in an appropriately ambiguous form the relations between troubled human beings, trapped in the divisions of the economic, and dogs who here offer something different.[1] Fiction has examined the position of the guest more often than philosophy, which tends to focus on the responsibility of the host, who is assumed to be in the position of power.[2] Philosophy has also typically assumed an answer in the negative to the questions: Can we humans be hospitable to other animals, and, even more interestingly, can animals be hospitable to us?[3] Or philosophy has simply neglected to examine its assumption that animals are excluded. Taken seriously, these two questions unsettle both hospitality and the setting of the borderline between animal and human. How is hospitality understood such that *either* by definition, as for Irigaray, true hospitality occurs between human beings (although she defies the tradition that implicitly sets it up between men)? *Or* by definition is absolute hospitality, as for Derrida, an open welcoming that cannot even specify that the guest or host would be human? Derrida includes in the long list of questions that we ask about animals: 'Does it offer hospitality? Does it offer? Does it give?' (Derrida 2008, 63).[4] His work would suggest examining the symptomatic in any confident assertion that specifies man as uniquely economic and as uniquely generous and hospitable. In other words, instead of considering such statements as constative, the reader might enquire into the motivation or desire that drives self-flattering statements about what man is, and privative statements about what the animal is *not* – what is at stake?

These questions relate furthermore to the not-quite-human humans, those to whom 'we' need not offer hospitality, yet cannot imagine offering us hospitality, because they do not meet the criteria we have set. They fall outside the borders set up which, in limiting hospitality, are thought to enable it. Hospitality to and from animals is a limit case, on the margin of the question of hospitality, but the boundaries applied to the human have to be examined in order to analyse the foundations of any inequality. In 'Hostipitality' Derrida challenges another thinker of hospitality, and a friend, Emmanuel Levinas, over the boundaries of hospitality.[5] Levinas seeks to have the most open understanding of the hospitable relationship – but claims that it is b*etween men*. His preferred term – which he distinguishes from *semblable* – is *brother*. Here I remember that he was born in 1906, and even more importantly perhaps, is writing in French. Nevertheless this term seems symptomatic of a problem – of potentially doing violence to otherness as sexual difference. In this essay and elsewhere, one of Derrida's responses to this closure is to open up hospitality to animals. The argument can be made that this is ethically right in itself and/or that it is only by including animals that we can be sure of not excluding some human beings. In 1979 at Cerisy, Derrida will assert: '[W]e shall have to ask ourselves, inevitably, what happens to the fraternity of brothers when an animal appears on the scene' (Derrida 2008, 12). The category of 'animal' is created by philosophy (natural science is another story) as that which is not us; animals do *not* speak, reason, laugh, pretend, invent technology and so on. Thus there has been a long-standing philosophical and political debate around defining the human with and against the animal, and so constructing the nature of 'man' (a term used advisedly) in a way that has typically evoked a significant division, if not an abyss, between human beings and other animals. The consequences have often been devastating both for animals and for those presented, or, to some extent at least, perceived as, animals in human form. For however secure a frontier seems to be, it can always be breached for better or worse.

I shall approach being a guest with respect to two questions – the most fundamental is that of animal hospitality, but I shall pause on the relationship between tourism (part of the hospitality industry) and hospitality. Today it is as tourists that those from the developed world, usually described in hospitality studies as *hosts* – particularly hosts to migrants from less economically favoured locations, sometimes with a former colonial relationship – most often experience being *guests* – particularly guests of those living in less economically favoured locations. When those locations are former colonies there is a further turn of the screw. Relatively wealthy tourists may be treated to a spectacular welcome as an appropriate return on their expenditure on their holiday. However, tourists who report their willingness to be that most desirable of visitors – the repeat customer who passes on recommendations, building a solid and growing market – often celebrate a reception that goes beyond what they have paid for. What is perceived as genuine warmth and hospitableness, something which exceeds the emotional labour purchased, is frequently the element most praised by tourists once their physical needs have been met. Hosts in the broadest sense can get pleasure from acting as genuine hosts in accordance with their cultural practices or individual preferences – it can be a more dignified position than being a wage slave or a beggar. Generosity is a supplement to waged labour when a waiter or guide chooses to act beyond the paid role. However, the complexity of the relationship between economic exchange, which might involve a simulacrum of hospitality, and a direct affective bond demonstrated in gifts, services, invitations or simply words and gestures, can make visitors suspicious – eager not to be duped or even exploited. In this essay, I shall examine the failure of hospitality for anxious tourists who feel unwelcome; then when they are welcomed, they respond inappropriately – the consequent end to hospitality leading to violence.

In *Derrida and Other Animals*, I began an analysis of Ndiaye's *Ladivine* focusing in particular on sections of the novel which take place in France, as well as on the relationship between Ladivine Sylla and her daughter Malinka, who renames herself Clarisse, and between Clarisse and her husband Richard Rivière.[6] Relations between these characters are damaged by the gaze of others, structured by hypostasised race and class differences, and by the internalisation of that gaze. Clarisse has to escape a mother defined socially and labelled by her daughter as a paid and unpaid servant;[7] then the reader discovers through a scene in a café that the mother is named by Clarisse's employer as a 'Negress'. However, the guilt for having obliterated this loving mother from her story of her life leaves her reserved as *une serveuse* (the perfectly smooth image of a waitress, wife, mother).[8] She is reserved or *contained* as a personality, never losing control or allowing her emotions to spill out; at the same time, she is reserved, in the sense of held back, in what readers assume is a minimum-wage, albeit respectable, job in the service sector that echoes the stasis of her domestic role.

The 'gift' of money, a use of tokens for exchange often presented by philosophers as one of many behaviours that is uniquely human, is persistently shown in the novel to be an inadequate substitute for love and time, a failure of communication. This is the case whether a monthly payment is made to the mother or to the wife and however much or however little they may be in need of financial assistance – since they have been left behind. These points are not unfamiliar in the history of literature. What is less typical in her rewriting of recurrent human anxieties is NDiaye's evocation of dogs to suggest some other kind of exchange of looks, rather than a hypostasising gaze, and some other kind of caring relation over time. Hospitality in the figure of the dog is an illuminating gift that allows others to act as hosts and guests. Ladivine Sylla and Richard Rivière finally meet at the end of the book, *with* a/the 'large brown dog' ('le grand chien brun').[9] In this essay, however, I shall focus on the long section of the novel that takes place in an unnamed foreign location (a very hot country), where Clarisse's daughter Ladivine, named after the grandmother she does not know, takes a holiday with her German husband Marko Berger and their two children.

The novel is organised by a complex series of flashbacks, or reflections by characters on past episodes, while the action moves between precise locations in Europe and this unknown land that may, or may not, be an African country formerly colonised by the British. The European episodes of the novel take place in the Île de France (near Paris), Bordeaux, Langon (a town in the Gironde *département* in southwestern France), Annecy (Savoy) and Berlin. Within these geographical spaces, where the characters live out their daily lives, the reader is given detailed points with which to map their journeys, for instance a shopping trip to Galeries Lafayette, a well-known department store in Bordeaux. In Berlin the key department store for the family is Karstadt, first the branch in Hermannplatz and then the one in Wilmersdorfer Strasse, Charlottenburg – places of work and consumption. In the unknown land no places and few characters have names; notable exceptions are the hosts, a local teenager called Wellington and a wealthy French couple, the Cagnacs.

This section of the novel is focalised by Ladivine, who may be considered an unreliable narrator in that she is flooded by feelings of guilt and images of her mother's violent death at the hand of her lover three years earlier. An only daughter's guilt at failing her lonely mother recurs across the generations in the novel: Clarisse denies her mother, and leaves her unable to act as host or guest to Clarisse's family; a good cook, she is not even allowed to bake treats for her grandchild. Ladivine moves to Berlin and does not support her mother when her father leaves; her husband and children do not visit Clarisse, although she is at least allowed to visit her adored grandchildren. Ladivine could be understood as depressed, her perceptions doubtful, her behaviour pathological, her mourning become melancholia. Her role in her mother's murder (which, she feels, inhabits her like an unwanted pregnancy) is at the edges of her consciousness. The reader knows that it is Ladivine's cold rejection of her mother's socially undesirable lover that was a trigger for his violence towards Clarisse, who had unconditionally welcomed him into her home and into her hospitable mother's home – the first time she felt able to invite someone to her mother's flat. The beautiful yellow dress that Ladivine bought on a shopping trip with her mother on her fateful last visit, a present Clarisse encourages her to buy for herself when she wanted to do her duty and purchase Clarisse a birthday gift, becomes a motif or linking thread in this section. Yet, alongside any theory that would explain away the welcoming dogs by disordered human perceptions, I would retain the possibility of animal-human hospitality.

Hospitality could be defined as a structure of welcoming difference, even if that is both too vague and too exclusive. NDiaye's name and the skin colour visible in photographs, in spite of what she describes as a typically French upbringing in 'la France profonde' by her French mother without her Senegalese father, have shaped her critical reception to a striking degree. Even critics who do not want to reduce this gifted stylist to someone who is damned if she does engage with racial difference in the postcolonial world and certainly damned if she does not, are likely to refer to this question if only to refute it (see for example Asibong 2013). From my perspective, whether or not it is ethnicity which is at issue, it is certainly clear that (in)hospitality is at issue, the refusal to welcome someone seen to be 'different'. In this chapter I shall focus on hospitality between those who, at the very least, do not share the same language or culture, at most involving a different species.

Famously, in French the common term for host is the same as the common term for guest (*hôte*). Many of the best-known writers on hospitality in French draw attention to this linguistic equivalence, not only Derrida, but also Anne Gotman and, more recently, Luce Irigaray.[10] There is no such mirroring in English, and so no such implicit drawing towards reciprocity in the act itself. However, we Anglophones can still find linguistic *aide-mémoires*: 'welcoming' is a present participle that can be used as an adjective. If we read 'welcoming' in 'welcoming animals' as a present participle, then this expression refers to the hospitality that is extended to animals. If 'welcoming' is treated as an adjective then it is animals that are hospitable. It is important to retain this double meaning of 'welcoming animals' that does not enforce reciprocity, but rather embodies a simultaneous opening to and from the other. However, this simultaneity is momentary: as soon as the phrase goes into a sentence, the possibility of placing the verb in the singular (if 'welcoming' is a participle: 'welcoming animals *is* a good thing – we enjoy welcoming animals into our home') or the plural (to agree with animals: 'welcoming animals *are* a good thing – dogs are often considered to be welcoming animals, greeting you as you walk through the door') removes the helpful ambiguity even before a complement is established. This kind of mutually reinforcing linguistic structure is often celebrated in French via the double genitive; both Jacques Derrida and Hélène Cixous discuss *l'amour du loup*, both the love felt by the wolf for another and the love for the wolf felt by another (Still 2015, 110-81). Moving away from an exclusive either/or structure allows the possibility of both/and, through which, for instance, the guest hosts the host by enabling the host to be a host – this will be animal hospitality as I find it in the figure of the dog in *Ladivine*.

The plurality in 'welcoming animals' should be heard as a collection of singularities, of singular animals, rather than as a universal plural covering all animals, which might lead the reader towards the reification of 'the animal' set against 'man'. To make this particularly specific, I am taking the example of an animal whose symbiotic relation with humans, welcoming and being welcomed, has a particularly long history: dogs. Instead of travelling through history and into prehistory to ask questions about whether domestication can be mutual rather than a process of enslavement, or in lieu of travelling through philosophy to investigate dogs from Plato to Levinas, I shall shortly turn to fiction as a place where dogs might figure hospitality in a particularly inhospitable world.

Hospitality as reciprocity: Luce Irigaray

The question of *reciprocity* is extremely important in Irigaray; this might even be *assumed* in the very title *Sharing the World* – except for our readerly insistence on returning to ourselves as the powerful (even if, perhaps especially if, guilty) subject, the one who has the power to share, even share out.[11] Neither the father who controls resources and allocates to each his part (keeping the lion's share for himself), nor the long-suffering mother baking the cake, sharing it out (keeping the smallest share for herself), would fit the Irigarayan dream of what could be. In the face of critical resistance to reciprocity today, it is important to draw out the implications of what Irigaray means by *sharing the world*. Reciprocity for Irigaray is above all human, experienced between two differently sexuate beings; nevertheless, she leaves in suspense the possibility of some kind of hospitable relation with animals that goes beyond the kindness of men.

Irigaray insists upon dialogue as one element of reciprocity; however, this is not only about the *logos* unique to men. In a dialogue each interlocutor will spend time silent, as a precondition of welcoming; each will spend time offering thoughts and responding to the other. She writes:

> The first word that has to be said to each other by way of welcome is our capacity for remaining silent. This sign of welcome shows that each one accepts to leave the circle of one's own discourse – or usual house of language – in order to listen to what the other wants to say, wants to address to him or her, from a horizon of language that is unknown to them.
>
> (Irigaray 2013, 48)

How do we think of reciprocity in a situation of real inequality? Forms of hospitality and communication with animals raise this question in an acute form. Traditional and classical models of hospitality have always referred to reciprocity (see for example Benveniste 1969, 88-91) and Homeric hospitality often assumes guest-friendship. This does not have to be immediate reciprocity: there can be a very significant time lag, even over generations, but there must be an implied promise of reciprocity. For Irigaray, '[e]ach subject alternately ought to occupy or assume the two poles so that hospitality can be potentially reciprocal and not reduced to a bipolar relationship between dominant-dominated, acting-acted, superior-inferior, but also nature-culture, body-spirit' (Irigaray 2013, 50). I would note her writing that 'hospitality ought to be – or can be – potentially reciprocal', which is an important distinction from 'is reciprocal'. In Irigaray's account, the other must not be considered as needy; her focus is less on material need than on emotional or spiritual desire. The other is not defined as lacking, but rather considered also for what they offer. We should not reduce the other to their need, although we must surely respond to a need – while perhaps always seeing what the guest brings. One problem with the theoretical assumption that the writer and reader are in the powerful position of host is that this leads to what Irigaray describes as charity inspired by mere moral obligation, with the would-be host behaving like a superior with an abstractly ideal attitude (ibid.: 51).

Much writing on hospitality since 1945 has, however, been fascinated by so-called absolute hospitality which absolutely rejects any element of the economic, taking that rejection of economy to the extreme point of refusing any return. This has gone alongside a persistent focus on the figure of the host as the one who must be completely open to the other, not even expecting a guest to arrive and certainly not imagining any reciprocity. This unexpected guest is imagined without any qualities, properties or property, naked. Derrida's hyperbolical Law of hospitality lies beyond debt, exchange or economy and thus even reciprocity, yet its relation to the laws of hospitality (the ethical code found, say, in Homer) is simultaneously one of mutual perversion and one of mutual need. However, many modern readers are fascinated by the absolute Law of hospitality and forget Derrida's point about the need for laws. This impossibilism can lead readers to wallow in the conviction that there is no true hospitality, focusing largely on their guilt concerning the suffering poor, especially (in postcolonial theory) those of another race.

Irigaray and animal hospitality

Like most philosophers, Irigaray suggests that certain traits are specifically human, and in *Sharing the World* and 'Toward a Mutual Hospitality', she sets out what would be properly human hospitality, asking: '[I]s this not always what is at stake with human being?' (Irigaray 2008, 43) She writes that: 'reproducing is not specifically human, unlike the aptitude for transforming sexual attraction from instinctive attraction, including procreative instinct, into desire and love respectful of our difference(s) and into cultural creation thanks to such difference(s)' (Irigaray 2013, 45). According to Irigaray, we need to discover what is really proper to us, for opening one's world 'calls for the capacity to return home' (ibid.: 52). Here, home, as she elaborates, is not a country or language but the more original identity shared by the whole of humanity, the universal two: man and woman. 'Humanity is differentiated in itself and it is such a difference that makes possible a world culture of hospitality without any fusion or confusion, complementarity, domination, or subjection of one with respect to the other.' We need to cultivate our own identity *and* the relation with the other in respect for our difference(s), beginning with gender (ibid.: 52). Furthermore, linguistic and other gestures with a view towards a mutual hospitality should, Irigaray argues, be invented by each one during the time of meeting – not from already existing civilisations – thus as human beings we would be transforming ourselves into works of art (ibid.: 51). This raises the problem of uniquely human language. Animals are traditionally represented as lacking relative to man and not only lacking conceptual language or reason but also creativity, although Irigaray's references to gesture and silence perhaps open her argument to a broader sense of communication.

Irigaray's opposition to showing charity, giving material, parental hospitality to someone considered inferior, more child-like, more lacking (ibid.: 46) is certainly relevant in terms of animals. Feeling sorry for suffering animals is one model privileged today by animal rights activists. While most philosophers of the past (Aristotle, Descartes and Heidegger, for example) are condemned by today's animal rights philosophers for their assertion of an abyss between man and animal, the work of Jeremy Bentham has been much praised. His turning the debate away from reason has indeed a real strength when pitted against the argument that it is acceptable to hurt or eat those, like chickens, who are deemed more stupid than ourselves. In his *Introduction to the Principles of Morals and Legislation*, he writes: 'The question is not, Can they *reason*? nor, Can they *talk*? but, Can they *suffer*?' (Bentham

1823, 311) The movement from the tradition of judging animals negatively for their assumed lack of reason or language, to urging the reader to focus on their capacity for suffering, is a significant leap forward for an Enlightenment philosopher. Nevertheless, Bentham in this instance, like his followers today, is defending animals by presenting them as pitiful.[12]

One aspect of the originality of Irigaray's work on this is that she is interested in what animals might offer to us on an emotional or spiritual level and not only in our need to look after animals. What an animal can give is perhaps something different from what a human being might provide, both more and less. And animals vary hugely – what a domesticated dog might offer to a human (after centuries of learning to communicate between species) is different from what an ape might offer or a butterfly might offer. In Irigaray's essay 'Animal Compassion' (2004), animals – and especially birds – look upon human suffering with compassion in fleeting encounters, seeming to understand, in the anecdotes she relates, when she is sad and in need of cheer. Importantly, the relationship is not about possession, possessions or appropriation. The language of hospitality is crucial for Irigaray, as well as pertinent to thinking about animals; it is not about the direct relation ('I feed you', 'I shelter you'), but the indirect hospitable 'to' or the reciprocal 'with' of sharing.

NDiaye's *Ladivine*

Hospitality and inhospitality in the section of *Ladivine* that takes place in an unknown land are experienced in three ways: first is the general situation of the tourist as stranger in a foreign land; within that context are a series of microsituations in the hotel, on a bus, driving in a hired car, in a museum – typical tourist experiences. Second, there are more particular encounters: on two occasions the Bergers are invited to eat or stay overnight by locals, in one case natives and, in the other, French incomers. Third is the sole instance of true hospitality: this is the radical welcome extended by the large brown dog to the grieving Ladivine.

The family had never before taken a holiday outside Germany, their homeland; even more strongly within the circle of the familiar, the *semblable*, they had always returned to the same modest place and to Marko's parents. Although Marko's potential for looking outside the circle has already been demonstrated by his marriage to a French woman, this decision to resist his parents' economic expectations for the first time is a significant and scarily expensive break with the everyday. Hopes are high: Ladivine considers they have nothing in common with those who 'were only expecting the usual profit from their holidays abroad' ('n'attendaient de leurs vacances à l'étranger qu'un profit ordinaire', NDiaye 2013, 161). However, as the epitome of insecure visitors, they will not be easy guests. Marko worries that their trip could became an 'example of the dreadful way in which the most naïve tourists let themselves be rooked' ('l'exemple de la manière affreuse dont se faisaient rouler les tourists les plus crédules', 160). His internet research before booking the holiday increases his anxiety, and he despairs at the thought of being unable to 'escape the lying and cheating' ('échapper au mensonge et à l'arnaque', 161), displaying 'ferocious determination not to be duped' ('la farouche volonté de ne pas se faire avoir', 162) as he imagines his parents' satisfaction at his failure. The greater the psychic investment, the greater the fear of this unknown which they have desired.

Unwelcome tourists

Passing encounters with other human beings in 'this unknown city' ('cette grande ville inconnue', NDiaye 2013, 155) are marked by inhospitality ranging from the casual to the extraordinary, almost a parody of Western terror of venturing off the beaten track and into hostile territory; however, no major harm comes to the visitors with the possible (albeit unlikely) exception of Ladivine's disappearance. Marko and the children fear going out and do not enjoy staying in; the hotel is not like the image in the brochure. The first disappointment is that their cases are stolen at the airport, and no one is interested in helping them. The clothes from the missing cases (and also clothes left in Berlin) reappear for sale by a woman wearing the yellow gingham dress that Ladivine bought in Bordeaux. The woman explains that she made the dress herself, that: 'The French copy everything we make' ('Les Français, ils copient tout ce que nous faisons', 230). The impossible is a literalisation of a figural inhospitality, mendacity and theft to the point of stealing clothes that they did not even bring.

NDiaye repeats the term 'unknown' (*inconnu*), which applies both literally and figuratively; by not naming the country, the city, or any landmarks, she ensures that these remain unknown, so that any reader, however well-travelled, also has the experience of not knowing, of not being able to orient herself, thus mirroring the experience of the characters in their anxious confusion.[13] The stranger's question, 'Where am I?', is never answered. The extraordinariness of the inhospitality is largely in the atmosphere – meteorologically hot but affectively cold. The adjectives 'cold' (*froid*) and 'closed' (*fermé*), together with a series of related terms, build up a deeply depressing image of the visitors' experience in ludic opposition to the hospitality industry's seeking to gain a competitive advantage by emulating a warm, open-hearted welcome. The holiday is in a thoroughly inhospitable environment, in a 'town in reality cold' ('une ville en réalité froide', 226), so unlike the image painted by the guidebook they bought in a Germany of decadent prosperity and exotically casual poverty. Marko is such a 'negligible intruder into this harsh and closed environment, he was perhaps asking himself what he was doing there' ('négligeable intrus dans ce milieu âpre et fermé, il se demandait peut-être ce qu'il était venu faire là', 226-27). Ladivine's experience, however, differs from that of her husband and children; she is recognised and welcomed by the stray dog of whom they are oblivious. The city is confusing in its topography; this is again both a common tourist experience, and possibly an authorial indication of state of mind. The distance from Wellington's house to their hotel seems short to Ladivine, when accompanied by her faithful friend; Marko proves, with masculine rationality, that it is long. His wife, he says, has 'exaltation, imposture, in short aberration' ('l'exaltation, de l'imposture, en un mot de l'aberration', 255) to fall back on – this is his interpretation of her behaviour as a guest, trying to respond to what she imagines is asked of her.

In inhospitable tourist locations, hotels for Western visitors sometimes make a special effort to be welcoming, cocooning visitors from any potential hostility, or even importuning, beyond the gate. The hotel in *Ladivine*, however, is a place, or even non-place, of gloom rather than cheer. The swimming pool, that staple of holiday brochures as a focus for pleasure in the sun, is heavily chlorinated and makes even the children grumpy and bored. The reader is left to worry whether the excessive use of bleach is to protect (seemingly unwelcome) guests from germs or whether it is a prophylactic response to potential contamination from the guests, rather like putting plastic under the sheets on beds, a sure sign of the expectations about their occupants. It is not only the Berger family who are sunk in gloom:

> A similarly closed and miserable expression would distort the faces of the few elderly people who also used to swim each morning in the little pool and who would never respond to Ladivine's timid greeting, pretending not to notice. . . . It was as if fate had condemned them to spend a hellish eternity in the confined space of the hotel and the pool.
>
> (Une semblable expression fermée et chagrine contractaient les visages des quelques vieilles gens qui se baignaient chaque matin également dans la petite piscine et qui jamais ne répondaient, feignant de ne pas le remarquer, au timide salut que leur adressait Ladivine. . . . Il semblait que le sort les eût condamnés à passer une infernal éternité dans l'espace clos de l'hôtel et de la piscine.)
>
> (267-68)

These elderly white-fleshed individuals never reply to the greetings of staff or fellow guests, as though these people were responsible for their martyrdom. The motif is thus one of imprisonment rather than hospitality: the children are grateful to be allowed out of the pool. When the family leaves the hotel, there is no exchange of looks, let alone smiles, with the staff; the manager looks disgusted, and does not reply to Ladivine's nod.

The Bergers, however, are not only unwelcome but discourteous guests in a downwards spiral which makes it difficult to determine causal antecedence. When they flee the city, Marko displays a complete lack of care for local drivers as he enjoys speeding in his powerful and luxurious, hired 4x4 jeep, a mark of superiority closely linked to Ladivine's father. As he overtakes rusty little old cars and over-loaded lorries, 'the driver would sometimes make an exceptionally aggressive gesture at Marko' ('le conducteur adressait parfois à Marko un vigoureux signe d'inimitié', 284). Wheels are a human invention (technology is part of the hominisation of man), a substitute for feet or paws, but without this luxury the 'dog' travels great distances in order to be with the one he cares for.

Two invitations

On two occasions the Berger family are entertained by locals; in both cases there is a move from the hope of hospitality to the death of hospitality. The first example is that of the teenager Wellington, 'open, friendly as no one in that city had ever been towards them up to that point' ('ouvert, amical comme personne ne l'avait encore été avec eux dans cette ville', NDiaye 2013, 234), who seemed to be waiting for them on the threshold of the culturally emblematic National Museum. It is not only that the boy is seductive, but that

> they felt alone and fragile in these places where their very appearance seemed to be a legitimate reason for an attitude of indifference, if not suspicion or cold hostility, towards them, which, as they were not used to this, they weren't happy about it, being keen basically to be recognised and appreciated as the good people that they had reason to think themselves.
>
> (ils se sentaient seuls et fragiles en ces lieux où leur simple aspect semblait être un légitime motif d'indifférence à leur égard, voire de méfiance ou de froide hostilité, et n'y étant pas accoutumés ils ne s'y faisaient pas bien, désireux au fond d'être aimés, d'être reconnus et appréciés comme les bonnes personnes qu'ils pensaient être à juste titre.)
>
> (234)

The postcolonial 'return gaze' makes a diptych with the racist gaze evoked in France by Ladivine's grandmother. Initially cautious, suspecting that this is really an economic transaction and that they will need to give Wellington money, Marko betrays the Western tourist's anxiety about different conventions of exchange: how much is appropriate here? Marko is always worried about not being generous enough. Ladivine has the dog to count on and so Wellington's friendship is of little import for her, but the rest of the family are 'desperate for human warmth' ('avides de chaleur humaine'). Thus Marko and the children are won over despite the museum context as a locus of national history, with terrible scenes of what the reader assumes to be colonial slave-master violence and torture in the paintings. Wellington describes the exhibits as though these visitors were blind to their significance and in need of words to *see*; Marko wonders if he wants them to feel guilty (237), another kind of return gaze. Yet, strange, in this country it is suddenly dark after light, and an equally strange reversal.: 'they had become Wellington's guests' ('ils fussent devenus les invités de Wellington', 240), invited to dine in his home; perhaps global Southern hospitality has finally been located. Indeed the hospitable hosts' lamb stew proves to be good (244), although the kind man cutting up Daniel's meat is wearing Marko's stolen shirt, and thus the possibility lurks that generosity masks rapaciousness, a wolf in lamb's clothing. However, all goes well until once again Ladivine is taken for a woman who was a guest at a wedding,[14] and she constructs a fiction in response.

On the first occasion when Ladivine is misrecognised, the situation is one of only vestigial hospitality: a local woman on a bus asks where she bought the dress that she wore to the wedding (218-19). At first Ladivine does not answer the question, but, as it seems clear she has been rude, she is moved to say that she bought the yellow dress in France in an attempt to respond to the woman's reaching out to her. But the woman replies that then she could not find it here, and it seems an inept subject to have introduced – the moment of connection is lost. Politeness overlaps with hospitality – it seems courteous for the guest to entertain the host with conversation, often by telling tales. But must those tales be true, or can the guest be creative, and thus invent herself as the ideal guest, producing something which seems emotionally true or inspired, as in the many *mauvaise honte* episodes of hospitality that Rousseau narrates in his *Confessions*?[15] At Wellington's house, Ladivine is again asked for the story of the wedding, this time by an old woman whom she perceives as an honoured matriarch. She thus becomes what the other seems to want of her and invents the story of a superb wedding. Richness is exuded by linguistic form (her abundant words are 'a golden tide' ['flots dorés']), wealth of detail and also by the content of fairy-tale luxury. The magnificent flowers are borrowed, she realises, from her mother's funeral, where her father provided lilies and white gladioli (248). However, her deception is recognised, or perhaps she had misidentified her host. The woman she saw as a high-status matriarch is in fact a 'mad old woman' ('une vieille folle', 251); she has made a category error, or she may have narrated the wrong story, since her hosts are not interested in that wedding. Wellington asks whether she knows the origin of the wealth she has described. 'The atmosphere cools, suddenly inhospitable' ('l'atmosphère refroidie, soudain inhospitalière', 251) to the point that they have to leave, their emotions a mixture of fear, even terror, and anger. Ladivine feels only irritation towards Marko

> both for having accepted so swiftly, and with such obvious gratitude, Wellington's invitation, and for having kept himself aloof from the role *she* had consented to play to make their hosts happy.
> (à la fois d'avoir accepté si vite avec une aussi manifeste gratitude l'invitation de Wellington et de s'être tenu à l'écart du rôle qu'elle avait consenti à jouer, elle, pour réjouir leurs hôtes.)
>
> (252)

If he had joined in, then Wellington would not have commented on the source of the bride and groom's riches; 'all that would have remained from their unexpected situation would be the memory of their exceptional ability to integrate' ('il ne serait resté de leur situation inattendue que le souvenir d'une formidable faculté d'intégration', 252), a good memory for the children, who are now miserable. They had entered 'with all the joy of their sincere and open hearts, all ready to give of themselves' ('avec toute la joie de leur coeur ouvert et cordial et tout prêt à se donner', 252). Instead, the meal has ended with a shameful escape in disgrace, the family shoved out by Wellington's sister and the door locked behind them with no care for their safety as they try to find their way back to the hotel in the dark.

This failed hospitality is followed by a real or imagined scene of great violence. Wellington appears in their bedroom and Marko pushes him off the balcony after a struggle – both husband and wife share this hallucination, if it is a hallucination, and both are convinced that their erstwhile host is dead and that the body has been cleared away. Yet the young man reappears as a servant in the home of their next hosts on the following day. A realistic explanation would point to the possibility that the healthy adolescent was able to survive a fall, but (from a certain perspective) the critical point is that Marko wishes him dead. NDiaye is sometimes represented as a magical realist or as drawing on the fantastic (including on the dustjacket of *Ladivine*). I prefer to say that she literalises metaphors – the emotional power of the figural is such that it is described, even seen, as really happening, which in itself is a not uncommon experience. Instead of writing 'she felt as a free as a bird', NDiaye describes becoming a bird and flying away; this has all the greater emotional resonance for readers (NDiaye 2009). So perhaps Marko, humiliated in the failure of the one experience of potentially being a welcome guest, in the hasty expulsion from Wellington's home like stray dogs chased away, wants to murder him – something often said. In the night he awakes, imagining that this teenager who turned from charming and seductively welcoming to judgemental, cold and uncaring – like the whole country – has come to dispossess him of what is most valuable, not just all their clothes and most of their money, but their very children. So he fights and kills that dangerous stranger, no longer a host but an intruder (the opposite of a guest). If the guest creates the host, the intruder constitutes the one who expels, and vice versa. The peaceful and calm, even timid, husband is bestialised by what he sees as an experience of being 'treated like dogs' ('traités comme des chiens', 253) rather than guests. He himself behaves like a disturbed dog: 'He began to sob, like a dog, Ladivine thought again, with stifled yaps' ('Il se mit à sangloter, comme un chien, pensa encore Ladivine, avec des jappements étouffés', 259) In one sense, Ladivine still feels linked to her family, since Marko provides her with a story that Wellington forced himself into their hotel bedroom; having driven them out of his family home, he has come to rob them of their children (to kidnap or even kill them). Ladivine knows there could be other more benign explanations, but the post hoc justification for Marko's (attempted) murder is necessary to hold the family together. Nevertheless, she becomes physically disgusted by Marko. Although she does not help Wellington as she would have helped her friend/dog, Ladivine does not objectify this young man, the one 'who had opened his door to us' ('qui nous avait ouvert sa porte', 268), as Marko does; indeed she persistently identifies him with her mother (267), the victim of a crime.

The second episode in which the Bergers are entertained is rather different, although it too ends with something close to expulsion. It is different, on the one hand, in that the hosts (the Cagnacs) are friends of Ladivine's father, a French couple to whom he supplies nearly new 4x4s that they sell at a huge profit. Although the Cagnacs may seem more natural hosts, since they are endebted to Ladivine's father for their lucrative franchise, Marko refuses to call them before setting off on the journey to their house, so that they are 'really obliged to welcome us' ('ils seront bien obligés de nous accueillir', 270) and cannot make the excuse of inconvenience.

After the incident with Wellington, the Bergers are seeking refuge with their own kind, yet cannot trust that hospitality will be offered freely. This incident is also different in all the trappings of extreme privilege enjoyed by the neo-colonial couple whom Ladivine finds corrupt and disgusting, from their appearance to the excessively copious French food that their servants produce,

> full of fat: pork cutlets covered with melted cheese, potatoes sautéed in goose fat, lettuce soaked in walnut oil, and finally thick pancakes stuffed with chocolate cream.
>
> (extrêmement gras: côtelettes de porc couvertes de fromage fondu, pommes de terre sautées à la graisse d'oie, salade de laitue confite dans l'huile de noix, et pour finir d'épaisses crêpes fourrées de crème au chocolat.)
>
> (see Jordan 2020, 301)

Once again, it is initially Marko and the children who are both the favoured guests and those who are delighted by the situation. They eat greedily, while Ladivine, excluded and furious, can hardly manage a bite, Cagnac groaning with satisfaction as they feast together. The reader might think the couple are simply being hospitable, but for Ladivine their pressing wine and greasy treats upon her family is a sign of a shared crime: 'the fatal bond that united the Cagnacs and her children and husband was holding firm thanks to that revolting food eaten together' ('le lien funeste qui unissait les Cagnac à ses enfants et à son mari se tendait solidement sous l'effet de cette nourriture révoltante avalée en commun', 302). Yet this corrupt communion is broken once Wellington reappears, suggesting that it was no more than a very general complicity in exploitation. As Wellington serves dinner, the Cagnac couple begin to display 'such coldness, such hostility' ('une telle froideur, une telle hostilité', 321) towards Marko and the children, who sink into gloom. Wellington smiles as Marko moans that he cannot go on: 'Marko had no more strength even to pretend that he was a guest simply overcome with exhaustion' ('Marko avait perdu toute force pour feindre au moins d'etre un convive simplement éreinté', 324), while the children cry that they want to go home. For their hostess: 'this is unbearable' ('c'est insupportable'), and indeed these are spectacularly ungrateful guests. The most likely explanation for the change of heart by their hosts would lie in their now having some specific knowledge of the violent episode with Wellington. However privileged their quasi-colonial lifestyle, these luxury car dealers are immigrant-guests in a postcolonial country and so to some extent dependent on the hospitality of the state. The reader, of course, relies on the perceptions of Ladivine, but the bizarrely rapid departure of her family in spite of her own disappearance in the forest may suggest that Marko feels distinctly at risk.

Welcoming dogs

The large brown dog or dogs in *Ladivine* are an image of absolute hospitality.[16] NDiaye places dogs at different points not only as companions bringing everyday comfort but also as abject beasts (especially in human form) and as potentially divine spirits. This approach is reminiscent of Derrida's contention that the rejection of the animal at the same time entails the exclusion of gods, for both fall outside the notion of the human as such (being neither *brothers* nor *semblables*) (Derrida 2000, 142).[17] So what does/do 'welcoming dogs' in *Ladivine* achieve for the reader with respect to an understanding of humanity, or hospitality, or inter-species co-existence and even love? The use of the term *friend*, 'she had never had such a friend before' ('un tel ami, jamais elle n'en avait eu auparavant', 303), which is how Ladivine describes the large brown dog, is critical to this hospitality. There is a common argument that there can be no hospitality between friends, based on a very particular and exclusive model of (male) friendship that can be traced back to Aristotle; it assumes an absolute bond, indeed an identification, between two friends such that a gift to your friend would be the same as a gift to yourself (see Still 2010, 93-142). This is not, of course, the only paradigm of friendship nor, I would argue, is it the most common one today. Indeed, both Aristotle and Montaigne argue that many relationships called friendship do not conform to the pure and true fusion which is their ideal. Aristotle claims that in order to get to the point of true friendship, the two men concerned must actively spend a certain amount of time together. Montaigne's position is rather different, since he falls instantly 'in friendship' with his friend, and the all too short time together comes afterwards. When a stranger offers friendship as the dog does to Ladivine, it is often initially a kind of hospitality or at least expressed as a kind of hospitality. In the end we might imagine that the dog does merge with Ladivine; this point is the end of hospitality in both senses: fulfilment and death.

The section of the novel that takes place in an unknown land begins: 'The dog was there, on the other side of the road, he was now there for her' ('Le chien était là, de l'autre côté de la rue, il était là maintenant pour elle', 141). The reader might well ask, 'Which dog?' When we first meet a dog in *Ladivine* it is Richard's parents' dog accompanying them on their first visit to see their grandchild; somewhat inhospitably, the *pater familias* expels him from his house bellowing: 'Get that beast out of there!' ('Sortez-moi cette bête de là!' NDiaye 2013, 81), not looking at the animal although the Alsatian gazes serenely at him. The dog has entered Ladivine's bedroom uninvited and lies with her in her cot – to Richard's horror – but Clarisse understands the communion between the child and the animal. The dog's care for Ladivine is subsequently demonstrated when, locked out, he nevertheless alerts the family when she is choking. In the unknown land an unknown dog, seemingly a stray although at one stage he is chained up outside a supermarket, is a constant caring presence.

It simply seems to Ladivine that things are happening and will happen in such a way that 'every morning when she came out of the hotel and her eyes grew used to the burning light, the large brown dog would be looking at her from the opposite pavement' ('chaque matin, quand elle sortait de l'hôtel et accoutumait ses yeux à la lumière ardente, le grand chien brun la contemplait depuis le trottoir d'en face', 143); he would then follow her wherever she went. The dog's giving without measure evokes a response and not simply a reaction in her; the response becomes responsiveness and responsibility between the two of them. If she thinks that they are going to be separated, '[s]he could not stop herself from slowing down, she wasn't afraid that she would accidentally lose him, but the worry that she imagined would flood his dog heart was painful for her own heart' ('Elle ne pouvait s'empêcher alors de ralentir son pas, elle ne craignait pas de le semer involontairement mais l'inquiétude qu'elle supposait devoir envahir son cœur de chien était pénible à son propre cœur', 143). The one *heart* echoes the other *heart*. The dog is love as a refuge where Ladivine feels 'sheltered from misfortune or misery, from failure or despair' ('à l'abri du malheur ou de la tristesse, de l'échec ou de la désolation', 155). She never doubts that the dog will follow and that is what he does, without ever giving preference to his own needs (201). This is expressed in simple poetic language (through repetition, internal half-rhymes or assonance, for instance), sometimes in very short paragraphs, with sequences of the imperfect tense to signal continuity and repetition. Derrida asks in relation to the animal looking at him:

> What does this bottomless gaze offer to my sight [*donne à voir*]? What does it 'say' to me, demonstrating quite simply the naked truth of every gaze, when that truth *allows me to see and be seen* through the eyes of the other, in the *seeing* and not just *seen* eyes of the other?
>
> (Derrida 2008, 12)

The gaze of the dog is critical in communication with Ladivine; she wishes her mother could have experienced that friendly, sympathetic look.

She meets the dog for the last time and, in one reading, metamorphoses into him at the point of death in the forest at night; he is tired after his long journey to find her. The physical begins to conjoin with the emotional or spiritual as she breathes in his sweaty perfume as the mark of his qualities:

> Such a smell would have disturbed her before, but knowing what a long way he had travelled to find her and what loyalty, what courage that smell testified to, she breathed it in with gratitude, with satisfaction.
> (Une telle odeur l'eût gênée avant mais sachant quel long chemin il avait parcouru pour la retrouver et de quelle fidélité, de quel courage cette odeur témoignait, elle la respira avec gratitude, avec satisfaction, 326).

From theories of *pneume*, the breath of life, to Irigaray's emphasis on the spiritual importance of breathing, the reader may perceive how easily the animal mutual sniffing takes on deeper tones of intimacy. Ladivine sleeps next to 'her friend', with her arm around his body as if he were her husband. The transformation into the dog, his ultimate hospitality to her, begins with her awareness of a new comfort with her body (which had weighed her down, a familiar reaction for many women who feel overweight) and enhanced senses spiritually and figuratively. She sees her own face at her side. When her family set off in the 4x4,

> [i]n her joy, in her pride at having found them again, all three of them, and thus to be able to take them under her protection, she was making little noises that she alone could hear, and which the wind of her running carried away immediately.
>
> (Dans sa joie, dans sa fierté de les avoir retrouvés tous trois et de pouvoir ainsi les prendre sous sa garde, elle poussait de petits cris qu'elle était seule à entendre, que le vent de la galopade emportait aussitôt, 328).

Once the family are back in Berlin, the new section of the novel begins with: 'The dog was there, on the other side of the road, he was now there for her' ('Le chien était là, de l'autre côté de la rue, il était là maintenant pour elle', 329); This is the exact phrase used earlier; the dog is now looking out for Ladivine's daughter.

Impossible hospitality alone, unmediated and uncomplicated by the laws of hospitality, is perhaps the most negatively theological and thus, for me, the least interesting aspect of hospitality. NDiaye's novel gives numerous examples of failed encounters according to the laws of hospitality, of inhospitality, and of relations soured by the inability to connect – in the face of misperceptions and misrecognitions in societies fractured by historical and present inequalities of class, race and sex. The episodes in the unknown land highlight the strangeness of European visitors' seeking a warm welcome in the sun, even as they agonise over the possibility that they will be exploited and struggle to be good guests. Rousseauian attempts at communication or communion end in physical or psychological violence (see Rousseau 1953). The analysis of such human interactions is important.

The animal, then, permits what is outlined by some thinkers as truly and uniquely human. Earlier in the story, when Ladivine gazes into the dog's eyes, she sees 'all the *humanity* and the unconditional goodness of the *animal*' ('toute *l'humanité* et l'inconditionnelle bonté de *l'animal'*, NDiaye 2013, 224, my emphasis). The large brown dog is as close as we get to unconditional, priceless hospitality: he lets the stranger in and cares for the stranger at any cost – even death – although the dog does seem to *choose* the other/stranger and so the impossibility of absolute hospitality (if you wish it to be so) inevitably returns. Ladivine longs to welcome and to be welcomed by the dog to the point of *becoming*, perhaps divine in some strange way as her name projects, and perhaps that loving human-animal. And perhaps the dog's greatest gift is then *potential reciprocity* – he is the host that enables the hospitality of the guest.

Notes

1 NDiaye (born 1967 in Pithiviers, France) has had great success as a novelist and playwright from an early age; not only have her books sold well, but she was awarded the prix Femina in 2001 for *Rosie Carpe*, and the prix Goncourt in 2009 for *Three Strong Women*. Her writing is a beautiful model of classic French, with strings of verbs in the

160 Judith Still

imperfect tense and a delicate use of the subjunctive. She moves between the everyday real, the poetic and what some have characterised as magic realism – what I would prefer to name, at least in the context of my essay here, the literalisation of the figural. I would like to thank Isha Pearce who first introduced me to NDiaye. My translations are provided throughout; unfortunately, I am not able to convey the wonderful pattern of echoes in sound, structure and signification that NDiaye deploys.

2 Postcolonial fiction has taken the perspective of the migrant, for example. Life-writing addresses the pleasures and tribulations of being a guest as often as being a host – Rousseau is an early example. Politeness manuals constitute another set of writings dealing with the guest; I would include advice for business travellers.

3 Derrida presents absolute hospitality to animals as a dream in *The Animal That Therefore I Am* (Derrida 2008, 37); this seems particularly appropriate to *Ladivine*.

4 David Wills's choice to translate *il* by 'it' is a not unreasonable decision when moving between a language which genders every noun, whether it refers to an animate being or not, and one that uses 'it' for objects. In English the translation would have to *choose* a sex unless it were to move to the plural. However, calling an animal (or even *the* animal) 'it' runs contrary to the spirit of Derrida's relentless questioning of the placing of an impermeable boundary between human and animal. See Vicki Hearne's poetico-philosophical account of horse and dog training, *Adam's Task: Calling Animals by Name*; in Chapter 7, 'Calling Animals by Name', she expresses her unease about calling animals 'it' or labelling them by putting scare quotes around their names rather than addressing them as subjects (Hearne 2007, 166-71). I shall call NDiaye's dogs 'he', but their sex is not necessarily given in the novel.

5 'Hospitality – if there is any – must, would have to, open itself to an other that is not mine, my hôte, my other, not even my neighbor or my brother (Levinas always says that the other, the other man, man as the other is *my* neighbor, my universal brother, in humanity. At bottom, this is one of our larger questions: is hospitality reserved, confined to man, to the universal brother? For even if Levinas disjoints the idea of fraternity from the idea of the 'fellow [*semblable*]', and the idea of neighbor [*prochain*] or of proximity from the idea of non-distance, of non-distancing, of fusion and identity, he nonetheless maintains that the hospitality of the hôte as well as that of the hostage must belong to the site of the fraternity of the neighbor). Hospitality, therefore – if there is any – must, would have to, open itself to an other that is not mine, my hôte, my other, not even my neighbor or my brother, perhaps an "animal" – I do say animal' (Derrida 2002, 356–420, 363).

6 See *Derrida and Other Animals: the Boundaries of the Human*, Chapter 6.

7 'She only consented to be the servant's daughter, that daughter called Malinka, within the walls of the little flat' ('Elle ne consentait à être la fille de la servante, cette fille qui s'appelait Malinka, qu'entre les murs de ce petit appartement', NDiaye 2013, 55). Her mother works as a cleaner.

8 Clarisse chooses to cut herself off from her roots, but: 'the heavy burden of a bad conscience weighed on her rib cage and prevented her, wherever she was, from being truly happy' ('la lourde charge de mauvaise conscience qui encombrait sa cage thoracique et l'empêchait, où qu'elle fût, d'être pleinement gaie', NDiaye 2013, 56). Shirley Jordan suggests that 'nomads' in NDiaye are not happy in assuming their nomadism, their lack of fixed location – unlike the postcolonial paradigm of mobility offered by Rosi Braidotti (Jordan 2007). Clarisse may have chosen 'exile', or succumbed to social pressure rather than having it forced upon her, but it is exile none the less. See also Jordan (2017).

9 There are a series of dogs in the novel which on the plane of realism cannot all be the same dog, yet, though Richard's mother has a dog killed (as we humans do), she is sure that 'he will return' ('il reviendra', NDiaye 2013, 104).

10 For bibliographic references and a discussion of *hôte* in Derrida and Gotman, as well as the way in which *hôte* is translated in Derrida, see Still (2010).

11 Irigaray's writing on hospitality is both urgent and original because she is directly addressing sexuate difference (see Still 2010, 2012). Her writing on hospitality includes: *Sharing the World* (Irigaray 2008), 'Toward a Mutual Hospitality' (Irigaray 2013) and 'Animal Compassion' (Irigaray 2004).

12 For a longer discussion of this debate, see Still 2015, 1–66 and Still 2019, 49–65.
13 Ladivine and Marko had, of course, explicitly desired a holiday somewhere, anywhere, *unknown* to his parents and their neighbours ('un lieu, quel qu'il fût, inconnu des vieux Berger et de Lüneburg en général', NDiaye 2013, 160).
14 This *unheimliche* doppelganger, or strange doubling, is one of many mysteries left unresolved, that the reader could explain away, but might want to leave hanging as relating to being away from home, the same and not the same. Ladivine could be descended from people in this country through her maternal grandmother.
15 NDiaye has claimed that she feels 'the cultural heir of Molière, Rousseau or Proust' (NDiaye 1997, 67).
16 I expand on the figure of the dog in Still (2016). This essay also addresses the question of a hospitality that opens itself up to an other that is not mine, while challenging the critique of (economic) reciprocity by many contemporary theorists of hospitality which can end up in an impossibilism by focusing uniquely on the absolute hospitality of the host.
17 Greek gods were fond of translating themselves into animal form, and indeed the line between these apparent antitheses (animal/divine) is crossed in many religions as gods take animal shape.

References

Asibong, Andrew. 2013. *Marie NDiaye: Blankness and Recognition*. Liverpool: Liverpool University Press.

Bentham, Jeremy. 1823. *Introduction to the Principles of Morals and Legislation*. 2nd edn. London: T. Payne and Son.

Benveniste, Emile. 1969. 'Hospitalité'. In *Le Vocabulaire des institutions indo-européennes*. Vol. I, 88–91. Paris: Minuit.

Derrida, Jacques. 2000. *Of Hospitality: Anne Dufourmantelle Invites Jacques Derrida to Respond*. Translated by Rachel Bowlby. Stanford, CA: Stanford University Press.

———. 2002 'Hostipitality: Session of January 8, 1997'. In *Jacques Derrida: Acts of Religion*, edited by Gil Anidjar, 356-420. London and New York: Routledge.

———. 2008. *The Animal That Therefore I Am*. Translated by David Wills. New York: Fordham University Press.

Hearne, Vicki. 2007. *Adam's Task: Calling Animals by Name*. New York: Skyhorse Publishing.

Irigaray, Luce. 2004. 'Animal Compassion'. In *Animal Philosophy: Essential Readings in Continental Thought*, edited by Peter Atterton and Matthew Calarco, 195-201. London and New York: Continuum.

———. 2008. *Sharing the World*. London and New York: Continuum.

———. 2013. 'Toward a Mutual Hospitality'. In *Conditions of Hospitality: Ethics, Politics, and Aesthetics on the Threshold of the Possible*, edited by Thomas Claviez, 42-54. New York: Fordham University Press.

Jordan, Shirley. 2007. 'La Quête familiale dans les écrits de Marie NDiaye: nomadisme, (in)hospitalité, différence'. In *Nomadismes de romancières contemporaines de langue française*, edited by Anne Simon and Audrey Lasserre, 147-57. Paris: Presses universitaires de France.

———. 2017. *Marie Ndiaye: Inhospitable Fictions*. Research Monographs in French Studies, 38. Cambridge: Legenda.

———. 2020. 'Food, Disorder and Disgust in Marie NDiaye'. In *Disorderly Eating in Contemporary Women's Writing*, edited by Shirley Jordan and Judith Still, Special Number of *Journal of Romance Studies* 20.2: 323–46.

NDiaye, Marie. 1997. 'Mon quatrième roman'. In *Tombeau du cœur de François II, Adeline et un voyage*, edited by Thierry Fourneau, Marie-Thérèse Humbert and Marie Ndiaye, 65-8. Tours: CRL.

———. 2009. *Trois femmes puissantes*. Paris: Gallimard, 2009.

———. 2013. *Ladivine*. Paris: Gallimard.

Rousseau, Jean-Jacques. 1953. *Confessions*. Translated by J. M. Cohen. Harmondsworth, Middlesex: Penguin.

Still, Judith. 2010. *Derrida and Hospitality*. Edinburgh: Edinburgh University Press.

———. 2012. '*Sharing the World*: Luce Irigaray and the Hospitality of Difference'. *L'Esprit créateur* 52.3: 40-51.

———. 2015. *Derrida and Other Animals: The Boundaries of the Human*. Edinburgh: Edinburgh University Press.

———. 2016. '"Welcoming animals" bei Derrida und Irigaray – unter besonderer Berücksichtigung des Hundes in Marie NDiaye's Roman *Ladivine*'. In *Perspektiven europäischer Gastlichkeit. Geschichte – Kulturelle Praktiken – Kritik*, edited by Burkhard Liebsch, Michael Staudigl and Philipp Stoellger, 374–94. Weilerswist: Velbrück Wissenschaft.

———. 2019. 'Thoughts from France on the Animal-Human Borderline: Derrida and Animal Rights Philosophers'. In *French Thought in the UK, or Sur-vie*, edited by I. Goh, 49–65. London: Routledge.

10

INDIGENOUS HOSPITALITY

Kim Scott's fiction, multinaturalism and absolute conditional hospitality

Russell West-Pavlov

In contemporary Australia, it has become common when opening official functions or events to make a brief statement that acknowledges the prior Indigenous custodial ownership of the land and thanks the Indigenous owners, whether present or not, for the opportunity to hold the event within a space under their jurisdiction. Less frequently, a matching 'Welcome Ceremony' may be held, in which Indigenous representatives formally welcome the participants in the event to their territory. The 'Acknowledgement of Country' and 'Welcome to Country' ceremonies are significant public gestures within the contemporary Australian polity. They indicate a widespread understanding of the ramifications of the violent and illegal infringement of Indigenous sovereignty upon which the modern Australian nation-state was founded (Cox 2014, 140-41). Such ceremonies imply that the acknowledgement of Indigenous ownership, if not sovereignty, prior to British colonisation in 1788, enshrined in the supreme court's 'Mabo' ruling of 1992 (Butt et al. 2001; Reynolds 1996; Stephenson and Ratnapala 1993), has become part of the nation's collective consciousness. They suggest a willingness to make gestures towards reparation not merely in the often remote business of the return of traditional, often sacred Indigenous lands, but also in the protocol of everyday administrative procedures and public life.

There has, however, been much debate about such ceremonies. Are they merely examples of 'politically correct' tokenism, as incoming Prime Minister Tony Abbott suggested some years ago (Maiden 2010)? Are they paternalistic gestures towards an ancient civilisation valued primarily as a tourist draw-card? Are they even an 'insult' to the white (supremacist) Australians who stake an equal claim to the land on the basis of two hundred years of (initially armed) appropriation (Bolt 2010)? Given the creeping curtailment of Indigenous rights – and civil rights more generally – including the rescinding of Indigenous Land Rights in the Northern Territory in the wake of the draconian Northern Territory Intervention from 2007 onwards, all supported by successive Australian governments until the present (Gray 2015; Scott 2015), the accusation of tokenism might appear justified. Paradoxically, the inauguration of successive Australian Federal Parliaments since 2008 by Indigenous Welcome Ceremonies has been almost contemporaneous with measures voted by those same parliaments (since the inception in 2007 of the Intervention) that are radically inimical to Indigenous welfare. These measures have rolled back Indigenous autonomy in the Territory, most conspicuously by the clawing back of control of traditional and sacred lands previously ceded to Indigenous communities (Gray 2015, 37). The 'Welcome' to Indigenous 'Country' becomes, in this context, a politically fraught and highly ambivalent gesture of vitiated hospitality.

This chapter approaches the very topical issue of hospitality by re-framing this central interrogation of social interaction across linguistic, cultural and geopolitical borders in terms of geography. The Indigenous tradition of 'Welcome to Country', perhaps merely a recent 'invented tradition' (Hobsbawm and Ranger 1983; O'Brien and Hall 2010), also reposes upon older traditions of cultural accommodation and reciprocal exchange that often structured interactions in the pre-colonial period, as well as the initially friendly 'first contact' dynamics from the early 1800s. Such traditions drew upon the primacy of 'Country' as the bedrock of all Indigenous culture, inserting human agency into the complexities of hospitality via the central, but always subordinating, notion of custodianship. Indigenous actors had (and have) a crucial role as the custodians and curators of 'Country'; but the ultimate Actor was (and is) 'Country' itself as the matrix of all life and thus as the real Subject and Agent of existence. A Welcome ceremony is thus always a derivative, secondary welcome, in which humans welcome other humans, but in consultation with 'Country' itself, on whose behalf they utter the words of welcome. Indigenous concepts of hospitality thus offer the possibility of recalibrating extant debates about hospitality in ways that relativise and resituate both the customary terms of the discussion and its ultimate implications for scholarship in the humanities, in addition to the possible policy decisions arising out of that scholarship.

The welcome of foreigners and the foreignness of welcome

The debates about the provenance and thus the authenticity of Indigenous welcome protocols, acrimonious yet central as they may be, also work to occlude the epistemological strangeness of the 'Welcome to Country' ceremony. These issues deserve some discussion. First, such ceremonies are illocutionary speech acts, that is, speech acts which, like 'I promise', semantically describe their own act in a circular, 'illustrative' manner (Austin 1962). Second, these ceremonies are not merely linguistic in nature. They are also performances in the sense of enacted ritual. Third, as a result of their linguistic-ritual nature, they become spatio-temporal gestures that inaugurate a specific *event* in a specific *venue* by appealing to a set of Indigenous concepts that are also spatio-temporal in nature – the enduring validity of 'Country' as the matrix of all life that is therefore the object of respect and circumspection. The 'Welcome to Country' is thus not merely a gesture of hospitality, but an invitation to pay due respect to immanent cosmic forces that are embedded in the earth and the landscape itself – whence, perhaps, the absence of a particularising article before 'Country'. Fourth, as just noted, in view of the fundamental ontological status that Indigenous lore (known as the Law) awards to Country as the very fabric of the cosmos, the 'Welcome to Country' ceremony tends, ultimately, to eclipse the human actors involved in the ritual. Although it is executed by human members of the specific Indigenous community concerned, the 'Welcome to Country' ceremony inevitably directs attention towards 'Country' itself as a site of agency which exceeds, or better, underpins and envelops human agency. Indigenous welcome thus stages a notion of hospitality that is absolute (in consequence of its cosmic dimensions) to the extent that it is absolutely conditional (because it places absolute ethical and existential demands on the human).

Stephen Muecke's mention of an Indigenous-inspired education programme conceived by Carol Oomera Edwards exemplifies some of these aspects of 'Welcome to Country' or 'Acknowledgement of Country' ceremonies (Muecke 2004). With a view to educating primary school children about Indigenous *Guyanggu* ('way of being'), Edwards suggests that they should learn to acknowledge the agency of place: 'Eventually we might address these presences, in a place, with whom we have become familiar, as we approach them: "Hello, only us mob coming, OK if we camp here again?"' (as quoted in Muecke 2004, 69). 'Country', as an all-embracing agency which underpins life, is everywhere:

> Relations can thus be established with any sort of place. Even classrooms. Children might be encouraged to perform a little ceremony each time they enter a place, to modify their behaviour at the threshold. They might be induced to address the room:
> 'Hello, my name is Tommy. OK if I spend a year with you here?'
> (ibid.: 69)

The hospitality offered by place, and the obligations it imposes, are both absolute because ubiquitous. 'Country' is everywhere. Country welcomes, in a manner which is always and everywhere conditional for all inhabitants or visitors, but for that reason, its hospitality is absolute.

Muecke concludes:

> In this example of the approach to place, children keep in mind that the place has a prior existence and history of its own long before they turn up. Their arrival and its impact are considered as addition to the place; in establishing a relationship to the place they acknowledge the prior existence of a context they now seek to become part of.
> (Muecke 2004, 69)

Despite this explanatory gloss, the imagined apostrophe ascribed to the fictive child may appear bizarre to us: first, because we may address God in apostrophic mode, but not, generally, places in all their concreteness; in fact, this may not constitute an act of apostrophe whose basis lies in absence as well as abstraction (Culler 1981, 135–54). Second, the banality of the places thus apostrophised (a camping park, a classroom) clashes with, and thus underlines, the latent sacrality that is thereby spoken into being. Yet, precisely because such places appear to be mere receptacles for transient populations, 'empty' of greater meaning, the protocol awards all the more strikingly a plenitude that indexes agency and matricial nurture.

What these somewhat odd examples set in scene, I would suggest, is a notion of hospitality that is far more radical than that evoked by many of the debates which, since Levinas and Derrida's decisive interventions, have been conducted about 'conditional' and 'unconditional' hospitality (e.g. Derrida 2000, 25; 2005, 6; Savić 2005). These examples of the hospitality afforded by 'Country' itself, and then, by proxy, offered by the Indigenous custodians or 'representatives' of 'Country', propose a possible answer to 'the recurring question about the possible location that would allow for a hospitable (or for that matter, "hostipitable") encounter actually to "take place"' (Claviez 2013, 3). Thomas Claviez's formulation frames the enduring tension between the ideal or conceptual horizons of hospitality and its realisation in actual practices. He frames this tension between the conditional and the unconditional within the notion of spatiality in manner highly pertinent to Indigenous Australia. In Indigenous thought, these two frames of hospitality are not so much reconciled as imbricated within one another in a manner that radicalises the entire construct of hospitality. This radicalisation of the question inserts it within a much larger framework, perhaps the framework of cosmic hospitality. By relocating the issue of hospitality to the level of a 'hyperobject' (T. Morton 2013) related, for instance, to other such issues as climate change, the global politics of 'extraction' or 'expulsion' (Sassen 2014), or global biopolitics (S. Morton 2013), it becomes possible to rearticulate the notion of hospitality in ways that integrate, for instance, Global South migration or the current European refugee 'crisis'. Both of these exemplary problematics of hospitality are deeply embedded in global complexes of geopolitics, economies of extracting resources and climate change (Klein 2016; McAdam 2014). Such global dimensions of hospitality, however, exceed the brief of this chapter, which is merely to explore how Indigenous texts work out that radicalisation of the question itself.

In *That Deadman Dance* (Scott 2010) and the co-autobiographical dialogue that preceded it, *Kayang & Me* (Scott and Brown 2005), Western Australian Noongar author Kim Scott has offered fictional explorations of first-contact Indigenous hospitality. My reading of these works will suggest that the language of welcome is crucial. If Scott's first two fictions (1993, 1999) focused largely on the destruction wrought upon Indigenous societies by white colonisation, his third and fourth texts (Scott and Brown 2005; Scott 2010) turn to the promising, if short-lived, period of amicable cohabitation on the Western Australian 'friendly frontier'. Hospitality has been a foundational theme, indeed, a textual performativity, within Scott's fiction from the outset: the title of the opening chapter of his début novel, *True Country* (Scott 1993, 13), is 'First Thing, Welcome'. We are introduced to the oeuvre to come by an exemplary gesture of Indigenous hospitality. In the later works, however, hospitality becomes an even more central and possibly redemptive concern:

> I live in Noongar country. . . . It was Noongar people who created society here, and their reactions to 'First contact'. . . offer[ed] mostly sound values upon which to build, and within which 'white' society could be accommodated.
>
> (Scott and Brown 2005, 207)

Literal welcome and axiological cosmic 'accommodation' go hand in hand as the Indigenous contribution to 'First Contact' encounters, which Scott's oeuvre performatively reiterates from the first readerly contact. The cumulative force of his oeuvre is to stage a textual hospitality that reposes upon a 'sense of place' which in turn is generative of a 'possibility of something more meaningful than a simple biological kinship' (Scott and Brown 2005, 79). This notion of a form of hospitality that exceeds 'mere' inter-human hospitality does not erase the distinction between conditional and unconditional hospitality. On the contrary, it radicalises that human hospitality in a manner suggesting, as I shall show, that *conditional* 'cosmic' hospitality may indeed be the location of transcendent 'absolute' hospitality. Whereas extant discussions see 'absolute/unconditional hospitality' as the impossible condition of possibility of 'conditional' hospitality, Indigenous thought would turn this aporia inside-out into the plenitude of Country. Country as the ultimate conditional provides the ethical imperatives and conditions of possibility of any practice and theorisation of hospitality.

Scott's novel, and the dialogical historical meditations that precede it, are about the failed cross-cultural dialogue between early European settlers and prior Indigenous inhabitants and custodians of the land. But Scott's texts are also, and more significantly perhaps, about the failed cosmic diplomacy between two ways of understanding the world, in which the language of hospitality sketches a crucial threshold or 'contact zone' between these two cosmologies, where Country itself is the very embodiment of Indigenous cosmology. Non-respect for the conditions of hospitality dictated by Country, and encountered at its existential and conceptual threshold, has dictated the contours of the Australian polity and the course of Australian politics ever since.

In order to elucidate this threshold encounter, a sort of hospitality at the door to a radically different cosmos, I shall draw upon Brazilian anthropologist Eduardo Viveiros de Castro's (2014) meditations on Amerindian cosmologies, which display some affinities with Indigenous Australian ideas of 'Country'. It may appear somewhat far-fetched to go to the Amerindian world to elaborate a theory of Australian Indigenous cosmological welcome, but there are ample reasons for considering these two Indigeneities of the Global South as close conceptual neighbours. Stuart Cooke's (2013) comparisons of Australian and Chilean Indigenous oral poetry and songs suggest that it is entirely plausible to posit cognate conceptual spaces across apparently far-flung realms of the Global South, while Tim Ingold's meditations upon circumpolar Indigenous cultures (2011) demonstrate another set of remarkably close analogies despite hemispheric distances. In particular, teasing out the common resonances between Scott's and Vivieros de Castro's interest in language, I propose translation as the basic operator of the cosmic hospitality envisaged by Kim Scott's 'modern' Indigenous cosmology. Translation does not make these ideas universal; rather, it facilitates their travel across various borders of hospitality to a multiplicity of locations.

Climbing the rock

By way of 'entry' into my subject – a turn of phrase that is by no means innocent, as I hope will become clear in what follows – I begin by looking in some detail at a passage from *Kayang & Me*, in which Scott describes the process of a rediscovery of Indigenous culture. Excavating beneath the grim remnants of an 'oppression culture' (Scott and Brown 2005, 17; explored earlier in Scott 1993, 1999) resulting from a white nineteenth-century genocide and dispersal that eradicated all but five per cent of the original Indigenous inhabitants of South-Western Australia (Scott and Brown 2005, 102), Scott describes a group of Noongar (South-Western Australian Indigenous) university students in search of a their heritage in Indigenous 'high culture . . . creation stories, language and songs' (ibid.: 17). Scott takes his student group on an excursion to a traditional sacred site under the tutelage of a local elder, Ralph Winmar: 'We were among a privileged few to be properly introduced to the intimacies of his home country, and welcomed with the songs and language of its ancestral spirits' (ibid.). The crucial terms here are those of 'introduction' and 'welcome'. In effect, the educational welcome afforded by Winmar to Scott's group is exemplary of Indigenous hospitality, brokering a protocol-based initiation and transition into 'Country'. If Winmar's welcome is couched in 'the songs and language of its ancestral spirits', the language of the literary text is not unrelated to those other forms of sacral language.

This episode of welcome also works as a welcome to the book. It precedes a description given by Scott's interlocutor and co-author, his aunt Hazel Brown, or 'Kayang [or Elder] Hazel', a few pages later (ibid.: 23-24), where she outlines the protocols of entry to certain territories and domains of Country within Noongar Indigenous culture. Hazel Brown recounts journeys with her father into traditional Wilomin country, where ritual fires had to be lit so as to alert the ancestral spirits to one's approach: 'You gotta stop here now, and make a fire. You gotta make smoke and let 'em know you're coming' (ibid.: 23). Only when the curlews, the embodiment of the Wilomin spirits, reply, can one proceed: 'That's the Wilomin people; they're letting us know. We're right now' (ibid.: 18).

Scott's description of a welcome to a cognate Country for quasi-outsiders (students of Indigenous descent who have little familiarity with traditional Noongar culture) thus works, chronologically, as a textual welcome to the subsequent, more intimate entrance protocol related to him by his aunt. We, as readers and true outsiders, are thus inducted, step-by-step, into the 'intimacies' of an encounter with

Country. (Chronologically, we are also taken back by successive temporal acts of introduction, from the moment of our own reading towards a moment of Indigenous cultural reconstruction on the cusp of the twenty-first century, then back to a moment, perhaps fifty or sixty years earlier, when previous generations still had immediate contact with the residual culture – customs, rituals, stories – of Country and the ancestors.)

But the act of crossing into Country via rituals of welcome inducts us into a form of hospitality that is not merely between one culture and another. Rather, it aids us in traversing a border that leads into what, according to the text, is a radically different cosmos. The transformation of the cosmos is indexed most obviously by the personification of the land:

> [Ralph Winmar] sent a group of us to climb the rocky side of that creative spirit, the Waakal – or at least that transformed remnant of it fenced within a small rectangle of the wheat belt somewhere around Quairading and York. On the climb we tasted water running out of the wound left by an ancestral Noongar's spear and, standing high on the Waakal's fossilised back, looked out over a tractor describing small futile circles in the paddock below us, and heard the bleating of distant tiny sheep. The breeze in our faces, and the air entering our lungs did not – despite the cleared paddocks and the fences and sheep and tractor – belong to any place known only as 'the wheat belt'.
>
> (ibid.: 17–18)

What may appear initially as a rather quaint form of anthropomorphisation (the rocky bluff *is* Waakal, the Noongar rainbow serpent who carved out and now regulates the rivers sustaining life across the land) is, more significantly, the trace of a transformation. The juxtaposition of rock and ancestral Dreaming being, which suggests a fusion of different temporal planes within the ongoing presence of the landscape itself, becomes something akin to one of Benjamin's 'dialectical images' that fuse the present and the past into a frozen 'now of recognisability' (Benjamin 2002, 473). Whereas Benjamin's 'dialectics at a standstill' (ibid.: 462) crystallise the conflicted movements of human history, though, what we see on the side of this rocky bluff rearing up out of the wheat belt is something that is not immobile but flowing, and not recognisable as human but radically strange and ahuman. Indeed, the space that the pilgrims enter is sacred: it does not 'belong to any place known only as "the wheat belt"' (Scott and Brown 2005, 18).

Scott's text suggests that the welcome into an Indigenous space is a welcome into a literally different and foreign space, albeit within the same empirical geophysical coordinates. This difference rests upon the fact that the relationships that structure that space, starting with the ritual passage across a threshold via the ceremony of welcome, are radically readjusted.

It might seem, at first glance, that what takes place on the slope of this rock is indeed a mediation between cultures: a Western culture on the one hand, embodied by the sceptical if curious students, and Indigenous culture, of which Ralph

Winmar is the custodian. According to this take on the scene, what Scott reverses is a revision of ethnology. It is, in a sense, ethnology in reverse. Ethnology in its usual form was a brainchild of Enlightenment thought. That Enlightenment thought envisaged a multiplicity of human cultures sharing the common background of a single natural world. The ethnologist effectively imposes upon the Indigenous person a divided view of the world that was central to the Enlightenment. The human subject is regarded as fundamentally distinct from the natural surroundings, thus freeing him from a pre-Enlightenment entanglement of humans and a world dominated by superstition. Ethnology claims that the Indigenous person is 'primitive' precisely because s/he is not aware of this distinction, and lives in a pre-literate, 'mythic' fusion with the natural world, which the ethnologist 'translates' into an 'explanation' of 'primitive thought' (Viveiros de Castro 2004, 4–5). The ethnological elucidation of Indigenous thought, which claims to make 'them' accessible to 'us', is simultaneously a confirmation of their nullity: it is an 'epistemocide' (Scholte, as quoted in Viveiros de Castro 2014, 100). Scott's text, in one reading, reverses the chronology. Resisting the nullification of Indigenous thought, he revives Indigenous culture and re-dignifies it, giving it full validity (albeit through what may appear as 'mere' anthropomorphisation) as a genuine reality. A semi-fictional narrative thus allows a sort of thought experiment that nonetheless presupposes an underlying consent to the separation of concept and world, so that no ultimate questioning of the Enlightenment paradigm really takes place. Such a reading, however, neglects the true radicalism of what Scott, very discretely, is seeking to achieve. It maintains the difference of cultures, if only to overcome it in defence of Indigenous cultures, upon the common 'ground' of the sacred site.

By contrast, what Scott performs textually, and Viveiros de Castro calls 'perspectivism', assumes a common transhuman continuum of cultures looking into a multiplicity of singular and incommensurable natures. Whereas nineteenth- and twentieth-century ethnology posited quite diverse cultures, say those of the European scholar-researcher and those of the Noongar Indigenous person, with their variously 'modern' and 'primitive' worldviews, both inhabiting an identical landscape, multinaturalism shifts the terms radically. This dual structure is turned inside out, chiastically, by Viveiros de Castro's implementation of Amerinidan cosmologies. Where Enlightenment thought imagines different (and *hierarchically different*) cultures arrayed against the stable 'background' of a single universal nature, Amerindian thought posits a single common 'personhood' gazing upon a multiplicity of natures. 'Persons' is a term that denotes nothing more nor less than an intention-driven perspective. 'Persons' can be humans, animals, indeed plants and other entities such as the moon (Viveiros de Castro 1998, 477). Personhood thus represents a realm of commonality, aside from bodily variations between, say, humans, jaguars, tapirs and moons. Scott discovers, for instance, that 'we are part of a continual rebirth because we carry the shape of the new moon at the base of our fingernails' (Scott and Brown 2005, 220). We find this frequently in *Kayang & Me*:

> As we were going down this bird started to talk.
> Well, the magpies started talking – magpies, like they're stickybeaks – they'll tell you when things and people are around.
> . . .
> You know, 'cause they'll tell you. They act as a signal. Like if human beings come that they know, they'll talk. These magpies, I don't think they were warning us, they were warning this other person, that we were predators or whatever.
>
> (ibid.: 210)

The 'other person' is a dingo – for whom the humans are co- or counter-predators. The magpie-persons are warning the dingo-person of the threatening presence of the human-persons. They are all persons within different natures with their corresponding predatorinesses.

This notion of person translates also into language: '"Nidja kwel maya wangin", I said. *The sheoaks are talking*; Maya wangin. . . . That's the wind talking' (ibid.: 221, 233). The wind is not part of nature as opposed to culture, but occupies the personhood-continuum within a multiplicity of natures. Likewise, in *That Deadman Dance*, the astute cross-cultural communicator Dr Cross ruminates about his Indigenous companions,

> Sometimes Wooral addressed the bush as if he were walking through a crowd of diverse personalities, his tone variously playing, scolding, reverential, affectionate.
> It was most confusing. Did he see something else?
>
> (Scott 2010, 46)

The answer might be: No: some*one* else. The 'perspectivism' that Viveiros de Castro finds in Amerindian worldviews, and that appears to be present in Scott's dramatised Indigenous world, puts all persons on a single continuum of intentional positionality, that is, of taking up a position in the world which is structured according to a set of practices and goals: 'Personhood and perspectiveness – the capacity to occupy a point of view – is a question of degree, context and position rather than a property distinct to a specific species' (Viveiros de Castro 2014, 57–58). The continuum of personhood is much more heavily populated in the perspectivist world than in the rarefied Enlightenment universe, where humans alone are on the non-natural side of the divide.

If a multiplicity of cultures gives way, here, to a singular continuum of personhood, what, then of the Enlightenment's putative universality of nature? In Scott's text, the being that crosses the threshold of welcome enters a space in which nature is other not merely because it segues into a community of persons, but also because it is in a constant process of transformation. Scott's description of the newly welcomed initiates' vantage point 'standing high on the Waakal's fossilised back, look[ing] out over a tractor describing small futile circles in the paddock below us, and hear[ing] the bleating of distant tiny sheep' (Scott and Brown 2005, 17) appears at first glance to describe an immobile adamantine world. It seems to fulfil all the criteria of the landscape aesthetics that objectify a landscape by cutting it out of the land and framing it within the distanced perspective of a viewer (Jullien 2014, 13–38). The tractor and the sheep, despite their minimal movements, are so distant that they are relegated to elements of a frozen backdrop panorama; even the rock itself, 'fossilised', is part of the backdrop, albeit very much in the foreground, a mere stable platform for the viewer. Or so it might seem. Yet such assumed stability represses genuinely seismic disjunctions such as the one discretely signalled by the article present in the turn of phrase 'standing high on *the* Waakal's fossilised back', which jolts the rock out of its zero-degree impassivity. That single article drives a wedge between apparently passive elements of the panorama and versions of the cosmos dormant within it. The perspective offered by the 'non-synthetic union' or 'alter-junction' (Kristeva 1969, 253, 257) of the materiality of the rock and the immateriality of the mythical Dreamtime being suggests a blending of utterly incompatible perspectives, which amounts not to a reconciliation or even a dialectical synthesis, but rather to a radically explosive productivity of multiple, oscillating realities. A 'fossilised' natural world cedes to a vibrant body among other bodies. Elsewhere, referring to another such Dreaming narrative embedded in the landscape, Scott writes, 'Dwoort baal kaat – *Dog his head*. . . . There had only been mute stone; now wild dogs howled and leapt into the sea through flames, were transformed into seals' (Scott and Brown 2005, 216–17, emphasis in original). 'There had been' and 'now' are not tense-based descriptors of transformed perception, but belong more fundamentally to a basally transformative and constantly transforming reality. The narrative of transformation reactivates the transformation in the landscape – better, the transformation that *is* landscape.

What is multiple here is not the realm of 'culture', as this is a shared domain of intentional perspectivalism. (Indeed, 'culture' is a term which may, within this optic, have to be discarded, because it no longer demarcates humans from nonhumans.) Difference resides instead on the side of 'nature' (once again, a term which may have to be jettisoned because the fundamental distinction upon which it depended has disappeared), or rather, with the things upon which 'persons' have a perspective. The same things now possess different 'natures' depending upon who sees them with an intentional gaze: 'all beings see ("represent") the world *in the same way*; what changes is *what they see*' (Viveiros de Castro 2014, 71). Where a human sees blood, a jaguar sees manioc beer; where a human sees a pool of mud, a tapir sees a ceremonial dwelling (these are Vivieros de Castro's recurrent examples, cf. ibid.: 62). Any entity may be several things at once, depending upon who is looking at it from which bodily perspective: 'What exists in multinature are not such self-identical entities differently perceived but immediately relational multiplicities of the type blood/beer. There exists, if you will, only the limit between blood and beer, the border by which these two "affinal" substances communicate and diverge' (Viveiros de Castro 2014, 73).

Indicative of this transformation embodied in 'immediately relational multiplicities' (ibid.: 73) in Scott's anecdote is the 'water running out of the wound left by an ancestral Noongar's spear' on the side of the mountain (Scott and Brown 2005, 17). The spring embodies a 'connection to a nurturing life source; as patience, as stillness, and welling' (ibid.: 220). This materialisation of the constant flow of life's renewability and fungibility also encapsulates, at a second degree, the rock's oscillation between a mineral solidity and mythical organicity. In a constant pattern of reciprocal transformation, '[r]ocks can set a narrative in motion', while narrative 'animate[s] the stone' (ibid.: 248). Narrative is not merely a mode of representation of this multiplicity of natures; narrative is a participant in this basal transformative multiplicity that makes the natural world multiple in itself.

At first glance, Viveiros de Castro's conceptual chiasmus (inverting a multiplicity of cultural perspectives upon a single nature into a single intentional perspective upon a multiplicity of natures) may seem neat, even elegant, but ultimately trite. The cross-over may be construed as reversing the terms of the debate in a way that appears too simple to be valid; it appears too clear-cut, replacing one set of binaries in a perfectly symmetrical manner with another. But if Viveiros de Castro's chiastic structure is neatly symmetrical, re-inscribing binaries in a different place, the conceptual and epistemological effects of this re-inscription are so turbulent that their unruliness can by no stretch of the imagination be conveniently cordoned-off or battened-down by binary concepts.

In a similar manner, in *That Deadman Dance*, the paradigmatic exchange of garments between coloniser and Indigene (Dr Cross's officer's tunic for Menak's cloak of kangaroo skin) may seem to be a simple chiastic swap, but the ensuing intermingling of natural and bodily odours cannot be so easily contained. It opens up beyond its own semi-closure, folded/enfolding/unfolding:

> The surprisingly soft and pliable kangaroo skin hung easily from Cross's shoulders, enclosing him in the smell of another man, a very different man of course, but a man for all that. *Noongar*, he remembered. The scent was not so much that of a body but of sap and earth, the oils and ochres and who knew what else of this land.
>
> (Scott 2010, 91-92)

The folding structure ('pliable', from the French *plier*, see Deleuze 1992) allows a subtle shift in emphasis from the man to the land. The gesture of welcome is an exchange which establishes a rapport, based on a chiastic, overlapping gift of garments. Its significance, however, is radically asymmetrical: on the one hand, the signifier of military hierarchy and continental conquest; on the other, the cloak which morphs into a metonym, or perhaps even a concrete element of the land itself. A sign of geopolitical hegemony is exchanged, in a ritual of welcome, for a participatory access to the land itself. Personhood is related to a generative force that embraces and exceeds humans, animals, trees, in a multiplicity which gives life: 'This author finds solace in being descended from a particular and distinctive region' (Scott and Brown 2005, 196); in other words, 'the sense of place' generates a 'possibility of something more meaningful than a simple biological kinship' (ibid.: 79).

What Scott inducts the reader into, along with his group of students, is anything but the 'Timeless Land' as represented in the classic Australian settler account of Indigenous culture (Dark 2002 [1941]). Rather, it is a cosmos that is transformation embodied through the constantly present oscillation between multiple and therefore productive states of being. The dynamic, renewing force of life, a constant production of the new, is what characterises the land: 'any life form must inevitably be in some way a manifestation of the land's spirit' (Scott and Brown 2005, 230). The welcome ceremony as induction or instruction takes the newcomer across a threshold into a world of thresholds, a world that is always already different from itself. The welcome is thus a spatial event, a crossing of a border into a zone in which the mythic past is embodied in the present as an 'abiding event' (Swain 1993, 22-25), that is, a temporal threshold constantly bringing forth futures whose site is the regenerative materiality of the land itself.

Scott concludes his meditations upon this student excursion by noting that 'an old spirit resides in the land and we, its people, are the catalyst of its awakening. It's a potential, a possibility, that still excites me' (Scott and Brown 2005, 18). This apparently romanticising rhetoric in fact conceals some immensely complex operations. The 'old spirit' in the land, now 'awakening', is equated with 'a potential, a possibility'. There are dynamics in the land, transformative possibilities that are inherently plural because transformation always potentially exceeds any limits placed upon it. Potential is thus always unlimited, making its trajectories 'lines of flight' that inevitably lead over the horizon of what is known. This process is however 'catalysed' by a new generation of human custodians who recognise their belonging to the land and thus join their energy with its energy: Scott's artistic statement thus 'disperses its maker's self into nature' (Macfarlane 2013, 240).

Scott, having travelled with his aunt Hazel Brown and heard her tales of nomadic mobility, notes that even for Indigenous people

> only a relatively small part of the continent is home, and beyond that you need introductions and the welcome of its people. Obviously, it's too simple to say 'the bush' is home. There are very many homes, which is another reminder that a single Indigenous Australia is a political construct, a consequence of colonisation.
>
> (Scott and Brown 2005, 243)

The land itself is multiple.

'Multinature' is thus not a single entity: 'Far from evincing the primordial identification between humans and nonhumans commonly ascribed to it, this precosmos is traversed by infinite difference (even if, or because, it is internal to each person or agent)' (Viveiros de Castro 2014, 66). Thus, 'multinature' is always already a multiplicity that balances permanently on the edge of a coming transformation: as

Simondon claims, '[t]he living lives at the limit of itself, on its limit' (as quoted in Deleuze 1990, 103; for the original see Simondon 1964, 260). The multiplicity of 'multinature' is thus both spatial and temporal in character. 'Multinature' is multiple because it contains co-existing incommensurables within itself, but also because this inherent instability makes it a generator of multiplicity in the sense of future possibilities that can neither be predicted nor pre-programmed, but by definition exceed the present, or that which is extant and given. The already multiple and self-different thing-(not)-in-itself becomes the site of transformation, while its capture by one gaze or another becomes a re-capture of the gazer by that multiplicity.

This very sketchy indication of what an Indigenous technique of welcome might mean in practice responds to a single episode early in one of Kim Scott's semi-autobiographical/oral-history-based ethnographies of 'first contact'. It seeks to give some initial indications of the ways in which a tradition of Indigenous hospitality may radicalise our existing notions of hospitality and the debates that have been conducted around the concept in recent years. In order to render concrete the implications of an Indigenous culture of welcome, I now turn back to *That Deadman Dance*, a novel that opens with a word of welcome.

'*Kaya*, hello'

We are welcomed to Kim Scott's 2010 novel *That Deadman Dance* by a Noongar greeting: '*Kaya*, hello' (Scott 2010, 1). At the threshold of the text, whose fictional world we are now entering, stands a threshold word. Bobby Wabalanginy is writing the word with damp chalk on slate: 'Nobody ever done writ that before, he thought. Nobody ever writ *hello* or *yes* that way!' (ibid.: 1). In the text, the word is in printed type on paper, but Bobby, using a piece of chalk that is as 'brittle as weak bone ... wrote on slate. Moving between languages, Bobby wrote on stone' (ibid.: 1). Bobby's writing is a transitional language, an oral medium transiting by way of the rock towards paper, migrating from Noongar to English. Yet the movement is also in the other direction: 'Nobody ever writ *hello* or *yes* that way!' (ibid.). Bobby, using the medium of writing, is not merely ushering Noongar into the realm of written language and English scriptural and pedagogical culture. He is also pulling English back into the world of Noongar knowledge, translating the English 'hello', using an English technology of inscription, back into Noongar and its universe of linked words and land, animals, rocks, water, trees. Bobby is a two-way welcomer, a two-way translator, standing on the threshold as he does. He guides the whites through his territory, and aids his people in negotiating their way through the white order that is irrupting into Indigenous 'Country'. In a manner which is both self-referential and fractal (like his protagonist, Scott 'carrie[s] a story deep within himself, a story [Bobby] gave him' [ibid.: 2]), the author does the same sort of threshold work, mediating between languages, cultures, Indigenous and settler peoples, welcoming both into each others' worlds. This cultural brokerage is underlined by the reiteration of 'Kaya' at the close of the prologue (ibid.: 5). It is also underlined by Scott's later publication of a bilingual poem with the title 'Kaya' that terminates each of its halves with the lines 'You are welcome on Whadjuk country' / 'Kaya, noonookat wandjoo, wandjoo nitja Whadjuk boodjar' (Scott 2017, 271, 272).

Cultural brokerage between humans on 'the friendly frontier' is one of Scott's concerns in *Kayang & Me* and *That Deadman Dance*: 'Delighted to meet you again, Mr Geordie Chaine, [Bobby] said. His words carried Cross's accent; it might almost have been Cross talking. *Kaya*, we say. The boy would not stop shaking Chaine's hand. His smile was infectious' (Scott 2010, 44-45). But, contrary to what such rehearsals of introductions might suggest, the primary emphasis in the text falls not upon a translation that introduces two human cultures to each other against the background of a single nature; rather, there is a radicalising equality of all beings (as persons) via a welcome into a constantly multiple, because constantly transforming, nature(s). As Scott himself writes of his own ventures into the Noongar language: 'Sometimes it's as if, learning to make the sounds [of the Noongar language] I remake myself from the inside out. As if, in making the sounds of the language of this land, I make myself an instrument of it' (Scott and Brown 2005, 236). The topology of self inverts the self from within, unfolding it into the land that provides the self's meaning and being. Language thus empties the self into the land, as does walking, which in turn transforms the self, 'dispers[ing] [the] self into nature', to quote Macfarlane (2013, 240) once again.

Thus 'Kaya' is only in a subsidiary sense a threshold between radically different languages. The linguistic act of welcome does not operate between two cultures, one of which would be 'closer' to nature, 'further' from Reason, than the other. Rather, the welcoming exchange is situated, simultaneously, between many 'persons', some of them very clearly on the side of what would be understood as Nature. 'There would thus be a single series – that of persons – instead of two, while the relations between "nature" and "culture" would involve metonymic contiguity rather than metaphorical resemblance' (Viveiros de Castro 2014, 82-83).

Something akin to this is experienced by Jak Tar, the runaway Scots sailor who marries the Noongar woman Binyang, thus forming one of *That Deadman Dance*'s paradigmatic 'friendly frontier' cross-cultural partnerships. He finds his status being negotiated by Manit, the wife of the local elder Menak – but also, apparently, by other actors:

> Jak, an object of discussion, looked around him. . . . A crow landed beside the pool and bent to drink. But it seemed very watchful. There were many crows in the trees, and now that they had been noticed they began to speak.
> (Scott 2010, 213)

It is in this context of lateral, multi-person communication that 'Kaya' takes place as an event of welcome:

> Manit slapped her thigh and laughed. Jak heard *Kaya*.
> He repeated the word.
> She looked into his face; gave a small, slow smile.
> (ibid.: 213)

Thus 'Kaya' constitutes a linguistic threshold between the various 'multinatures' of things themselves. Significantly, 'Kaya' may signify both 'hello' and 'yes' (ibid.: 1). It is already multiple in character. 'Kaya', then, which may not be perfectly translatable into the English 'hello', actually transpires to be always-already-in-translation-itself, as is, indeed, 'hello' (Lucy 2015). In other words, the term to be translated is itself a translative space. It is not a threshold between 'cultures', because it no longer needs to broker the 'metaphoric' correspondences between actors who are in fact 'metonymic' neighbours of one another as inhabitants of a continuum of personhood. Rather, the word translates between and within 'multinatures' themselves. That 'multinature' is manifest here, within the linguistic fabric of the word, in the internal ambivalence between 'hello' and 'yes'. As Viveiros de Castro summarises: 'To translate is to take up residence in the space of equivocation'(Viveiros de Castro 2014, 89) or semantic ambivalence. (An approximation of the 'spatialisation' of this welcome can be seen in a public art manifestation of Scott's bilingual 'Kaya' poem, which can be found 'etched into 68 pre-cast concrete panels that circle the perimeter of the podium level of the Perth stadium. . . . The entire composition features at the stadium's eastern entrance' [AustLit 2018, n.p.])

Correspondingly, translation is no longer accomplished against the background of some set of common assumptions, or a common language that mediates the languages being negotiated, just as disparate cultures no longer meet against the mediating background of a single universal nature. Rather, there is simply a world of differences that are to be traversed. Perhaps the only common denominator between the entities to be translated is the act of translation itself, not a substratum against which they could be translated. As François Jullien notes, 'One is either in one language *or* another – there is no more a background-language than a background-world' (as quoted in Viveiros de Castro 2014, 73). Translation is not a triangulation between one thing and two words. Rather, translation passes through the thing, which is multiple and already different within itself. For, 'only the incommensurate is worth comparing' (ibid.: 90).

The internal ambivalence between 'hello' and 'yes' opens up a space of productivity, especially through the affirmative resonances of the latter meaning. 'Kaya' is thus an operator of welcoming affirmation that inaugurates the new. The differences – not dislocations – internal to things- and words-(not)-in-themselves thus produce a field of dense relationships of transformation. Thus Muecke, in his recent work on the Indigenous Australian narrative traditions of the Arrernte, imagines 'this Indigenous Australian world to be only one, rather than one thus bifurcated [between heaven and earth, good and evil, material and transcendence, etc.], and one infinitely enriched by the powers of those multiple ancestors embodied in the landscapes and in the living things' (Muecke 2016, 42). It is only one, that is, not hierarchically divided between humans and nature, culture and barbarism; and it is infinitely enriched by the generative temporalities of which it consists.

'Kaya' thus takes on a particular resonance in this context. It is a threshold word, or rather, it is a word that means threshold and, in a fairly banal way, is a threshold between semiotic systems. More importantly, however, by virtue of the entanglement between language and the world in Indigenous cosmologies, it is also a material operator, a space of welcoming transition which signals itself as such.

The literary text as 'multinature'

Commenting upon the various instances of textual welcome in Kim Scott's fiction, Quinlivan notes that in *Benang* (1999), the protagonist Harley 'introduces himself directly to the reader in the first chapter' (Quinlivan 2014, 10: n. 3). This description reduces the textual welcome to an instance of human-to-human relationship, whereas the opening words of *That Deadman Dance*, as I have shown, welcome the human newcomer into an inhuman 'multinature'. Nevertheless, having expanded the notion of welcome to a much larger framework than is customary in hospitality theory, the significance of the manner in which the human reader is welcomed in Scott's texts remains a central question. Notwithstanding the shift of emphasis from the human to the cosmic that Scott's textual instantiations of Indigenous welcome perform, and the relativisation (and setting-in-relation) of human agency that ensues, I turn my attention now, by way of conclusion, to the consequences for scholarship and activism of Scott's 'multinaturalism'.

Having related one of Kayang Hazel's stories, retold to her grandson, about an infringement of welcome protocols, in which an 'unwelcome' juvenile interloper intrudes upon another tribe's sacred ground, Scott concludes:

> Transcribing this story, I realised it was about respect for cultural authority and traditional ownership, and that, like Graeme [Hazel's grandson and the intended audience], I was being welcomed and warned at the same time.
> And you, our reader?
>
> (Scott and Brown 2005, 256)

Scott's ostentatious metalepsis and his elaborately eighteenth-century phatic address (cf. West 2001) extends an already multi-layered narrative. The first level of embedding is the story of a boy in the wrong place, an invader who has not completed the protocols of welcome. His footprints can be found in the rock where he is killed for trespassing on others' territory; his killer's footprints are also engraved in the rock just behind his. The story, then, is embedded, even inscribed in the landscape. The second level of embedding is that of Kayang Hazel's narration of the story during a camping trip with her sister Audrey and grandson Graeme, to whom the tale is told; the telling happens at the place of its literal inscription in the rock, epitomising the way 'language and culture and place went together; sometimes . . . a place demands a certain song. . . . Rocks can set a narrative in motion, animate the stone' (Scott and Brown 2005, 248). The third level of embedding is that of the narrator Kim, who hears the story as it is retold by Kayang Hazel, recording and transcribing it. The fourth level of embedding, of course, is that of ourselves as the multiple readers of the text. The story, in its multiple loci of enactment, is both a narrative welcome to a certain site in 'Country', a fusion of place, language and narrative, and an injunction to use such knowledge well, that is, not to infringe the protocols of welcome that introduce us to the transformative power of place.

Here it becomes clear that the distinction between 'conditional' and 'unconditional' (or 'absolute') hospitality is rendered redundant within Indigenous hospitality; there is no unconditional welcome because the entirety of the cosmos is bound in relationships of reciprocal obligation. At the same time, the productivity generated by welcome opens up the putative constraints, so that the 'conditional' welcome ultimately harbours within itself an inherent, unlimited generosity. That generosity of the land has much in common with 'unconditional' hospitality. However, the generous hospitality of 'Country' is not instantiated here as the impossible horizon that renders the 'conditional' hospitality possible (Still 2010, 8–9); rather, it emerges as a materiality of generativity within the world of nature, housed in the productive difference within places themselves. There are, of course, two sets of footprints in the rock, which speak beyond the retributive scenario they record and found another form of narrative community that redeems the infringement of welcome they witness.

This multiple embedding within what is ultimately a generative 'multinature' is the final destination of Viveiros de Castro's 'symmetrical anthropology' in which 'multinature' co-produces knowledge (here I am modifying his formulation, cf. Viveiros de Castro 2014, 41). By way of a negative example, Viveiros de Castro observes that ethnology 'in deciding the rules of the comparative [cultural] game, reveals itself to stand outside its bounds. And if this recalls Agamben's idea of the state of exception, it's because that's the idea (the very same one) . . .' (Viveiros de Castro 2014, 86; ellipsis in original). Here Viveiros de Castro refers to Agamben's description of the way in which sovereign power must call itself into existence, found its own authority by a self-creating *diktat*, so that sovereign power always entails the potential to suspend the rule of law it has inaugurated – in the state of exception in which civil rights are bracketed off. Viveiros de Castro is well aware that Agamben's central scholarly referent, Carl Schmitt, sees the modern point of origin of this state of exception in the realm of lawlessness that reigns in the colonies of the 'New World' (Agamben 1998, 36; Schmitt 2006, 86–100, 126–38; West-Pavlov 2011, 2015). The ethnographer, then, follows in the footsteps of the colonial conqueror, the settler and the plantation overseer, exercising rampant violence outside the controlling framework of his own civilised values.

In contrast to this violently 'asymmetrical' ethnography, which reduces the object of knowledge to 'bare life', casting it into a space of lawlessness, and thus standing outside the self-constitutive zone of its own epistemic jurisdiction, Viveiros de Castro privileges 'the other, subjacent comparison that . . . implicates the observer in his relationship with the observed'. He continues, in a pivotal move in his argument, by noting that '[t]his kind of implication is also known as *translation*' (Viveiros de Castro 2014, 86). As soon as the theoretical 'person' is welcomed into an implicated relationship with the other, she or he engages with the differential equivocation at the core of the other as it is regarded from one perspective or another, so that the difference within the thing-(not)-in-itself begins to resonate with one's own multiplicity. The subject as well as the object of ethnography becomes translated – not to mention ethnography itself. As a consequence, the 'objects' of anthropological study 'are taken as the agents, instead of the patients, of theory' (ibid.: 84). This ethnography thus inevitably engages, as the work of a 'person' among other 'persons' (some of them not recognisably human), with the generative translative multiplicity of 'multinature'. It produces a reality which is different from itself in a processual, transformative manner – in which translation is an ongoing, creative process.

This also applies because ideas themselves behave like 'multinatural' things-in-process. Ideas are part of the world and inhabit the same spaces, ambivalently, as commonly intentional modes of understanding radically different, but co-existing, universes. The work done by ethnography, comparison, 'then, would not only be our principle analytic tool but also our raw material and ultimate horizon. . . . Things could not be otherwise, once every comparison is seen to be a transformation' (ibid.: 85). Put differently, ethnography would be a 'matter of actualizing the innumerable becomings-other that exist as virtualities of our own thinking' (ibid.: 93) – and indeed, of our own material existences. Is this not too far-fetched, does it locate a symmetrical ethnography in a too-extensive everywhere? Carol Oomera Edwards's already cited anecdote about a schoolroom 'acknowledgement of Country' shows that Indigenous culture, and the transformative encounter with Indigenous culture, does not just happen 'out there' in remote areas or in a mythical outback (see Drew 1994), but pertains to every inch of the Australian continent – or even of the globe. This reach implicates classrooms and offices and homes and even the realm of thinking, reading and writing: all are potentially sacred spaces, regulated by the rules of 'Country' and absolute conditional hospitality.

What might this mean for the discipline of literary studies? The act of reading, an initiation into a 'multinature' via the welcome protocol of a literary instantiation of Indigenous hospitality, engages the reader with a cosmos in process, a cosmos that is generative, new and ever surprising. Almost programmatically, Scott says, 'The way to keep country and culture alive . . . is to have its people welcoming and introducing others into its stories' (Scott and Brown 2005, 257). Once again, it is worth stressing that this 'welcome' is not merely between human actors whose identities are somehow already fixed. For within this perspective, the form of literary narration is not neutral, notionally extracted from the translative ambivalence and generativity of the 'multinature' it describes. That would be to place the writer in the same position of immunity as was adopted by the traditional ethnographer. Rather, the literary work is implicated in the translative ambivalence with which it engages. Providing a useful analogy for the notion of text that is implied by his text, Scott recalls, 'Kayang said her dad used to receive message sticks in stamped envelopes; old forms utilizing a new system. The type of wood was itself part of the message, indicating the region from where it had been cut and sent' (ibid.: 237). The epistolary artefact is split, multiple, ambivalent, linking disparate orders in the same way as the sacred rock site. To that extent, Scott seems to be suggesting that the literary text is itself an element of 'multinature', generating potentiality out of its own virtual dynamic. He formulates this sense of productivity through an extended meditation upon the Noongar lexemes for his own literary activity:

> The usual Noongar word for paper is *bibool*, taken from one dialect's word for paperbark tree. Paperbark trees often stand beside *bily*, our dialect's word for river, which is almost the same as the word for navel. The earth around them is called *boodjar*, and to be pregnant is to be *boodjari*.
>
> Whichever way we put it, writing – to be a writer – is to offer sustenance and life. It is also, as in so many matters of creation and fertility, about intimacy.
>
> (ibid.: 247)

Scott suggestively raises the possibility of re-thinking the thresholds of transformative hospitality at any number of points within the humanities, the literary disciplines (whether critical or creative or both), the teaching profession, the learning community, the business of storytelling and our common existences within the built environment and the natural landscape. All of these are to be understood as processual 'multinatures' in which points open onto other points to generate nomadic trajectories and 'lines of flight' (cf. Ingold 2015) where 'persons' engage with other 'persons' in events of reciprocal transformation.

References

Agamben, Giorgio. 1998. *Homo Sacer: Sovereign Power and Bare Life*. Translated by Daniel Heller-Roazen. Stanford, CA: Stanford University Press.
Austin, John L. 1962. *How to Do Things with Words*. Oxford: Oxford University Press.
AustLit. 2018. 'Kim Scott: "Kaya", Poem, 2016'. *AustLit Database*. www.austlit.edu.au/austlit/page/10031440 (accessed 13 October 2018).
Benjamin, Walter. 2002. *The Arcades Project*. Translated by Howard Eiland and Kevin McLaughlin. Cambridge, MA: Belknap Press of Harvard University Press.
Bolt, Andrew. 2010. 'Don't Welcome Me to My Own Country'. *Herald Sun* blog, 15 March. www.blogs.news.com.au/heraldsun/andrewbolt/index.php/heraldsun/comments/dont_welcome_me_to_my_own_country/ (accessed 23 January 2014).
Butt, Peter, Robert Eagleson and Patricia Lane. 2001. *Mabo, Wik & Native Title*. 4th edn. Sydney: Federation Press.
Claviez, Thomas. 2013. 'Introduction: "Taking Place": Conditional/Unconditional Hospitality'. In *The Conditions of Hospitality: Ethics, Aesthetics, and Politics at the Threshold of the Possible*, edited by Thomas Claviez, 1-9. New York: Fordham University Press.
Cooke, Stuart. 2013. *Speaking the Earth's Languages: A Theory for Australian-Chilean Postcolonial Poetics*. Amsterdam and New York: Rodopi.
Cox, Emma. 2014. 'Sovereign Ontologies in Australia and Aotearoa-New Zealand: Indigenous Reponses to Asylum Seekers, Refugees and Overstayers'. In *Knowing Differently: The Challenge of the Indigenous*, edited by G. N. Devy, Geoffrey David and K. K. Chakrabarty, 139-57. New Delhi: Routledge.
Culler, Jonathan. 1981. *The Pursuit of Signs: Semiotics, Literature, Deconstruction*. London: Routledge, Kegan Paul.
Dark, Eleanor. 2002 [1941]. *The Timeless Land*. Sydney: Angus & Robertson.

Deleuze, Gilles. 1990. *Logic of Sense*. Translated by Mark Lester with Charles Stivale. New York: Columbia University Press.

———. 1992. *The Fold: Leibniz and the Baroque*. Translated by Tom Conley. Minneapolis: University of Minnesota Press.

Derrida, Jacques. 2000. *Of Hospitality: Anne Dufourmantelle Invites Jacques Derrida to Respond*. Translated by Rachel Bowlby. Stanford, CA: Stanford University Press.

———. 2005. 'The Principle of Hospitality'. *Parallax* 11.1: 6-9.

Drew, Philip. 1994. *The Coast Dwellers*. Ringwood, VIC: Penguin.

Gray, Stephen. 2015. *The Northern Territory Intervention: An Evaluation*. Melbourne: Monash University, Castan Centre for Human Rights Law. www.monash.edu/law/centres/castancentre/our-research-areas/indigenous-research/the-northern-territory-intervention/the-northern-territory-intervention an-evaluation/right-to-social-and-cultural-rights.

Hobsbawm, Eric and Terence Ranger (eds.). 1983. *The Invention of Tradition*. Cambridge: Cambridge University Press.

Ingold, Tim. 2011. *Being Alive: Essays on Movement, Knowledge and Description*. London: Routledge.

———. 2015. *The Life of Lines*. London: Routledge.

Jullien, François. 2014. *Vivre de paysage, ou L'Impensé de la Raison*. Paris: Gallimard/NRF.

Klein, Naomi. 2016. 'Let Them Drown: The Violence of Othering in a Warming World'. *London Review of Books* 38.11: 11-14.

Kristeva, Julia. 1969. *Semiotiké: Recherches pour une sémanalyse*. Paris: Seuil.

Lucy, Niall. 2015. 'Introduction'. In *A Dictionary of Postmodernism*, edited by Niall Lucy, with John Hartley and Sam Lucy-Stevenson et al., 1-2. Chichester: John Wiley-Blackwell.

Macfarlane, Robert. 2013. *The Old Ways: A Journey on Foot*. London: Penguin.

Maiden, Samantha. 2010. 'Tony Abbott reopens culture wars over nods to Aborigines'. *The Australian* Online, 15 March. www.theaustralian.com.au/archive/politics/tony-abbott-reopens-culture-wars-over-nods-to-aborigines/story-e6frgczf-1225840660428 (accessed 16 March 2013).

McAdam, Jane. 2014. *Climate Change, Forced Migration, and International Law*. Oxford: Oxford University Press.

Morton, Stephen. 2013. *States of Emergency: Colonialism, Literature and the Law*. Liverpool: University of Liverpool Press.

Morton, Timothy. 2013. *Hyperobjects: Philosophy and Ecology after the End of the World*. Minneapolis: University of Minnesota Press.

Muecke, Stephen. 2004. *Ancient & Modern: Time, Culture and Indigenous Philosophy*. Sydney: UNSW Press.

———. 2016. *The Mother's Day Protest and Other Fictocritical Essays*. London: Rowman and Littlefield.

O'Brien, Amanda and Lex Hall. 2010. 'Ernie Dingo Claims the First Welcome', *The Australian* Online, 17 March. www.theaustralian.com.au/archive/in-depth/ernie-dingo-claims-the-first-welcome/story-e6frgd9f-1225841577128 (accessed 25 January 2011).

Quinlivan, Natalie. 2014. 'Finding a Place in Story: Kim Scott's Writing and the Wirlomin Noongar Language and Stories Project'. *JASAL: Journal of the Association for the Study of Australian Literature* 14.3: 1-12.

Reynolds, Henry. 1996. *Aboriginal Sovereignty: Three Nations, One Australia?* Sydney: Allen and Unwin.

Sassen, Saskia. 2014. *Expulsions: Brutality and Complexity in the Global Economy*. Cambridge, MA: Belknap Press of Harvard University Press.

Savić, Obrad. 2005. 'Introduction: Unconditional Hospitality'. *Parallax* 11.1: 1-5.

Schmitt, Carl. 2006. *The Nomos of the Earth: The International Law of the Jus Publicum Europaeum*. New York: Telos.
Scott, Kim. 1993. *True Country*. Fremantle: Fremantle Arts Centre Press.
———. 1999. *Benang: From the Heart*. Fremantle: Fremantle Arts Centre Press.
———. 2010. *That Deadman Dance*. Sydney: Picador.
———. 2017. 'Kaya'. In *The Fremantle Press Anthology of Western Australian Poetry*, edited by John Kinsella and Tracy Ryan, 270-72. Fremantle: Fremantle Press.
Scott, Kim and Hazel Brown. 2005. *Kayang & Me*. Fremantle: Fremantle Arts Centre Press.
Scott, Rosie (ed.). 2015. *The Intervention: An Anthology*. Salisbury South, SA: Griffin.
Simondon, Gilbert. 1964. *L'individu et sa genèse physico-biologique*. Paris: PUF.
Stephenson, M. A. and Suri Ratnapala (eds.). 1993. *Mabo – A Judicial Revolution: The Aboriginal Land Rights Decision and Its Impact on Australian Law*. St. Lucia: University of Queensland Press.
Still, Judith. 2010. *Derrida and Hospitality: Theory and Practice*. Edinburgh: Edinburgh University Press.
Swain, Tony. 1993. *A Place for Strangers: Towards a History of Australian Aboriginal Being*. Cambridge: Cambridge University Press.
Viveiros de Castro, Eduardo. 1998. 'Cosmological Deixis and Amerindian Perspectivism'. *The Journal of the Royal Anthropological Institute* 4.3: 469-88.
———. 2004. 'Perspectival Anthropology and the Method of Controlled Equivocation'. *Tipití: Journal of the Society for the Anthropology of Lowland South America* 2.1: Article 1. www.digitalcommons.trinity.edu/tipiti/vol2/iss1/1 (accessed 16 November 2017).
———. 2014. *Cannibal Metaphysics: For a Post-Structural Anthropology*. Translated by Peter Skafish. Ann Arbor, MI: Univocal.
West, Russell. 2001. 'To the Unknown Reader: Constructing Absent Readership in the Eighteenth-Century Novel: Fielding, Sterne and Richardson'. *Arbeiten aus Anglistik und Amerikanistik* 26.2: 105-23.
West-Pavlov, Russell. 2011. 'The Time of Biopolitics in the Settler Colony'. *Australian Literary Studies* 26.2: 1-19.
———. 2015. 'Said, Space and Biopolitics: Giorgio Agamben's and D. H. Lawrence's States of Exception'. In *The Geocritical Legacies of Edward W. Said: Spatiality, Critical Humanism, and Comparative Literature*, edited by Robert Tally Jnr, 17-41. New York: Palgrave Macmillan.

11

'YES TO WHO OR WHAT ARRIVES'

Hospitality and property in contemporary art

Anthea Buys

Since the late 1990s art concerned with relational encounters and positive social change has come to be recognised as a genre of contemporary art,[1] achieving visibility even on the least public-spirited of mainstream platforms at contemporary art fairs and at commercial galleries. Under the extensive influence of what we might provisionally call 'socially-engaged art',[2] many contemporary art institutions have in recent years begun to address the topic of hospitality as a means of interrogating the relationship of the professional art community to its perceived outside. Either implicitly or explicitly drawing on Jacques Derrida's notions of hospitality, as presented in *Of Hospitality* and *On Cosmopolitanism and Forgiveness,* a spate of public programming in museums, galleries, academies and alternative spaces has appropriated such terminology with a view to signalling an activist concern for audience development, a 'radical' break with a notion that the world of contemporary art is hermetic and unwelcoming. In 2012 the SMART Museum of Art at the University of Chicago organised the exhibition *Feast: Radical Hospitality in Contemporary Art,* which focused on 'sharing food and drink to advance aesthetic goals' (Feast 2012, n.p.). More recently, *freethought,* a collective of scholars commissioned as co-artistic directors of the 2016 Bergen Assembly, organised a public lecture by curator Laurence Rassel entitled 'On Radical Hospitality'.[3] The latter was held at the Hordaland Kunstsenter (Hordaland Art Centre) in Bergen in December 2015.

However, far from being radical, the appropriation of the tropes of hospitality is inherited from established artistic practice. The invitation of everyday life into the rarified sphere of culture – in which gesture artists have often assumed the role of host and regulator of the presence of 'non-art' content in their work – can be traced as far back as twentieth-century European modernism;[4] such practices persist to the present day. It is not unusual to find contemporary artworks in which the artist literally plays host to non-artist others, who are invited (and sometimes coerced) to participate in situational works as actively contributing guests or as ostensible co-authors. The recent Venice Biennale of Art, entitled 'Viva Arte Viva!', offered us a highly visible example: an installation called *Um Sagrado Lugar (A Sacred Place)* (2017). Credited to the Brazilian artist Ernesto Neto and the Huni Kuin (an indigenous people from Brazil and Peru), this installation occupied a central place in one of the two main exhibition venues, the Arsenale. Neto created a nest-like environment in which visitors to the exhibition were invited to 'hang out', in the words of *New York Times* reviewer Holland Cotter (Cotter 2017, n.p.), and participate in discussions and religious ceremonies conducted by Huni Kuin representatives. Following Cotter's description, Neto invited members of the Huni Kuin, as part of the work, to be present in the installation for the duration of the biennial's preview and opening days. Dressed in traditional ceremonial attire, these individuals were both Neto's guests and second tier hosts (Neto himself being the primary host) to exhibition visitors during this exclusive period of the biennale's presentation (ibid.). Neto's objective was problematically unclear: on the one hand he used his invitation to the privileged platform of the Venice Biennale to extend access to this social setting to the Huni Kuin group. At the same time, their presence as his guests was tightly circumscribed: their proper territory was his installation; while occupying this space, they were expected to demonstrate an indexical relationship to their ostensibly real home, their villages in rural Brazil and/or Peru.[5] Instead of disrupting traditional divisions, Neto's solicitations were premised on a form of hospitality that is highly conditional and serves to reify a preconceived narrative of the redemptive power of art.

Neto's piece is but one recent example of an endemic preoccupation in Eurocentric art since the twentieth century.[6] Drawing on a selection of historical and contemporary examples since the mid-twentieth century, this chapter considers the engagement of art with the concept and practice of hospitality. The incursion of the theme of domestic hospitality into the field of art is itself an enactment of the idea that contemporary art extends an invitation to its outside. However, at both the normative and the reflective level, some of the most prominent instances of hospitality-as-art fail to move beyond appropriations in their interrogation of the conventions of hospitality itself. The examples considered in this discussion all identify homes or house-like spaces – that is, enclosed, built environments to which access is limited – as the contested ground of social interaction. And in each case, the power of the artist to '[intervene] in the condition of hospitality' (Derrida 2000, 149), to grant access to an otherwise prohibitive space, is contingent on a relationship to the private property market (even if as a disavowal). In Theaster Gates's *Dorchester Art and Housing Collaborative (DAHC)* (2009–ongoing),[7] for example, the artist purchased an abandoned two-storey house in a depressed neighbourhood of Chicago and refurbished it as 'a site of community interaction and uplift' (Gates 2009-ongoing, n.p.). While living in an old shopfront next door, Gates created a library, a slide archive and a 'soul food kitchen' for use by residents of the area (ibid.). According to Gates's website, the project 'empowers community members to engage in the movement of radical hospitality by physically transforming their surroundings and filling them with beautiful objects, diverse people and innovative ideas' (ibid.).

Decades earlier, in 1974, Gordon Matta-Clark made the now-famous intervention *Splitting* in a house that was purchased by his dealers as a property investment and was soon to be demolished. Rather than using this site to offer hospitality to a community, Matta-Clark sliced the house in half, rendering it effectively uninhabitable, and casting a shadow on the values of conviviality and belonging that are associated with the home. Both Gates and Matta-Clark treat the house as a site marked by ethical positions. However, while Gates affirms the ethical duty of the master of the house to promote the wellbeing of his guests, Matta-Clark challenges the grounds of this mastery by literally cutting across the thresholds of the master's domain. In both cases, probing the relations between host and guest, private and public, as played out through metaphor, allusion and other non-literal means, is shadowed by a real, inflexible jurisdiction: access is governed by ownership.

This uneasy collusion of capital and critique emerges from, and speaks to, a ubiquitous culture of private wealth, in which the concept of home is entwined with that of ownership. However, whether guided by Marxist politics or other positions, there are artists who have explored systems of spatial and social relations that disavow the notions of property and entitled access. In his long-term project entitled *New Babylon* (1956–1974), Dutch artist Constant Nieuwenhuys (hereafter 'Constant')[8] proposes an alternative to the separation of private and public space in the service of work and the accumulation of wealth. In line with a critical position common amongst his contemporaries (including those belonging to the Situationist International, of which he was a founding member), Constant maintained that postwar (European) cities were being designed to accommodate private automobile transport and a hierarchical division of labour.[9] Constant experimented with an array of spatial and architectural arrangements for a future form of urbanism in which rights of movement and abode would not be contingent on the ownership of property or on the related powers of permission and invitation. Presented through a collection of sculptures, speculative maps, drawings depicting ambiguous architectural environments and descriptive texts, *New Babylon* remained an intentionally unrealised (and unrealisable) work of spatial and social transformation.[10] This speculative city of the future would rely on technology to automate all forms of functional labour, and this same technology would enable freedom of movement on an unprecedented scale. In contrast to works by Theaster Gates and Gordon Matta-Clark, in which hospitality is staged or subverted in the context of privileged access, *New Babylon* proposes the irrelevance of private property, and therefore of its most potent symbol, the house. This unsettles the conventional terms of hospitality, through what Derrida calls a '"derange[ment]"' of 'the trace of a frontier between the public and the non-public, between public or political space and individual or family home' (Derrida 2000, 49-50).[11]

Despite their vast differences in approach, Gates and Constant seem to share an 'ethos' that places importance on the equitable distribution of space and resources, as well as access to aesthetic experiences. Though Constant, for instance, never directly discloses an interest in ethics, it is clear that both artists work from an embedded ethical position. For Derrida, hospitality is inseparable from a negotiation of ethics, and the home is at the centre of this nexus. As Derrida writes, 'the problem of hospitality [is] coextensive with an ethical problem', which is staged as a contention over access to the home (ibid.: 149). 'It is always about answering for a dwelling place, for one's identity, one's space, one's limits, for the ethos as abode, habitation, house, hearth, family, home.' (ibid.: 149-51). In *On Cosmopolitanism and Forgiveness*, this view is clearer still: 'Insofar as it has to do with the ethos, that is, the residence, one's home, the familiar place of dwelling, inasmuch as it is a manner of being there, the manner in which we relate to ourselves and to others as our own or as foreigners, *ethics is hospitality*; ethics is so thoroughly coextensive with the experience of hospitality' (Derrida 2001, 16-17). Not only is the house the site of ethical deliberation and delimitation, but the corollary is posed as well: an 'ethos' becomes an 'abode', a home of sorts. This is implied in the common use of the word 'ethos' to describe a culture or a common sensibility. The community in possession of an 'ethos' has created a 'realm of sedimented practices', 'a domain of exclusion, the passage into or across which is regulated by a certain *logos*' (Mouffe 2007b, n.p.). This *logos* is the foundation of the separation between art and its outside, and thus for the emergence of the idea that the outside can be ushered into the ambit of art at the discretion of artists, curators, critics and others professing custodianship of the discipline.

The ethics of hospitality in contemporary art

Nicolas Bourriaud begins his seminal publication *Relational Aesthetics* (1998; translated from French into English in 2002) with an anecdote recounting the transformation of an artist into a host. He describes a scene that has since been cited prolifically:

> A metal gondola encloses a gas ring that is lit, keeping a large bowl of water on the boil. Camping gears [*sic*] is scattered around the gondola in no particular order. Stacked against the wall are cardboard boxes, most of them open, containing dehydrated Chinese soups which visitors are free to add to the boiling water to eat. This piece, by Rirkrit Tiravanija, produced for the *Aperto 93* at the Venice Biennale remains around the edge of any definition: is it a sculpture? an installation? a performance? an example of social activism?
>
> (Bourriaud 2002, 25)

Untitled (Twelve Seventy-One) (1993) is one of several works by Tiravanija to use the serving of food as 'a means to allow a convivial relationship between audience and artist to develop' (Bishop 2012, 56). Though given little more attention by Bourriaud than the passage transcribed here, the work is a foundational example in his formulation of the concept of relational art. As emerges later in the book, and in subsequent efforts by other authors to circumscribe this field, relational art is characterised by actions traditionally associated with hospitality and domesticity or artistic incursions into people's ordinary home environments.

Bourriaud introduces the slightly more general term 'relational aesthetics' to describe 'an art form where the substrate is formed by intersubjectivity, and which takes being-together as a central theme' (Bourriaud 2002, 15).[12] In his view, relational art transgresses the threshold between art and (non-art) everyday life, because it invites those who are not artists to join in the creation of the artwork in an essential capacity by manifesting the artwork itself as a social interaction. Unlike minimalist art, which called on viewers to 'complete' the work in a phenomenological way by situating their space in relation to it, the work in relational art subsists precisely in the inter-human encounter. In *Artificial Hells: Participatory Art and the Politics of Spectatorship*, Claire Bishop questions the priority Bourriaud gives to 'the production of . . . forms of conviviality' (Bishop 2012, 277), noting that the prominence of participatory or relational art might be symptomatic of a consolidation – rather than a dissimulation – of power in the art world. The current robustness of participatory art

> could be seen as an heroic narrative of the increased activation and agency of the audience, but we might also see it as a story of our ever-increasing voluntary subordination to the artists' will, and of the commodification of human bodies in a service economy (since voluntary participation is also unpaid labour).
>
> (ibid.: 277)

As the profile of Tiravanija's soup kitchen demonstrates, it is not uncommon for works based on an invitational premise to result in encounters that primarily affirm the artist's accomplishment as a host. Tiravanija's transformation of the exhibition space into a self-service kitchen clearly evokes domestic hospitality by replicating the commonplace gesture of offering one's houseguests refreshments. In this manner, the artist identifies the exhibition as his realm, over which he has jurisdiction not only to invite outsiders into his space but also to regulate the activities and behaviours permitted there. Tiravanija's work further alludes to a well-known collaborative project from 1971 by Gordon Matta-Clark, Caroline Goodden, Rachel Lew, Suzanne Harris and Tina Girouard, an artist-run café called *Food*. Matta-Clark is credited with designing and programming the café, which regularly invited artists to cook meals for a paying clientele of fellow-artists. In recent years, particularly given the rise in scholarly interest in hospitality (and community-oriented art) *Food* has surfaced in several key texts, including Bourriaud's, and has thus become something of a canonical example in the genre. In echoing its basic premise – the artist's serving food – Tiravanija also implicitly invokes the authority of art-historical precedent. Thus armed with historical and institutional authority, he assumes the identity of host; the visitors' participation is on his terms, and on the conditions inherited from the conventions of institutional art exhibitions.[13]

There is a clear analogy between this form of invitation (and subsequent incorporation) of the 'ordinary world' into the realm of art and Derrida's understanding of 'traditional hospitality' which colludes with power (Derrida 2000, 55). The host – the one who is in a position to grant or deny hospitality to a stranger – has sovereignty over his domain, at least to the extent that the stranger respects the boundaries excluding him or her from it. 'No hospitality, in the classic sense, without sovereignty of oneself over one's home', Derrida writes (ibid.: 55). In other words, in order to be a host, to bestow or deny access, one has to have staked out a territory that makes of some desirable guests and of others 'parasite[s] or enem[ies]' (ibid.: 61, 45). For Derrida hospitality is inevitably concerned with a relation to foreignness, but for foreignness to fall within the logic of the host-guest relation, it must be attributable to a *subject*. Hospitality is granted as a 'right' to 'the foreigner remaining foreign', as a 'pact' between 'contracting parties' such as a 'familial or ethnic group' (ibid.: 23). For this right to be conferred, Derrida notes, both parties must 'be equipped with nameable identities and proper names' (ibid.: 23). They must be implicated in the ethos of a name, a community, a common law, which regulates their alienation from one another. From within the limits of this ethos, one can offer hospitality to a foreigner without any threat to one's territory or self-sameness.

As Bishop argues, the discourse of relational art asserts the viewer's assumption of power. The viewer is supposedly transformed from a supplicant guest-viewer into a subject who shares the artist's sovereignty as an author of the work. This transformation also ostensibly entails a progression from passivity to activity, through which the viewer is shaken out of a kind of ignorant stupor and conscientised into participation. One of Bourriaud's central, and most controversial, assumptions is that this kind of transformation leads in turn to transformation in the world outside the work, and so encourages convivial social interactions *per se* (not only in the context of art). Bourriaud suggests that Tiravanija's *Untitled (Twelve Seventy-One)* could be an instance of 'social activism', in addition to its interest purely as a work of art (Bourriaud 2002, 25). Drawing on Rancière's central argument in the essay 'The Emancipated Spectator', Bishop problematises this link, pointing out that

> [t]he binary of active/passive is reductive and unproductive, because it serves only as an allegory of inequality. . . . To argue . . . that social participation [in art] is particularly suited to the task of social inclusion risks not only assuming that participants are already in a position of impotence, it even reinforces this argument.
>
> (Bishop 2012, 38)

Gates's *DAHC* differs from *Untitled (Twelve Seventy-One)* and many of the pieces Bishop addresses in *Artificial Hells*; rather than staging a temporary interactive situation, the work constitutes a permanent intervention in an urban environment. In this way, Gates elides the separation between art and its outside by collapsing the artwork and external social realities into a single phenomenon. According to an interview by Tim Adams in *The Guardian*, Gates finances his urban refurbishment projects through the sale of more conventional art objects (Adams 2015, n.p.). Gates works with an established commercial gallery, White Cube in London, and in 2015 presented the exhibition *Martyr Construction* as part of the Venice Biennale. The predominantly sculptural works that circulate through such channels, many of which are made using reclaimed materials from the buildings Gates has purchased, are related indexically to the *DAHC* and to Gates' more recent refurbishment project, the *Stony Island Arts Bank*.[14] On the basis of this relationship, Gates has indirectly 'sold' the *DAHC* to the art establishment in what he candidly describes as 'a hustle' (Colapinto 2014, n.p.). The 'hustle' has also been instrumental in mythologising *DAHC* as a piece of art activism. According to an article by John Colapinto in *The New Yorker*, Gates himself acknowledges that 'the impact of *DAHC* has been largely symbolic', and that the project has in fact effected little social transformation in the neighbourhood (ibid.). However, Gates's gallery, his personal website, and most of the now-extensive media coverage of his work paint the project (and Gates himself) as 'activist'.

Boris Groys in a recent article in the influential online contemporary art journal, *e-flux Journal*, defines 'art activism' as 'the ability of art to function as an arena and medium for political protest and social activism' (Groys 2014, n.p.). Groys claims that activist art is unique to 'our time', a 'new phenomenon' that is 'quite different from the phenomenon of critical art that became familiar to us during recent decades' (ibid.). He continues:

> Art activists do not want to merely criticize the art system or the general political and social conditions under which this system functions. Rather, they want to change these conditions by means of art – not so much inside the art system but outside it, in reality itself.
>
> (ibid.)

Groys's claim that activist art is particular to the contemporary era is difficult to accept given the extensive history of activist art in the twentieth century (or even further back if we include the political provocation of Gustave Courbet's paintings of labourers in the late nineteenth century).[15] To give Groys the benefit of the doubt, though, he seems to be concerned primarily with artistic practices that bring about tangible social change through actions that are technically indistinguishable from community service or political activism 'in reality itself'. *DAHC* is an apt example of this type of art, since the work subsists in creating the conditions for greater access to culture in a neighbourhood where municipal services fail to provide it. Groys, however, overlooks another crucial operation of activism, namely its distinctness from service. The facilities and access Gates provides through the *DAHC* constitute a service to neighbouring residents, but they cannot alone be construed as activism. While an artist may be able discreetly to offer a service to the public, without announcing it, activism requires public knowledge of the act. It is the visibility of Gates's activities that makes them 'activist' in nature, or 'activating', in that they are tacitly meant to encourage similar behaviour and thinking in a broader context. The instructive nature of activism presupposes an ethically corrective potency, an exemplary action or message. In this light, it is Gates's hospitality – his generosity as the master of the house – that is presented as exemplary.

'Yes to who or what arrives' 191

In 'Aesthetic Separation, Aesthetic Community',[16] Rancière identifies the mechanism by which art is supposed to effect political awareness or social change as an assumed causal relationship between the configuration of a work and a desired outcome. In the case of Tiravanija's food-based works, for example, Bourriaud assumes that knowledge of the incongruity of contexts created by the availability of self-service soup inside an art gallery – where both the consumption of food and the touching of artworks are usually prohibited – will eventually lead, in a more general context outside the circumstances of the exhibition, to the promotion of more convivial interpersonal relations. This form of 'critical art', Rancière writes, takes for granted a 'direct road from intellectual awareness to political action' (Rancière 2011, 75). It 'define[s] a straightforward relationship between political aims and artistic means: the aim is to create an awareness of political situations leading to political mobilization' (ibid: 74). Clearly though, this assumed causality could be effective only if the work's audience thought and acted uniformly, not only drawing the same conclusions from what is seen or heard but also having identical perceptual experiences before the work. In other words, this view is inhospitable to readings that may reject the ethical trajectory of political activation, and thus further closes the spaces of art precisely as it purports to open them. Through this inherent contradiction, 'critical art' becomes stultifying rather than politically mobilising; in Rancière's words, '[t]he very same thing that makes the aesthetic "political" stands in the way of all strategies for "politicizing art"' (ibid.). The ethics of conviviality and consensus that characterise the mediation of Gates's work are an effect of the presiding discourse of contemporary participatory art. As Bishop points out, this discourse often submits artworks to ethical rather than critical criteria, evaluating them for their effectiveness as social interventions rather than in terms of artistic interest.[17] Importantly, in these contexts 'ethics' is taken not as a philosophical disposition, or as the scene of a tension between 'the laws' of hospitality and a giving over of oneself to the other (Derrida 2000, 81), but as a moral position inherited from neoliberal democracy. Reading Rancière, Bishop argues that ethics is 'instrumenatliz[ed] as a strategic zone in which political and aesthetic dissensus collapses' (Bishop 2012, 28). In Rancière's own words, when '[a]rt is summoned . . . to put its political potentials at work in reframing a sense of community, mending the social bond, etc.', 'politics and aesthetics vanish together in Ethics' (as quoted in Bishop 2012, 27). Art is neutralised in its capacity for contradiction and difference; the model hospitality performed in the *DAHC* and works like it is revealed to be inhospitable to forces which might challenge its presuppositions.

Hospitality after houses

Rancière maintains that this neutralising order, which exists across disciplines and social situations, overwrites the potential for dissensus and antagonism with consensus. In each of its instances, it is a manifestation of what Rancière calls 'the police', an ordering principle embedded in societies, the essence of which 'lies in a partition of the sensible that is characterised by an absence of void and supplement' (Rancière

2010, 36).[18] Rancière elaborates that society 'is made up of groups tied to specific modes of doing, to places in which these occupations are exercised, and to modes of being corresponding to these occupations and places. In this matching of functions, places and ways of being, there is no place for any void. It is this exclusion of what "is not" that constitutes the police-principle' (ibid.). Contrary to '*the* law of absolute, unconditional, hyperbolic hospitality' that says 'yes *to who or what turns up*' (Derrida 2000, 75, 77), Rancière's 'police' principle is comparable to 'the laws' of hospitality (ibid.: 77). These are the 'conditions, the norms, the rights and the duties that are imposed on hosts and hostesses, on the men or women who give a welcome as well as the men or women who receive it'. The practice of hospitality, Derrida argues, proceeds by way of an aporia, 'at the frontier between two regimes of law' (ibid.), where the absolute openness to the other of unconditional hospitality is moderated by the necessity of choosing to grant access. Without the act of choice, this constitutive excision and exclusion, *the* law 'wouldn't be effectively unconditional', for it would not '*have to become* effective, concrete, determined. . . . It would risk being abstract, utopian, illusory, and so turning over into its opposite' (ibid.: 79). Martin Hägglund's reading of Derrida supports the converse too: the laws are necessarily perverted by *the* law of unconditional hospitality, since there is no hospitality without 'the risk of an evil visitation' (Hägglund 2008, 104). Hägglund continues: 'Hospitality can never be reduced to the invitation of an other who is good. . . . Even the other who is welcomed peacefully may turn out to be an instigator of war, since the other may always change' (ibid.).[19] The other may also misrepresent or deceive.

If, as Derrida maintains, the house is symbolic of the enclosed domain of conditional hospitality, its doors and windows are what incontrovertibly open it to the unknown, to the outside, to potentially threatening guests. Derrida writes: 'in order to constitute the space of a habitable house and a home, you also need an opening, a door and windows, you have to give up a passage to the outside world [*l'etranger*]' (Derrida 2000, 61, translator's parenthesis). Gordon Matta-Clark's various 'building cut' projects were concerned precisely with the built-in vulnerability of the physical structure of the house, as expressed, under normal circumstances, in its thresholds with the outside. Matta-Clark foregrounded the metaphorical significance of these commonplace structural 'punctures' by creating additional, and often spectacular, incisions in the architectural surfaces with which he worked. *Splitting* is one of the best-known examples of these works. Pamela M. Lee recounts the construction of the work in her 2001 study of Matta-Clark's production, *Object to Be Destroyed: The Work of Gordon Matta-Clark*. After using a chainsaw to cut two parallel vertical lines through the centre of the house, he and the builder Manfred Hecht 'scored and chiseled away all the block reinforcing the foundation', effectively lowering and grading the foundation on one half of the house (Matta-Clark, as quoted in Lee 1999, 18). Then, using building jacks, they removed four remaining blocks that held the half above its abraded foundations and were able to lower and tilt it, contriving a narrow, wedge-shaped rift that bisected the building (see Figure 11.1).

This piece dramatises the perforation of the home's limits through a violent gesture that literally destabilises the house, opening it to anything that may arrive

FIGURE 11.1 Gordon Matta-Clark, *Splitting*, 1974, Englewood, New Jersey.
Source: © Estate of Gordon Matta-Clark/Centre canadien d'architecture/cca.qc.ca

from the outside. Without creating the conditions for a participatory encounter between a guest and a host, Matta-Clark shows that the 'limitations of hospitality are . . . exposed to what they seek to exclude, haunted by those who – rightly or not – question the legitimacy of the determined restrictions' (Hägglund 2008, 104). Matta-Clark produced several more works in which the external thresholds of residential buildings were cut into, each time in a building that was identified for demolition in advance of speculative property development.[20] Like Gates, Matta-Clark addressed the phenomena of inequitable access and the effects of capital on urban development through the transformation of discarded properties. However, for Matta-Clark, the impending destruction of the buildings to which he often gained access presented the opportunity not to save them, but to interrogate the kinds of inhabiting to which a building is able to play host.

In the serial project *Fake Estates* (1973), Matta-Clark bought a number of inexpensive, tiny lots of 'surplus land' on auction.[21] As Lee writes, these lots were located in Staten Island and Queens as '"leftover" parcels from lots drawn by architects and city planners' (Lee 1999, 99). In a similar vein to Gates's property refurbishments in Southside, Chicago, Matta-Clark saw the act of purchasing these lots as an artistic gesture, a performative work in its own right. The lots were oddly sized, often sandwiched between buildings and with no potential for use. All of them were uninhabitable, and many were invisible to the public or described in the auction catalogue as entirely inaccessible. Matta-Clark's only intervention after purchasing the lots was to document them through banal, inventory-like texts and black and white photographs. Unlike Gates's 'real estate' works, the *Fake Estates* lots had no potential for recuperation or occupation. They could never have been used in the ostensible creation of community or as sites for Matta-Clark to exercise hospitality. At face value they created a schism between the notions of property, ownership and hospitality, pointing to the culpability of the property market in somewhat carelessly designating and denying spatial value. The *Fake Estates* lots, which in Matta-Clark's own words could be 'owned but not experienced' (as quoted in Lee 1999, 103), are a preposterous urban excrescence: they challenge the logic of the well-apportioned city, cutting into its grid of progress and order with the force of a Deriddean void and supplement. Recalling Rancière, the *Fake Estates* are places where there are no corresponding 'functions' or 'ways of being'. They are the 'is not' that is overlooked and excluded from the 'police' city.

Matta-Clark's style of appropriation of urban spaces could not have changed more dramatically in the short time that passed between the opening of *Food* in 1971 and the building cuts and *Fake Estates*. The same might be said of his position on community and hospitality. I would argue that Matta-Clark began in these later works to explore the possibility of a form of hospitality that acknowledges 'the ever present possibility of antagonism' (Mouffe 2007a, 8). Through breaking open private residential spaces to the outside and thus potentially to public exposure, Matta-Clark lays bare the highly conditional, strategic hospitality facilitated by urban property development, and the inherent vulnerability of the house to whomsoever or whatsoever may arrive. *Fake Estates* continues this critique by reserving spatial pauses in the logic of the city of useful constructions, effectively preventing the complete closure of this order. Borrowing from Rancière's lexicon, these voids function as dissensual operators. They represent 'different presuppositions, assumptions that are certainly unreasonable from the perspective of our oligarchic societies and the critical logic that is its double' (Rancière 2011, 48).

Although Matta-Clark breaks away from the narrative of restoration and 'uplift' ubiquitous in neoliberal city development strategies and in the art that often accompanies them, his work, like Gates's, is premised on a degree of assent to the values associated with real estate development and gentrification. Moreover, its meaning takes place through the processes of construction, destruction, acquisition and territorial manipulation that are already part of the technical arsenal of urban development. In most cities today, this 'matching of functions, places and ways of being' (Rancière 2010, 36) bears the legacy of Le Corbusier's influential assertion that the city should be organised around the efficient passage between places of work and homes.[22] However, the heightened and continuing organisation of cities around the world since the Second World War has also resulted in the displacement of people who are not served by the work-home schema. In the 1980s, not long after Matta-Clark was active in the New York art scene, Martha Rosler's project *If*

You Lived Here . . . (1989) exposed the vast extent of New York City's housing crisis as a result of the influx of urban capital at the time. *If You Lived Here . . .* was presented to the public in the form of a series of three exhibitions, numerous public meetings and a panel discussion that brought together artists, critics, groups of the homeless and lobbyists. A book was subsequently published by the Dia Foundation (which commissioned and hosted the project), serving as a record of the exhibition series and panel discussion, as well as an extension of that work (Rosler and Wallis 1998). These manifestations were revisited in the 2009 exhibition *If You Lived Here Still*, at 141 Essex Street in New York, with Rosler presenting her extensive archives from the original project. According to Rosalyn Deutsche, 'the project emphatically challenged the notion that urban spatial arrangements express the unified interests of coherent society' (Deutsche 1998, 46), thus foregrounding the ineluctable presence in the city of various groups of people who were not acknowledged within the existing urban structure. The project responded explicitly to a statement that Ed Koch, New York mayor at the time, addressed to those threatened by diminishing social housing: 'If you can't afford to live here, mo-o-ove!!' (exhibition documentation, in Rosler and Wallis 1998, 44).[23]

Rosler's exhibitions and public interventions are notable in that they resist framing the homeless as a homogenous community, as is often the fate of the poor who become the subjects of artists' projects (recall, for instance, that the *DAHC* addresses 'the community'). Even more importantly, *If You Lived Here . . .* proposes that the plurality of experienced homelessness warrants recognition in its own right, as a presence and an existential orientation that is not articulated merely by a lack of access to housing, but as a substantive set of relations to the city. In its own right again, the phenomenon of widespread urban homelessness seems to call for scrutiny of the notion that the house is central to the possibility of community, containment and giving place. Constant developed many of the central ideas related to *New Babylon* in response to a particular instance of voluntary homelessness. The sculpture widely accepted as the first *New Babylon* model, *Design for a Gypsy Camp in Alba* (1956) (see Figure 11.2), was based on a mobile built environment he proposed to the municipality of Alba as an alternative to fixed housing for a nomadic community that often settled on the outskirts of the town (Stamps and Pineda 2016, 102).[24] Constant's proposal acknowledged the need for shelter and enclosed environments, but resisted using the concepts of home and privacy. For Constant, it seems, the concepts of 'house' and 'home' were not coextensive, and it was equally possible to eschew the possession of a home and still benefit from provisional forms of housing.

Design for a Gypsy Camp does not resemble a conventional city plan or model except, perhaps, in its scale and its allusion to the aesthetics of architectural models; it is displayed horizontally, on a table, below eye-level, in order to facilitate an easy overview from above. Rather, the sculpture evokes mobility through overlapping, staggered arcs connected to a central hub by wires resembling bicycle spokes. Viewed from above, the wheel-like form suggests continuous motion, but from the side, the gaps between the arcs suggest a multifaceted interior space in which passage is not hindered by walls or regulated by doors. This open design is developed in later works and in Constant's writing on *New Babylon*, which describes its component parts, or 'sectors', as

> a quite chaotic arrangement of smaller and larger spaces that are constantly mounted and dismounted by standardised mobile construction elements such as walls, floors and staircases. . . . People are constantly moving around and travelling, and there is no need for them to come back to the same place, which would soon have been changed anyhow.
>
> (Nieuwenhuys 2016, 214)

This system replaces distinct private and public spaces with a 'playground', in which the occasional need for seclusion is satisfied by temporary enclosed quarters, much like public hotel rooms (ibid.). No individual or group of inhabitants commands the ability to regulate access or movement; thus the categories of guest and host seem to dissolve.[25] Mark Wigley suggests that even without subjects to uphold these categories, hospitality is still conceivable in these terms because architecture

FIGURE 11.2 Constant (1920–2005). *Ontwerp voor een zigeunerkamp in Alba/Design for a Gypsy Camp in Alba*, 1956. Model, stainless steel, aluminium, plexiglass, oil on wood, h. 13,7 cm Æ 125 cm. Collection Kunstmuseum Den Haag, NL.

Source: Tom Haartsen ©Constant/Fondation Constant c/o DACS, London

always already implies a host (even if this host is not an entity that occupies or presides over a building) (Wigley 2016). This is not to say that an architectural structure simply takes the place of a host (becoming a form of surrogate subject), since it is at the same time the place where hospitality occurs, but that hosting (and by implication, the presence of guests) happens wherever there is architectural space (cf. ibid.: 38). Presumably influenced by Derrida, although he does not refer directly to Derrida's writing on hospitality, Wigley observes that as a work of architectural hospitality *New Babylon* 'tries to undo its own authority, removing as many constraints as possible in order to offer the widest and deepest welcome but wants to be undone again and again by the people, actions and ideas that it hosts' (ibid.: 39). This 'relentless labour of deconstruction' entails 'the invitation and embrace of the unknown guest that necessarily undermines the designer and even design itself' (ibid.: 38). Like Hägglund, Wigley recognises that the unconditional invitation must extend to an other who is potentially violent or antagonistic, in order to avoid the 'greater violence' of exclusion (ibid.: 38).

Constant seems to have acknowledged that *New Babylon* would have to be vulnerable to the possible arrival of a violent other. This is particularly visible in the paintings he produced towards the end of his engagement with *New Babylon*, in which ambiguous scenes of violence are placed at the entrance to characteristic labyrinth environments. In the 1971 painting *Erotic Space* (see Figure 11.3), a naked woman lies in the foreground, partially cropped by the bottom edge of the canvas. She appears to be bleeding, while a menacing silhouette – perhaps her attacker – looms in the background. Another painting of this period, *Entrée du labyrinth* ('Entrance to the Labyrinth') (1972), shows an extensive grid of scaffolding and transparent, coloured walls – a clear signal that this is a view into a section of *New Babylon*. Again in the foreground, an ambiguous shape is obscured by what resembles a blood stain. It is unclear whether the stain is inside the imitative perspective of the painting, or whether it sits on the surface of the painting, as though the blood had come from the world outside. More of these nebulous red forms are scattered in the middle-ground, to the left and the right of the main labyrinth perspective, seeming neither to resemble figures nor fully to represent static marks left by an earlier act of violence. In yet another painting from 1972, *Le Massacre de My Lai* ('The Massacre of My Lai'), the reference to violence is much clearer.[26] Two mutilated bodies lie sprawled in a featureless landscape flanked by the ladders and scaffolding of a multilevel *New Babylon* sector.

A telling absence of critical reflection on Constant's depiction of violence in the later *New Babylon* works seems to suggest that this apparent departure from the ideals of creativity and liberty represents a contradiction to the utopian vision he otherwise put forward. Even in the exhibition *Constant, New Babylon. To Us, Liberty*, curator Laura Stamps translates this development in the work as Constant's disillusionment with an unattainable ideal, and a concession to the violence and destruction ubiquitous in the 'real world' (Stamps and Pineda 2016, 190).[27] An alternative reading, one that accepts the possible consequences of unconditional hospitality, is that *New Babylon* echoes Derrida's words and says 'yes *to who or what turns up*'. In this case, the appearance of violence in *New Babylon* follows on from the porous thresholds seen in earlier instances of the work.[28] Constant is unequivocal in his rejection of privileged spatial access, stating that in *New Babylon* '[e]very place is accessible to all. The whole earth becomes home to its owners' (Nieuwenhuys 1998, 161). His use here of the term 'owners' is deliberately paradoxical, since universal access and ownership are clearly mutually exclusive concepts, particularly in a context in which the notions of wealth, labour and resources are eschewed.[29]

It is difficult to imagine a situation more at odds with the privatised performances of hospitality in contemporary art settings, in which no hierarchies are really transgressed and no violence is done to systems of violent exclusion. That *New Babylon* has been revisited in the present in a major museum exhibition – and revisited moreover as an exemplary instantiation of hospitality – calls the broader current interest in hospitality into question, and clearly foregrounds its connections

FIGURE 11.3 Constant (1920–2005). *Erotic Space*, 1971. Oil on linen, 165,0 x 175,0 cm. Signed and dated "Constant '71'" bottom centre in black paint on red fond. Collection Kunstmuseum Den Haag, NL.

Source: Tom Haartsen ©Constant/Fondation Constant c/o DACS, London

to capital. Reversing the order of the cases discussed in this essay, a creeping anxiety about property ownership comes to light, culminating in a scenario in which critical artistic practice and property speculation can become indistinguishable from each other. One obvious interpretation is that this is simply an instance of the art world's absorbing, or rather 'welcoming', previously excluded elements into its ambit. But we have already seen how the very terms of this relational structure are fraught by, and in fact take for granted, the power art ostensibly sets out to colonise. With the art market, the property market, critical practice and ethical positions as intimately mingled as they are in Theaster Gates's system of financing and refurbishing properties, for example, it is unclear precisely which element plays guest and which host. It is important to note that, rather than representing a progressive transgression of thresholds, this ambivalence connotes the exclusion of the possibility of dissensus. The direct outcome of this exclusion is that the many proclamations of hospitality touted as radical or critically illuminating artworks in fact perform a conservative and highly conditional form of conviviality.

Notes

1. I have used the word 'genre' here rather than the more conventional 'medium' in order to accommodate multidisciplinary and cross-medium artistic practices that are concerned primarily with participation or community.
2. The nomenclature of 'work' in this genre is contested, with different authors naming it differently, while each variance reflects individual critical priorities. Claire Bishop, for instance, has called it 'participatory art' (Bishop 2012), while Grant Kester prefers to speak about 'dialogical' art (Kester 2004, 10). In each case, these differences in naming also circumscribe the author's field of reference, excluding potential examples not strictly relevant to the particular discussion. My intention at this point is the opposite: to indicate a very general field of influence on institutional programming by art concerned with the 'inter-human' encounter (this adjective is used by Nicolas Bourriaud (Bourriaud 1998, 6)).
3. Bergen Assembly is a triennial exhibition held in Bergen, Norway. The inaugural event took place in 2013.
4. The Situationist International famously called for the integration of art and everyday life. Through practices such as psycho-geographical exploration and mapping of their immediate surrounds, they imported activities such as walking, map-making and psychological interpretation. The presumed power of the artist was brought into particular focus in the late 1960s in Europe and America through the 'institutional critique' movement, which was identified with artists such as Hans Haacke, Marcel Broodthaers and Andrea Fraser, amongst others. Alexander Alberro and Blake Stimson's 2009 collection, *Institutional Critique: An Anthology of Artist's Writings*, offers a thorough overview of this field.
5. Notably, the credit information in the exhibition showed a familiar disparity in the quantity of biographical information given about Neto and his co-authors. The label of the work included the following details: 'Ernesto Neto: ★ 1964 Brazil, lives in Rio de Janeiro / Huni Kuin, or Kaxinawá, indigenous people living in the Brazilian state of Acre, and in Peru, the Amazonian forest' (exhibition label, n.p.). This replicated the convention in modern European ethnographic museology of giving the tribal and broad geographical provenance of cultural objects collected from non-European, and especially rural and pre-industrial, societies, rather than the names of the individual creators.
6. I use the term 'Eurocentric' to refer to canonised Euro-American art, instead of the more commonly used adjective 'Western', because the latter term fails to acknowledge, on the one hand, the centrality of European art in canonical art history, and on the other, the

continuing centralisation of the global art world's intellectual and commercial power in Europe.
7 This work was formerly known as the *Dorchester Projects*, and is still sometimes referred to using this title.
8 Constant used only his first name in professional contexts; this essay follows the convention by referring to him as 'Constant'.
9 See Simon Sadler's *The Situationist City* (1998: 25-26).
10 Constant's work has been the subject of a fairly recent survey exhibition entitled *New Babylon: To Us, Liberty*, coproduced by the Gemeentemuseum in Den Haag and the Reina Sofia Museum in Madrid (Reina Sofia, 20 October 2015–29 February 2016; Gemeentemuseum, 28 May–25 September 2016).
11 Derrida introduces this idea in relation to the invisible, non-physical presence of technologies such as the internet, email and satellite transmissions that cut across the physical thresholds separating private and public space. For Derrida the transgression of boundaries entailed in this spatial duality leads to reflection on an aporia, the inevitable vulnerability of these thresholds, their necessary solicitation of transgression. In addition, however, Derrida begins to enunciate thought-provoking observations about the spatiality of transmission technology (the internet, satellites, etc.), as well as the implications for our understanding of mobility and the ontology of intangible entities, among other notions. While it does not lie within the scope of this chapter fully to explore such concerns, Derrida's sense of the relationship between technology and hospitality resonates strongly with Constant's hypothesis that future technologies would demand a revision of theories of mobility, privacy and the uses of space.
12 I differentiate between 'relational aesthetics' and 'relational art' in order to avoid potential confusion between specific reference to Bourriaud's concept and more general reference to a field of artistic practice.
13 As with Tiravanija's other food-based works, the self-service soup kitchen was open only during the hours of the exhibition and according to the other customs of access that pertain in such environments (such as having to purchase tickets, observing any prohibitions against photographing or touching specified works, and similar limitations).
14 The latter opened during the 2015 Chicago Architecture Biennale in December 2015.
15 The most frequently cited instance of pre-twentieth-century work is probably Courbet's 1850 painting *The Stonebreakers*, which was destroyed in the Second World War. Michael Fried discusses the painting in detail in *Courbet's Realism* (1990: 261–63).
16 The version of the essay cited here appears in *The Emancipated Spectator* (Rancière 2011).
17 Bishop's observation is not without its own difficulties, however, since she takes for granted a self-evident standard of artistic merit against which participatory artworks can be critically evaluated.
18 In *On Cosmopolitanism and Forgiveness*, we see that the legislative nature of conditional hospitality resonates strongly with the notion of 'the police'. Derrida gives context to the association of hospitality with law as follows: '[I]n defining hospitality in all its rigour as a law . . . Kant assigns to it conditions which make it dependent on the state sovereignty, especially when it is a question of *the right of residence*. Hospitality signifies here the *public nature (publicité)* of public space, as is always the case for the juridicial in the Kantian sense; hospitality, whether public or private, is dependent on and controlled by the law and the state police' (Derrida 2001, 22).
19 Implicit in this claim is Hägglund's thesis that Derrida sees unconditional and conditional hospitality as indissociable on practical and logical – rather than ethical – grounds. 'On the one hand, unconditional hospitality is indissociable from conditional hospitality, since it is the exposure to the visitation of others that makes it necessary to make conditions of hospitality, to regulate who is allowed to enter. On the other hand, unconditional hospitality is heterogenous to hospitality since no regulation finally can master the exposure to the visitation of others' (Hägglund 2008, 104).
20 The 1975 work *Conical Intersect*, for example, involved cutting a torqued cone shape from the exterior wall into an apartment building in the central Les Halles-Plateau Beauborg

district of Paris (22–29 rue Beauborg). The building's imminent demolition was to make way for what is today the Centre Georges Pompidou.
21 This project is sometimes referred to as *Reality Properties: Fake Estates* (Lee 1999, 98).
22 This argument is presented comprehensively in Le Corbusier's *The City of Tomorrow and Its Planning* (1987).
23 The statement was reproduced as a wall text in the first of the three exhibitions, *Home Front*, which ran from 11 February to 18 March 1989.
24 I have not seen Constant's designs for this housing solution, and the account of the origin of *Design for a Gypsy Camp* as a serious proposal to the Alba municipality may be purely apocryphal. The link between Constant's encounter with the nomadic community and his inspiration to begin work on *New Babylon* is sound, however, and is reiterated by Constant himself in various interviews and texts. See, for example, Constant's interview with Hans Ulrich Obrist (Obrist 2003, 171-72).
25 This recalls Derrida's own reliance in *Of Hospitality* on the double meaning of the French etymology of the word *hôte,* which can refer to both host and guest.
26 The title of this painting is a direct reference to the My Lai Massacre of the Vietnam War that occurred in 1968.
27 This position was presented in the wall text accompanying the display of these paintings in the exhibition. In line with the conventions of museum exhibitions, this kind of text is not attributed to an author, but seems rather to speak 'for the museum', and with the museum's authority. However, since Stamps is credited as the primary curator and researcher for the exhibition, I attribute this point of view to her. The text is reproduced in the exhibition catalogue (Stamps and Pineda 2016, 190-91), and, likewise, the authorship is unattributed.
28 What may be disconcerting about Constant's use of violent imagery is that it is unclear whether or not he condones the violence that appears in the late *New Babylon* paintings. In *Erotic Space*, the brutalised female figure is clearly linked to a more playful erotic image suspended in front of the black silhouette, suggesting that she might have been complicit in her attack. Similarly, in *Entrée du labyrinth* ('Entrance to the Labyrinth'), the bloody forms are at moments oddly vital.
29 This is not comparable, for example, to the Marxist principle of labourers' collectively owning the means of production, since nothing is produced or gained in *New Babylon*.

References

Adams, Tim. 2015. 'Chicago Artist Theaster Gates: "I'm Hoping Swiss Bankers Will Bail Out My Flooded South Side Bank in the Name of Art"'. *The Guardian*, 3 May. www.theguardian.com/artanddesign/2015/may/03/theaster-gates-artist-chicago-dorchester-projects (accessed 19 August 2016).
Alberro, Anthony and Blake Stimson (eds.). 2009. *Institutional Critique: An Anthology of Artist's Writings*. Cambridge, MA and London: MIT Press.
Bishop, Claire. 2012. *Artificial Hells: Participatory Art and the Politics of Spectatorship*. London and New York: Verso.
Bourriaud, Nicolas. 2002 [1998]. *Relational Aesthetics*. Paris: Les Presse du Reel.
Colapinto, John. 2014. 'The Real-Estate Artist'. *The New Yorker*, 12 January. www.newyorker.com/magazine/2014/01/20/the-real-estate-artist (accessed 19 August 2016).
Cotter, Holland. 2017. 'Venice Biennale: Whose Reflection Do You See?'. *The New York Times*, 2 May. www.nytimes.com/2017/05/22/arts/design/venice-biennale-whose-reflection-do-you-see.html (accessed 18 February 2020).
Derrida, Jacques. 2000. *Of Hospitality: Anne Dufourmantelle Invites Jacques Derrida to Respond*. Translated by Rachel Bowlby. Stanford, CA: Stanford University Press.
———. 2001. *On Cosmopolitanism and Forgiveness*. Translated by Mark Dooley and Michael Hughes. London and New York: Routledge.

Deutsche, Rosalind. 1998. 'Alternative Space'. In *If You Lived Here: The City in Art, Theory, and Social Activism: A Project by Martha Rosler*, edited by Martha Rosler and Brian Wallis, 45-66. New York: The New Press.

Feast. 2012. 'Feast: Radical Hospitality in Contemporary Art'. SMART Museum of Art, The University of Chicago. www.smartmuseum.uchicago.edu/exhibitions/feast/ (accessed 20 December 2019).

Fried, Michael. 1990. *Courbet's Realism*. Chicago and London: The University of Chicago Press.

Gates, Theaster. 2009-ongoing. *Dorchester Art and Housing Collaborative (DAHC)*. www.theastergates.com/project-items/dorchester-art-and-housing-collaborative-dahc (accessed 18 February 2020).

Groys, Boris. 2014. 'On Art Activism'. *e-flux Journal* 56. www.e-flux.com/journal/on-art-activism/ (accessed 21 October 2015).

Hägglund, Martin. 2008. *Radical Atheism: Derrida and the Time of Life*. Stanford, CA: Stanford University Press.

Kester, Grant. 2004. *Conversation Pieces: Community and Communication in Modern Art*. Berkeley, Los Angeles and London: University of California Press.

Le Corbusier. 1987. *The City of Tomorrow and Its Planning*. London: Courier Corporation.

Lee, Pamela M. 1999. *Object to Be Destroyed: The Work of Gordon Matta-Clark*. Cambridge, MA and London: MIT Press.

Mouffe, Chantal. 2007a. 'Art and Democracy: Art as an Agonistic Intervention in Public Space'. *Onlineopen.org*. www.onlineopen.org/art-and-democracy (accessed 20 December 2019).

———. 2007b. 'Artistic Activism and Agonistic Spaces'. *Art & Research: A Journal of Ideas, Contexts and Methods* 1.2. www.artandresearch.org.uk/v1n2/mouffe.html (accessed 10 May 2016).

Nieuwenhuys, Constant. 1998. 'Outline of a Culture'. In *Constant's New Babylon: The Hyperarchitecture of Desire*, edited by Mark Wigley, 160-65. Rotterdam: 010 Publishers.

———. 2016. 'Lecture at the Institute of Contemporary Arts, London, 1963'. In *Constant, New Babylon. To Us, Liberty. Exhibition Catalogue*, edited by Laura Stamps and Mercedes Pineda, 210-15. Ostfildern: Hatje Cantz.

Obrist, Hans Ulrich. 2003. *Interviews*. Vol. I. Edited by Thomas Boutoux. Milan: Edizioni Charta.

Rancière, Jacques. 2010. *Dissensus: On Politics and Aesthetics*. London: Bloomsbury.

———. 2011 [2009]. *The Emancipated Spectator*. London and New York: Verso.

Rassel, Laurence. 2015. 'On Radical Hospitality'. Unpublished Public Lecture, 5 December 2015. Bergen: Bergen Assembly and Hordaland Kunstsenter.

Rosler, Martha and Brian Wallis (eds.). 1998. *If You Lived Here: The City in Art, Theory, and Social Activism: A Project by Martha Rosler*. New York: The New Press.

Sadler, Simon. 1998. *The Situationist City*. Cambridge, MA and London: MIT Press.

Stamps, Laura and Mercedes Pineda (eds.). 2016. *Constant. New Babylon. To Us, Liberty. Exhibition Catalogue*. Ostfildern: Hatje Cantz.

Wigley, Mark. 2016. 'Extreme Hospitality'. In *Constant, New Babylon. To Us, Liberty. Exhibition Catalogue*, edited by Laura Stamps and Mercedes Pineda, 38-49. Ostfildern: Hatje Cantz.

INDEX

Abbott, Tony 163
Abelard, Peter 23, 25–6, 31, 35n5, 35n6, 35n7, 35n8, 36n22; on *Invisibilia Dei* 26; writings (*Planctus* 26–7; *Theologia christiana* 26)
Abraham 5, 61, 64–6; as Ibrahim 5
Achebe, Chinua: *Things Fall Apart* 79–80
Adams, Tim 189–90
Adorno, Gretel 116
Adorno, Theodor 15, 59, 69–70, 72, 115–17, 123n5; on home 59; writings (*Prismen* 116; *Prisms* 123n5)
Africa 79, 90; Central 91; North 95, 111
Agamben, Giorgio 179; 'bare life' 179
Algeria 9, 18, 108, 110–13, 115, 118–19, 123, 123n1
Algiers 111, 123
alterity: absolute 47, 51; radical 68
Altieri, Charles 14, 23
Anidjar, Gil 5
animal(s) 143–50, 157–9, 160n3, 160n4, 160n5
apartheid 16–17, 75, 77–8, 86–7, 99, 100, 104; post-apartheid 16, 76, 87
aporia 13, 15, 21, 25, 35, 43, 56, 117, 136, 167, 192, 200n11; aporia as 'non-road' or 'non-passage' 3, 55
Aristarkhova, Irina 85
Aristotle 24–5, 149, 157
Ashcroft, Bill 17; 'postcolonial utopianism' 87
Athanasiou, Athena *see* Butler, Judith

Augustine, St. 31; writing (*Confessions* 114)
Australia 9, 16, 127, 163, 168

Badiou, Alain 106n4
Baker, Gideon 77, 83–4
Bantustan 17, 100
Barolong 16, 75–6, 80–3, 88
Bauman, Zygmunt 98
Bechuana 80, 88
Beckett, Samuel 59–72 *passim*; writings (*Malone Dies* 72; *Molloy* 15–16, 59–72 *passim*; *Murphy* 61; *The Unnamable* 65, 70, 72); *see also Molloy*
Bell, Avril 75
Benjamin, Walter 18, 113–16, 121, 169; writing ('The Work of Art in the Age of Mechanical Reproduction' 114)
Bentham, Jeremy: *Introduction to the Principles of Morals and Legislation* 149–50
Benveniste, Emile 78
Biko, Steve 76–9, 82–4, 87, 89–90, 91n4; Black Consciousness 76–9; colonial abuses of hospitality 77–9
Bishop, Claire 188–9, 191, 199n2, 200n17; writing (*Artificial Hells* 188–9)
Blackwood, Algernon 53
Blanchot, Maurice 67
Blatty, William Peter: *The Exorcist* 54
Bloch, Ernst 17; Blochian not-yet 87
Bloch, Robert: *Psycho* 15, 54
body 99–102, 105, 135–7, 140, 148, 158, 172–3, 188; and consciousness 101; national 100; and spirit 102

Index

Boers 16, 76, 81–3, 85, 88
Bourriaud, Nicholas 187–9, 191, 199n2; convivial sociability 20; writing (*Relational Aesthetics* 20, 187)
Brontë, Emily: *Wuthering Heights* 15, 51
Brown, Hazel 166–76, 178, 180–1; *see also* Scott, Kim
Bürger, Gottfried August: 'Leonore' 50
Burke, Edmund 48–9; writing ('Case for the Suffering Clergy in France' 48–9)
Burney, Frances 49; writing (*Brief Reflections Relevant to the Emigrant French Clergy* 49)
Butler, Judith 72n1; in dialogue with Athena Athanasiou 137, 141
Buys, Anthea 4, 20

Caminero-Santangelo, Byron 79
Capella, Martianus 36n11; writing (*The Marriage of Mercury and Philology* 27)
Catholic 29, 48–9, 111; anti-Catholic 49
Charles I, King 102
Chennells, Anthony 86–9
Choi, Susan: *A Person of Interest* 129
Chrétien, *see* De Troyes, Chretién
Christ 26, 61, 114
Christianity 25, 97; Christian courtly love 32
Cixous, Hélène 16, 18, 108–23 *passim*, 147; on Algeria 108, 110–13, 115, 118–19, 123; on dreaming/dreams 109–10, 115–19, 121–3; on life and death 108–10, 118–19; on loss 108, 110, 112–15, 117, 122; on mourning 108–9, 112–13, 117, 122–3; and veils 18, 113, 115, 120; writings (*FirstDays of the Year* 110; *Hyperdream* 109–10, 113–20, 122; *Illa* 123; *Insister of Jacques Derrida* 117; '*La Baleine de Jonas*' 121; *Le Prénom de Dieu* 121; 'Letter to Zohra Drif' 111; 'My Algeriance' 110–11; *Portrait of Jacques Derrida as a Young Jewish Saint* 109, 123n2; *Reveries of the Wild Woman* 111–13; '*Savoir*' 120; *Three Steps on the Ladder of Writing* 118; with Derrida, *Veils* 113, 120)
Claviez, Thomas 166; writing (*The Conditions of Hospitality* 9)
Coetzee, J. M.: *Disgrace* 98–9
Colapinto, John 190
Collins, Wilkie: *The Haunted Hotel* 53
colonialism 20, 75, 77–9, 83, 88–9; anti-colonial 112; neocolonial 19, 156; postcolonial 17, 75–6, 86–7, 98, 153, 156; precolonial 16, 76, 79–80, 164

cosmos 20, 165, 167; in process through reading 179–80; transformation of 169–74
Cotter, Holland 185
'Country' (Indigenous Australian) 20, 163–9, 175, 179–80; *see also* 'Welcome to Country'
Courbet, Gustave 190; artwork (*The Stonebreakers* 200n15)
cupiditas 29, 34

Davis, Colin 47
dead, the 9–10, 108, 118, 120
death 18–19, 108–23 *passim*, 157, 159
democracy 16, 76, 86–7
Derrida, Jacques 2–5, 7, 9–12, 15, 18, 24, 25, 27, 35, 41–8, 50, 54–6, 60, 75–7, 83–4, 89, 108–10, 113–23, 132, 143–4, 147–9, 157–8, 160n3, 160n4, 166, 185–9, 191–2, 194, 197–8, 200n11, 200n18, 200n19; *arrivant* 6, 10, 13, 47, 112, 122; conditional (also commonplace, ordinary) hospitality 2–4, 10, 12, 14–15, 17, 20, 42–56 *passim*, 60, 77, 81, 110, 133–4, 166–7, 179, 185, 192, 200n18, 200n19; on death 108–9, 117–18; 'derangement' of the public-home threshold 186, 200n11; *différance* 46; hauntology 119; *histos* 118, 120; hospitality and spectrality 10, 47; hospitality to animals 143–4, 158, 160n3, 160n5; hostipitality 5, 10, 12, 15, 21, 44, 46, 50, 56n2; interimplication of culture and hospitality 75; the Law (also *The* law or *the* law) of absolute (or unconditional) hospitality 3–5, 13, 43, 45, 55–6, 117, 120, 148–9, 192; laws of (conditional) hospitality 3–5, 13, 43–5, 55–6, 117, 132, 149, 159, 191–2; on mourning 108; the *question* of hospitality 2; *revenant* 118, 122; *tallit* 120–1; unconditional (also absolute, hyperbolical, pure; impossible, radical) hospitality 2–4, 6, 10, 12–15, 17, 25, 31, 42–56 *passim*, 56n3, 64, 66, 77, 83–4, 121, 143, 148–9, 156, 158–9, 160n3, 161n16, 166–7, 179, 192, 200n19; writings (*Adieu to Emmanuel Levinas* 2–3, 5–6, 10, 41–3, 46–7); *The Animal That Therefore I Am* 160n3; '*Fichus*' 115–17; *The Gift of Death* 116; *HC for Life, That Is to Say...* 108–9, 121; 'Hospitality, Justice and Responsibility' 2; 'Hostipitality' 56n2, 56n4; 'Hostipitality:

Session of January 8, 1997' 144, 160n5; *Of Hospitality* 43, 184, 201n25; *On Cosmopolitanism and Forgiveness* 42, 184, 187, 200n18; 'Plato's Pharmacy' 120; *Politics of Friendship* 122; 'A Silkworm of One's Own' 114, 120; *Specters of Marx* 42–3, 47, 72, 122; for *Veils, see* Cixous, Hélène)
Descartes, René 149
De Troyes, Chrétien 14, 23, 27–9, 35n7, 35n8, 36n11, 36n13; writing (*Erec et Enide* 27–9)
Deutscher, Rosalyn 195
Dickens, Charles: *The Mystery of Edwin Drood* 98–9
displaced populations 1–2
dogs 19, 145–7, 150–9, 160n4, 160n9, 161n16
Doyle, Arthur Conan 106n5
Drif, Zohra 18, 111, 113, 118, 123n1
Dufourmantelle, Anne: 'Hospitality – Under Compassion and Violence' 2; *see also* Derrida, Jacques, *Of Hospitality*

Edwards, Carol Oomera 165, 180
Eggers, Dave: *Zeitoun* 129
England 48, 52
Enlightenment, The 8, 17, 101, 150, 170–1
Eriugena, John Scottus: *Periphyseon* 24
Europe 1, 9, 19, 48, 145, 199n4; European 5, 16, 22, 60, 79, 95, 99, 102–3, 127, 137, 143, 146, 159; European 'crisis' 95

Fanon, Frantz 78
Fasselt, Rebecca 9, 16–17, 19, 20, 22
foreigner 3–4, 7, 10, 17, 43–4, 97–8, 119, 122, 164; hospitality to 187–9; transplanted heart as 104; *see also* stranger
foreignness 115, 189; Cixous on '(most) intimate' 118–19, 122; of welcome 164–8
Foucault, Michel 133, 135; *dispositif* 133; on security and biopolitics 133; writing (*Security, Territory, Population* 133)
France 18, 48, 103, 115, 123n1, 145–6, 159n1
French (language) 110, 112, 115–16, 122, 123n1, 123n4, 144, 147, 159–60n1
Freud, Sigmund 60; *see also* unheimlich
friendship 11, 18, 84–5, 88, 91n5

Gates, Theaster 20, 185–7, 189–91, 193–4, 199; artworks (*Dorchester Art and Housing Collaborative (DAHC)* 185, 189–91, 195, 200n7; *Martyr Construction* 190; *Stony Island Arts Bank* 190)
German (language) 110, 115–17, 120
Germany 97, 150–1
Gevisser, Mark: *Lost and Found in Johannesburg* 106n9
ghost 10–11, 15, 20, 41, 47, 50–3, 67, 102, 111, 118, 122; Banquo's ghost in *Macbeth* 43, 45, 50; etymology 47
Gibson, Nigel 78
global warming 1
God 25–6, 31, 47, 114, 121, 141, 165
Gordon, Lewis R. 78
Gothic writing 14–15, 41–3, 47–56; affect (terror and horror) 47–8, 50, 53–4; ghosts in 15, 41, 43, 45, 47, 50–3; guests in 41–54 *passim*; hosts in 41–54 *passim*; violence in 42–9, 54–5
Gotman, Anne 147
Gottfried, *see* Von Strassburg, Gottfried
Gramsci, Antonio 16
Green, D. H. 29
Green, Michael 76, 82, 87
Greenblatt, Stephen: *Renaissance Self-Fashioning* 106n7
Groys, Boris 190; and *e-flux Journal* 190
guest 2, 7, 10, 15–17, 19, 24, 41–54 *passim*, 59, 67, 76–8, 80, 82–4, 95, 97, 102, 106n9, 118, 122, 131, 141, 143–59 *passim*, 185–6, 188–9, 192–3, 196–7, 199, 201n25; etymology 4–5, 12–13, 45–6; as parasite 45–6, 51–2

Hägglund, Martin 192, 197, 200n19
Hayman, David 61
heart 98, 100, 154, 156, 158; heart transplant 104–5; Mr Darvall and the victim's sacrifice 105; *see also* Nancy, Jean-Luc
Hecht, Manfred 192
Heidegger, Martin 149; *Mitsein* 8; writing (*Being and Time* 117)
Herder, Johann Gottfried 97
Hesiod 24
Hitchcock, Alfred (director): *Psycho* 54
home 3–4, 6, 7, 9, 15–16, 21, 24, 77–8, 80–2, 84, 86, 88, 97–8, 100, 105, 111, 115, 119, 131, 138, 140–1, 146–7, 149, 153, 155–6, 161n14, 174, 180; in Beckett's *Molloy* 59–72 *passim*; and contemporary art 185–95, 198; in Gothic writing 43, 45–7, 52; security of 61–2; as shared identity of man and woman (Irigaray) 149
'homeland' (South African) 77, 99–100

homelessness 20, 59, 195
homeliness 59, 61–2, 67, 71–2
Homer 24, 148–9
hospitalities 1–2
hospitality 1–21 *passim*, 23–9, 31, 33, 35, 41–56 *passim*, 59–60, 64, 66, 68–72, 75–91 *passim*, 95–7, 99–103, 105, 108–12, 114, 117–18, 121–2, 126–8, 131–5, 138–9, 141, 143–59 *passim*, 160n5, 161n16, 163–9, 175, 178–81, 184–99 *passim*, 200n18, 200n19; absolute(ly) conditional 165, 180; to animals (*see* Derrida, Jacques; Irigaray, Luce); conditional (*see* Derrida, Jacques); cosmic 166–8; ethics of 43–7, 54–6, 68, 70, 78–80, 187; and heart transplant 104–5; Indigenous 166–75; languages of 79, 84, 91; medieval hermeneutical 25–7; unconditional (*see* Derrida, Jacques); unconditionally absolute 20
host 2–7, 9–10, 15–16, 19, 24, 41–54 *passim*, 60, 66, 76–86, 95, 97–9, 102, 105, 108, 131, 141, 143–59 *passim*, 185–6, 184–9, 192–3, 196–7, 201n25; etymology 4–5, 12–13, 45–6; as hostage 5–6, 10, 14–15, 42, 45–7, 52, 77, 108; sacramental 33, 35, 54, 102
hostess 5, 43, 80, 91n3, 192
hostility 5, 14, 16, 21, 44, 51–2, 96–7, 110, 152–3, 156
hôte 5, 45–6, 56n2, 147, 154, 201n25; host as constituted by guest 7; as phantom 47; as animal 160n5
house 2, 5, 6, 20–1; in Beckett's *Molloy* 59, 62, 65–7, 71; and contemporary art 185–7, 190–2, 194–5; hospitality after houses 191–9
Hughes, Heather 86

Indigenous: culture 164, 168–70, 174–5, 180; lands and rights 163–4
Innocent III, Pope 29
intruder 15, 17, 81, 103–5, 155; *see also* Nancy, Jean-Luc
inventio 28–9
Invisibilia Dei see Abelard, Peter
ipseity 3, 45–6
Irigaray, Luce 19, 143, 158–9, 160n11; on animal hospitality 149–50; on hospitality as reciprocity 147–9; on language and silence 11–12; writings ('Animal Compassion' 150; *Sharing the World* 7–8, 11, 147, 149, 160n11; 'Toward a Mutual Hospitality' 149, 160n11)

James, M. R. 53
Jew 18, 111; Jewish 110–12, 120, 123n2; Wandering 50
Johnson, David 86
Jordan, Shirley 160n8
Jullien, François 177

Kant, Immanuel 45–6, 200n19; writing (*To Perpetual Peace* 43)
Kaya 175–8
Kayang 168, 178, 180
Kermode, Frank: *The Sense of an Ending* 98
King, Stephen: *The Shining* 15, 41, 54–5
Koch, Ed 195
Kristeva, Julia 14

Ladivine (Marie NDiaye): hospitality to animals in (*see* Derrida, Jacques; Irigaray, Luce); unwelcome tourists in 151–6; welcoming dogs in 156–9
land 105, 163, 167, 169, 172–6; generosity of the 179; language and the 176; as multiple 174; ownership of 98–9
Le Corbusier 194; writing (*The City of Tomorrow and Its Planning* 201n22)
Lee, Pamela 192–3; writing (*Object to Be Destroyed* 192)
Le Fanu, J. Sheridan: 'Carmilla' 51–2
Levinas, Emmanuel 12, 15, 18, 35, 35n4, 44, 46–7, 64–5, 118, 147, 160n5; on the feminine Other 6–7; hospitality towards the *semblable* 144; *il y a* ('there is') 70; language as goodness, friendship and hospitality 11; language as preconceptual sensibility 24; metaphor for modes of travelling 64–5; the self as persecuted host 5–6; welcome as cultural-conceptual disruption 24; welcome of the face 2; writings (*Otherwise than Being* 11; *Totality and Infinity* 2, 6, 9, 11, 45)
Lewis, Matthew: *The Monk* 15, 49–50, 52
Lindqvist, John Alvide: *Let the Right One In* 54
Lingis, Alphonso 65
Lish, Atticus: PEN America interview 129–30; writing (*Preparation for the Next Life* 18, 126, 128–41); *see also Preparation for the Next Life*
Locke, John 17, 102; writings (*An Essay concerning Human Understanding* 100–1; *A Letter concerning Toleration* 101)

Macfarlane, Robert 176
MacGillivray, Catherine 110

Magaziner, Daniel R. 79
Maldonado-Torres, Nelson 78
Marais, Mike 6, 15–16
Marebon, John 31, 35n5, 35n6
Matabele 16, 76, 81–5, 87–8
Matta-Clark, Gordon 20, 186, 188, 192–4; artworks (*Conical Intersect* 200–1n20; *Fake Estates* 193–4, 201n21; *Splitting* 186, 192–3; with Caroline Goodden, Rachel Lew et al *Food* 188, 194)
Mauss, Marcel 17, 96, 105, 105n2
Mbembe, Achille 87
Mediterranean (Sea) 1, 95, 105n10; *The Med* 105
Merkel, Angela 95
Mews, Constant 25
mfecane 16, 76, 79
Mhudi (Sol Plaatje): exceptional moments of individual welcoming in 84–6; hospitality beyond the nation in 86–91; interracial hospitality in 81–4; pastoral hospitality in 79–81
migrancy 18–19, 106n10, 126–8, 132–3, 135–8; US policy on 126–30, 132
migrant 6, 18–19, 22, 90, 96, 126–30, 132, 134–6, 139–41; 'migrant crisis' 9
migration 2, 18–19, 84, 86, 90–1, 135, 144, 166; and the *mfecane* 75–6; mobility and 90–1; narratives 128–30, 132; and the US Department of Homeland Security (DHS) 126–8
Miller, J. Hillis: 'The Critic as Host' 12–13, 46
Miller, Jacques-Alain 68
mobility 9, 19, 75–6, 83, 86, 90, 91, 126, 128, 131–3, 135–9, 200n11; and circulation 133–5; regulation of 131
Moir, John: *Hospitality: A Discourse Occasioned by Reading His Majesty's Letter in Behalf of the Emigrant French Clergy* 49
Molloy (Samuel Beckett): *Bildung* in 61, 63; haunt/haunting in 16–17, 60, 65, 67; identifying thought in 60, 64, 69, 70; language in 60, 63–70; the outsider in 59, 61, 65, 69–70; recognition in 15, 61, 64, 68, 70–1, 72n1; travel in 60–1, 64–5; the 'unhomely' in 60, 65, 70, 72; vagrancy and the vagrant in 60–1, 63, 66, 68, 71; waiting in 63–4, 67–9, 71; wandering in 15, 61, 71
Montaigne, Michael Lord of 157; writing ('That to Philosophise is to learne how to Die' 115–16)
More, Hannah 49

Mpe, Phaswane 89
Muecke, Stephen 165, 177
multinaturalism 163, 170, 178
'multinature(s)' 172–81; the literary text as 178–81
Murray, K. Susan 27
Muslim 131, 139

Nail, Thomas 132; writing (*The Figure of the Migrant* 126)
Nancy, Jean-Luc 15, 17, 19, 103–5; *l'intrus*/'the intruder' 17, 103; plural singularity 11; saying and said 11; singular plural 3–4, 8–9, 11, 13–14; writings (*Being Singular Plural* 105; '*L'Intrus'*/'The Intruder' 103)
nation 75–6, 82, 84, 86–9, 104, 127, 132; modern Western conceptions of 97; nation-state 127–8, 132, 163
native 16–17, 75, 98, 103
NDiaye, Marie 19, 143, 145–51; critical reception 164; literary biography 159–60n1, 161n15; writing (*Ladivine* 19, 145–6, 150–9, 160n3, 160n7, 160n8, 160n9, 160n13, 160n14); *see also Ladivine*
Nesbit, Edith 53
Neto, Ernesto (and the Huni Kuin) 185, 199n5; *Um Sagrado Lugar* ('A Sacred Place') 185
neural mirroring 24–5
New York City 195
Nietzsche, Friedrich 105
Nieuwenhuys, Constant 20, 186–7, 195–9, 200n8, 200n10, 200n11; artworks (*Constant, New Babylon. To Us, Liberty* (exhibition) 197; *Design for a Gypsy Camp in Alba* 195–8, 201n24; *Entrée du labyrinth* 197, 201n28; *Erotic Space* 197–8, 201n28; *Le Massacre de My Lai* 197, 201n26; *New Babylon* 186, 195, 197–9)
Noongar 20, 166–70, 173, 175–6, 181
north 1, 9; north-south 9–10, 13
North (Global) 13, 21

Odysseus 61, 65–6
Oliphant, Andries 86
Oran 112–13, 119, 121, 123n2
Other (Levinasian) 2, 6, 8, 11; Absolute 15; also: absolute other 44–8, 51, 54, 56n4; absolutely other 121; Levinasian other 64–5; Face of the Wholly 47; Wholly 10; *see also* alterity
Ovid (Publius Ovidius Naso) 102, 119

Parzival (Wolfram von Eschenbach): hospitality to the stranger in 29–33; *triuwe/triwe* in 30–1, 36n15; welcoming intellectual daring in 29–33

Paul, St. 26, 36n22

'person' (in the 'perspectivist' sense) 170, 172, 176, 179–81

personhood 17, 97, 103, 136; in Amerindian thinking 170–1, 173, 177; Locke's puzzle concerning 101

Phelps, J. M. 82

Pistorius, Oscar 103

Plaatje, Sol 75–6, 79–86, 88–91; and the South African Natives' Land Act 75, 83, 86–7, 90, 91n1; writings (*Mhudi* 75–6, 79–91; *Native Life in South Africa* 75, 86; *Sechuana Proverbs* 80); see also *Mhudi*

Plato 147

Pope, Alexander: Translation of the *Odyssey* 52

Preparation for the Next Life (Atticus Lish): deportation and 127, 134–5; dispossession in 126, 135–9; securitisation of bodies in 135–7, 140; securitisation of migrancy in 126–33; securitisation of mobility in 133–4, 136–7

property 184–6, 193–4; market 185, 194, 199; ownership 186, 194, 199

Protestant 48, 95, 97

Purves, Maria 48

Quinlivan, Natalie 178

Rabinovitz, Rubin 61

Radcliffe, Ann: *The Italian* 15, 49–50

Rancière, Jacques 20–1, 191–2, 194; policing 20–1; the 'police' 191–2, 194, 200n18; writings ('Aesthetic Separation, Aesthetic Community' 191, 200n16; 'The Emancipated Spectator' 189)

Rassel, Laurence: 'On Radical Hospitality' 184

reciprocity 3–4, 27–8, 82, 85, 88, 161n16; in Black-white relations 78; in conditional and unconditional hospitality 46, 48, 53, 77; and hospitality in Irigaray 147–9; in the host-guest relationship 147, 159

refugee 1, 19, 43, 90, 96, 113, 116; refugee 'crisis' 19, 104, 166

Ricoeur, Paul 14

Robinson, Fred Miller 64

romance 14, 23, 27–35; and Gottfried's *Tristan* 33–5; medieval chivalric 27–9; and Wolfram's *Parzival* 29–33

Rosler, Martha 20, 194–5; and the Dia Foundation 195; exhibitions and writings (*If You Lived Here ...* 194–5; *If You Lived Here Still* 195)

Rousseau, Jean-Jacques 154, 159, 260n2; writing (*Confessions* 154)

Royle, Nicholas 62, 65–6, 72

Saint-Amour, Paul K. 83

San, The 83, 88

Schmitt, Carl 60, 179

Scott, Kim 16, 20, 164–81 *passim*; on language and story 178–81; on negotiating Indigenous culture 168–75; and Ralph Winmar 168–70 (see also *Kaya*); writings (*Benang* 178; *That Deadman Dance* 20, 166, 171, 173, 175–8; *True Country* 166; with Hazel Brown, *Kayang & Me* 20, 166–75, 178–81)

security 126–41 *passim*; biopolitics of 133; and circulation 127, 133–5; discourse and practices 127–9; in *Preparation for the Next Life* 130–41; and the (US) Department of Homeland Security (DHS) 126–7, 129, 131, 141; see also Foucault, Michel

settler 16, 20, 77, 79, 167, 175, 179

Shakespeare, William 47, 106n7; literary appropriations of *Macbeth* 49–50, 54; two orders of hospitality in *Macbeth* 43–5; writings (*Hamlet* 43; *Macbeth* 14–15, 43–5, 49–50, 54)

Simmel, Georg: 'The Stranger' 98, 103

Simondon, Gilbert 174–5

Sinclair, Mary 53

Situationist International 186, 199n4

SMART Museum of Art (University of Chicago): *Feast: Radical Hospitality in Contemporary Art* 184

south 1, 9, 19; south-south 9–10, 13

South Africa 9, 16–17, 76, 90; and Bantustans 100; in Biko 78–9; hostility to aliens 96, 98; South African Union 75, 90; transition to democracy 86–7; and the Truth and Reconciliation Commission 104

South (Global) 13, 21, 166–7

spectrality 9–11, 42, 47, 118; spectral hospitality 14–15

Stamps, Laura (curator): *Constant: New Babylon. To Us Liberty* 197, 201n27

Stanzel, F. K. 63

Steiner, Tina 76, 85

Still, Judith 5, 13, 19–21, 84, 90, 91n5, 161n12, 161n16; writing (*Derrida and Hospitality* 9, 12, 123n1, 123n3; *Derrida and Other Animals* 145, 160n6)
Stock, Brian 25
Stoker, Bram: *Dracula* 15, 52
stranger 4–5, 29, 31–2, 54, 56n4, 84–5, 87, 95, 106n5, 120, 128, 132, 141, 155, 157, 189; and absolute alterity 51; in Beckett's *Molloy* 60, 62, 68, 70; caring for the 159; and heart transplant 104; and hospitality 43–6, 55; as intruder 103; in *The Little Stranger* 42–3; the tourist as stranger 150; and wandering/homelessness 98

Taylor, Jane 17, 19
Tennyson, Alfred: 'Ulysses' 123
Tiravanija, Rirkrit 187–9, 191, 200n13; artwork (*Untitled (Twelve Seventy-One)* 187, 189)
tourism 143–4
tourist 19, 144–5; *see also Ladivine*
Townshend, Dale 9, 11, 14–15, 19, 20
transgression 2, 4, 13, 18, 21, 108, 199, 200n11
transition 2, 4, 8, 9, 13, 76, 86–7, 118, 168, 178; a society in 80; South African transition to democracy 76, 86
translation 8, 52, 84, 111, 123n4, 160n1, 160n4; as hospitable border-crossing 168, 176–80; showing the antinomies between the laws and *The* law of hospitality 13
triuwe/triwe see Parzival
Trump, Donald 1, 19, 127

Ulysses 64; *see also* Odysseus
uncanny 105, 116; in Beckett's *Molloy* 62, 64–5, 68, 72; *see also unheimlich*
unheimlich 10, 12, 15, 116, 161n14; in Beckett's *Molloy* 60, 65
United Nations: Development Program (UNDP) 126; High Commission for Refugees (UNHCR) 1
United States 1, 90, 126–32, 135, 138–9; control of migration to the 126–8; as 'deportation nation' 127; immigration policy 9; in *Preparation for the Next Life* 128–32, 135, 138–9; *see also* security
utopianism: postcolonial 76, 87

vampire 51–2, 54
Venice Biennale (of Art) 185, 190

violence 42, 49, 54–5, 59, 77, 83, 90, 112–13, 144, 153, 155, 179, 197–8; and hospitality 43–6, 145
visitation 2, 6, 9, 15, 42, 48, 62, 67, 83, 192, 200n19
Viveiros de Castro, Eduardo 20, 166–7, 170–80; 'perspectivism' 170–3; 'symmetrical anthropology' 179; and translation 177; *see also* multinaturalism; 'multinature'
Von Eschenbach, Wolfram 14, 29–33, 35, 36n13, 36n21, 36n22; writing (*Parzival* 23, 29–33); *see also Parzival*
Von Strassburg, Gottfried 14, 33–5, 36n13, 36n25; transformative hospitality in 33–5; writing (*Tristan* 33–5)

Walpole, Horace 15; writing (*The Castle of Otranto* 47–8)
Waters, Sarah: *The Little Stranger* 14, 41–2, 45, 48, 56n4
Watson, David 2, 9, 16, 18–19
Wehrs, Donald 9, 14, 20, 35n7, 36n11, 36n19
welcome 4, 6, 7, 11, 15, 19, 47, 51, 54, 60, 76–7, 80–3, 87, 89–90, 112, 117, 119, 144, 159, 163–81 *passim*, 192, 197; of foreigners in Indigenous Australia 164–8; Indigenous protocols of 164, 166, 168, 180; in Indigenous stories 178–80; Irigaray on 148; to medieval literary expressive particularity 27–9; radical welcome 150; in Stoker's *Dracula* 52; in Waters's *The Little Stranger* 41–3; *see also Mhudi*; welcoming
'Welcome to Country' 20, 163–6; *see also* Country
welcoming 30, 31, 35, 46, 51, 53, 143, 146–8, 199; as present participle and adjective 147; textual difference 24; *see also Ladivine*; *Parzival*
Weller, Shane 70
West-Pavlov, Russell 7, 9, 16, 19–20
Wigley, Mark 196–7
Williams, Cynthia Schoolar 85
Williams, Merle A. 9, 11, 16, 18–19
Wolfram, *see* Von Eschenbach, Wolfram
writing 115, 122–3, 175, 180–1; Cixous and/on 109–10; *Kaya* and 175; Moran in Beckett's *Molloy* 66–70

Xenia 96
xenophobia 96, 103, 126

Zaccaria, Paola 13; writing ('The Art and Poetics of Translation as Hospitality' 13)

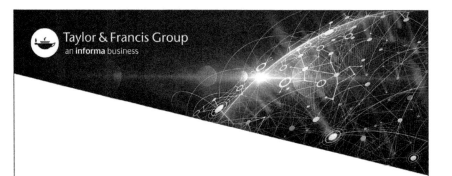